THE NATIONAL ORIGINS
OF POLICY IDEAS

THE NATIONAL ORIGINS
OF POLICY IDEAS

KNOWLEDGE REGIMES IN
THE UNITED STATES, FRANCE,
GERMANY, AND DENMARK

John L. Campbell
Ove K. Pedersen

Princeton University Press
Princeton and Oxford

Copyright © 2014 by Princeton University Press

Published by Princeton University Press, 41 William Street, Princeton, New Jersey 08540

In the United Kingdom: Princeton University Press, 6 Oxford Street, Woodstock, Oxfordshire OX20 1TW

press.princeton.edu

ISBN 978-0-691-15031-4

Library of Congress Control Number: 2013957458

British Library Cataloging-in-Publication Data is available

This book has been composed in Minion Pro 10/13

Printed on acid-free paper ∞

Printed in the United States of America

10 9 8 7 6 5 4 3 2 1

To Kathy and Anne

Contents

Tables and Figures

Acronyms

UNITED STATES

AEI	American Enterprise Institute
AFL-CIO	American Federation of Labor and Congress of Industrial Organizations
CAP	Center for American Progress
CBO	Congressional Budget Office
CBPP	Center on Budget and Policy Priorities
CEA	Council of Economic Advisors
CRS	Congressional Research Service
DLC	Democratic Leadership Council
EPI	Economic Policy Institute
GAO	Government Accountability Office
MIT	Massachusetts Institute of Technology
NCPA	National Center for Policy Analysis
NRC	National Research Council
OMB	Office of Management and Budget
OTA	Office of Technology Assessment
PPI	Progressive Policy Institute
RFF	Resources for the Future

FRANCE

ATTAC	Association for the Taxation of Financial Transactions and for Citizens' Action/Association pour la Taxation des Transactions Financières et pour l'Action Citoyenne
CAE	Council of Economic Analysis/Conseil d'Analyse Économique
CAS	Center for Strategic Analysis/Centre d'Analyse Stratégique
CEPII	Center for International Prospective Studies/Centre d'Études Prospectives et d'Informations Internationales

CEPREMAP   Center for Economic Research and Applications/Centre pour la Recherche Économique et ses Applications

CES   Economic and Social Council/Conseil Économique et Social

CNIS   National Council for Statistical Information/Conseil National de l'Information Statistique

CNPF   National Council of French Employers/Conseil National du Patronat Français

CNRS   National Center for Scientific Research/Centre National de la Recherche Scientifique

COE   Employment Advisory Council/Conseil d'Orientation pour l'Emploi

Coe-Rexecode Center for Economic Observation and Research for the Expansion of Economy and Enterprise Development/Centre d'Observation Économique et de Recherches pour l'Expansion de l'Économie et le Développement des Entreprises

COR   Retirement Advisory Council/Conseil d'Orientation des Retraites

CREST   Center for Research in Economics and Statistics/Centre de Recherche en Économie et Statistique

DARES   Directorate for the Coordination of Research, Studies and Statistics/Direction de l'Animation de la Recherche, des Études et des Statistiques

DGTPE   General Directorate of the Treasury and Economic Policy/ Direction Générale du Trésor et de la Politique Économique

DREES   Directorate of Research, Studies, Evaluation and Statistics/ Direction de la Recherche, des Études, de l'Évaluation et des Statistiques

ENA   National School of Administration/École Nationale d'Administration

ENSAE   National School of Statistics and Economic Administration/ École Nationale de la Statistique et de l'Administration Économique

FN   National Front/Front National

IDEP   Institute for Enterprise/Institut de l'Enterprise

IFRAP   French Institute for Research on Public Administration/ Institut Français pour la Recherche sur les Administrations Publiques

IFRI   French Institute of International Relations/Institut Français de Relations Internationales

INSEE	National Institute for Statistics and Economic Studies/ Institut National de la Statistique et des Études Économiques
IRES	Institute for Economic and Social Research/Institut de Recherches Économiques et Sociales
MEDEF	Movement of French Enterprises/Mouvement des Entreprises de France
OFCE	Center for Economic Research/Observatoire Français des Conjonctures Économiques
RPR	Rally for the Republic/Rassemblement pour la République
UDF	Union for French Democracy/Union pour la Démocratie Française
UMP	Union for a Popular Movement/Union pour un Mouvement Populaire

GERMANY

ARGE	German Consortium of Economic Research Institutes/ Vorsitzenden der Arbeitsgemeinschaft der Wirtschaftswissenschaftlichen Forschungsinstitute Deutschlands
BDA	Federation of German Employer Associations/ Bundesvereinigung der Deutschen Arbeitgeberverbände
BDI	Federation of German Industries/Bundesverband der Deutschen Industrie
BMWI	Federal Ministry of Economics and Technology/ Bundesministerium für Wirtschaft und Technologie
CDU	Christian Democratic Union/Christlich Demokratische Union Deutschlands
CEE	Council of Economic Experts/Sachverständigenrat zur Begutachtung der Gesamtwirtschaftlichen Entwicklung
CSU	Christian Social Union/Christlich-Soziale Union
DFG	German National Science Council/Deutsche Forschungsgemeinschaft
DGB	Federation of German Trade Unions/Deutscher Gewerkschaftsbund
DIW	German Institute for Economic Research/Deutsches Institut für Wirtschaftsforschung
FDP	Free Democratic Party/Freie Demokratische Partei
FES	Friedrich Ebert Foundation/Friedrich Ebert Stiftung

HWWA	Hamburg Institute for International Economics Archive/ Hamburgisches-Welt-Wirtschafts-Archiv
IAB	Institute for Employment Research/Institut für Arbeitsmarkt und Berufsforschung
Ifo	Institute for Economic Research at the University of Munich/ Institut für Wirtschaftsforschung an der Universität München
IfW	Kiel Institute for the World Economy/Institut für Weltwirtschaft
IMK	Institute for Macroeconomic Forecasting/Institut für Makroökonomie und Konjunkturforschung
INSM	Initiative New Social Market Economy/Initiative Neue Soziale Marktwirtschaft
IW	The Cologne Institute for Economic Research/Institut der Deutschen Wirtschaft Köln
IWH	Halle Institute for Economic Research/Institut für Wirtschaftsforschung Halle
KAS	Konrad Adenauer Foundation/Konrad-Adenauer-Stiftung
LMU	Ludwig Maximilian University in Munich/Ludwig Maximilians Universität München
MPIfG	Max Planck Institute for the Study of Societies/Max-Plank-Institut für Gesellschaftsforschung
RWI	Rhine-Westphalia Institute for Economic Research/ Rheinisch-Westfälisches Institut für Wirtschaftsforschung
SM	Foundation Market Economy/Stiftung Marktwirtschaft
SOWI	Bundeswehr Institute of Social Sciences/ Sozialwissenschaftliches Institut der Bundeswehr
SPD	Social Democratic Party/Sozialdemokratische Partei Deutschlands
WSI	Economic and Social Research Institute/Wirtschafts und Sozialwissenschaftliches Institut
WZB	Berlin Social Science Research Center/ Wissenschaftszentrum Berlin für Sozialforschung
ZEW	Center for European Economic Research/Zentrum für Europäische Wirtschaftsforschung

DENMARK

AC	Danish Confederation of Professional Associations/ Akademikernes Centralorganisation

ADAM	Annual Danish Aggregate Model
AE	Economic Council of the Labor Movement/ Arbejderbevægelsens Erhversråd
AKF	Danish Center for Governmental Research/Anvendt Kommunal Forskning
CARMA	Center for Labor Market Research/Center for Arbejdsmarkedsforskning
CASA	Center for Alternative Social Analysis/Center for Alternativ Samfundsanalyse
CEPOS	Center for Political Studies/Center for Politiske Studier
CEVEA	Center-Left-Academy/Tænketanken Cevea
DA	Confederation of Danish Employers/Dansk Arbejdsgiverforening
DI	Confederation of Danish Industry/Dansk Industri
DR	Danish Regions/Danske Regioner
DREAM	Danish Rational Economic Agent Model
DSGE	Dynamic Stochastic General Equilibrium Model
DØR	Danish Economic Council/De Økonomiske Råd
FAOS	Employment Relations Research Center/Forskningscenter for Arbejdsmarkeds-og Organisationsstudier
FTF	Confederation of Professionals/Funktionærernes og Tjenestemændenes Fællesråd
LGDK	Local Government Denmark/Kommunernes Landsforening
LO	Danish Confederation of Trade Unions/Landsorganisationen i Danmark
MILASMEC	Micro-Data Labor Supply Model of the Economic Councils
SFI	Danish National Center for Social Research/Det Nationale Forskningcenter for Velfærd
SMEC	Simulation Model of the Economic Council
TFV	Think Tank for Future Growth/Tænketanken Fremtidens Vækst

INTERNATIONAL

EU	European Union
IMF	International Monetary Fund
INTOSAI	International Organization of Supreme Audit Institutions
OECD	Organization for Economic Cooperation and Development

Preface

Although we did not realize it at the time, this project began when we decided during a quiet stroll along the Danish sea coast in 2004 to write a short paper about the role of ideas in public policymaking. Since then it has taken us to 11 cities in four countries. During our travels we had the pleasure of talking with many fascinating people and dining in many wonderful restaurants and cafes. We met some of the smartest people in politics as well as a few of the most paranoid. Our interviews with them were so riveting that in one case we lost track of time and missed our train back to Copenhagen, much to the amusement of those we were interviewing at the moment. We survived a restaurant fire and witnessed a street brawl. We watched pickpockets plying their trade in the Paris subway. We sat at the conference table used by Jean Monnet when he planned for the European Coal and Steel Community after the Second World War. We raced along the German autobahn one dark and rainy night at 125 miles per hour while the taxi driver flashed his lights and cursed cars in front of us for not going faster! We saw a couple dozen enormous tractors block traffic outside Christian Democratic Union headquarters in Berlin as farmers protested CDU agricultural policies. We passed through countless security check points in Washington, D.C. We visited the White House. We saw the parade grounds in Nuremberg where Hitler addressed mass rallies during the heydays of the Third Reich and where the Allies later held the Nazi top brass for trial and eventual execution. And along the way we collected and processed 15,000 or more pages of interview transcripts and documents. In the end we tried to write a book that will be of interest to a wide range of readers in the social sciences and beyond who are curious about how ideas are produced and disseminated to policymakers and used to affect public policy.

Many people helped us along the way. They include Magnus Paulsen Hansen, Antje Vetterlin, Magali Gravier, Vivien Schmidt, and Mogens Lykketoft who helped arrange interviews for us, as did the German and French embassies in Copenhagen and the Danish embassy in Berlin. Charles Quincy, Jordan Osserman, Jaclyn Wypler, Andreas Birkbak, Noah Glick, and John Mei helped gather, code, and organize data from websites, interviews, and organization documents. Mike Massagli, Gretchen Wright, Peter Marsden, Kathryn Lively, and Kathleen Sherrieb offered sage advice about developing coding schemes. Anne Ivey, Stephanie Morgan, Deborah Edwards, and Bo Bøgeskov were an enormous help when it came to managing the project's funding.

We owe special thanks to everyone who agreed to be interviewed for this project and especially those who agreed to read and give us feedback on the chapters for which we interviewed them once they had been written. Because some of them preferred not to be identified, we refrain from reporting their names here. Nevertheless, this project would not have been possible without their generosity and help, for which we are extremely grateful.

We thank as well a number of people who commented on various aspects of this project along the way or provided comments on drafts of chapters and in some cases the entire manuscript. These include Denise Anthony, Edward Ashbee, Mark Blyth, Susana Borrás, Robert Boyer, David Brady, Marc Dixon, Marie-Laure Djelic, Francesco Duina, Marion Fourcade, Mauro Guillén, Peter Hall, Peter Katzenstein, Patrick Le Galès, Kathryn Lively, Cathie Jo Martin, Bruno Palier, Martin Møller Boje Rasmussen, Andrew Rich, Ann Sa'adah, Vivien Schmidt, Len Seabrooke, Kathleen Sherrieb, Diane Stone, David Strang, Wolfgang Streeck, Ruy Teixeira, and Kathleen Thelen. Special thanks go to three reviewers—John A. Hall, Nick Ziegler, and Elizabeth Popp Berman—who provided extensive and extremely helpful comments on an early version of the full manuscript. And, of course, we would be remiss not to thank Eric Schwartz, our editor at Princeton University Press, who helped guide the project to its completion. We benefitted as well from presenting portions of the analysis in seminars at the Social Science Research Council in New York City, Dartmouth College, Boston University, Duke University, Harvard University, the Massachusetts Institute of Technology, CEPREMAP, Alborg University, Copenhagen University, Krakow University, Hokkaido University, Columbia University, Brown University, McGill University, University College–Dublin, Sciences Po, Koç University, the Australian National University, and the Copenhagen Business School. We benefitted tremendously from a manuscript review seminar sponsored by the John Sloan Dickey Center for International Understanding at Dartmouth, for which we owe special thanks to Ken Yalowitz and Christianne Hardy Wohlforth.

Financial support was provided by the U.S. National Science Foundation (SES-0813633), the Copenhagen Business School through its World Class Project funds, the Nelson A. Rockefeller Center at Dartmouth College, and the Department of Business and Politics (formerly the International Center for Business and Politics) at the Copenhagen Business School. In a similar vein, special thanks go to Finn Jung Jensen, former president of the Copenhagen Business School, and Alan Irwin, Dean of Research at the Copenhagen Business School.

Finally, we must thank our wives, Kathy Sherrieb and Anne Bøttger. They provided more moral support to us than we probably deserved throughout this project. For these and many other reasons we dedicate this book to them with much love and affection.

John L. Campbell   Ove K. Pedersen
Lyme, New Hampshire   *Copenhagen, Denmark*

THE NATIONAL ORIGINS
OF POLICY IDEAS

1

Knowledge Regimes and the National Origins of Policy Ideas

Two conservative congressional staff members in Washington, D.C., Ed Feulner and Paul Weyrich, were frustrated in 1971 by the lack of timely policy-relevant research on Capitol Hill. Their frustration peaked when an impressive and potentially influential briefing paper about the supersonic transport prepared by a prominent conservative think tank arrived a day *after* Congress voted on the issue—too late to influence the vote. Frustration led to action. In 1973, with the help of wealthy benefactors like the beer tycoon Joseph Coors, they established the Heritage Foundation, an aggressive policy research organization dedicated to quickly producing and disseminating conservative policy analysis to members of Congress so that conservative ideas would have greater influence on policymaking. It worked. Notably, in 1980 the Heritage Foundation provided Edwin Meese, the head of Ronald Reagan's transition team, a hefty volume called *Mandate for Leadership*, a conservative blueprint for transforming all aspects of public policy and intended as a guide for the incoming administration. It was a best seller in Washington for weeks and reputedly guided the administration's initial budget cutting efforts at a time when conservatives believed that excessive government spending was causing inflation and economic malaise in America. The Heritage Foundation's reputation soared, marking the beginning of a seismic change in how policy research organizations operated in Washington.[1]

Since then and thanks to challenges associated with the rise of globalization and the transformation of advanced capitalism, policy research organizations in the United States and Europe have undergone major changes as people have tried to use policy analysis and other ideas to more effectively influence policymaking and solve national economic problems. But they have done so in nationally specific ways. This book explains these changes as they unfolded in the United States, France, Germany, and Denmark. In doing so it answers several pressing yet much neglected questions: Where do the ideas come from over which policymakers fight and that affect policymaking and public debates? How has this changed with the onset of globalization? And, most important, how has all of this varied across different types of advanced capitalist countries? In short, this book is about the national origins of policy ideas. Its arguments bear directly on critical debates about the nature of globalization, the rise of neoliberalism, the orientation of comparative political economy, and fundamental theories of organizational and economic sociology.

Researchers in the social sciences have long debated whether policy analysis, economic theories, and other sorts of ideas as well as self-interests affect policymaking in advanced capitalist countries. Many now agree that ideas matter a lot. Peter Hall, for instance, showed that big intellectual policy paradigms like Keynesianism and then neoliberalism shaped economic policy after the Second World War. Mark Blyth revealed how policymakers used ideas as weapons in their political struggles to reform taxation and government spending. Frank Dobbin argued that deep-seated values regarding the appropriate relationship between the state and economy influenced the development of national transportation policies. And others, particularly Vivien Schmidt, explained that cognitive and discursive structures helped frame policy debates in different ways in different countries.[2]

We accept that ideas matter for politics. Our concern, however, is that those who have shown that ideas are important have paid remarkably little attention to how these ideas are *produced* and *disseminated* in the first place and how this varies across countries and over time. So this book is not about how ideas matter or why policymakers choose one idea over another. It is about the organizational and institutional machinery by which these ideas

---

[1] Rich 2004, pp. 53–55; Smith 1991, pp. 194–202; Weidenbaum 2009, p. 96.

[2] Blyth 2002; Dobbin 1992; Hall 1989b, 1993; Schmidt 2002, 2001. The literature on how ideas matter is extensive. Other examples include Babb (2001), Béland and Cox (2011), Berman (1998, 2006), Campbell (2002, 1998), Goldstein and Keohane (1993), Katzenstein (1996), McNamara (1998), and Rueschemeyer and Skocpol (1996).

are produced in different ways in different countries. This is especially important because variation in this machinery helps explain how policy ideas themselves differ across time and place. To our knowledge this is the first study of its kind.

The book focuses on how policy research organizations like think tanks, government research units, political party foundations, and others that produce and disseminate policy ideas are organized, operate, and have changed during the past 30 years or so in our four advanced capitalist countries. In each country these organizations constitute what sociologists call an organizational field—a community of organizations whose participants engage in similar activities and interact more frequently with one another than with organizations outside the field.[3] We call fields of policy research organizations and the institutions that govern them *knowledge regimes*. Knowledge regimes are the organizational and institutional machinery that generates data, research, policy recommendations, and other ideas that influence public debate and policymaking.

Policymakers need the information produced by knowledge regimes insofar as the policy problems they confront often involve ambiguity and uncertainty. They need it to make sense of these problems. Sense making is often a contested process involving varying degrees of competition, negotiation, and compromise—often involving power struggles—over the interpretation of problems and solutions for them. A knowledge regime, then, is a sense-making apparatus.[4] Just as sense making occurs in different ways in organizations depending on how they are organized individually, it also occurs in different ways in knowledge regimes depending on how they are organized as a field. Sense making is especially important and difficult for policymaking during periods of crisis when ambiguity and uncertainty are extreme because problems are unfamiliar and conventional policy prescriptions no longer work. During periods of crisis sense making can take a long time and may involve changing the sense-making apparatus itself.[5] This is just what happened in nationally specific ways in our four knowledge regimes beginning in the late 1970s and early 1980s.

---

[3]DiMaggio and Powell 1983; Dobbin 1992, 1994; Fligstein 1990; Fligstein and McAdam 2012; Schneiberg 1999, 2002, 2007; Schneiberg and Bartley 2001; Scott 2008.

[4]The term "sense making" is from organizational theory and is generally described as a process involving a set of organizations and institutions that help people interpret the problems they face and determine how to tackle them (e.g., March 2010; Weick 1995). Political economists also recognize that policymakers face uncertainty and ambiguity and thus need to interpret—that is, make sense of—their situations and do so often in ways that facilitate change (Blyth 2011; Mahoney and Thelen 2010a; Orren and Skowronek 1994; Streeck and Thelen 2005, chap. 1).

[5]For examples of lengthy sense-making episodes during times of economic crisis, see, for example, Blyth (2002) and Hay (2001).

Analytic Arguments

Our overarching argument is that policy ideas have national origins and the way they are produced is largely determined by nationally specific institutions. In substantiating this claim, however, we offer four additional analytic arguments. The first three provide new insights into previous research on globalization and the rise of neoliberal ideas, comparative political economy, and organizational convergence. As we are about to explain, we identify and begin to fill important gaps in these three overlapping research literatures and challenge some of their key claims. The fourth analytic argument constitutes our causal model of the national construction of knowledge regimes. Our interest in these things stems from our long-standing curiosity about institutions and institutional change.[6]

The End of the Golden Age and the Rise of Globalization and Neoliberalism

Sense making and knowledge regimes became especially important in advanced capitalist countries during the era of economic globalization whose onset was marked by the end of the Golden Age of postwar capitalism—a period of strong economic growth, welfare state development, and general prosperity enjoyed by many advanced capitalist countries during the first three decades after the Second World War.[7] The end of the Golden Age was accompanied by the onset of a stagflation crisis where economic stagnation and inflation increased simultaneously during the 1970s and 1980s. We will have more to say about this later in the chapter. But for now what is important is that stagflation discredited conventional Keynesian policy ideas in many advanced capitalist countries and triggered what some have called a "war of ideas" in North America and Europe in which political opponents used theories, data, ideology, and rhetoric as weapons in the fight over economic policy.[8] These ideas varied widely from left to right across the political spectrum and across countries and were all attempts to make sense of this unprecedented situation.[9] Among them, *neoliberalism*—the call for less public

---

[6]See, for example, Campbell (2004), Campbell and Pedersen (2001a), and Pedersen (2010, 2011).

[7]Marglin and Schor 1990. Others have described the Golden Age as a period of "embedded liberalism" (Ruggie 1982) and advanced "Fordism" (Piore and Sabel 1984). This is not to say that the advanced capitalist countries were without problems during the Golden Age or that their experiences were all the same. There was much variation. In particular, two of our European countries, Germany and France, had to rebuild after the devastation of the Second World War, whereas Denmark and the United States did not.

[8]Blyth 2002, pp. 258–59; Fourcade-Gourinchas and Babb 2002; Stiglitz 2009, p. 211; Weidenbaum 2009, p. 29.

[9]These ideas were derived from a wide variety of perspectives including neo-Marxism, institutional economics, industrial policy, post-Keynesianism, neoliberalism, public choice theory, and

spending, lower taxes, especially on business and the wealthy, and less state intervention into the economy—figured prominently. And once ideas like these were adopted they had far-reaching consequences for how successfully economies performed.[10]

Much attention has been paid to globalization and the end of the Golden Age and how it transformed the advanced capitalist countries after the 1970s thanks to pressures associated with increased international capital mobility, new telecommunications technologies, the emergence of free-trade zones like the European Union, and more. New forms of economic organization resulted, such as the emergence of global outsourcing, international commodity chains, and network-like corporate structures.[11] New economic and social policies appeared too, including sometimes the scaling back of welfare states and tax burdens.[12] What is missing in this literature, however, is attention to the rise of knowledge regimes as a means of searching for new ideas about how to make sense of and cope with globalization and its challenges. For instance, David Held and colleagues' well-known *Global Transformations* offered an impressive analysis of how globalization caused a variety of political, economic, and cultural changes around the world. But they provided little discussion—or even recognition—of where the ideas came from with which people tried to make sense of these changes.[13]

Following Max Weber, who argued that ideas are an important starting point for the development of capitalism, we argue that knowledge regimes became more important for advanced capitalist countries as policymakers and others grappled with the challenges of globalization.[14] Put differently, this is an age when policymakers strive to recognize and improve their country's institutional competitive strengths and rely increasingly on the production of policy-relevant knowledge to do so.[15] This is why overlooking the significance and transformation of knowledge regimes is a serious omission in the research on globalization and the end of the Golden Age. By correcting this we illuminate a previously unexplored dimension of the breakdown in consensus on economic management that followed the end of the Bretton Woods system in the 1970s and the demise of the Golden Age.

monetarism, among others (Blyth 2002; Fourcade 2009; Fourcade-Gourinchas and Babb 2002; Mudge 2008; Prasad 2006).

[10]For detailed discussions of the nature of neoliberalism and its persistent effects, see, for example, Crouch (2011) and Schmidt and Thatcher (2013).

[11]DiMaggio 2001; Gereffi 2005.

[12]Steinmo 1993; Swank 2002.

[13]Held et al. 1999.

[14]Weber 1958.

[15]Pedersen (2010), for instance, shows that the academic discussion of national institutions and institutional competitiveness seeped into policymaking discourse and guided policy reform from the 1970s.

But the manner in which knowledge regimes help policymakers make sense of and deal with the challenges of globalization varies across countries. This is important for understanding the international diffusion of neoliberalism. Several scholars have argued that neoliberal ideas diffused internationally since the end of the Golden Age as globalization began to occur. In particular, researchers have claimed that this resulted in tendencies toward international convergence on a common set of political and economic outcomes, such as certain forms of market reregulation and welfare retrenchment.[16] As Frank Dobbin and his colleagues remarked with reference to the globalization literature, "The power of global models is increasingly taken for granted even in studies focusing on domestic economic and political conditions."[17] We offer two arguments in this regard. First, we challenge albeit cautiously that neoliberalism is as taken for granted today as many believe. We show that the adoption of neoliberalism at least by national councils of economic advisors was highly uneven across our four countries and in one case was largely rejected. Second, although some researchers have also noted this sort of unevenness they attributed it to the fact that neoliberal ideas were translated (or not) into local practice by way of political and economic institutions already in place. In other words, national political-economic factors mediated the degree to which neoliberalism was adopted from one country to the next. We argue, however, that the structure and practices of knowledge regimes—not just political and economic institutions—also had important mediating effects. This is because knowledge regimes are where neoliberal ideas were often formulated and debated, and because the nationally specific organization of knowledge regimes affected how these and other ideas were crafted in the first place. This leads to our second argument—one that bears directly on literature in comparative political economy and the issue of national diversity.

Comparative Political Economy

Knowledge regimes are just as important for modern political economies as policymaking and production regimes at least insofar as knowledge regimes produce the ideas that inform what political and economic elites do. However, policymaking and production regimes have received the lion's share of attention from comparative political economists. Much of their work dwells on how policymaking and production regimes respond to globalization in nationally specific ways. This work emerged in two waves. The first was about *policymaking regimes*, which were scrutinized closely in the 1980s and 1990s by social scientists like Peter Evans, Dietrich Rueschemeyer, and Theda Skocpol, whose

---

[16]Lane 2005; Simmons et al. 2008; Thatcher 2005.
[17]Dobbin et al. 2007, p. 450. See, for example, Crouch (2011), Fourcade-Gourinchas and Babb (2002), Harvey (2005), and Simmons et al. (2008) on the diffusion of neoliberalism.

volume *Bringing the State Back In* set the tone for much of this research.[18] Policymaking regimes involve the organization and governance of states, political parties, and other political institutions. They vary across countries in many ways. For instance, policymaking is more centralized bureaucratically in some policymaking regimes than others. Elections are based on winner-take-all rules in some policymaking regimes but proportional representation in others. In turn, some policymaking regimes feature considerably more political parties and tend more toward compromise than others. And some policymaking regimes rely more heavily on the career civil service than others. Research shows that all of these factors influence how policy is made and contributes to different national styles of policymaking.[19]

The second wave in comparative political economy involved the analysis of *production regimes*. It emerged in the late 1990s and early 2000s thanks largely to the emergence of the so-called Varieties of Capitalism School, pioneered by Peter Hall and David Soskice, who wanted to bring the analysis of firms back into comparative political economy. Their edited collection *Varieties of Capitalism: The Institutional Foundations of Comparative Advantage* remains the classic statement of this perspective. They assert that the important roles of firms and other economic actors were overshadowed for years in comparative political economy by studies of policymaking regimes. Production regimes involve the organization of economic activity through markets and other market-related institutions, which govern the interrelationships among firms, customers, employers, employees, and owners of capital. Some production regimes are dominated by large firms while others are dominated by small and medium-sized firms. Some firms are owned by families, others by diverse shareholders, and still others in part by the state. Some firms depend on equity and bond markets for finance while others depend on banks or the state. Some production regimes have strong unions, employer associations, and corporatist bargaining while others do not.[20] Researchers demonstrated that all of these factors influenced how well national economies adjusted to economic challenges, problems, and crises.

One of the most important contributions of the Varieties of Capitalism School was to show that different institutional combinations sometimes create synergies that help improve overall economic performance in ways that would not happen otherwise. Such synergy is typically called *institutional complementarity*. Generous universal welfare state provisions, for instance,

---

[18]Evans et al. 1985.

[19]For further important statements of bringing the state back into policy analysis, see, for example, Hicks and Kenworthy (1998), Katzenstein (1978), Schmidt (2002), and Steinmo et al. (1992). In a related vein, some scholars compared national styles of policymaking (e.g., Richardson 1982; Vogel 1986).

[20]Hall and Soskice 2001b; Hancké et al. 2007a; Soskice 1999.

may enhance labor market flexibility such that the political institution helps improve the performance of the economic institution. Not all institutional combinations do this.[21] Robert Boyer is one of the few to argue that complementarities sometimes break down as circumstances change and institutional combinations become dysfunctional. Nor in his view are institutional complementarities necessarily self-evident; sometimes they must be discovered much as investors spot opportunities for arbitrage—all of which is to say that institutional complementarities are often as much a matter of perception and intentional action as they are of institutional structure per se.[22]

Comparative political economists now often characterize national political economies in terms of combinations of different types of policymaking and production regimes and the institutional complementarities they entail.[23] And their work has provided countless insights into how advanced political economies operate. But they err in ignoring the important role that knowledge regimes play in all of this. After all, policymakers use the ideas emanating from knowledge regimes to formulate and implement the public policies that affect how production regimes are organized and operate and, in turn, how successful they are.[24] It stands to reason, then, that knowledge regimes may constitute an additional source of institutional complementarity insofar as the analysis and advice they generate help leaders in the policymaking and production regimes make sense of and resolve problems and thus improve national economic performance. Similarly, the institutional complementarity that knowledge regimes provide may break down as circumstances change. How all this happens depends on the nationally specific ways in which knowledge regimes are organized.

It is surprising that such a blind spot for knowledge regimes exists because a rich literature has emerged on how ideas matter for policymaking, and because some prominent representatives of the policymaking and production regime literatures, such as Peter Katzenstein and Peter Hall, respectively, have contributed to it![25] Several researchers explored the conditions under which different types of ideas, such as policy programs, cognitive paradigms, public sentiments, and frames, influence policymaking.[26] Others addressed the methodologies by which this can best be studied.[27] However, this work largely

[21]Hall and Soskice 2001a; Crouch 2005.
[22]Boyer 2005a, 2005b. See also Campbell (2011), Hall (2005), Höpner (2005, p. 343), and Streeck (2005).
[23]See, for example, Amable (2003), Campbell (2011), Campbell and Pedersen (2007b), Hancké et al. (2007b), and Kenworthy (2006).
[24]Blyth 2002; Campbell and Lindberg 1990; Fligstein 1990; Hall 1989a.
[25]Hall 1992, 1993; Katzenstein 1996. See also Blyth (2002, 1997) and Schmidt (2002, 2001, 2000).
[26]Blyth 2002; Campbell 2002, 1998; Goldstein and Keohane 1993; Katzenstein 1996; McNamara 1998.
[27]Berman 1998; Béland and Cox 2011, pt. 1.

ignores where these ideas come from in the first place and how knowledge regimes are important in that regard.

There is also much excellent work that in one way or another suggests that economic ideas conform to and influence the broader political economy in nationally specific ways. For instance, some scholars have studied why Keynesianism and then monetarism emerged and were adopted in different times and different ways across countries.[28] In particular, Peter Hall's edited volume *The Political Power of Economic Ideas* is an important study of the diffusion of Keynesianism.[29] And Marion Fourcade-Gourinchas and Sarah Babb argued that the stagflation period was accompanied by the rise of neo-liberal ways of thinking about economic policy and showed how economists played important roles in this in several countries.[30] Others have examined how neoliberalism emerged and diffused across less developed countries too thanks in part to the efforts of U.S. political and financial interests pushing the so-called Washington Consensus but with nationally specific results.[31] Virtually all of these researchers argued that these ideas had to be translated and fit into national political and economic institutions. But to explain how this happened, they tended to focus on the activities of strategically placed politicians, technocrats, and professional economists—particularly academics—operating within a few state agencies, such as central banks and finance ministries. In other words, they had little to say about the policy research organizations many of these people inhabited or conversed with or how these organizations went about their business either individually or collectively.

Some scholars explored how in nationally specific ways policymakers framed various policy ideas in order to make them normatively palatable to the public.[32] Yet the role of knowledge regimes was largely ignored—an important omission insofar as it is not just politicians and their handlers, but often organizations within knowledge regimes that created these frames in the first place and modified them if they were not effective.

A few researchers have written about independent, nonprofit, private think tanks. However, only a few of them discussed these organizations in connection with other types of policy research organizations, such as those associated with either the state or political parties, as an entire national field.[33] And with the exception of a few edited volumes, their work lacked cross-national

[28]Hall 1989a, 1989b, 1992, 1993; Hay 2001; Blyth 2002.
[29]Hall 1989b.
[30]Fourcade-Gourinchas and Babb 2002.
[31]Dezalay and Garth 2002; Harvey 2005.
[32]Katzenstein 1996; Schmidt 2001, 2002.
[33]Medvetz 2012; Rich 2004.

comparisons.[34] Other researchers were more attentive to cross-national differences in how policy ideas were produced but only with examples from the early part of the twentieth century, when national political economies were vastly different from today. We have in mind here especially Dietrich Rueschemeyer and Theda Skocpol's collection titled *States, Social Knowledge, and the Origins of Modern Social Policies*.[35]

Finally, some studies have shown how the economics profession developed and how this influenced some of the ideas to which policymakers were exposed in different countries. They too pay less attention than we would like to our principal concerns—how policy research organizations operate in the first place, and how policymaking and production regimes influence knowledge regimes.[36] For instance, Marion Fourcade's excellent book *Economists and Societies*, which analyzed the development of the economics profession in France, Britain, and the United States, focused on the relationships between economists and universities but downplayed the role of economists in policy research organizations, particularly outside the state.[37]

In short, although all these literatures are insightful, they shed less light than one might hope on how knowledge regimes are organized, operate, and vary across countries today and how they have evolved. The analysis of knowledge regimes is the linchpin that connects these disparate literatures. As such, the analysis of knowledge regimes constitutes the third analytic leg of a three-legged stool along with the analysis of policymaking and production regimes upon which comparative political economy should rest. Until now that leg has been largely missing. We correct this problem by showing that knowledge regimes are intimately connected with policymaking and production regimes in nationally specific ways. And in doing so, we offer two sets of insights into comparative political economy.

The first set is about policy paradigms. Paradigms are cognitive frameworks including core assumptions and causal arguments about which policies are effective in different situations—frameworks that constrain the range of policies that policymakers and others are likely to consider and support. Those who have studied the role of ideas in policymaking have discussed how one policymaking paradigm is replaced by another.[38] For instance, several researchers have argued that Keynesianism was replaced by neoliberalism in various countries since the 1970s. And they have frequently taken for granted

---

[34]See, for example, Desai (1994), Medvetz (2012), Ricci (1993), Rich (2004), and Smith (1989). For comparative exceptions see Abelson (2002), McGann and Weaver (2000), Stone and Denham (2004), and Stone et al. (1998).

[35]Rueschemeyer and Skocpol 1996. See also Furner and Supple (1990) and Hall (1989b).

[36]Babb 2001; Dezalay and Garth 2002; Fourcade 2006, 2009.

[37]Fourcade 2009; Fourcade-Gourinchas and Babb 2002.

[38]Blyth 2002; Campbell 2004, chap. 4; Hall 1992, 1993.

that these paradigms are, as Grace Skogstad points out, "internally coherent ideas that are . . . largely incommensurable with the paradigms that replace them."[39] In light of our evidence we argue against this view on two counts. First, paradigms are not hegemonic. One can exist alongside another in competition for long periods of time. Second, contrary to the implication of much of this literature, the shift from one paradigm to another does not involve an abrupt break but rather is an incremental and evolutionary process where bits and pieces of two or more paradigms may comingle in the analysis and policy prescriptions on offer.[40]

Our second set of insights for comparative political economy pertains to the Varieties of Capitalism School. As we noted earlier, the Varieties of Capitalism School considers only complementarities involving policymaking and production regimes, whereas knowledge regimes are another possible source of institutional complementarity for the rest of the political economy. Indeed, our analysis shows that when people perceive that these complementarities break down—that is, that their knowledge regime no longer provides the analysis, advice, and other ideas deemed useful for making sense of and coping with their country's political-economic problems—they try to change them in ways that they hope will rejuvenate such complementarity. And they do so in nationally specific ways that may involve, for instance, centralized planning or coordination, decentralized competition, trial-and-error experimentation, and haphazard muddling through. This is just what happened in our four countries as the Golden Age waned, globalization emerged, and people struggled to cope with stagflation and other problems. Three important implications follow from this insight. Complementarities are not fixed; they are dynamic. Efforts to create (or re-create) them are not necessarily successful despite their best intentions. And perception matters insofar as efforts to change knowledge regimes depend on people believing that their knowledge regimes have become dysfunctional in the first place. As such there is nothing automatic or mechanistic about this. And there are no functionally preordained outcomes. Ours is not a functionalist argument. Insofar as the Varieties of Capitalism School has been accused of functionalist reasoning, our research helps chart a way out of that dilemma.[41] Moreover, we focus our attention on the breakdown of institutional complementarities and unpack how actors seek to make sense of and restore them in different ways in

---

[39]Skogstad 2011, p. 239.
[40]Schneiberg (2007) makes a very similar argument about different organizational models coexisting and sometimes competing with each other. Also see Campbell (2004, chap. 3) on institutional change as bricolage. Crouch (2011) and Schmidt and Thatcher (2013) reflect on why policy paradigms, notably neoliberalism, persist even in the face of much evidence that they are misguided.
[41]Hancké et al. (2007b) reviews this functionalist critique.

different countries—something that the Varieties of Capitalism School has largely neglected.

Recognizing the dynamic nature of the institutional complementarities associated with knowledge regimes can also help resolve what some consider to have been the Achilles' heel of comparative political economy in general and the Varieties of Capitalism School in particular—lack of a satisfactory theory of change. A number of people have argued that researchers in these traditions have excelled in distinguishing between types of political economies and how they perform but that they have not done well in explaining how they change, especially in gradual or incremental ways.[42] This is why, for example, Wolfgang Streeck, Kathleen Thelen, James Mahoney, and their colleagues have worked hard to identify different patterns and mechanisms of incremental change in advanced capitalist countries.[43] We contribute to this effort by showing that when people perceive a breakdown in institutional complementarity, their efforts to restore it can lead to significant incremental change. This is counterintuitive insofar as scholars often argue that institutional complementarities are a source of *stability* whereas we show that they can also be a source of *change*.[44] However, we also show that the way this played out in our four knowledge regimes was nationally specific, which leads to our third argument—one that bears on convergence theory and the issue of national similarity.

Convergence Theory

In contrast to researchers in comparative political economy who emphasize the persistence of nationally specific institutional characteristics, other researchers have argued that these differences may fade under certain circumstances. Notably, many scholars have argued that globalization and the end of the Golden Age precipitated convergence—or isomorphism as it is often called—among countries in the advanced capitalist world. Convergence theory was pioneered in organizational and economic sociology by John Meyer and his colleagues who argued that a "world culture" or "world polity" has emerged by which nation-states have adopted similar organizational and institutional arrangements, norms, and ideas about how to configure political systems, state structures, educational systems, and the like. Nation-states did so, they argued, in order to cultivate legitimacy within the international community by doing what other leading nation-states and international organizations defined as being appropriate.[45] Others expanded on these insights, arguing that this occurred as a result of several causal

---

[42]For discussion of this criticism, see Hancké et al. (2007b).

[43]Mahoney and Thelen 2010a; Streeck and Thelen 2005.

[44]For arguments about how institutional complementarities serve as anchors preventing change, see, for example, Campbell (2010) and Crouch (2005, pp. 30–31).

[45]Bartley 2007; Boli and Thomas 1999; DiMaggio and Powell 1983; Dobbin et al. 2007; Frank et al. 2000; Meyer et al. 1997a, 1997b; Strang 2010; Thomas et al. 1987.

mechanisms including the *coercive* power of international actors, such as the International Monetary Fund; the *normative* learning facilitated by nongovernmental organizations and professionals; or the *mimicry* by one nation-state of other prominent nation-states' practices.[46] Typically, normative and mimetic mechanisms hold pride of place in these arguments, particularly when organizations in a field are uncertain about their environments and how to cope with them.[47] But in each case the result is the same—a tendency toward convergence.

Similarly, as noted above, some scholars have argued that the rise of globalization and the end of the Golden Age have been accompanied by a tendency toward convergence across nation-states on common neoliberal ideas where national governments, for instance, "race to the bottom" by competing against each other to attract and maintain investment capital by creating the most favorable investment climate possible with low taxes and limited government spending and regulation. *Competition* is the causal mechanism posited here.[48] But others have argued that the diffusion of neoliberalism has been driven too by coercive, normative, and mimetic mechanisms.[49]

To be sure, all of this work has been very fruitful and generated lots of interesting research. But critics have identified two problems with it. First, much of it, especially by Meyer and his colleagues, albeit quite sophisticated methodologically, is a bit superficial insofar as it relies on the analysis of large cross-national datasets that do not permit digging deeply into how certain ideas or organizational and institutional structures and practices may take on nationally specific characteristics and maintain them over time. On closer inspection seemingly similar ideas, structures, and practices often vary quite a bit across countries—even when they are pushed upon nation-states by international organizations like the United Nations or European Union. Terrence Halliday and Bruce Carruthers, for example, found that even though a set of internationally accepted benchmarks for the development of bankruptcy law was devised in the late 1990s, the degree to which they were adopted by different nation-states varied widely depending on the political and economic institutions and circumstances of each country.[50]

[46]Dobbin et al. 2007; Simmons et al. 2008.

[47]Mizruchi and Fein 1999. But see Dobbin et al. (2007) for a more balanced approach that considers coercive and competitive mechanisms as well, and Garrett et al. (2008) who argue that competition and learning are the most important mechanisms.

[48]Some argue in particular that various forms of capitalism are converging on a common liberal type (Harvey 2005; Lane 2005; Thatcher 2005). For discussions of the "race to the bottom" thesis especially regarding neoliberal tax policy, see, for example, Crafts (2000), Dehejia and Genschel (1999), Hallerberg (1996), McKenzie and Lee (1991), and Steinmo (1993, pp. 29–30).

[49]Babb 2007; Crouch 2011; Fourcade 2006; Fourcade-Gourinchas and Babb 2002; Harvey 2005; Mudge 2008, 2011; Simmons et al. 2008.

[50]Halliday and Carruthers 2010. Francesco Duina (1999) found much the same thing with respect to the adoption of EU directives by member states.

Second, researchers who establish that convergence has occurred often do not adequately substantiate their claims about which mechanisms have caused it: normative, mimetic, coercive, or competitive. Assumptions are often made, particularly that learning and copying are often involved, but little if any empirical evidence is provided to that effect. Thankfully, some recent scholarship has started to address this issue, but more work needs to be done.[51]

Our analysis of knowledge regimes documents that all four convergence mechanisms were at work in our cases. Moreover, they tended to operate in nationally specific combinations. There was much competitive mimicry and partisan coercion in the United States. State coercion and international normative and mimetic learning were especially pronounced in France. Coordinated normative and mimetic learning were evident in Germany. And consensus-based normative learning and state coercion were important in Denmark. More important, the results of those mechanisms differed significantly from what convergence theorists claim—that is, evidence of convergence was uneven and limited. Our cases show that each knowledge regime changed gradually and incrementally since the 1970s but that their evolution occurred in ways that were constrained by already existing political and economic institutions as well as the availability of certain resources. The U.S. knowledge regime remained competitive and bifurcated between clearly distinct public and private policy research organizations; the French knowledge regime remained largely statist; the German knowledge regime remained coordinated and continued to privilege semi-public research organizations; and the Danish knowledge regime continued to exhibit a remarkable orientation to negotiation, consensus making, and reasoned debate. In this regard our argument resembles those of researchers operating in the tradition of comparative political economy and sometimes the Varieties of Capitalism School who have shown that institutional change tends to be incremental and path-dependent thanks to a number of factors that limit the range of options from which people can choose when change is afoot.[52] Put bluntly, then, insofar as our research is concerned convergence theories are right about the mechanisms of change but misleading about the outcomes.[53]

---

[51] The criticism is long-standing (e.g., Buttel 2000; Mizruchi and Fein 1999; Schneiberg and Clemens 2006; Dobbin et al. 2007). Recent work that tries to empirically pin down which mechanisms are at work includes, for example, Bartley (2007), Halliday and Carruthers (2007, 2010), and Simmons et al. (2008).

[52] Campbell 2010, 2004; Campbell and Pedersen 2001b; Hall 2007; Halliday and Carruthers 2010; Mahoney and Thelen 2010a; Pierson 2000a; Thelen 1999; Steinmo 2010; Streeck and Thelen 2005.

[53] The term "convergence mechanisms," or "mechanisms of institutional isomorphic change" as DiMaggio and Powell (1983) first referred to them, is itself misleading insofar as normative, mimetic, coercive, and competitive processes may be operating without necessarily leading to widespread convergence on a particular structure or practice, which is what is often implied.

A Model of the National Construction of Knowledge Regimes

With all of this in mind we can now present our model of the national construction of knowledge regimes—a model based on the comparative historical analysis presented in subsequent chapters. To begin with, knowledge regimes produce the analysis, advice, and other ideas that others have shown often influence public policy. But knowledge regimes themselves are shaped largely by the nationally specific policymaking and production regimes with which they are associated. Challenges to and changes in production and policymaking regimes often cause changes in knowledge regimes, which is not surprising insofar as institutional change in one area of a political economy can cause change in another particularly when people believe that institutional complementarities have broken down and try to renew them.[54] Extending Boyer's insights, noted earlier, the breakdown of institutional complementarity is particularly evident when actors (1) perceive that the knowledge regime is no longer useful for policymakers trying to make sense of and solve economic problems and (2) take steps intentionally to change them in order to make them more useful. *Perception* and *intention* are the telltale signs.[55]

However, knowledge regimes and the ideas they produce are not necessarily just simple reflections of material political and economic interests. Knowledge regimes may enjoy a degree of independence from the policymaking and production regimes depending on institutional and other circumstances. And there are no guarantees that even though actors try to change knowledge regimes they will succeed or their efforts will lead to more effective public policy. As a result, ours is not an argument about the functional *inevitability* of certain outcomes but rather an argument about the functional *intentions* of actors to build institutions and organizations that they hope will be useful. Even when people intend to behave rationally the social contexts within which they operate are often so complex and unpredictable that their intentions are not always fulfilled.[56] So ours is an institutional middle-ground argument that extends some of our earlier work on the international diffusion of neoliberalism and on the nature of ideas,

[54] Amable 2003; Campbell 2010; Crouch 2005; Hall and Soskice 2001a; Streeck 2009. Fligstein and McAdam (2012) make a similar argument about the relationship among organizational fields in general.

[55] Challenges to and changes in production and policymaking regimes do not necessarily or immediately trigger changes in the structure of knowledge regimes. They may simply stimulate efforts within the existing knowledge regime structure to produce new ideas. Structural change occurs only after people begin to suspect that new ideas adequate for coping with the problems at hand are not forthcoming from the existing knowledge regime and therefore believe that adjustments to it are required. It is this later situation with which we are concerned.

[56] Prasad 2012, p. 251.

policymaking, and institutional change.[57] In short, knowledge regimes are nationally specific constructions whose structure and practices are largely determined by—but not reducible to—the surrounding policymaking and production regimes.

Several very important clarifications are necessary. First, we cannot stress enough that ours is not a functionalist argument. Sometimes elites respond to a perceived breakdown of institutional complementarity through a centrally planned process where, for example, political leaders suspect that the policy research organizations upon which they rely no longer provide analysis and other ideas that are useful to them in coping with the country's current problems and so they take steps to change and improve the situation. This might involve establishing brand-new types of policy research organizations or encouraging those that already exist to operate in different ways. In contrast to this top-down process, at other times responses may be much more decentralized and piecemeal. But regardless of how centralized or decentralized the response is it often involves much trial-and-error experimentation and casting about for ways to generate better policy analysis and other ideas. At best such muddling through allows people only to hope that whatever adjustments they make to the knowledge regime will in fact produce better ideas.[58] Put differently, even the best of intentions do not always produce the results envisioned. This is why there are no guarantees that the adjustments made—regardless of the nationally specific form they take—will necessarily improve the knowledge regime's institutional complementarity vis-à-vis the rest of the political economy.

Second, we do not mean to suggest that the actors involved actually conceive of and articulate their problems as "breakdowns of institutional complementarity." This is an analytic concept that we use to describe what happens and is based on our interpretations of the data at hand—particularly what people told us during interviews. Nor do we argue that their intentions are to change knowledge regimes in toto. The reality is that their reform efforts are generally much less encompassing and focus on some but certainly not all of the policy research organizations within their knowledge regimes. Again, this underscores the fact that the reform process is often much about piecemeal trial-and-error experimentation, puzzling, and muddling through.

Finally, ours is not a naïve view where all the ideas emanating from knowledge regimes necessarily influence policymakers. Things are messier than that. First, knowledge regimes are not monolithic but rather constellations of

---

[57]On the diffusion of neoliberalism, see Campbell (2004), Campbell and Pedersen (2001b), and Pedersen (2011). On ideas, see Campbell (1998, 2002) and Pedersen (1991). On institutional change, see Campbell (2004, 2010).

[58]The importance of muddling through, puzzling, and trial-and-error experimentation for policymaking is well known (e.g., Heclo 1974; Kingdon 1995; Lindblom 1959).

policy research organizations sometimes competing and sometimes cooperating with each other. So depending on their nationally specific institutional arrangements knowledge regimes may produce a variety of ideas from which policymakers may pick and choose. Second, these choices often depend not only on the persuasive powers of people in the knowledge regime but also on powerful political and economic interests. In other words, there is no guarantee that policymakers will rely on the analyses and ideas that knowledge regimes generate. Third, there are feedbacks in play. If policymakers choose to incorporate some of the ideas produced by knowledge regimes into policy, then these policies may have subsequent effects on the policymaking and production regimes themselves. Given all the causal complexities involved, evidence that knowledge regimes matter as an important source of institutional complementarity rests on our findings in each country that actors realized their knowledge regimes had become dysfunctional for the rest of the political economy and as a result tried to improve them.

The basic causal relationships are illustrated in figure 1.1. Our concern, however, as we have already explained, is not with these feedbacks or the direct impact of ideas on policymaking, which have already been explored by those arguing that ideas matter for public policymaking. Instead, our focus is largely on the initial nationally specific causal effects that policymaking and production regimes have on knowledge regimes and that knowledge regimes have on the ideas they produce. The relationships with which we are concerned are represented by the solid causal arrows in figure 1.1 as opposed to the dotted arrows, which represent the relationships that others have already studied. All of these relationships, of course, constitute some of the most important power dynamics in advanced capitalist countries insofar as actors in all three regimes struggle within various institutional and resource constraints to influence the production and dissemination of policy-relevant ideas. Policymaking and production regimes are in effect dynamic power structures that involve the mobilization of resources and that can change over time. So are knowledge regimes.

Our approach does not subscribe to a strictly Marxist, Gramscian, or otherwise materialist line of argument in which the ideas produced by knowledge regimes can somehow be reduced to powerful economic interests or otherwise represent the hegemonic interests of a ruling class.[59] To be sure, these interests are part of the story, although more so in some cases and at some times than others. But the influence of policymaking regimes, not to mention experts and analysts themselves, is too important to permit this sort

---

[59]Classic statements are from Gramsci (1971) and Marx and Engels (1970), but see also Bourdieu (2001). More recent versions focusing on policy research organizations include Domhoff (2010, chap. 4) and Dye (1995, chap. 9).

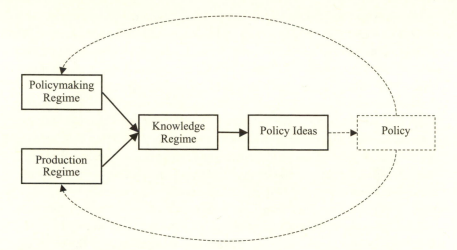

Figure 1.1. The National Construction of Knowledge Regimes and Their Effects

of economic reductionism. Nor, however, do we subscribe to the opposite idealist position, such as that articulated by Karl Mannheim, who argued that sometimes idea producers are free-floating intellectuals immune from the influence of political and economic forces.[60] Adjudicating this debate is not our main concern. Nevertheless, we will address the issue occasionally because our evidence shows that things are more complicated than either of these views suggests and that the sharp distinction between materialist and idealist views is misguided. In other words, knowledge regimes may enjoy a degree of independence from the production and policymaking regimes depending on institutional circumstances.[61] We will show, for example, that thanks to differences in the institutional configuration of production and policymaking regimes private money holds sway over knowledge regime activities more in the United States than in France. Independence also stems from the fact that knowledge regimes are populated in varying degree by experts and professionals. As others have shown, thanks to their professional norms experts often insist on

---

[60]In fact, Mannheim (1936) was torn over the issue. He argued that intellectuals can be either free-floating and quite independent or willing to sell their services to powerful political and economic interests. Gouldner (1979) muddies things further by arguing that intellectuals in modern society present themselves as free-floating intellectuals serving the interests of the general public but in fact conspire to turn their intellectual capital into power for themselves.

[61]For an elegant theoretical adjudication of a similar middle-ground position, see John Hall (1993). Of course, Max Weber (1946, p. 280) staked out the middle ground too when he argued famously that ideas are sometimes like independent switchmen occasionally diverting the course of otherwise interest-based action.

a modicum of autonomy in their work and tend to resist excessive interference or control by political or economic elites.[62] The independence of experts and professionals also depends on institutional circumstances and is perhaps most obvious in our German case where universities often work closely with policy research organizations. We will show as well that because the role of professional economic science became increasingly important in our knowledge regimes the knowledge producing function gradually gained more independence from the policymaking and production regimes, especially in France and Denmark.

Finally, policy research organizations do not operate in isolation from one another. Nor do knowledge regimes. As a result, structures, practices, and ideas may diffuse within and across knowledge regimes in ways that involve convergent tendencies. However, the manner in which this occurs is heavily mediated by the nationally specific arrangements of knowledge, policymaking, and production regimes. In particular, institutional and resource constraints limited the degree to which convergence occurred within and across our four knowledge regimes. Hence, despite mechanisms that may *encourage* convergence they do not necessarily *result* in convergence. Convergence may be blocked, and even if it is not it may still be partial and very uneven.

It is worth mentioning that there is also an emergent literature on "social knowledge making" to which our model and research speaks. This is an effort by scholars to understand how knowledge in the social sciences and humanities is produced. They are influenced by the sociology of knowledge literature and research in the production of knowledge in the natural sciences. This is a new field, and its proponents have called for research exactly along the lines we develop in this book. In particular, they have urged research into cross-national and historical variations in "knowledge sites" where people engage in a variety of knowledge producing practices that are influenced by other fields of actors in the political and economic environment. They have called as well for research into the interaction and interrelationships among knowledge sites to see whether there has been a diffusion and convergence across countries in knowledge and knowledge producing capacities.[63] These are issues that lie at the heart of this book and for which we offer many insights.

---

[62]On the autonomy of professionals and experts, see Abbott (1988), Brint (1994), Collins and Evans (2007), Freidson (1994), and Ziegler (1997).

[63]The literature on social knowledge making is well represented in an edited volume by Charles Camic, Neil Gross, and Michèle Lamont (2011a). It includes chapters representing a number of extensive studies of different types of social knowledge making. Their recommendations are detailed in the introductory chapter (Camic et al. 2011b, pp. 29–32).

Knowledge Regimes, Globalization, and the End of the Golden Age

We will substantiate our analytic arguments through historical and compara-tive analyses showing that the knowledge regimes in the United States, France, Germany, and Denmark underwent significant changes in their structures and practices as a result of the political-economic crisis that erupted in the 1970s and 1980s. A bit of historical background is in order here, followed by a brief summary of each chapter that lies ahead.

As is well known, the 1970s and 1980s was a period when economic globalization was developing rapidly, and as a result, all the advanced capi-talist countries experienced problems that brought the Golden Age of post-war twentieth-century capitalism to an end. The Golden Age was based on several things. First was a settlement between capital and labor. This took different forms in different countries, but the essence everywhere was an agreement to link wage increases to productivity growth. The resulting wage restraint helped bolster retained earnings, which provided investment neces-sary for growth. Second, welfare states were built up as a protection against unemployment and other social ills and, following Keynesian principles, as a vehicle for stimulating demand and therefore economic growth. Third, the United States was the world's postwar hegemonic economic power. It pur-sued macroeconomic policies that stimulated demand in America, which provided a market for foreign imports that helped bolster economic growth overseas. Moreover, U.S. foreign direct investment in Europe also helped spur economic growth there. Fourth, all of this was carried out in an environ-ment of international currency stability thanks to the Bretton Woods system of pegged but adjustable exchange rates, which provided a check against pro-longed bouts of inflation. Economies prospered. As table 1.1 shows, the ad-vanced capitalist countries as a whole averaged healthy productivity growth, nearly full employment, low inflation, and balanced government budgets for much of the 1960s and early 1970s.

However, the Golden Age began to teeter in the mid-1970s and the post-war settlement started unraveling. Economic growth had created jobs and re-duced unemployment during the Golden Age. But, as a result, the threat of unemployment became less effective in disciplining wage demands. This was compounded by the fact that memories of high unemployment in the 1930s faded as the older generation began to retire. Similarly, the availability of more generous welfare benefits weakened the wage moderating effects of unemploy-ment. Workers continued to demand higher wages even though productivity growth rates were beginning to decline now that the initial benefits of postwar investment in the modernization of manufacturing capacity and infrastruc-ture had been realized. Labor conflicts broke out in the late 1960s in many

Table 1.1. Economic Performance in 17 Advanced Capitalist
Countries, 1960–1989

	1960–73	1974–79	1980–89
Average annual productivity growth (%)	3.8	1.6	1.5
Average annual unemployment (%)	2.2	4.1	6.8
Average annual inflation (%)	4.5	10.0	6.4
Average annual government budget deficit (% of GDP)	0.1	2.9	3.9

Note: The countries include Australia, Austria, Belgium, Canada, Denmark, Finland, France, Germany, Italy, Japan, the Netherlands, New Zealand, Norway, Sweden, Switzerland, the United Kingdom, and the United States.

Source: Kenworthy (1997, tables 3 and 7).

countries. With wages rising faster than productivity, profits and retained earnings were squeezed, capital formation and investment were constricted, and economic growth began to falter. In turn, firms raised prices so inflation heated up. To spur growth governments turned even more toward Keynesian demand stimulus policies, but this increased government budget deficits and debt, which contributed further to inflationary pressures. Stagflation began to materialize. Table 1.1 reveals that in the advanced capitalist countries from the mid-1970s through the 1980s productivity growth deteriorated, unemployment and inflation escalated, and governments ran larger budget deficits.

Making matters worse, the Bretton Woods system, which depended on countries being committed to defending their currency pegs, began to wobble. As economic growth slowed and demand stimulus followed, pressure mounted for governments to let their currencies float in an effort to improve exports. This was exacerbated by the deterioration of U.S. economic hegemony. America's trade surplus shrank in the face of stiffer competition from Europe and Japan. The U.S. government began to run into budget deficit problems thanks to Keynesian stimulus policies and the costs of the Vietnam War. And the dollar became overvalued. The Bretton Woods system collapsed in 1971 when the United States abandoned it. Governments turned increasingly to devaluation in order to stimulate growth and resolve balance of payments problems associated with wage escalation and economic stagnation. Inflationary pressures mounted further. And the expectation of greater inflation fueled additional wage demands. A vicious cycle was unleashed that was exacerbated by increased capital mobility thanks to the inability of national governments to maintain adequate capital controls. Finally, OPEC hiked oil prices in 1973 and 1979, compounding all of these problems, amplifying inflation, and contributing to two deep recessions in the advanced capitalist world. Since then economic globalization and in Europe the advancement of the single market project made life even more difficult as countries struggled to assert and maintain their competitive economic advantages.[64]

What matters here are not the particulars of how all of this played out in the United States, France, Germany, and Denmark, but rather that the end of the Golden Age and the rise of globalization set in motion challenges to and changes in their policymaking and production regimes. These, in turn, caused changes in their knowledge regimes as everyone struggled to make sense of and manage new problems. People began to recognize that their knowledge regimes had become dysfunctional in the sense that they were not providing ideas useful for resolving these problems. They tried to improve them accordingly. Put differently, the institutional complementarities afforded by each knowledge regime for the rest of its political economy broke down and movements to reform them followed. This played out differently in each country and stemmed from various crises that people described for us during our interviews for this book.[65] But in each case new policy research organizations emerged, some of the old ones reformed their structures and practices, and the manner in which they interacted often changed. These stories are told in the four chapters that follow in part I.

In chapter 2 we explain that through the late 1970s the U.S. knowledge regime was dominated by a number of prominent state policy research organizations and several rather scholarly private ones too. But after that as stagflation gripped the country the United States experienced what several people described for us as an increasing *crisis of partisanship* that was marked by a continuing escalation in ideological rancor, polarization, and divisiveness in Washington. This entailed the proliferation of a more competitive and often contentious set of private policy research organizations thanks to numerous sources of tax deductible private funding from corporations and wealthy individuals, and a fragmented and porous political system. This led to a war of ideas that grew increasingly vicious. The presence of a number of private policy research organizations meant that there was an important degree of separation of one part of the knowledge regime, which had important connections

---

[64]This general history is well documented, for example, by Eichengreen (2008), Judt (2006), Marglin and Schor (1990), and Piore and Sabel (1984). For detail on the rise and fall of the Bretton Woods system and problems of escalating international capital mobility, see Kapstein (1994), McNamara (1998), and Pauly (1998). The literature on how states and policymakers have tried to cope with all of this, especially in the context of economic globalization and Europeanization, is vast. For well-cited examples from comparative political economy, see Boyer and Drache (1996), Garrett (1998), Lash and Urry (1987), Swank (2002), Weiss (2003), and several essays in Kitschelt et al. (1999) and Morgan et al. (2010).

[65]We do not lightly invoke the term "crisis" here or elsewhere. In effect, this is how people described situations to us during the course of our interviews for this project.

to the production regime, from another part that was embedded within the policymaking regime. Paradoxically, as the crisis of partisanship reached an unprecedented level in the late 1990s and early 2000s, cooperation among some of these organizations broke out across the political divide due to the efforts of those who sensed the disastrous consequences of such mean-spirited partisanship for the country and for the credibility of their research organizations. In effect, people sensed twice that their knowledge regime's institutional complementarity vis-à-vis the rest of the political economy had broken down and tried twice to fix it: first by ramping up more aggressive and competitive private policy research organizations and then by engaging in more cooperative activities. Meanwhile, policy research organizations in the state, which had substantial analytic capabilities, did not change much and continued to exhibit a surprising amount of cooperation as they had all along. As a result, the U.S. response to a perceived breakdown in the knowledge regime's institutional complementarity with the rest of the political economy involved lots of muddling through via a mix of decentralized experimentation and a limited amount of coordination.

The French struggled too in the aftermath of the Golden Age. In chapter 3 we show that this involved a knowledge regime that was dominated almost exclusively during the 1970s and 1980s by the state thanks to France's strong statist traditions. However, the political-economic problems of this period persisted and precipitated what some people we interviewed described as a *crisis of ideas* within the state—the realization that this statist knowledge regime was too insulated and therefore suffered a dearth of fresh thinking. In turn, policymakers began to encourage the development of new semi-public policy research organizations outside the state as well as new ones inside it in an effort to cultivate new ideas. This externalization strategy was very much a part of France's move away from *dirigisme*—central state-led economic development—and involved the gradual if partial separation of the knowledge regime from the policymaking regime, which earlier had been virtually indistinguishable from each other. And there were a few efforts to establish private policy research organizations too. But it took a long time for people to realize that the knowledge regime had become dysfunctional and that it no longer complemented the rest of the political economy, so change was slower than in the United States and orchestrated in a more top-down centralized manner but in the end still with a considerable amount of experimentation and casting about in hopes of success. There was never such a full-scale war of ideas in France as there was in America, although in a sense the state tried to start one, or at least some modest skirmishes, by financing these new organizations. As a result, the French knowledge regime became more fragmented with many of its policy research organizations insulated from each other in their own niches and engaging in comparatively little competition or cooperation. Eventually, the state recentralized some of their activities but without returning to the heavy handed ways of dirigisme. So, like the United States, the French tried twice to restore institutional complementarity: first by decentralization and then by recentralization. Insofar as there is any cooperation or coordination among French organizations it is still among those in or closely affiliated with the state.

We show in chapter 4 that the German knowledge regime was coordinated through a number of mechanisms that reflected Germany's long-standing formal corporatist institutions as well as the country's strong multiparty proportional representation system of government. However, contrary to what one might expect given these institutional legacies, there were also a considerable number of more informal coordinating mechanisms. Both formal and informal mechanisms facilitated compromise in the knowledge regime despite the continued presence of political-ideological divisions in the policymaking regime. The German knowledge regime was also more decentralized than any of the others due to Germany's federalist state, which funded and helped to organize and coordinate many important semi-public policy research organizations throughout the Länder. Much of this has been in place for a long time. So was a strong emphasis on scientific analysis as an important ingredient in economic policy advice. Yet we were told that a *crisis of corporatism*, which followed the end of the Golden Age, led eventually to an expansion of private policy research organizations, not to mention lobbyists, which increased competition in the knowledge regime. This was a decentralized effort to reform the knowledge regime through a kind of trial-and-error process based upon various privately organized initiatives, but it was blended with somewhat more centralized coordination too, such as deliberate efforts by the state to improve the scientific quality of policy analysis and advice emanating from the semi-public policy research organizations. Doubts and concerns about the knowledge regime's complementarity with the rest of the political economy came into full view as people grew concerned over the crisis of corporatism. In this regard, Germany may be witnessing the initial salvos of an emergent war of ideas although one that is tempered by the persistence of its long-standing coordination mechanisms. Reunification in 1990 also increased the number of policy research organizations and, in turn, competition for resources and analytic credibility.

Finally, and in stark contrast with the escalating war of ideas in the United States, a war of ideas subsided in Denmark after the mid-1980s. As we explain in chapter 5, this was due to the fact that the Danes perceived what was described to us as a *crisis of ideology* among the political parties as the Golden Age faded away. Policymakers and others realized that the old ideological battles between the left and the right were counterproductive and that thinking based on objective empirical analysis should guide policymaking in order to resolve the economic malaise that first beset Denmark in the 1970s. They recognized that their knowledge regime had grown dysfunctional and in effect that its complementarity for the rest of the political economy had atrophied. This led then to a great deal of consensus making in the knowledge regime. But this was amplified as well by three additional factors. First, Danes established a taken-for-granted national consensus about the core socioeconomic principles that should orient policymaking—something we did not find in the other countries and that stemmed from Denmark's particular experience as a small country. Second, the state centralized its control over the knowledge regime playing a major role in improving the quality of scientific policy analysis. Third, much decision making in Denmark's policymaking and production regimes was based on systems of corporatist negotiations, which were once tripartite but in important areas became more complex, inclusive, and expert oriented over the years—a pluralist turn that reflected the crisis of ideology. Given the state's presence in the knowledge regime and the extensive system of corporatist negotiations that permeate this society, the interpenetration and lack of separation among knowledge, policymaking, and production regimes is extensive although diminishing slowly. As a result, the Danish knowledge regime shares particular features with its French and German counterparts. It is an example of an increasingly centralized and planned response to the perceived breakdown of the knowledge regime's institutional complementarity but one that involved much negotiation and consensus making. And recently a few small private policy research organizations have emerged too.

Overall, then, transformations in each country's knowledge regime were driven by challenges to and changes in their policymaking and production regimes that emanated from the end of the Golden Age and the advent of globalization. In each case, the institutional complementarities that knowledge regimes had once afforded countries during the Golden Age appeared to deteriorate. And as people began to realize that their knowledge regimes no longer provided the analysis and advice necessary to make sense of a new set of political-economic problems they moved to change them. However, this unfolded as comparative political economists would expect in nationally specific ways thanks to the institutional differences involved. The broad story lines are summarized schematically in figure 1.2.

We conclude part I with a brief Reprise where we consider the theoretical implications of the evidence presented so far for research in comparative political economy. Here we elaborate on the arguments and criticisms we introduced earlier in this chapter. We also discuss how our evidence sheds light on the issue of the relative independence of policy analysts and their ideas from political and economic forces that might seek to influence them. Finally, we show how our findings suggest the need for researchers interested in policy research organizations in general and think tanks in particular to reevaluate

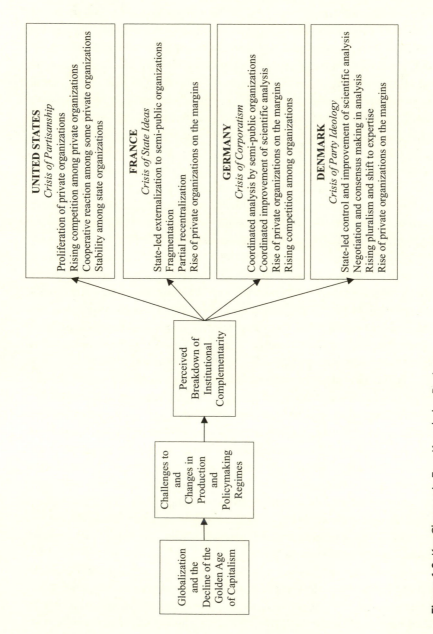

Figure 1.2. Key Changes in Four Knowledge Regimes

some of the organizational typologies they use in their work. Theoretical considerations for the analyses presented in part II are included at the end of each chapter there.

In part II we refocus and in light of the four national cases address the issues of convergence and the influence of knowledge regimes. Two things are at issue here. First is whether the national character of knowledge regimes has diminished, as some would expect, in the face of globalization and other forces by which organizational structures and practices as well as policy ideas diffuse within and across knowledge regimes. Second is whether at the end of the day knowledge regimes and the policy research organizations of which they are made actually influence policymaking.

We take up convergence in chapter 6. To begin with, we show that the quality of policy analysis improved across knowledge regimes and policy analysts tended to agree increasingly on common analytic practices, such as appropriate databases, econometric methodologies, and forecasting models. Then we demonstrate that in every country policy research organizations began to converge on similar dissemination practices, such as use of the Internet and new media, by which they channeled their analysis and recommendations to policymakers and others—practices that tended to resemble those of American advocacy organizations. Both trends were evident within and across knowledge regimes. And in both cases normative, mimetic, coercive, and competitive mechanisms were responsible for these changes. But they often worked in nationally specific combinations. Moreover, convergence was extremely uneven and partial because there were significant obstacles to the wholesale diffusion of these practices across countries and organizations. These stemmed from the unique resource and institutional constraints that knowledge regimes and the rest of the political economy posed, such as the availability of private or state funding for policy research organizations, peculiar tax laws, corporatist and statist legacies, deep-seated political traditions, electoral systems, and more. As a result, although each knowledge regime underwent significant change, national differences persisted in how each one was organized and operated. In short, we found patterns of only limited convergence that were at odds with what many organizational and economic sociologists and others would have expected especially during times of great uncertainty like the end of the Golden Age and the rise of globalization.

In chapter 7 we address the degree to which knowledge regimes influence policymaking. For reasons that we explain in that chapter establishing influence is a devilishly tricky business that we can only begin to address. Two questions are in play. First, do *individual* policy research organizations influence policymakers' thinking? We find that for methodological reasons it is enormously difficult to determine which policy research organizations are influential on an individual basis.[66] Notably, the evidence offered to us by people in these organizations by which they try to measure their organization's influence, such as the number of times they are cited in the media or invited to make presentations to policymakers, is by their own admission often circumstantial at best. Second, do knowledge regimes as *fields* of policy research organizations affect the nature of the ideas that policy research organizations tend to produce in the first place and then disseminate to policymakers and others? Put differently, does the nationally unique character of a knowledge regime tend to produce nationally unique policy analysis and advice? Based on content analysis of reports from national councils of economic advisors in our four countries we find that the arguments, analyses, and policy recommendations from these councils reflect the arrangement of the knowledge regimes in which they are located. This field-level approach sheds light on key debates about the nature of ideas and politics. At stake here is an argument in the globalization literature—and similar in some ways to convergence theory—which suggests that the rise of globalization led policymakers across countries to adopt a common set of neoliberal supply-side ideas. We find, however, that insofar as these reports are concerned the rise of supply-side and especially neoliberal thinking since the 1970s was incomplete, gradual, and uneven within and across our four countries. These perspectives did not become hegemonic paradigms. Nor did their emergence necessarily constitute a sharp break with the older Keynesian approach. In some countries the end of the Golden Age and the onset of stagflation and globalization brought Keynesianism to its knees. But in other countries it did not. As a result, these cases provide further evidence about the limits of convergence and diffusion across countries. And they demonstrate that the structure of knowledge regimes affects the content of the ideas that they produce.

Finally, part III wraps things up. There chapter 8 briefly reviews our main findings and in light of our analysis reflects on a normative question: Which knowledge regime is best? Finally, because we have explored new and largely unchartered territory in our analysis of national knowledge regimes, we offer in a Postscript some suggestions for a research agenda for the future, including

[66]For general discussions of the pitfalls of showing how ideas influence policymaking, see, for instance, Berman (1998, chap. 2), Blyth (1997), Parsons (2007, chap. 4), and Campbell (2004, chap. 4). The literature on think tanks argues that demonstrating influence is difficult for several reasons. First, definitions of influence are often vague. For instance, one researcher defined it as "the success by experts in making their work known among a set of policymakers so that it informs their thinking on or public articulation of policy relevant information" (Rich 2004, p. 153). Second, an organization's influence may vary over time, over different phases of the policymaking process, and across policy areas (Weidenbaum 2009, chap. 7). Third, the target of influence may vary and include policymakers, their staff, career civil servants, and/or the general public (Abelson 2002).

especially questions and propositions for scholars to consider regarding globalization and neoliberal diffusion, comparative political economy, and convergence theory.

The Nature of Ideas and Knowledge Regimes

Let us clarify our key terms. When we refer to policy *ideas* we have in mind arguments that specify causal relationships, such as that between tax or welfare policies and economic performance, over certain periods of time. They are based on paradigmatic theoretical or ideological assumptions. They are often substantiated with data and analyses of various sorts. They are often framed rhetorically in ways designed to appeal to policymakers and their staff, the general public or other audiences, sometimes by invoking widely held values, opinions, or attitudes in society. And they are often articulated in explicit opposition to competing ideas.[67] For example, certain versions of neoliberalism became influential during the 1980s in the United States. Neoliberals often argued that less government involvement in the economy would improve economic performance—an argument that was rooted in the fundamental principles of neoclassical economics as practiced by conservative economists. It was frequently substantiated by the Laffer curve, a formal model intended to show that declining tax rates would be more than offset by rising revenues stemming from increased economic growth. It was framed with Jeffersonian images of a big, centralized, and expanding government whose consequences were devastating to the country and that could best be brought under control by limiting politicians' access to revenues. It was typically juxtaposed to Keynesianism, which favored a more active role of government in the economy.[68] Ideas like this emerge from analysts and others in policy research organizations in knowledge regimes who are trying to make sense of their country's political-economic problems. Ideas like this are often contested. When they become widely accepted and taken for granted—that is, legitimate—they become part of an institutionalized knowledge base for policymakers and others.

The distinction between a regime and a field is subtle but important. As noted earlier, a *field* is simply a particular set of organizations. Of course, a

---

[67]For detailed discussions of the multidimensional nature of policy "ideas," see, for example, Berman (1998), Block (1996), Campbell (1998, 2002), and Goldstein and Keohane (1993). Our view on these issues is similar to those of scholars who have recently studied the production of "social knowledge," which entails descriptive information and analytical statements about social phenomena, normative recommendations based on such statements, and technologies and tools of knowledge making, such as epistemic principles, cognitive schema, theoretical models, and the like (Camic et al. 2011b, p. 3).

[68]Campbell 1998. To be sure, neoliberalism had different meanings for different people. For a discussion of its many facets and interpretations, see Colin Crouch (2011).

field often consists of niches—that is, sectors or subfields—of actors who are relatively more similar to one another and more closely associated with one another than they are with others in the broader field. For example, private think tanks in Washington tend to interact more with each other than with government research units like the president's Council of Economic Advisors, the Congressional Budget Office, and the Government Accountability Office.

Fields in knowledge regimes consist of combinations of different types of policy research organizations. As discussed at length in the literatures on ideas and think tanks there are four ideal types.[69] First are private *scholarly* research organizations, sometimes referred to as universities without students. These are staffed with scholars, professional researchers and analysts, sometimes with joint university appointments. They produce expert research monographs and journal articles much like those found in academia as well as analytical reports. They also tend to be politically and ideologically nonpartisan. Second are private *advocacy* research organizations. They tend to be more politically and ideologically partisan. And they are less concerned with conducting rigorous policy research than with consuming, packaging, and aggressively disseminating the research and theories of others in brief policy papers and through the media in order to influence the ideological climate, public debate, and public policy. Lobbyists are not part of this world because they do not do much if any policy research and because they only push ideas on behalf of individual paying clients. Third are *party* research organizations. These are formally associated with political parties and provide a source of expert advice and analysis for party members. Fourth are *state* research organizations. These may be either directly affiliated with specific government departments and ministries or serve the legislative or executive branches more generally. The other three types are located in civil society—by which we mean that they are not part of the state apparatus per se. We use the terms "scholarly," "advocacy," "party," and "state" research organizations throughout the book. However, as we quickly discovered, particular policy research organizations do not always fit neatly into any single ideal type.

Regimes are more than just a field of organizations like these. Regimes also involve mechanisms of governance that constrain and enable the activities of organizations in the field. Put differently, regimes consist of both a field of organizations and the institutions—that is, the rules, monitoring, and enforcement mechanisms—that guide their behavior. These institutions can be formal, such as laws and legislative mandates, or informal, such as professional norms.[70]

[69]Blyth 2002; Hall 1993, 1992; Rich 2004; Stone 2004; Weaver and McGann 2000.
[70]Our focus on knowledge regimes as fields of organizations should not be confused with work on either "epistemic cultures," which focuses on interactions among knowledge producers within individual organizations like scientific laboratories (Knorr Cetina 1999; see also Hage and Mote

We have distinguished among three types of regimes in national political economies—policymaking, production, and knowledge regimes—which in our view should constitute the three legs of comparative political-economic analysis. Conceptually these can be viewed as ideal types each having their own discrete set of organizations and institutions governing their behavior. However, in reality things are more complicated. For example, the policymaking regime's tax code prohibits nonprofit think tanks in the U.S. knowledge regime from lobbying politicians. But no such rules apply in the other countries. Furthermore, the presence of corporatist institutions in Germany and Denmark's production regimes and their absence in the United States have significant effects on the types of policy research organizations found in each knowledge regime and the degree to which policy research organizations cooperate with each other or not.

Two implications follow from this that will be documented in subsequent chapters. First, the degree of separation between regimes is sometimes blurry. Put simply, just as three circles in a Venn diagram may overlap, so too may the structures and practices of policymaking, production, and knowledge regimes. Second, the degree of separation between each of these three types of regimes may change. Indeed, all three types of regimes are dynamic, and that dynamism accounts for shifts in separation. For instance, immediately after the Second World War virtually all French policy research organizations were located within the state. Hence, the separation between the policymaking and knowledge regimes was virtually nil. But later the French prime minister funded the development of policy research organizations affiliated with the main political parties and encouraged them to operate independently from the state, thus increasing the degree of separation between the knowledge and policymaking regimes.

Notes on Methods

We focus on the United States, France, Germany, and Denmark because these are typically offered as good examples of liberal, statist, and corporatist types of advanced capitalist countries, respectively.[71] Hence, their policymaking and production regimes are sufficiently different from one another to facilitate interesting cross-national comparisons about their relationships to national knowledge regimes. In brief, researchers often describe the United States as having a decentralized, open, and competitive policymaking process and a lib-

---

2008), or work on "epistemic communities," which focuses on interactions within networks of individual knowledge producing experts (Haas 1992).

[71]Crouch and Streeck 1997; Dore et al. 1999; Kenworthy 2004; Katzenstein 1978; Schmidt 2002; Thelen 2004; Hall and Soskice 2001b; Ziegler 1997.

eral production regime in the sense that there is comparatively little state intervention or other forms of economic coordination beyond what the market provides. France is famous for a centralized, closed policymaking process and much state coordination of markets. Germany is known to have compromise-oriented policymaking and corporatist coordination in the production regime. Denmark, however, is a less well-known case. And contrary to conventional wisdom it is a hybrid that blends elements of the other three, particularly a strong central state and corporatist bargaining. It is also a small country compared to the others, which has important implications for its knowledge regime.[72]

For each country we drew a sample of each of the four types of policy research organizations described earlier. We contacted them to arrange interviews with top-level administrators, often presidents or executive directors, and occasionally senior researchers or other senior staff members. We talked at length with 101 people in 75 organizations between April 2008 and August 2009.[73] We also collected policy documents and if they were available annual reports from each organization for 1987, 1997, and 2007 or years as close to these as possible. We explored each organization's website too. We based the analysis for the book on data gathered from these sources but especially the interviews. And we adopted an inductive approach to these data. So, for example, our descriptions of each knowledge regime as a field and our definitions of the crises that triggered change in them emerged from the interviews; we did not impose them on the data. Readers interested in learning more about our sampling procedures and our methodologies for handling these different data

[72]Campbell and Hall 2006; Campbell and Pedersen 2007a, 2007b; Kenworthy 2006; Kjær and Pedersen 2001; Pedersen 2006a, 2006b. Some people advised us as well to examine policy research organizations attached to international organizations, such as the OECD, IMF, and European Union. International organizations like these have become an increasingly popular subject for research (e.g., Djelic and Quack 2010; Djelic and Sahlin-Andersson 2006; Marcussen 2000). Studying them would have been worthwhile, but the scope of this project was already sufficiently large that adding another set of policy research organizations was simply more than we were prepared to handle given the resources at our disposal. As it turned out, however, little mention was made of these organizations during the course of our interviews, except for the fact that they were cited as increasingly important sources of data and occasionally methodological expertise. In other words, to a significant degree the knowledge regimes we studied are nationally oriented and inwardly focused.

[73]We interviewed 35 people in 19 organizations in the United States (April 2008 and August 2009), 21 people in 19 organizations in Denmark (May and July 2008), 23 people in 19 organizations in France (June 2008), and 22 people in 18 organizations in Germany (April, May, June, and August 2009). Some of the people we interviewed have since moved on to other organizations or changed their professional titles. All references to their organizational affiliations and titles are to those they held at the time we interviewed them. Moreover, some people we interviewed asked us not to reveal their identities. So in the chapters that follow we report the identities only of people who gave us written permission to do so.

sources, including the reliable coding of interviews, should read the appendix at the end of the book.[74]

Although we have drawn heavily on the comparative political economy literature in formulating this project we depart from some of its conventions. First, we do not describe the world in terms of just two types of capitalism—liberal and coordinated market economies—as the Varieties of Capitalism School does.[75] Others have argued convincingly that there are important differences across countries within each of these two broad types.[76] Indeed, we subscribe to a more diverse classification of types: liberal, corporatist, and statist.[77] Second, our methodology is different from that of most comparative political economy studies, which are based typically on aggregate quantitative data, such as those available from the OECD, case studies utilizing secondary literature and documents, or some combination of both.[78] In addition to primary organizational documents and secondary literature we rely heavily on in-depth interviews with people who work in, run, and have extensive first-hand experience with prominent policy research organizations in our four knowledge regimes.[79] Few studies in comparative political economy rely heavily on interviews, which we have found to be extremely useful. We urge others to use them in future research.

Similarly, although we have drawn on the sociological literature on convergence that takes the field of organizations as the unit of analysis, we depart from some of its common practices too. Instead of using quantitative data from a large population of organizations, we are using interview data from a sample of organizations in our four fields of interest.[80] And instead of simply trying to establish whether convergence of some sort has occurred in the field, as many sociologists have done with great skill, we have used our interviews to identify the mechanisms that caused convergence and other sorts of change to happen or not. In this regard, we have heeded the warnings of those who urge

[74]See also Campbell et al. (2013), which details our innovative method for interview coding.
[75]Hall and Soskice 2001a.
[76]Crouch and Streeck 1997; Hancké et al. 2007b.
[77]Katzenstein 1978; Schmidt 2002; Zysman 1983. This, of course, does not exhaust all possible types (e.g., Hancké et al. 2007b; Weiss 1998).
[78]For examples of these conventional methodologies of comparative political economy, see, for instance, Garrett (1998), Hall and Soskice (2001b), Hancké et al. (2007a), Kitschelt et al. (1999), and Swank (2002).
[79]Because knowledge regimes are much like organizational fields, they are social constructions defined to a significant degree by the "mutual awareness among participants in a set of organizations that they are involved in a common enterprise" (DiMaggio and Powell 1983, p. 148). Interviewing prominent people with such mutual awareness is an excellent way to determine how these regimes are organized and operate.
[80]For examples of the conventional quantitative methodologies of organizational field analysis, see Meyer et al. (1997a, 1997b). An exception closer to our approach is Jacoby (2005).

researchers to empirically identify causal mechanisms rather than just assert them in lieu of good evidence.[81] Finally, to the best of our knowledge using content analysis of important policy documents as we have done with reports from the national councils of economic advisers to determine whether convergence in ideas has occurred is a novel approach. It is also rare in the literature on globalization and the rise of neoliberalism, not to mention the literature on how ideas matter for policymaking.[82]

Overall, then, this book explores the structure and practices of national knowledge regimes and how they changed in each of our four countries as a result of forces set in motion by the demise of the Golden Age of postwar twentieth-century capitalism and the rise of globalization. This includes an analysis of the internal dynamics of the knowledge regimes themselves and especially how the relationships among policy research organizations evolved. But it also includes an analysis of the dynamic relationships among knowledge, policymaking, and production regimes more broadly. This is a study of experts, intellectuals, political operatives, and other elites involved in policy analysis and advising as they work formally and informally in organizations and surrounding institutional environments. As a result, this study offers new insights for and challenges to the received wisdom on globalization and neoliberalism, comparative political economy, and convergence theory. In short, this is a study of the comparative political economy and sociology of policy knowledge during the globalization era. It is the first time such a systematic and extensive cross-national study has been done on this subject. It is also one of the few efforts to blend the insights and theories of these two socials science disciplines. But it also has important differences from each discipline in terms of how we envisioned the project initially, the types of data we collected, and, of course, some of the key conclusions we reached.

To be clear, this is a study that focuses on economic policy. Had we looked at different policy areas, such as defense, foreign policy, or environmental policy, we might have found different things and drawn different conclusions about each country's knowledge regime. Had we examined them for earlier or later time periods things also might have looked different. In particular, we did most of our research just prior to the 2008 international financial crisis, in response to which our four knowledge regimes may eventually change a lot.

---

[81]Campbell 2004; Dobbin et al. 2007; Hedström and Swedberg 1998; Mizruchi and Fine 1999. In this regard we are following the lead of Halliday and Carruthers (2007, 2010), whose comparative analysis of the international development and diffusion of bankruptcy law guidelines was based on extensive interviewing in order to identify mechanisms promoting and inhibiting cross-national diffusion.

[82]One important exception is Stephany Mudge's (2008, 2011) work on the rightward shift toward neoliberalism in the platforms of European political parties.

Each of the next four chapters examines a knowledge regime in a particular country. For each case we sketch the production and policymaking regimes with which the knowledge regime is associated. We map the structure of the knowledge regime—that is, the various types of organizations that populate its field—as it existed around 2008, the period for which we have the most recent data. We also discuss the interactions among different types of organizations within the field, paying particular attention to competitive and cooperative interactions. And we explain how its structure and practices are governed by various formal and informal institutions found in the knowledge regime itself as well as the surrounding policymaking and production regimes. Finally, we examine how and why the knowledge regime came to be as it was in 2008—especially as it was influenced by challenges to and changes in the policymaking and production regimes that were set in motion by the demise of the Golden Age and the advent of globalization.

We turn now to our first case, the United States. This is the knowledge regime where we encountered the most extreme stories of no-holds-barred competition and conflict, organizational bloodletting, and even paranoia.

I

THE POLITICAL ECONOMY OF KNOWLEDGE REGIMES

2

The Paradox of Partisanship in the United States

The U.S. knowledge regime is often described as a highly competitive marketplace of ideas.[1] Advocates of various policy ideas battle each other in order to influence the thinking of national policymakers. Indeed, several people in Washington used precisely this metaphor in describing the situation to us in April 2008. So we were surprised to learn that there was recently also a significant amount of cooperation among research organizations in Washington. And we were especially amazed when people told us that this was occurring not only among organizations on one side or the other of the political spectrum but also among organizations from both the left and the right. This was a paradox insofar as cooperation across the political center had developed at a time when ideological and political partisanship and polarization had escalated to unprecedented heights between the Republican and Democratic Parties. Nevertheless, the American knowledge regime remains the most competitive of the four we discuss in this book.

[1] Abelson 1992, 2004; Feulner 2000; Gellner 1995.

We were surprised as well by two other things. First, although the literature on policy research organizations tends to draw clear distinctions between scholarly and advocacy organizations in the U.S. case, we discovered that considerable blurring had occurred.[2] Organizations long known as being quite scholarly adopted some practices typically associated with advocacy organizations, and organizations long known for their advocacy work adopted some practices typically associated with scholarly organizations. And a third generation of organizations emerged recently that strategically blended important features of both scholarly and advocacy types in order to intensify competition even more in the knowledge regime. Second, the literature on comparative political economy has often described the U.S. state as having limited state capacities relative to other advanced capitalist countries. In particular, the U.S. state is described as having an underdeveloped civil service.[3] Yet we discovered that American state research organizations are often large and well resourced and have substantial and sophisticated analytic capabilities. The prominence of these organizations and their close proximity to policymakers suggest that at least in this case the U.S. civil service and its state capacities are quite well developed.

We begin with some background about key features of the political-economic environment that shaped the knowledge regime. Next we describe what the U.S. knowledge regime looked like when we performed interviews in Washington.[4] We turn then to the story of how it developed since the early 1980s to assume its present form. This is a saga of the proliferation of private research organizations, escalating competition, and eventually a *crisis of political partisanship* that threatened the credibility of many policy research organizations and engendered, paradoxically, cooperation among policy research organizations across the political divide. All of this started as people struggled to make sense of the challenges to and changes in production and policymaking regimes that were set in motion by problems associated with the end of the Golden Age of postwar twentieth-century capitalism and the rise of globalization. Analytically speaking, proliferation and then cooperation were two initiatives taken to improve the knowledge regime's institutional complementarity vis-à-vis the rest of the political economy after people perceived that their knowledge regime had become dysfunctional—that it was no longer producing analysis and other ideas adequate for solving the country's economic problems.

[2]Ricci 1993; Rich 2004; Smith 1991. Medvetz (2012) has also discovered this blurring of organizational types.
[3]See, for example, Fourcade (2009, pp. 34–35), Skowronek (1982), Steinmo (2010, chap. 4), and Weir and Skocpol (1985). Many have argued that the U.S. state is "weak" in this sense relative to European states. This view, however, has been criticized by Block (2008), Campbell and Lindberg (1990), and Prasad (2012).
[4]Not all policy research organizations involved in national politics are in Washington. However, our sampling method turned up only ones that were located there.

The Political-Economic Environment

Observers often characterize the United States as a liberal production regime.[5] There is considerable competition among firms and the federal government's enforcement of antitrust law prevents much interfirm coordination. Business associations are not nearly as well developed and important in organizing the interests of corporations in the United States as they are in many European countries. There are a few large general business associations, notably the U.S. Chamber of Commerce and the National Association of Manufacturers, each claiming several thousand corporate members. But unlike the situation in Europe, there are no peak associations representing business in labor-management bargaining.[6] Instead, the focus of U.S. business associations is on politics and lobbying. Furthermore, in striking contrast to Germany and Denmark corporatism is absent in the United States.[7] All of this is important because it means that in the United States business does not speak with a unified voice. Moreover, the fact that firms in the United States depend more heavily on stock and bond markets for finance than do firms in our other countries means that their political activities as well as those of wealthy individuals and foundations are closely tied to swings in the financial markets.[8]

Labor is poorly organized and unions are notoriously weak in the United States when compared to most European countries. Only about 8% of the private sector employees and 36.4% of public sector employees belonged to a union in 2005. Across the economy only 12% of employed workers belonged to a union—down from a record high 35% in 1955.[9] Only 13.5% of the work force is covered by collective bargaining agreements.[10] Throughout this period unions embraced a conservative "business unionism" strategy whereby they often limited their focus to wages and benefits rather than more ambitious political or social reforms.[11] And, of course, there was no true labor or social democratic party in the United States. The fact that unions are so weak and oriented toward business unionism means that they do not dedicate nearly as many resources to policy research and related activities as business firms do. This imbalance is much greater in the United States than in Europe.

[5]Hall and Soskice 2001a; Soskice 1999. Others have shown, however, that the degree to which the United States fits this categorization varies considerably across sectors and over time (Campbell et al. 1991).
[6]Peak associations are confederations whose members are either unions or employer associations.
[7]Domhoff 2010, p. 48; Hall and Soskice 2001a, p. 31; Hollingsworth 1997; Salisbury 1979.
[8]Deeg 2010; Zysman 1983.
[9]Freeman 2007, chap. 5; Fantasia and Voss 2004, chap. 2.
[10]Visser 2009.
[11]On the origins of business unionism, see Hattam (1993). This has changed somewhat since the 1980s, especially as the AFL-CIO, America's largest labor federation, has taken a more liberal and aggressive stand in politics (Fantasia and Voss 2004).

Insofar as the policymaking regime is concerned, the United States has only two major political parties that compete in elections based on winner-take-all rules rather than proportional representation as in our three European countries. Both the Republican and Democratic Parties are weak and poorly disciplined by European standards. This is partly because people running for Congress or the presidency raise much of their campaign financing themselves rather than getting it from their party, which makes them less dependent on party resources and therefore makes it more difficult for the party leadership to control them than is true of their European counterparts. Indeed, private money plays a huge role in American politics. For example, in 2008 presidential candidates and candidates for Congress spent about $5.3 billion—virtually all of it coming from private contributions.[12]

The motivation for spending so much private money in electoral campaigns and the like is so that contributors can gain access to policymakers and encourage them to attend to their interests.[13] Access is also widespread thanks to the fact that political power in the United States is fragmented as a result of the separation of powers between the legislative and executive branches of government, which are frequently controlled by different political parties. There are dozens of congressional committees and subcommittees affording outsiders access to the policymaking process. Similarly, thanks to a long history of filling political offices through patronage appointments, the permanent civil service has many more political appointees than in our three European countries, which by many accounts ought to afford outsiders additional avenues of access to policymakers.[14] When a new government is elected, many personnel in cabinet bureaucracies, administrative agencies, and congressional committees are replaced with new appointees in what amounts to a political spoils system.[15] This system is often referred to as a "revolving door" through which people frequently move into and out of government jobs.

We will show that all of this affects the U.S. knowledge regime. For example, private policy research organizations constitute a much larger portion of the U.S. knowledge regime than they do in European ones because corporations, philanthropic foundations, and wealthy patrons are willing and able to fund them depending on gyrations in the private capital markets.[16] Second, the absence of peak associations means that business tends to be less united

---

[12]http://www.opensecrets.org/. Accessed December 2010.
[13]Clawson et al. 1998, chap. 3.
[14]Fourcade 2009, pp. 34–35; Skowronek 1982; Steinmo 2010, chap. 4; Weir and Skocpol 1985.
[15]Fourcade 2009, pp. 34–35.
[16]Abelson 1992; Braml 2004, chap. 5; Gellner 1995. Abelson (2004, 2000, 1998) argued as well that America's undisciplined party system means that politicians are less likely to toe the party line and are therefore more inclined to seek policy advice and expertise from private policy research organizations, further encouraging their development.

and coordinated in how it tries to influence policy research than is the case in Europe. The same is true for labor. In particular, business and labor peak associations play especially important roles in the Danish knowledge regime. Third, a two-party winner-take-all electoral system tends to encourage more political partisanship and less compromise than multiparty, proportional representation systems.[17] Partisanship spills over into the knowledge regime and encourages aggressive competition among policy research organizations. Finally, the state's fragmented structure as well as its revolving door afford private policy research organizations and others plenty of opportunities to proffer policy advice to policymakers.[18]

Mapping the Field: The Knowledge Regime Today

Compared to those of other countries the U.S. knowledge regime is marked by a fragmented structure of scholarly, advocacy, and state policy research organizations. It is unique as well because it is bifurcated into distinct and well-populated public and private sectors. It is worth noting in this regard that our view of the field differs significantly from two other otherwise excellent treatments of policy research organizations in the United States. One is Andrew Rich's *Think Tanks, Public Policy, and the Politics of Expertise,* and the other is Thomas Medvetz's more recent *Think Tanks in America.* Both of these ignore the important role that state policy research organizations play in the world of policy analysis and advising in the United States.

Private Scholarly Research Organizations

Private policy research organizations in America are often called think tanks. There were over 100 private think tanks in Washington in the mid-1990s and over 300 nationwide.[19] Almost everyone we interviewed agreed that among the most prominent were a small set of scholarly organizations, many of which have been around since the 1960s or earlier, such as the Brookings Institution, the Century Foundation, the Urban Institute, and Resources for the Future (RFF). Along with Brookings and Urban, the American Enterprise Institute (AEI) is one of the largest and best known scholarly research organizations in Washington. Brookings and AEI are full-service organizations—that is, they work on a wide range of domestic and international policy issues rather than focusing on a small subset, such as RFF, an organization specializing in environmental economics. Most scholarly research organizations are financed

[17]Steinmo 1993.
[18]Abelson 1992; Fischer 1991; Ricci 1993.
[19]Gellner 1995; Rich 2004. Among these, we visited several of the most prominent according to Weidenbaum (2009, chap. 3) and Rich (2004, p. 84).

privately by philanthropic foundations, wealthy patrons, and corporate grants. Some, notably Brookings, have accumulated endowments that support some of their operations. Urban is unique insofar as it depends more on federal contracts and competes for these with private consulting firms.[20]

These policy research organizations are classified as 501(c)(3) organizations under the federal tax code, which allows people and organizations who make financial contributions to them to receive a generous tax deduction for their charity. This is unique to the United States and one reason why the American knowledge regime has a much larger private sector than our European countries. Under the tax code these organizations technically serve "educational" purposes and must refrain from activity that could be viewed as propaganda, political campaigning, or attempting to influence legislation.[21]

As is well known, what makes these organizations "scholarly" is the quality and style of their research. It is often based on in-house data analysis and frequently published either as lengthy research reports resembling academic journal articles or as books.[22] Brookings, AEI ,and the Urban Institute have their own book publishing operations. AEI publishes about 20 books a year.[23] Brookings also publishes numerous scholarly articles, including the famous journal *Brookings Papers on Economic Activity*, which routinely features articles by renowned university scholars as well as in-house researchers.

These organizations are like universities without students.[24] They hire people, often with PhDs, to do research. Their researchers enjoy considerable professional autonomy to pursue their own research agendas, have no teaching responsibilities, and are often encouraged to seek external funding to support their work. They publish occasionally in academic journals and may even receive tenure after a probationary period. Kevin Hassett, a senior fellow at AEI, explained that AEI and Brookings have a very similar model: "You bring in PhD economists where you've asked them to do both academic work and participate in policy debates and we leave them alone." A big difference between these organizations and universities is that their research is more applied and engaged in policy debates than is typically the case for university researchers. A senior researcher at Brookings told us that her "think tank colleagues tend to be less steeped in the academic literature, and more steeped or interested in how [their work] is going to play in a public policy forum or world."[25]

[20]Interview with Robert Reischauer, Urban Institute.
[21]Obach 2010.
[22]Rich 2004; Medvetz 2012.
[23]Interview with Karlyn Bowman, AEI.
[24]Joel Darmstadter, RFF, compared his organization favorably to top academic departments of natural resources at Yale University and the University of Michigan.
[25]Interview with Isabel Sawhill, Brookings Institution.

The scholarly nature of these organizations was impressed upon us several times during our interviews. For instance, the AEI's Kevin Hassett showed us an extensive cross-national database on tax rates that he developed and that was the basis for a paper he was scheduled to deliver to the economics department at Princeton University. A senior researcher at the Urban Institute explained that they have a staff that develops its own complex and very expensive statistical models for analyzing large databases and probably consumes the lion's share of the organization's budget and person hours each year.[26] Officials at the Center on Budget and Policy Priorities (CBPP) and the Economic Policy Institute (EPI) explained as well that they do sophisticated policy analysis using statistical models.

The scholarly research organizations span an ideological spectrum. The Century Foundation and EPI positioned themselves on the left.[27] Brookings is often described as being centrist, which is consistent with the fact that of its two last presidents one came from a Democratic and the other a Republican administration.[28] The Urban Institute has a similar reputation if not slightly left of center, as does CBPP.[29] CBPP's 2005 promotional brochure describes it as "socially liberal, fiscally conservative, and academically rigorous . . . [and] organized around a commitment to low-income citizens." AEI is frequently described as being the center-right complement to Brookings. The Hudson Institute is another conservative organization that claims credit in its 2008 annual report for doing pioneering research on welfare reform and charter schools in the 1990s and the Bush administration's faith-based community initiatives program in the 2000s. The Heritage Foundation is an even more conservative organization that lists in its 2007 annual report Margaret Thatcher as a patron and espouses freedom of choice in education, health care, and other matters as well as the "unshackling" of American entrepreneurs. Also on the right for economic policy is the Cato Institute, well known for its libertarianism.

How scholarly some of these organizations, such as the Heritage Foundation, really are is a debatable point that we will address shortly. What is important now is that positioning organizations on the ideological spectrum is sometimes tricky.[30] For example, Brookings' managing director insisted that his organization was ideologically neutral, reiterating that they did not recruit people based on either their political or ideological views. Yet others said that Brookings tends to be staffed more by Democrats than Republicans and called it center-left.[31] But the president of EPI was incensed when we happened to

[26]Interview with Rudolph Penner, Urban Institute.
[27]Interviews with Christy Hicks, Century Foundation; Lawrence Mishel, EPI.
[28]Interview with Isabel Sawhill, Brookings Institution.
[29]Interview with senior official, PPI.
[30]Nevertheless, our assessment corresponds closely with those in Rich (2004, p. 230).
[31]Email correspondence with Joel Darmstadter, RFF. See also Weidenbaum (2009, p. 20).

remark that some people we interviewed had described Brookings as center-left and AEI as center-right. His response was an exasperated, "Bullshit!" He then explained that the boards of directors and funding streams of both these organizations had healthy representation from the business community. His point was that there was nothing really leftist about Brookings or most other organizations around Washington and that Brookings and AEI were actually two peas in the same ideological pod.

His comment is revealing. What passes for left-wing and right-wing in the United States is different from in Europe. There are no truly left-wing political parties in America by European standards. Similarly, there are very few truly leftist policy research organizations in the United States. EPI is the only one in our sample that even comes close insofar as a significant portion of its funding comes from labor unions, it is engaged with social democratic organizations in Europe and it touts social democratic policy recommendations at home. On the other hand, right-wing organizations like Heritage and Cato are oriented further to the right than many of the conservative policy research organizations we visited in Europe, especially in Germany where they subscribe to a social market ideology that accepts a significant level of government social spending to buffer citizens from the vicissitudes of the market. Generally speaking the political-ideological continuum in the United States is skewed rightward compared to our European countries. The center-left in America is comparable to what Europeans would call a centrist and more likely a center-right position.

Blurred Distinctions between Scholarly and Advocacy Organizations

Advocacy organizations are less interested in doing research than taking it from elsewhere to support their ideological or political position. William Antholis from Brookings said that some organizations in Washington tailored their research conclusions to fit their political and ideological agendas. Others questioned the quality of work done by these organizations too. EPI's president explained, "Yeah, there are a lot of shops that are set up that pontificate and come up with what I would consider pseudo-social science . . . I call it pretend social science, and it has the language of it, the look of it, and it's total crap."

We mentioned earlier that classifying organizations as scholarly is sometimes difficult. Consider the Heritage Foundation. Established in 1973 it was the first advocacy research organization in Washington. It devised a new business model that was less concerned with scholarly research than advocating policies from a conservative viewpoint. Heritage is generally acknowledged to have changed the game among Washington think tanks, which were "pretty sleepy places until this scrappy, energetic new organization arrived."[32]

[32]Karlyn Bowman, AEI, quoted in Weidenbaum (2009, p. 31).

Nowadays Heritage staff conducts dozens of policy briefings for government officials and testify frequently before Congress. In 2006, its staff wrote over 1,000 op-ed essays for newspapers around the country. Historically it had few academic pretentions.[33] And according to one of its vice presidents, Stuart Butler, they have developed an extensive outreach program at the state level to put pressure on congressional representatives to support conservative legislation. However, Butler said that they have been moving in a more scholarly direction lately by hiring PhD economists and doing more sophisticated data analysis.[34] Robert Reischauer, president of the Urban Institute, confirmed this, observing that "Heritage and even Cato have gotten more seriously scholarly" over the past few years. Nevertheless, others said that Heritage and Cato were still more interested in advocacy work than anything else.[35] And one of Heritage's new economists told us that although they now do some academic quality research there is still a tension between scholarly and advocacy goals. Before his research is released publicly staff makes sure that it "fits into the Heritage view of the world," but that it is also substantively and methodologically correct.[36] In short, they still straddle the fence.

The Hudson Institute is another tough case to classify. According to some observers it was one of the earlier research organizations to break with norms of neutrality and academic objectivity by hiring staff willing to push a more dogmatic line of argument than older scholarly organizations. But it now claims to have become more scholarly insofar as about a third of its researchers hold adjunct university professorships and the organization has moved away from opinion work, such as appearing on talk radio and blogging.[37] In contrast, some organizations may have moved in the opposite direction. One person told us that outreach and advocacy rather than research—what he called "Heritage-ization"—has occurred increasingly across a large segment of the think tank community. He said, for example, that in 2009 under the direction of Arthur Brooks, its new president, AEI began moving slowly away from more academic research and increasingly hired journalists to do the kind of quick response, conservative work that AEI did not do in the past. Brooks himself has cosigned op-eds with highly partisan and conservative

[33] Weidenbaum 2009, p. 29; Rich 2004, pp. 53–55.
[34] Despite the apparent increase in hiring of PhDs, only about 30% of the expert staff at Heritage held this degree in 2005. This is substantially less than at most other private policy research organizations that we visited for which Medvetz (2012, p. 134) gives the following figures: Brookings (75%), AEI (65%), Urban (60%), Hudson (50%), EPI (50%), the Century Foundation (45%), Cato (45%), Center for American Progress (35%), Progressive Policy Institute (20%), and CBPP (10%).
[35] Interviews with Karlyn Bowman, AEI; senior official, German Marshall Fund; Lawrence Mishel, EPI. See also Dezalay and Garth (2002, pp. 129–35).
[36] Interview with senior fellow, Heritage Foundation.
[37] Email correspondence with senior official, Hudson Institute, and Rich (2004, pp. 46–47).

congressional leaders, such as Representative Paul Ryan (one-time Republican vice presidential candidate and close ally with the ultra-conservative Tea Party movement), which his predecessor at AEI would never have done.[38]

In some cases, the trend toward more aggressive advocacy work has been pushed by wealthy benefactors. For instance, the Cato Institute has long tried to cultivate a reputation as a venerable libertarian research center unafraid to cross party lines. But two of its founding members—the conservative billionaire brothers Charles and David Koch—tried recently to install their own people on Cato's board and, according to Cato's chairman, get the institute to supply its brand-name research and scholars to Koch-financed political advocacy groups, such as Americans for Prosperity, which has strong ties to the Tea Party movement. Worrying that such a move would destroy Cato's credibility and alienate its other funders, the institute resisted the move. In response the Koch brothers filed a lawsuit against the institute.[39]

The Progressive Policy Institute, founded in 1989, is a centrist advocacy organization. One PPI senior official said that it was a "Third Way" operation favoring the sort of policies touted by Bill Clinton and Tony Blair. PPI does some research but lots of other things too. He claimed that it is the first "progressive" think tank concerned mostly with generating policy solutions rather than scholarly research. Others confirmed that PPI also does a lot of "messaging," that is, disseminating their ideas quickly, clearly, and concisely as policy briefs and reports in order to change the debate in Washington like Heritage did during the Reagan era.[40]

Another advocacy organization doing some scholarly work is the conservative National Center for Policy Analysis, founded in 1983. John Goodman, its founder, president, and chief executive officer, told us that some of the NCPA's policy proposals were included in the Contract for America—a set of eight conservative policy promises that helped Newt Gingrich and other conservative Republicans win control of the U.S. House of Representatives in 1994 for the first time in 40 years. One thing that set the NCPA apart from many scholarly organizations was that Goodman dictated what his researchers worked on: "We get very involved in the product and go back and forth [with the researcher] and have more direction." He explained, for instance, that the organization routinely funds a certain university economist to research tax policy and that at one point Goodman "talked him into doing it a different way" in

[38]Email correspondence with senior official, Hudson Institute. The Tea Party movement emerged initially as a vehement grassroots reaction against the Obama administration's proposed health care reform but subsequently morphed into a more complex movement funded in part by wealthy conservative benefactors (Skocpol and Williamson 2012).

[39]http://www.nytimes.com/2012/03/06/us/cato-institute-and-koch-in-rift-over-independence.html?pagewanted=all. Accessed June 2012.

[40]Interview with Stuart Butler, Heritage Foundation.

order to demonstrate the benefits of a flat tax, which he then convinced some conservative politicians to advocate. Moreover, the NCPA "is focused more on marketing than other organizations." That is, rather than publishing in respectable academic outlets they publish reader-friendly work for politicians and the public.

The most innovative example of the blurring of advocacy and research is the Center for American Progress, which in many ways represents an ascendant third-generation business model among Washington policy research organizations. Established in 2003 as the brainchild of John Podesta, former chief of staff to President Bill Clinton, CAP was inspired by some of the conservative advocacy organizations, particularly the Heritage Foundation, which had excellent communications capacities designed to frame ideas in clear and compelling ways and quickly transmit them to policymakers and the public. CAP wanted to do the same but with a substantial research component. And like Heritage and the Progressive Policy Institute, when we visited them CAP was developing policy blueprints that it hoped would help guide the next presidential administration. However, as Sarah Rosen Wartell, CAP's executive vice president for management, told us, CAP "leapfrogged" the Heritage model in two important ways. First, CAP established a sister organization, the Center for American Progress Action Fund. CAP is a 501(c)(3) policy research organization, but the Action Fund is a 501(c)(4) organization permitted by law to participate in political campaigns and lobbying work as long as it is dedicated to promoting "social welfare" and the common good.[41] CAP was the first full service operation to develop this model. These two organizations are located in the same building and work together closely. In fact, many people employed by CAP are also employed by the Action Fund. Second, CAP developed rapid response "messaging strategies," such as a daily email publication called the *Progress Report*, which addresses pressing issues in an advocacy way but that provides citations to research so that people can check CAP's facts. CAP often works on very short-term projects including rejoinders directed to politicians and the press to counter what it believes to be inaccurate or misleading claims by conservatives. Sometimes they can issue these rejoinders in a matter of hours over the Internet, through press releases, or through other media. Since we completed our interviews other organizations have adopted the CAP model, including the Heritage Foundation, which established its own 501(c)(4) organization, Heritage Action for America.[42]

[41] In contrast to lobbying firms, which operate on a for-profit basis, 501(c)(4) organizations are nonprofits like their 501(c)(3) sisters.

[42] We were told by someone off the record that this new organization was close to the Tea Party movement, which angered some of the Heritage Foundation's long-time congressional allies.

There is an important distinction between advocacy work and lobbying. Lobbying is a central feature of Washington politics.[43] We were told on one occasion that we should be talking to people on K Street in Washington where many of the lobbying firms reside because lobbyists have been an increasingly important source of legislative ideas.[44] These ideas, however, tend to be technical, very specific, and tuned to the narrow interests of individual paying clients; they are not the broader programmatic ideas that concern us here. In contrast, the 501(c)(3) organizations of interest to us are forbidden legally from spending more than a small fraction of their budgets on what would technically be considered lobbying—that is, they cannot appeal explicitly to politicians to vote a certain way on legislation or write legislative language for them. Lobbying organizations fall under a different tax designation, which permits them to do all of this on behalf of paying clients. Stuart Butler's explanation of how this was handled at the Heritage Foundation was typical of what we heard in many organizations: "The simple test to make sure that you're safely within bounds is to say we think this is a good bill. We think this is a bad bill. When you cross the line or are getting close to the line is when you [say we] think this is a bad bill *and you should vote against it*. If you avoid that conjunction you're fine" (our emphasis). We heard virtually the same thing at the Cato Institute.[45]

It is debatable whether the technical distinction between advocacy work and lobbying is simply splitting hairs. But it is an important fact of life that policy research organizations take very seriously. The Brookings Institution's William Antholis explained, "There are all kinds of 501(c)(3) restrictions, but we want to walk right up to the line and we've got a general council and we've got lawyers that we bring in to look at where the line is." He added later in an email to us that their general counsel regularly coaches its research directors and scholars on what does and does not count as lobbying.

But why are these legal restrictions so important? Policy research organizations say that they avoid crossing the line into lobbying because they do not want to jeopardize either their 501(c)(3) tax status—and thus their funding— or their integrity. The Cato Institute's Brandon Arnold explained:

> Maybe most importantly is our tax status. If you cross that line
> you're subject to have your donations not be tax deductible. But in
> a broader sense I think it's part of our institutional integrity. I think
> the closer you get to that line, the closer you get to the fights that
> happen on Capitol Hill . . . I think you really risk sacrificing your

[43]Steinmo 2010, p. 184.
[44]Interview with Robert Reischauer, Urban Institute.
[45]Interview with Brandon Arnold, Cato Institute.

institutional integrity. We try to stay very far away from that and try to be very, very principled.[46]

The Heritage Foundation had similar concerns. At one point because they did so much advocacy work they had a heated internal debate about whether they should change their tax status entirely and engage in lobbying but decided against it in part because they thought it would undermine their brand and trustworthiness.[47] Nevertheless, in 2010 they revisited the issue and agreed to set up Heritage Action for America.

Two additional observations are necessary about all of the private policy research organizations. First, they are not all equal in terms of resources. The Urban Institute spends nearly $70 million annually.[48] Brookings has an annual operating budget of about $62.9 million and owns its building.[49] Heritage is also rich with annual expenditures of about $50 million a year.[50] AEI spends about $25 million annually.[51] In contrast, CBPP spends about $18.7 million annually, while CAP spends about $16.1 million.[52] NCPA and the Hudson Institute also have small annual budgets of $6.5 million and $10.2 million, respectively.[53] EPI spends only $5.6 million.[54] Second, they depend largely on private financing thanks to their 501(c)(3) tax status.[55] Tax law in our European countries does not reward this sort of generosity with hefty tax deductions. However, private money still matters in Europe. The big difference is that it comes from organized interests there, notably business and labor peak associations, thanks to the corporatist institutions in those countries and goes to only a few policy research organizations in a more centralized manner.

The Absence of Party Research Organizations

In contrast to those in France and Germany, political parties in the United States do not have much in the way of policy research organizations.[56] Although some private policy research organizations have strong political profiles they

---

[46]The distinction between advocacy research and lobbying is blurred further by the fact that lobbyists sometimes commission research studies from policy research organizations and, as a result, have an increasing impact on public policy research (interviews with senior official, Hudson Institute, and Brandon Arnold, Cato Institute).

[47]Interview with Stuart Butler, Heritage Foundation. See also Braml (2004, p. 57).

[48]Urban Institute annual report 2007.

[49]Brookings Institution annual report 2007.

[50]Heritage Foundation annual report 2007.

[51]AEI annual report 2007.

[52]CBPP annual report 2007; CAP annual report 2006.

[53]NCPA annual report 2007; Hudson Institute annual report 2008.

[54]EPI annual report 2003–5.

[55]Bai 2007; Rich 2004.

[56]Abelson 1998, 2000, 2004.

are not affiliated *formally* with a political party—that is, they are neither organized nor funded by a party. This is not to say, however, that the two do not work together *informally*. CAP and the Heritage Foundation have close ties with the Democratic and Republican Parties, respectively. The Progressive Policy Institute (PPI) was created by the Democratic Leadership Council (DLC), which represents the right wing of the Democratic Party, to generate fresh ideas for the so-called New Democrats. However, neither PPI nor the DLC have official connections with the Democratic Party per se.[57]

By law policy research organizations must remain politically nonpartisan and unaffiliated with political parties or candidates running for public office. Virtually every organization we spoke with in Washington said that to do otherwise would jeopardize their 501(c)(3) federal tax status and therefore their funding. Isabel Sawhill from Brookings explained how this worked for their Project 2008—an effort to evaluate the positions of the candidates running for president that year:

> And we're really careful about keeping it nonpartisan, so that we
> would not, for example, go to Obama [a Democrat] and say you
> should do X unless we were also going to McCain [a Republican]
> and saying we think X. . . . It's not a private kind of activity geared to
> just one candidate. It's totally in the public domain, and if someone
> here decides to work—wants to work more closely with the can-
> didate, they have to take a leave of absence. We've had people that
> have done that.

Brookings made sure, she said, that all of its activities surrounding the 2008 campaign were nonpartisan and that their comparison of the candidates' policies was "scrubbed by our legal advisors to make sure it in no way seems biased or unfair." Brookings' managing director noted that their vice presidents and communications staff are very sensitive to the partisanship issue.[58]

The Surprising Prominence of State Research Capacities

Others have argued that the U.S. state does not have as extensive a career civil service as many European states and that this encourages dependency on outsiders for policy analysis and advice. Indeed, the initial growth of private policy research organizations after the Second World War was driven in part by a demand among policymakers for policy expertise not currently available to them from state organizations. Nevertheless, in the United States there is a set of prominent government organizations that also has extensive and

---

[57]Interview with senior official, PPI.
[58]Email correspondence with William Antholis, Brookings Institution.

sophisticated research capacities.[59] Some receive their mandates from Congress, such as the Government Accountability Office (GAO), Congressional Budget Office (CBO), and Congressional Research Service (CRS). GAO, for instance, does policy evaluation research for Congress and has an Applied Research and Methods team that provides methodological guidance to its researchers.[60] Some of this work is very technical, such as forecasting government finances.[61] Similarly, CBO does high-powered statistical modeling to estimate for Congress the effects of its policies on the federal budget and the economy. Emphasizing the seriousness with which they approach their work, one CBO analyst told us that it is done almost exclusively in house:

> Because part of the process for building a model isn't just to have a model but it's actually to learn something about the way the economy works and to learn something about how to think about these policies. There's a building of human capital that really needs to go on and if all you're doing is supervising and taking results from somebody, you're not going to have the full human capital development that you need.[62]

The CRS is also a sophisticated operation whose 400 analysts provide reports upon request to Congress on an enormous range of policy issues. It maintains its own extensive databases and for years was the only nonuniversity organization with access to the vast datasets of the Inter-University Consortium for Political and Social Research at the University of Michigan.[63] According to our interviews all of these organizations routinely hire university-trained researchers, many of whom hold PhDs. And they have all developed strong internal organizational cultures of professionalism and nonpartisanship. In some cases, such as CBO, a mandate of being nonpartisan was inscribed in their enabling legislation.[64]

Much the same story holds for research organizations in the executive branch, such as the President's Council of Economic Advisers (CEA), the Office of Management and Budget (OMB), and certain divisions in the Department

---

[59]For discussions of the underdeveloped U.S. civil service, see, for instance, Fourcade (2009, pp. 34–35), Skowronek (1982), Steinmo (2010, chap. 4), and Weir and Skocpol (1985). For further discussion about how this leads policymakers to be dependent on private policy research organizations, see Abelson (1998), Coleman (1991), Gellner (1995), and James (1993), who argued that a weak civil service is associated with poor policy analysis capabilities within the state. This may be so in some policy areas but not in the United States for economic policy.

[60]Interview with senior official, GAO.

[61]Interview with Gene Dodaro, GAO.

[62]Interview with Douglas Hamilton, CBO.

[63]Interview with senior official, CRS.

[64]Bimber 1996, chap. 8; Joyce 2011.

of Treasury. According to our interviews, these are often considered to be the three top economic research, modeling, and forecasting agencies working for the president, although high-powered technical work is also done elsewhere in the executive branch.[65] Both the Fed and Treasury have hundreds of PhD economists on staff. The Fed routinely hires new PhDs out of graduate school and is a training ground for many of the people who do econometric modeling in Washington as well as on Wall Street.[66] Andrew Samwick, former chief economist at the CEA, told us that he had worked at CEA with economists at the Fed who were as good or better than those you would find at some of the best university economics departments. He added that when he was coming out of his PhD program at MIT he understood that "[u]nless you got a burning desire to teach graduate students and unless you got an offer at one of the recognized top five places, you should be giving the Fed a lot of thought" as a place to go to do high-quality research. He also had high praise for the people working at Treasury, CBO, and other government agencies. In short, these places are at least as good as and often better than the best private scholarly policy research organizations. Indeed, when we asked one CEA analyst whether he ever discussed his work with people at leading scholarly think tanks in Washington, he replied that "AEI and Brookings aren't the places to go. Those guys are pointy-headed academics who've got their head in the clouds, okay?"[67]

Everyone we asked in these organizations insisted that their organizations were nonpartisan politically. Thanks to their legislative mandates many simply provide research services and research-based policy advice for policymakers when requested. For instance, GAO's director stressed that his organization was "nonpartisan, professional, fact-based." This is one reason, according to a staff member, why when a member of Congress asks GAO to do a study, the

---

[65]In an email one person told us off the record that the amount and quality of original research done by CBO, GAO, and CRS surpassed that done in the executive branch by CEA and OMB. Bimber (1996) suggests that this is because policy research organizations serving Congress have to answer to two political parties in the House and Senate whereas policy research organizations serving the president serve only one party. According to the email Treasury was a possible exception. And several executive branch agencies still have excellent policy shops, such as the Department of Housing and Urban Development and the Department of Health and Human Services, which do large amounts of research and some of which commission studies from academics and sometimes places like the Urban Institute. However, we focus on only those that turned up in our sampling frame.

[66]Interview with senior official, CEA. The Fed employs about 200 PhD economists (http://www.federalreserve.gov/econresdata/theeconomists.htm. Accessed January 2012).

[67]Interview with senior official, CEA. Other government officials distinguished their research from academic research insofar as theirs is more applied. One GAO official said, "We will do work that you would look at and say, well, it looks like academic research to me, but we wouldn't do it for the sake of sort of improving world knowledge. We would do it to help decision makers address a specific set of issues, so we're focusing on our client [Congress] in terms of trying to have research that is useful, rather than pure research in the sense that science does pure research."

agency prefers that the request be signed by both a Republican and Democrat.[68] CRS makes sure that its work is politically balanced too by thoroughly vetting it in-house before release.[69] Similarly, we were told at CBO that "[t]here aren't all that many places in Washington where you can call up and get an answer that doesn't have any slant to it. . . . This is a place where [we're] just trying to give you the information."[70] In fact, CBO's general council told us that they have gone to great lengths to avoid even the slightest appearance of partisanship, such as by forbidding their researchers from participating in conferences sponsored by organizations trying to affect public policy. Underscoring the organization's commitment to nonpartisanship, a CBO senior analyst offered us two stories about former directors who stood up to powerful politicians in both parties and told them that the agency's analysis did not support their views—acts that could have put their jobs at risk politically. In one case, the director told Speaker of the House Newt Gingrich that a capital gains tax cut would not pay for itself as Gingrich and other Republicans had insisted. In another case, the director told the Democrats, much to their chagrin, that the Clinton health plan represented a huge expansion of government.[71]

This is not to say, however, that all state policy research organizations are immune from partisan influence. For instance, despite the dispassionate analysis its staff does, the chair and appointed members of CEA are expected to drum up support for the president's economic policy proposals even if most economists predict on the basis of academic theory that these policies might not help the economy. The politically appointed members of the Federal Reserve Board are subject to various pressures from Wall Street, Congress, and the White House, although we have no evidence that they necessarily succumb to these pressures or that their analytic staff is affected by them.[72] And the president's OMB has often been accused of partisanship despite the fact that its analyses have had to conform more or less to those done by CBO.[73]

Other government agencies, departments, and committees, such as the Census Bureau, the Bureau of Labor Statistics, the Bureau of Economic Analysis, the Social Security Administration, and the Joint Committee on Taxation in Congress, also have research capacities. A few organizations with extensive

[68]Interview with senior official, GAO. We heard elsewhere, however, that GAO tends to become more embroiled in partisan activities than CRS or CBO because members of Congress often make requests of GAO to bolster their own political positions.

[69]Interview with senior official, CRS.

[70]Interview with senior official, CBO.

[71]Interview with Douglas Hamilton, CBO. These and similar episodes are documented in detail in Joyce (2011). The strong nonpartisan nature of CBO, CRS, and GAO analyses is well documented in Bimber (1996, chap. 8) and Joyce (2011).

[72]Rose 2005, pp. 89–90.

[73]Bimber 1996, chap. 8; Dickinson 2005, pp. 150–55.

research capacities are largely independent from the government in the sense that their research does not require review or approval by either the executive or legislative branch. One is the Federal Reserve.[74] Another is the National Academy of Sciences, and in particular its National Research Council (NRC), which is a nonprofit private organization operating under a government charter. The NRC is a bit different from the rest insofar as it does contract work almost exclusively for the government and provides advice on various scientific and technical matters. In this regard it is a bit like some of the semi-public research organizations we found in Europe that we discuss in later chapters. It appoints committees of outside experts who pour over all the relevant scientific literature on a topic, such as welfare reform, synthesize it, strike a consensus, and provide the government with a list of options about how it might proceed to craft policy.[75]

The state research organizations tend to be much better resourced than the private ones. For instance, GAO has expenditures of about $507 million a year and staff of around 3,200 people.[76] The NRC has a professional staff of about 1,000 and a budget of $280 million.[77] CRS has about 488 staff members and a $52.6 million budget.[78] CBO has a budget of about $46.8 million, about 250 employees, and a professional staff of whom about 75% hold advanced degrees, mostly in economics or public policy.[79] CEA, however, which has only about 30 staff, pales in comparison to the rest. The Federal Reserve Board has about 2,000 staff and a $350 million budget, and the Treasury Department posts outlays of about $490 million, although in both cases this covered much more than just their research, policy analysis, and related operations.[80]

Several further points are in order. First, the prominence of these state policy research organizations makes sense despite the fact that many scholars have characterized the U.S. state as having a weak civil service. After all, during the postwar period throughout the advanced capitalist countries, including the United States, states have taken more active roles in managing national economic affairs. This has entailed the expansion of their analytic capacities. And more specialized experts—particularly economists—have come to play

---

[74]By law its Board of Governors is appointed by the president and approved by the Senate but its monetary policy decisions are not subject to their consent.

[75]Interview with Michael Feuer, NRC. See also Blair (2011).

[76]GAO annual report 2007.

[77]Blair 2011, pp. 299, 308.

[78]The Library of Congress Budget Justification FY 2008 (http://www.loc.gov/about/reports/budget/fy2008.pdf. Accessed January 2013).

[79]http://www.cbo.gov/aboutcbo/factsheet.cfm. Accessed January 2012.

[80]Budget of the U.S. Government 2009, Treasury Department, Table 4.1 (http://frwebgate.access.gpo.gov/cgi-bin/multidb.cgi. Accessed January 2011). Staff memo to Federal Reserve Board of Governors, December 16, 2011 (http://www.federalreserve.gov/foia/files/2011_boardbudget.pdf. Accessed January 2013).

an increasing role in economic policymaking.[81] Second, the separation of powers ensures that several research organizations work only for the legislative branch, such as GAO, CBO, and CSR, while others work only for the executive branch, such as OMB and CEA. Hence, the organization of these policy research organizations parallels the state's fragmented structure. Third, virtually anybody in Congress can directly request research from GAO, CBO, CRS, and NRC. In Europe politicians must ask the relevant ministry to approve the request and then make the request of the appropriate policy research organization. This is probably why political parties in the United States do not have much in the way of a policy research apparatus—politicians do not need it.

Universities on the Periphery

Universities play a peripheral role in this knowledge regime, principally as a training ground for its researchers. But this is beginning to change. On the one hand, competition between Washington's research organizations and universities has increased. For instance, William Antholis at Brookings told us that his colleagues increasingly "see our competitors as the best universities around the [country] and around the world." Others agreed especially in terms of recruiting research staff.[82] On the other hand, there is cooperation too. Many of the organizations we visited had academics on their advisory board, consulted with them on research issues, and hired them in temporary, visiting, or part-time research positions. Brookings, Hudson, and RFF, among others, all have university fellows programs. Some research staff holds adjunct positions at universities. When NRC conducts a study it generally constructs its expert panels with people from universities.[83] The three members of CEA are drawn from universities, as are some of the economists they pick to work with them while in office. We also heard several stories about research staff collaborating with university scholars, such as seeking feedback on drafts of their work prior to its public release. In some cases the relationships between policy research organizations and universities are ongoing and formal. For example, the Brookings Institution publishes an academic journal, *The Future of Children*, in partnership with Princeton University, and for many years RFF published its books through Johns Hopkins University Press.[84]

That said, many of the people we interviewed in Washington did not have a high opinion of most university research, which they considered to be too far removed from the applied policy-relevant work they favored. Illustrating

---

[81] Fourcade 2006, 2009, chap. 2. The CEA, for instance, was established by the 1946 Employment Act to provide the president with professional economic advice (http://www.whitehouse.gov /administration/eop/cea/about. Accessed January 2012).
[82] Interviews with Karlyn Bowman, AEI; Ted Hand, RFF.
[83] Interview with Michael Feuer, NRC.
[84] Interviews with Isabel Sawhill, Brookings Institution; Joel Darmstadter, RFF.

the irrelevance of most academic research, a former Federal Reserve Board economist explained that one day he needed an article on monetary policy in one of the main academic economics journals. He walked around to all the economists on his floor at the Fed asking if they had a copy. None did!

> The reason was that the focus of the economic profession in the study of monetary policy had wandered so far from the things you need to understand day to day to do monetary policy. . . . I forget what the question was, but it turned out that the people at the Fed didn't feel like they needed to have the *Journal of Economics* on their desk. . . . You go and look at the papers that are being published. Most of them have no real impact on policy.[85]

EPI's president made the same point in a less conciliatory way, saying, "One of the things that I think you learn in this business is that not that many in academia actually have that much to offer. Those who do don't know what to do with what they know, and they write it in ways that are inappropriate for having an impact."

Things were, as we shall see, much different in Europe. In particular, many high-profile German policy research organizations have formal ties with nearby universities. And academics often run these research shops. In France, policy analysts have at least since the mid-1990s reached out to academics for additional policy analysis and input. And in Denmark, academic economists constitute a "brotherhood" that we were told is very influential in policymaking circles. The reasons for this have much to do with institutional arrangements in those countries. German policymakers had long off-loaded policy research and advising functions to semi-public policy research organizations, French policymakers became disenchanted with the analysis and advice they received from their state policy research organizations, and Danish policymakers turned away from a system of ideological to more expert-oriented policy advising.

Let us review the major effects we have seen so far that the policymaking and production regimes have had on the organization of the U.S. knowledge regime. To help, we preview some things that we will discuss in subsequent chapters. To begin with, consider the policymaking regime's effects. First, the knowledge regime is marked by a plethora of private policy research organizations, dependent in almost every case on private funding thanks in part to tax laws that offer generous incentives for charitable giving. In our European countries, notably France, where tax laws create few such incentives and

---

[85]Interview with Keven Hassett, AEI.

where private money plays a limited role in politics, private funding is scarce and there are few private policy research organizations. Second, contrary to expectations, there are a number of very well-resourced state research organizations in the United States. Some are located in the executive branch, some are located in the legislative branch, and some are independent of both. This is a reflection of the separation of powers and institutional fragmentation of the U.S. state. Third, there are no formal party research organizations in the United States. This stems from the fact that policymakers have at their disposal many state policy research organizations that they can ask for research without having to use a political intermediary, such as a cabinet minister's office, as they do in our European cases. This sort of direct access to state research organizations reduces the need for politicians to have alternative research capacities such as their parties might otherwise offer.

The production regime also had significant effects on the U.S. knowledge regime. Notably, because labor is weakly organized compared to our European countries there are few private policy research organizations funded by the labor movement. Things are different in Germany and Denmark where labor is better organized. Furthermore, although individual corporations may fund various policy research shops in the United States, corporate support for this is not centralized as it is, for instance, in Denmark where business is organized into centralized peak associations with their own analytic capacities. Finally, the rightward skewing of political ideologies among the private policy research organizations in the United States relative to their European counterparts stems from the lack of much funding from organized labor as well as the absence of corporatist institutions that tend to facilitate ideological moderation, as we shall see in Germany and Denmark. Of course, the absence of a labor or social democratic party in the American policymaking regime is important as well in this regard.

The prevalence of many private policy research organizations in the United States makes for a very competitive marketplace of ideas. We discuss this next. Later on we will explain how problems associated with the end of the Golden Age and the rise of globalization created such competition in the first place as people tried to recalibrate the knowledge regime and improve its institutional complementarity for the rest of the political economy.

A Competitive Marketplace of Ideas

The American knowledge regime is extremely competitive compared to its European counterparts. And competition is located almost entirely on the private side. This involves not only promoting policy ideas but also competing for funding, staff, media attention, and more.

Competition and Private Organizations

Private policy research organizations have become much more competitive since the early 1980s in marketing their policy ideas. The president of one organization told us, "When we started out think tanks didn't market anything. . . . Now today everybody does this. . . . For the market as a whole [there] is a lot more effort put into this than there used to be." He summed it up a few minutes later by telling us, "There really is a marketplace for ideas."[86] We heard on many occasions that competition is rooted in the proliferation of private research organizations during this period, a subject that we discuss in detail later. And this competition occurs not only between organizations on the left and right but also among ideological brethren.[87] Indeed, there is a real concern in some quarters about losing control of your good ideas to political and ideological allies. For instance, when we asked at PPI whether they sent their research papers out for review so that external experts could check for quality, a senior official said that they did not. Why? "Quite honestly one of the reasons we don't is because if we did we'd be afraid that someone else would try to steal the idea and publish it, so we don't do that now. . . . We have had issues, and I won't name the organizations, but . . . it's a competitive field."

In addition to competing in the realm of ideas, there are several additional sides to this competition. One of the most important is over *funding*. While some of the larger organizations like Brookings have a fairly secure financial base, other organizations need to compete for funding. One reason that our contact at PPI worried about getting credit for ideas was that he needed to demonstrate to prospective funders that those ideas were from his organization not someone else's. He explained, "It's a competitive business in reality. You're competing—there are a number of organizations out there that compete with the same funding sources. . . . A lot of us go to the same—we're funded by some foundations, some individual donors, and a lot of them are on the same list for other think tanks."

The competition for funding was exacerbated by changes in the policymaking regime. First, was the emergence of a new brand of political organization—the so-called 527 organization whose special tax status, thanks to changes in campaign finance law, allows it to raise money for election campaigns in unlimited amounts. These 527s burst on to the political scene during the 2004 presidential campaign. They raise money from many of the same deep-pocket donors upon whom policy research organizations rely. According to a senior official at PPI, nowadays "[t]he money is spread out. It's not just going to think

---

[86]Interview with John Goodman, NCPA. See also Ricci (1993, pp. 15–16) and Smith (1991, chap. 9).
[87]Interview with senior fellow, Heritage Foundation.

tanks. So while there's more think tanks, there's also sort of more of these third—these political organizations—527s, which don't do any policy stuff. . . . I'd say that's a big change." Second, political efforts to limit government spending have reduced funding for some private policy research organizations. The Reagan administration, for instance, reduced government support for places like the Urban Institute because they did a lot of evaluation research of government programs that the administration wanted to abolish anyway.[88] As the pool of available funds shrinks, competition for them expands. Competition for funding is much more intense in America than in our European countries, where much of it is provided by the state on a more stable basis.

Changes in the production regime also amplified competition for funding. Corporate mergers during the past 25 years reduced the number of firms willing to give money to policy research organizations. Funding also diminished when the economy faltered in the 1980s and after 2006 as donors cut funding.[89] And because foundations and other donors tightened their belts the past few years there has even been talk of mergers among some policy research organizations.[90]

Another area of increased competition involved attracting good *research staff*, particularly economists. For instance, as early as 1987 the Urban Institute worried that "[w]e face increased competition for staff from universities and other research organizations."[91] We heard at RFF that the salaries of economists had gone through the roof such that RFF has started to have trouble hiring and retaining them. Moreover, universities can offer tenure, better working hours, and occasionally tuition breaks for someone's children.[92] We heard the same story at AEI where someone said, "There's just a huge amount of competition in the academic world for a lot of people, and so one of the changes in the think tank world . . . we simply can't afford to bring a lot [of scholars] here we'd like to bring here. We can't pay the kinds of university salaries."[93] But the competition over recruitment is not just with universities. These organizations

[88] Interview with Rudolph Penner, Urban Institute.
[89] Interview with senior fellow, Heritage Foundation. According to email correspondence from Karlyn Bowman, AEI, thanks to the plunging stock market following the 2008 financial crisis, policy research organizations, such as AEI, took big budgetary hits and had to lay off staff, shift people to per diem salaries, and cut costs in other ways.
[90] Interview with Christy Hicks, Century Foundation. Robert Reischauer, the Urban Institute, waxed nostalgic about the good old days in this regard: "When I came to Brookings in 1970—I can't remember who it was—a foundation came down at the end of their fiscal year and said we have to get rid of $1 million. $1 million was real money in 1970. What are some good ideas in budget and social policy? And [my colleague] and I went in a room and wrote two pages." They got the money.
[91] Urban Institute annual report 1987, p. 4.
[92] Interview with Ted Hand, RFF.
[93] Interview with resident fellow, AEI.

also compete with each other. For instance, EPI's president told us that CAP did not have any PhD economists on staff because "I hired the last one away from them. He became my research director last year."

Changes in the policymaking regime have affected recruitment competition too. From the 1960s through the 1980s congressional staffs grew and, as a result, so did their need for research analysts. New government research organizations were also established like CBO. So demand and competition for research talent grew.[94] Furthermore, the arrival of a new political regime in Washington increases competition for some research organizations thanks to the revolving door phenomenon. We were told several times that if the Democrats won the White House in 2008, a lot of people from Brookings and the Urban Institute would probably be offered government jobs. And if the Republicans won, the same thing would happen at the Heritage Foundation and AEI.[95]

Ultimately, of course, organizations need funding, staff, and other resources in order to compete effectively for the attention of policymakers. But this has increasingly involved competing for *media attention* too. As one researcher at the Urban Institute explained, the competition for attention is ultimately directed at policymakers but often works "through a complicated chain of press and staff."[96] The multiplication of new forms of media further complicates things. Christy Hicks at the Century Foundation explained this to us at length when we asked her what some of the big challenges have been for her organization:

> Competing in an ever-crowded field in a era that's all about the sound clip, and people who are getting their news and information in very different ways . . . who are accessing their information online, and through social networking, and sort of dealing with things like search engine optimization, and things like that . . . where you have to get your whole message out in 30 seconds, which is definitely not natural to academics or think tankers. . . . That's the world that we're living in, and it's only going to go more that way. . . . I believe that it

---

[94]Interview with Robert Reischauer, Urban Institute. The competition for research talent may have been exacerbated by the fact that the gulf between academic and policy-oriented research grew from the 1980s, thus limiting the pool of available talent. Academic research became increasingly compartmentalized and narrowly focused, moving to the margins of public life. Theorists cannot move easily into government or policy research organizations, and researchers interested in practical policy issues are sometimes second-class citizens in academia compared to theorists. As one of our respondents said off the record in an email, "In my think tank and government life, I've sometimes been involved in hiring brand new, brilliant PhDs who come to the Washington world thinking that they can devote their time to writing abstract articles for academic publications. They don't last long." (See also http://www.nationalaffairs.com/publications/detail/devaluing-the -think-tank. Accessed May 2012.)

[95]Interview with senior official, CRS.

[96]Interview with Rudolph Penner, Urban Institute.

is a challenge for us and I believe for other organizations. . . . Just as we figure out how to use cable television, now we have to figure out how to use online social networks. Just when we figure out how to write for the Internet, now we've had to figure out blogs, and video—online videos. Just when we've figured out—just started putting our own websites up, now we have to figure out to rein in YouTube and ForTV, and other things like that. . . . It's a huge challenge for my organization, and I believe it's a huge challenge for any organization.

Others shared this sentiment. Even a small research organization like PPI realized that the competition for media attention was one that is waged against all the other private research organizations in the field. It boils down to being "relevant."[97] In other words, these organizations needed to remain visibly engaged in the multimedia public discourse. Many people we interviewed concurred. The Heritage Foundation's Stuart Butler said that this was an acute problem insofar as reaching young staffers in Congress was concerned:

One of the problems that we face with the web, and I think every major organization, you go on the web, and you look at a website, and that website could be three men and a coffee machine, or it could be an institution of 500 people. . . . So, we have issues associated with how do you keep reputation and brand in this sort of cacophony of noise of the web. And that's a thing we do struggle with. I think all the major groups struggle with that. . . . I mean, almost nobody sends hard copy like that to anybody anymore. And you look at young staffers, and you have to say . . . where do they get the information from? Well, it's not from dialing up Heritage Foundation saying can you send something over? It's where? And so we have to think about that. So, there have been a lot of profound changes in the way we try to maintain our brand and approach in this sort of noise of the web.

However, maintaining relevance and public visibility also depends on producing *quality research*—another area of competition. The Century Foundation's Hicks explained that this often involved a balancing act. Her organization "wants to be seen as both serious and relevant . . . we want to be relevant otherwise there's no reason for us to exist. But we have to be serious too and sort of being serious and navigating YouTube and *The Daily Show* is a challenge; it's just a challenge, but it's a challenge we have to figure out how to meet, because I'm sure my friends on the right are already figuring it out, and taking greater

---

[97]Interviews with senior official, PPI, and Christy Hicks, Century Foundation, who both used the term.

advantage of that." Heritage's Stuart Butler echoed her sentiment explaining that Heritage needs to connect high-quality research with an effective media outreach strategy. To do so, according to Butler, Heritage has started moving into more sophisticated, large-database econometric work in order to compete effectively with other large research organizations and the government, which is important in order to maintain their reputation and brand in ways that will help them penetrate the noise of the web. Organizations like the Urban Institute and CBPP already have these capacities and view this as a competitive advantage relative to places like Brookings and Heritage.[98]

Finally, and often closely related to the issue of research quality, was the problem of establishing and maintaining an organizational *identity and reputation* in an increasingly crowded field. Without that an organization would have a difficult time distinguishing itself from the pack and thus competing effectively for funding, media visibility, and the attention of policymakers.[99] For instance, EPI's president remarked:

> We very consciously say to ourselves internally that we have to be above the industry standard, and that's because we're liberal, left wing, right? I think if we're not . . . I think we are more vulnerable, and I think our greatest asset is, in fact, our credibility for putting out analysis and numbers that people can rely on, and some of the conservatives say they might not like our interpretation, but they— you know, find us pretty credible.[100]

But the problem of maintaining identity had become a problem even for large, well-established organizations. We were told at the libertarian Cato Institute, for example, that they worry a lot about being confused with other groups that are conservative on social or foreign policy issues, which Cato is not.[101]

Competition and State Organizations

Things are different among state research organizations where competition is more subdued. This surprised us insofar as the separation of powers might be expected to foster competition among policy research organizations in

[98] Interview with Robert Reischauer, Urban Institute.

[99] Interviews with Robert Reischauer, Urban Institute; senior fellow, Heritage Foundation.

[100] People at CBPP said virtually the same thing about their organization.

[101] Interview with Brandon Arnold, Cato Institute. Readers may be taken aback by Arnold's insistence that Cato is closer to the left on various social issues. These would also include, for instance, gay marriage, abortion, and the legalization of marijuana, things over which libertarians believe individuals should have free choice. But in terms of economic policy, which is our concern in this book, libertarians and the Cato Institute fit squarely into the conservative camp because they advocate limited government intervention and free markets.

the legislative and executive branches that work on similar problems, such as CBO and OMB, respectively. To be sure, there is competition for personnel.[102] And they each try to produce the most accurate budget forecasts and analyses as possible and in doing so keep an eye on what each other are doing.[103] But according to our interviews competition in other respects was usually negligible. For instance, there is little competition over funding because each organization is nestled within bigger government agencies or departments and so depends on the larger entity's appropriations from Congress. In the extreme, NRC accepts only no-bid contracts from Congress.[104]

The level of competition among state research organizations is limited as well by their enabling legislation—an important artifact of the policymaking regime, which according to many of our interviews results in a loose division of labor. For instance, Congress established GAO, which now conducts program evaluations, policy analyses, investigations, and financial audits. It set up CBO to do budget analysis. CRS is supposed to do policy analysis. Moreover, in 1976 these agencies established a Research Notification System to keep each other informed about their ongoing and planned studies in order to avoid duplicating each other's activities.[105] Whereas all of these collect and analyze data, NRC does not.[106]

The division of labor is not perfect but normally does not create problems.[107] We were told stories about various state research organizations working on similar topics and even developing competing analytic models. But as one senior researcher told us, this is "a friendly competition in the sense that we look at what they do and we learn from what they do. We try to do it better."[108] Sometimes conflicts occur that require reconciliation, as happened, for example, when the CBO discovered that the GAO was doing a cost estimate on a new piece of legislation. CBO's general council met with the GAO director to sort things out and GAO closed down the job. But instances of conflict like this are rare.[109] Indeed, relationships among state research organizations tend to be more cooperative than conflicted. For instance, the head of the GAO explained

[102]Interview with senior official, CRS.

[103]CBO was established initially by Congress to provide budget analysis for the House and Senate with which they could check and if necessary challenge the figures coming from the OMB. The idea was to provide Congress with independence from the executive branch when it came to budget issues. CBO was supposed to help keep OMB honest. CBO does not compete with OMB per se, but its work is used in the competition between Congress and the president (Joyce 2011, chaps. 1–2).

[104]Interview with senior official, NRC.

[105]Joyce 2011, p. 30.

[106]Interview with senior official, CRS. See also Bimber (1996, p. 79) and Joyce (2011, chap. 2).

[107]Interview with senior official, CEA, and off-the-record email correspondence.

[108]Interview with Douglas Hamilton, CBO.

[109] Interview with Robert Murphy, CBO.

that his staff has periodic meetings with their counterparts at CBO and CRS to keep them apprised of and get feedback on GAO's strategic plans for serving Congress as well as discussing specific tasks that they are undertaking to make sure that they are not duplicating each other's work. He said, "We have very good, constructive working relationships with them. We each have our own niche of work that we do. But since we're working for a common client in terms of the Congress, we work together with them to make sure that we're providing the type of support to the Congress that it needs." Similarly, CRS collaborates with CBO and GAO on virtually a daily basis.[110]

The same is true in the executive branch where one might expect organizations like the CEA, Treasury, and OMB to vie for attention and influence in the White House. However, the activities of this "troika" as it is known are coordinated either by the National Economic Council, established in 1993, in the office of the president or by a special assistant to the president. This dampens the possibility for turf wars. As a result, there is generally much information sharing and communication among CEA, Treasury, and the National Economic Council. To the extent that competition occurs it involves the really big policy debates like whether the government should do an economic stimulus this way or that way. Even there, however, the competition is mostly over pushing ideas up the chains of command *within* organizations and into the Oval Office. In the Bush White House, for example, there was little interorganizational infighting over economic policy. This stemmed as well from the fact that the troika leadership did not want to have disagreements or debates in front of Bush that could jeopardize their jobs or those of their staff. So, bureaucratic constraints also imposed a modicum of cooperation.[111]

Sometimes policy research organizations supporting Congress cooperate informally with those supporting the president. For instance, CBO and OMB both work on budget analysis. Their career staffs speak the same language, hold the same general professional views, have the same orientation, work on similar issues, and, therefore, often communicate collegially with each other. And when they agree with each other on budget issues, they can convince policymakers to embrace the analysts' point of view.[112]

Overall, then, state research organizations experienced much less competition than research organizations in the private sector thanks to the effects of

---

[110]Interviews with Gene Dodaro, GAO; senior official, CRS.
[111]Interviews with Andrew Samwick, former CEA chief economist; senior official, CEA. Stories of interorganizational cooperation among state research organizations are supported by our documents. For instance, the 2007 annual report from CRS reports much cooperation among CRS, GAO, and CBO, among other government agencies. Similarly, the CEA's 2008 annual report notes much cooperation among the troika in producing economic forecasts that underlie the administration's budget proposals.
[112]Joyce 2011, pp. 208–12.

the policymaking regime, in particular the legislatively mandated division of labor and stable funding. But the policymaking regime increased competition in the private sector. Changes in campaign finance law encouraging the creation of 527 organizations as well as reductions in public spending for some policy research shops increasingly pitted think tanks against one another for funding. Shifts in control of the government and with it migration of personnel between government and think tanks through the revolving door fueled competition for staff. So did the expansion of the state's policy research capacities. Changes in the production regime ramped up competition too. Notably, corporate mergers, dips in the stock market, and economic downturns reduced available funding. And the birth of an entirely new media sector, including cable news and the Internet, created such a din that it exacerbated competition among policy research organizations to be heard in public discourse. However, as we mentioned briefly earlier, one of the most important factors amplifying competition in the private sector since the 1970s was the proliferation of new policy research organizations. And this was in effect a response to the perceived deterioration of the knowledge regime's complementary relationship with the rest of the political economy. This requires explanation.

The Roots of Proliferation

We heard repeatedly in our interviews that the proliferation of private policy research organizations and as a result escalating competition among them was probably the most important change in the U.S. knowledge regime since the 1970s. Some of this involved the rise of so-called Mickey Mouse organizations, which were often simply fronts for a few business interests to influence policymaking. But it also entailed the entrance of more substantial policy research organizations.[113]

What caused this proliferation? The story begins in the production regime with the end of the Golden Age of postwar twentieth-century capitalism in America, the rise of globalization, and with it the emergence during the 1970s and 1980s of a number of challenges to the U.S. political economy. Unemployment averaged 4.8% per year from 1960 to 1973 but jumped to 7.2% during the 1980s. Over the same period productivity growth shrank from 1.9% to 0.8% per year, government budget deficits rose from 1.9% to 4.6% of GDP, and inflation accelerated from 3.2% to 5.5% per year after peaking in the late 1970s at 8.5%.[114] Where Richard Nixon had declared famously in 1971 that "We are all Keynesians now," by the end of the decade policymakers and others worried

[113]Interviews with Brandon Arnold, Cato Institute; Lawrence Mishel, EPI; Karlyn Bowman, AEI; Joel Darmstadter, RFF.
[114]Kenworthy 1997, tables 3 and 7.

that Keynesianism did not provide solutions to these problems.[115] As people looked for new ideas to make sense of this unprecedented set of challenges, new policy research organizations were born. In other words, people perceived that the institutional complementarity between the knowledge regime and the policymaking and production regimes had broken down and people moved to restore it.

This began with perceptions among conservatives that liberal Keynesians controlled the government and were unable to make sense of and handle these problems. As a result, conservatives in the 1970s began to build a number of more aggressive advocacy organizations, led by the pioneering Heritage Foundation.[116] Wealthy benefactors began to offer money to set up 501(c)(3) research organizations that shared their ideological views. Some like AEI refused to take money for doing work whose conclusions were ideologically preordained, which is what some patrons wanted, but others like the Heritage Foundation were less reluctant.[117] Stuart Butler at Heritage admitted that his organization was "created as an institution designed to promote the general objectives of American conservatism—so it has a philosophy, unlike say Brookings or Urban, in the sense of a conscious philosophy."[118] Others on the right followed suit, such as the Cato Institute, founded in 1977, and the NCPA, founded in 1983. Liberals eventually countered by establishing their own organizations, such as CBPP in 1981, EPI in 1986, and PPI in 1989.[119]

Proliferation received additional boosts from changes in the policymaking regime after the 1994 midterm election, when the Republicans seized control of the House of Representatives for the first time in 40 years, and after the 2000 election, when George W. Bush won the White House and the Democrats no longer controlled either the House or the Senate. In response Democrats saw the need for new organizations to generate and disseminate fresh policy ideas. CAP, in particular, was created in 2003 as a result of this political situation because progressives on the left wanted better messaging techniques to get their ideas to policymakers and the public in order to push back against the Republicans.[120]

But proliferation was driven as well by changes in the production regime. The economy was strong in the late 1990s and early 2000s so the availability of funding to support these organizations increased and they flourished.[121] As

---

[115]Quoted in Skidelsky (2009, p. xiv).
[116]Rich 2004; Ricci 1993; Smith 1991.
[117]Interview with Karlyn Bowman, AEI.
[118]A senior official at PPI also said that places like the Brookings Institution and the Urban Institute were less ideological than some of the more recent entrants to the field, including PPI.
[119]Interviews with Rudolph Penner, Urban Institute; senior official, PPI. This history is detailed in Medvetz (2012), Rich (2004), and Ricci (1993).
[120]Interviews with senior official, PPI; Sarah Rosen Wartell, CAP.
[121]Interview with senior fellow, Heritage Foundation.

one respondent put it, "The stock market boom of the late '90s filled the endowments of foundations and just—you know there became a multiplicity of players out there."[122] Initially, most of the money came from conservative families and foundations, but after the rapid growth of the information technology sector in the 1990s—another important change in the nation's production regime—liberal money from Silicon Valley and other places became available too, although by at least one account money from the left is still less than that from the right.[123]

In sum, challenges to and changes to the country's production and policymaking regimes precipitated a proliferation of private policy research organizations as people searched for new ideas to make sense of the nation's economic troubles. Analytically speaking, the institutional complementarity between the knowledge regime and the policymaking and production regimes broke down insofar as people felt that the knowledge regime no longer provided analysis and advice adequate for making sense of and solving these troubles. As people perceived that the knowledge regime had become dysfunctional they moved to fix things by transforming its private side by creating in an ad hoc decentralized manner a number of new policy research organizations. In doing so, however, they helped create another problem: a crisis of political partisanship. According to one observer, the fact that a number of conservative foundations gave large sums of money to a few conservative and rather aggressive advocacy think tanks to devise fresh policy ideas helped the Republicans capture the House in 1994—a victory that elevated political partisanship to unprecedented heights with surprising ramifications for the knowledge regime.[124]

A Crisis of Partisanship

Almost everyone we spoke with in Washington said that political partisanship had become increasingly acrimonious and nasty over the past 20 years. Political partisanship is not necessarily a bad thing in a democracy if it facilitates vigorous yet civil debate and does not lead to political gridlock. Washington politics have always been partisan. The problem was that since the mid-1990s partisanship grew so extreme and polarized ideologically that it became increasingly hard for Republicans and Democrats to agree on much of anything.[125] This crisis of partisanship, as it was described to us, had such

---

[122]Interview with Lawrence Mishel, EPI.
[123]Interview with senior official, PPI. For a discussion of the emergence and influence of ideologically liberal money for politics from the private sector during the 2000s, see Bai (2007).
[124]Interview with Robert Reischauer, Urban Institute.
[125]Edsall 2012; Hacker and Pierson 2010.

surprising consequences for the knowledge regime that is worth explaining how extreme the situation became.

Setting the stage for us, one former congressional staffer explained that "Washington has become so partisan in everything. I mean, I was on the Hill for six years in the early '80s, and it was a Democratic Congress. It was while Reagan was President, and it was a pretty partisan time, but nothing like now."[126] A senior fellow at the Heritage Foundation said that escalating partisanship turned increasingly mean-spirited and polarized over the past 20 years such that nowadays, "[p]eople are at each other's throats all the time. They never take a break." Many people we interviewed regretted this turn of events. The Cato Institute's Tom Palmer summed up many respondents' sentiments:

It's . . . soul destroying. Washington is a blue team/red team town. You have the blue team; everything is blue. You're supposed to do blue things. Red team, everything is red, and you're all supposed to hate each other. . . . The other team members are evil . . . I think it's not healthy.

Sometimes it gets personal. One researcher told us that they had been invited recently with their spouse to a Washington dinner party. They were the only conservatives there, and "[a]t times it was just uncomfortable, and that wouldn't have been true in the '70s or '80s. You would have been able to bring a lot of people together who had different points of view, but now we've all sort of gone into our own neighborhoods, and that, I think, is a very sad development."[127] Someone else said that partisanship had been growing for a long time, but within the last three years or so it had started to metastasize in private research organizations where some people began launching malicious ad hominem attacks on each other.[128] Others concurred that partisanship had spilled over into some think tanks, and one implied that it may have contributed to the establishment of some of the newer advocacy research organizations.[129]

Nevertheless, many people were quick to argue that it was not nearly as bad as it was among politicians. When we asked one think tank president whether the level of partisan rancor was worse in Congress than among policy research organizations, his response was emphatic: "Oh! A hundred times more sir! No, if it was just Brookings, NCPA, the American Enterprise Institute, we'd

---

[126]Interview with senior official, CBPP.
[127]Interview with Karlyn Bowman, AEI.
[128]Interview with Rudolph Penner, Urban Institute.
[129]Interviews with Tom Palmer, Cato Institute; senior official, PPI; John Goodman, NCPA; Isabel Sawhill, Brookings Institution.

all be having a good time. But you get the two parties on the Hill, it gets very bitter."[130] Indeed, several people reported that they continued to have good relationships with others in think tanks associated with political ideologies different from their own. For example, Kevin Hassett, at AEI, told us about testifying recently at a congressional hearing where he presented a table of data. Someone from the Brookings-Urban Joint Center on Taxation checked the numbers and found mistakes. What happened next is instructive:

> Now in a partisan town, you could imagine that [he] would call up the *Wall Street Journal* and *Washington Post* and try to embarrass me, but he didn't. He said "Hey Kev, your table was wrong, you should [check the numbers] . . . and correct your testimony." And I did. I think that is an example of a very high level of collegiality.

It is hard to be sure, but there may be several reasons for the relatively low level of acrimony among these organizations compared to the two political parties. One may be the fact that their boards of directors as well as staff at least at places like Brookings, Urban, and some others consist of both liberals and conservatives. Another may be the tax code. After all, as we have said, for tax purposes it is important that these organizations remain nonpartisan and willing to provide help and information to anyone who asks for it regardless of their political persuasion, which means that engaging in partisan attacks is risky business.[131] Finally, these organizations and others such as CBO, GAO, and CRS are staffed with lots of professionals who have bought into an organizational culture of nonpartisanship.[132]

Although the state organizations we spoke to were nonpartisan they were not immune from the effects of rising partisanship in Washington. For example, in 1995 after the Republicans gained control of the House they threatened to cut funding to some state research organizations that they suspected of Democratic partisanship—if not shut them down entirely. According to its general council, CBO received a letter to that effect demanding to see data on who they had been working for over the past 20 years. And GAO, where he worked previously, lost a third of its budget because the Republicans thought that GAO was catering to Democratic interests. In truth, most of GAO's work

---

[130] Interview with John Goodman, NCPA.
[131] Interview with senior official, PPI.
[132] Medvetz (2012) notes that private think tanks in Washington have increasingly had to balance whatever partisan profiles they may have had with a professional persona—often reaching out to academics and academically trained experts—to develop a more credible presence in the field. On the high level of professionally based nonpartisanship within government policy research organizations like CBO, GAO, and CRS, see Bimber (1996) and Joyce (2011).

is done for whichever party controls Congress because that is the party that drives GAO's agenda by making most of the requests to the agency.[133]

In some cases partisanship led to paranoia. We interviewed someone at a state organization who initially balked at talking with us when we arrived even though we had arranged the interview weeks in advance. He was extremely suspicious of who we were and why we wanted to talk to him. Eventually, things loosened up and we had a good interview, but he was still very concerned that we preserve his anonymity. When we were done we asked why he had been so hesitant initially. He explained that things had changed in Washington, especially after the younger George Bush became president, and he had been instructed not to speak with anyone from the press anymore. So, he became wary of granting interviews to anyone.

In another interview someone told us that nowadays it was difficult if not impossible to work with groups or individuals too far out on the ends of the political spectrum. Why? Because if word got out, then some people might say that they did not want to work with an organization that was hanging around with "extremists." Some organizations on the left, for instance, were very upset with Brookings for doing things with the Heritage Foundation. As a result, rather than having discussions in an organization's offices, people would do so on the Mall or other public places where they were less likely to be noticed. But even that was no longer safe because cell phone cameras were ubiquitous. According to one Washington veteran:

> You have to be a little more careful who you're seeing when somebody's got a camera, you know, and they just take a picture, oh, you're standing next to so and so. I mean, it may seem trivial, but it isn't, and therefore you've got to make some more broader—you've got to make broader decisions about who over the long haul are you prepared to work [with]. . . . Some people will look at that, and say, "I'm not working with some organization that hangs out with those guys." And we'll hear—we've heard that.[134]

The origins of such vicious partisanship were clear in our interviews. Virtually everyone we spoke with marked the Clinton administration as the turning point where partisanship turned nasty—especially, according to the Cato Institute's Tom Palmer, thanks to Clinton's attempt to overhaul the health care

---

[133]Interview with Robert Murphy, CBO. In response, GAO's director moved strategically to cultivate allies outside the agency by encouraging staff to interact with their counterparts in other government research organizations. GAO also tried to work more transparently in order to quell suspicions in Congress that it might be operating in politically partisan ways.
[134]Interview with Stuart Butler, Heritage Foundation.

system. He said that things continued to deteriorate when Republicans won the House in 1994 and then impeached Clinton but that they hit an even lower point during the Bush-Cheney era.

Many have attributed the crisis of partisanship to increasingly sluggish economic growth and wage stagnation, persistent if not rising demand for government programs, and therefore increasingly vicious political battles over resources and their distribution.[135] But there were also important institutional changes in the policymaking regime that contributed to the crisis of partisanship. First, according to Stuart Butler, who has been at the Heritage Foundation since 1979, during the 1980s and especially the 1990s the Republican Party leadership decided to impose much tighter discipline on its members in Congress by beefing up the whipping system—that is, rewarding members who toed the party line with committee chairmanships and the like. This strategy was perfected under Newt Gingrich's leadership in the 1990s. Democrats followed suit. Second, there was much gerrymandering during this period. Congressional district boundaries were redefined in ways that made them safer for incumbents running for reelection in the American winner-take-all system, which tends to amplify partisanship anyway compared to the European proportional representation systems. Because it was easier for incumbents to win, the number of moderates in Congress diminished.[136] Third, political "bomb throwers," who traffic in sensationalistic, nasty, and uncivil arguments to advance their political causes, became more common in Washington.[137] Some said that certain advocacy organizations had fueled the political polarization in Washington by engaging in bomb throwing, the ad hominem attacks mentioned earlier, and similar activities.[138]

Some people said that an important production regime development—the emergence of the new media—exacerbated the crisis of partisanship. One person explained that the 24-hour news cycle, YouTube, smash mouth talk radio and cable television, the blogosphere, and other information outlets fueled rancorous debate.[139] Indeed, people at CBPP told us that venues like these wanted a liberal and a conservative to attack each other and engage in verbal food fights. CBPP's analysts, they said, were lousy guests because they provided nuanced answers to questions, which precluded the sort of slugfest the media wanted.[140] Others complained that powerful interest groups, such as MoveOn.org, which mobilizes financial support for the Democrat Party

[135] Edsall 2012; Hacker and Pierson 2010.
[136] Interview with Karlyn Bowman, AEI.
[137] Interview with Robert Reischauer, Urban Institute.
[138] Interview with William Antholis, Brookings Institution.
[139] Interview with senior fellow, Heritage Foundation.
[140] Interviews with senior officials, CBPP.

through the Internet, have used the new media in ways that further aggravate partisan acrimony.[141]

The upshot of this crisis of partisanship was that policy research organizations began to be tarred with politically partisan brushes. This led to some of the most surprising discoveries for us about changes in the American knowledge regime.

Credibility and the Paradox of Partisanship

Proliferation, rising competition, and the subsequent crisis of partisanship in Washington politics led paradoxically to increased cooperation among private sector research organizations. There were two reasons for this. The first was that they began to experience serious credibility problems. They worried increasingly that fewer and fewer people took them seriously and were willing to acknowledge that they were operating objectively in a nonpartisan fashion.[142] A senior official at CBPP put it well:

> Starting in the '80s, accelerating in the '90s, you have an increasing number of people in Washington who see the world as "you're with us or you're against us," and they don't—in some sense, some of them don't believe there is such a thing as objective, careful analysis. They don't believe that somebody can analyze these issues without being tainted by whatever beliefs they have, and so increasingly you get that, and it's frustrating to us when you see sometimes people identify us as a liberal leaning organization, implying that they can then ignore what we're doing, because that must taint our thinking. . . . There are certain lawmakers on the Hill, certain pundits, and so on, who will simply say, "if you believe in these kind of policies then I can't pay attention to anything you say, because I believe you'll cook the numbers."

Another senior official at CBPP concurred, saying, "If you care about not just research, but policy and policy decisions, and the direction of our country, it's just very hard to enter into that debate in a way without somebody saying that you are partisan."

Some organizations were more susceptible to criticisms of partisanship than others. In particular, CAP was targeted during our interviews. The Heritage Foundation's Stuart Butler, for instance, told us that CAP simply wanted

---

[141]Interview with Stuart Butler, Heritage Foundation.
[142]http://www.nationalaffairs.com/publications/detail/devaluing-the-think-tank. Accessed May 2012.

George W. Bush out of the White House and liberal Democrats to take over. In contrast, he said, Heritage was less partisan than CAP because Heritage had attacked the Bush administration's Medicare drug benefit reform and some other Bush proposals. As he put it:

> We always say that when you [CAP] oppose something that Nancy Pelosi and Harry Reid [Democratic leaders in the House and Senate, respectively] support, let us know, will you? And when you tell us you've hired Republicans, tell us. They'd never tell us this. So, there's a partisan difference, which is very, very important. . . . They are much less of a think tank. . . . They are activists. They use information to try to achieve political objectives. I think that for them to be called a think tank actually besmirches the whole idea of a think tank, and I think if you ask people—the center-left organizations that I deal with, they have nothing to do with the Center for American Progress.

Conceiving of the Heritage Foundation as less partisan was hard for us to swallow given its long-standing advocacy of conservative Republican policies. Nevertheless, the point remains that people in these organizations worried that rising partisanship in Washington politics had jeopardized the credibility of research organizations in the knowledge regime.

But the crisis of partisanship created a second problem too. Politicians were either unable or unwilling to tackle the nation's most serious policy problems, notably growth of the huge middle-class entitlement programs, Social Security and Medicare, and the federal government's mounting fiscal deficits and debt. Several people pointed out that today's highly polarized political atmosphere meant that more and more politicians believed that they were better off just opposing everything the other side wanted rather than striving for compromise as they might have done 20 years ago. This made it harder to deal with big problems whose solutions could be achieved only if Democrats and Republicans worked together.[143] Thus, political gridlock emanating from a crisis of partisanship in the policymaking regime stymied solutions to these looming entitlement and fiscal problems.

The combination of escalating partisanship, flagging credibility, and political gridlock led to a surprising outcome in the U.S. knowledge regime: private policy research organizations on both sides of the political spectrum began to work together for the common good of both the knowledge regime and the country. Echoing what most of our respondents said, the president of one

[143]Interviews with senior official, CBPP; Stuart Butler, Heritage Foundation; Isabel Sawhill, Brookings Institution; Rudolph Penner, Urban Institute.

think tank told us, "There's more left-right cooperation than I've ever seen before."[144] We heard several examples of this. For instance, Brookings and AEI ran a Joint Center for Regulatory Studies from 1998 to 2008.[145] Urban and Brookings established a Tax Policy Center in 2002 with tax experts who had served in both Republican and Democratic administrations. And in 2007 a group of Democratic and Republican legislators, worried about excessive and escalating partisanship in Washington, established the Bipartisan Policy Center—a think tank seeking bipartisan solutions to economic and other national problems.[146]

Beyond these formal efforts Brookings and the Heritage Foundation assembled an informal and ideologically diverse group of budget experts from various policy research organizations, which, according to one member, the Urban Institute's Rudolph Penner, intended "to see if there was anything at all in the world we could agree on in terms of confronting what we all think is a devastating fiscal situation." The group tried to find areas of possible compromise and issued a report for politicians outlining these possibilities in early spring 2008. But Penner explained that the group's formation was also a response to the rising partisanship in Washington that had become especially vicious in the early 2000s and that was beginning to infect policy research organizations and manifest as the nasty personal attacks we mentioned earlier. In his words, "I think people reared back and said, 'Hey, wait a minute, this is not the right scholarly way to go,' as it were, and I think there's been a reaction to that. And one of the reactions is this group that I talked about where we've got Brookings, and Heritage, and AEI and all of us together trying to solve a problem."

Another example of cooperation like this was the Fiscal Wake-Up Tour, organized by people from Brookings, Heritage, AEI, PPI, and the Concord Coalition, a policy research organization specializing in budget issues. The idea was to alert state and local policymakers, academics, civic leaders, the media, and others to the magnitude of the country's fiscal problems. The hope was that by doing so people would put pressure on their representatives in Washington to do something about them. Members of the Fiscal Wake-Up Tour did not agree on how to solve the nation's fiscal problems, but they agreed that they needed to act together to raise a red flag about them.[147] Stuart Butler, one of the founders of the Fiscal Tour, told us that the motivations were to influence the policymaking agenda in a bipartisan fashion, overcome some of the credibility problems that had been plaguing their organizations, and address the big problems that politicians had been too scared to touch. This is one reason why

[144]Interview with John Goodman, NCPA.
[145]The Joint Center was replaced in 2008 by the AEI Center for Regulatory and Market Studies.
[146]http://bipartisanpolicy.org/bipartisanship. Accessed May 2012.
[147]Interviews with Isabel Sawhill, Brookings Institution; senior official, PPI.

they convinced David Walker, then head of GAO, to participate. The logic was that if two of the largest policy research organizations on the left and right—Brookings and Heritage—came together with the blessing of the government's top accountant, then people would sit up and take notice.[148]

In contrast to the informal Brookings-Heritage group that Penner described, which tried to influence the policymaking agenda through direct but quiet contact with policymakers, the Fiscal Tour had a formal declaration, had actively sought media attention, and by the time we showed up in Washington had visited over 30 cities to influence the policymaking agenda in a more indirect way.[149] Another cooperative group created to address fiscal concerns that politicians were avoiding was the so-called Four Cs, which included CBPP, the Concord Coalition, the Committee for Responsible Federal Budget, and the Committee for Economic Development.[150]

These are not the only instances of increased cooperation in response to credibility problems and partisan gridlock. The Urban Institute convenes what they call "First Tuesday" meetings each month where experts from various scholarly and advocacy organizations and policymakers are invited to participate on panels dedicated to a difficult policy issue, such as entitlement programs or tax reform. They also hold "Thursday Child" meetings, which are similar but devoted to policies that affect children. According to Rudolph Penner, some of these things have been going on for a long time, but "[t]here's been a proliferation of meetings of those kinds" around Washington since the early 1990s. He continued, explaining that "[t]here's recently been a lot more desire to invite each other to those kinds of sessions we have on First Tuesdays, or sessions AEI might have, or Brookings." John Goodman of the conservative NCPA concurred, adding that his organization recently "formed a group called the Consensus Group, which is an ongoing group where the right and center think tanks can come together and meet from time to time and try to find common ground."

The Urban Institute's president, Robert Reischauer, who has been involved in this world for over 30 years, put it all in historical perspective, saying, "There has been a distinct improvement in interaction at the professional level among the staff [of these organizations]. So we have many things here where a Heritage person or a Cato person might come and Brookings does too. And when Heritage has something, you know, talk with one of our people, or Brookings

---

[148]Interview with Stuart Butler, Heritage Foundation. Others eventually joined the effort including the Committee for Economic Development, the Association for Government Accountants, the American Institute of Certified Public Accountants, the American Association for Retired Persons, the Committee for a Responsible Federal Budget, and various state treasurers and auditors.

[149]Interview with Rudolph Penner, Urban Institute.

[150]Interview with senior official, CBPP.

[persons], and so I mean, in 1970, 1985 that never would have happened." Others agreed but lamented that there was still not enough of this cooperation in Washington.[151]

To be clear, cooperation among politically and ideologically diverse organizations is not uniform. Judging from the number of times their annual reports mentioned cooperating with organizations across the ideological spectrum, AEI, Urban Institute, Heritage Foundation, and Brookings appeared to be more interested in this sort of thing than some of the other private think tanks we visited in Washington.[152] Nor is cooperation like this an entirely new phenomenon. We heard a few stories about long-standing efforts to cooperate in a bipartisan fashion. Notably, since the 1930s the Century Foundation has been organizing bipartisan task forces to research tough policy issues.[153] And several people told us that there has frequently been informal collaboration among individual researchers at different organizations through their personal networks.[154] Still, virtually everyone we spoke with said that this sort of activity had been on the rise since the mid-1990s and they hoped it would continue.[155] This stands in especially sharp contrast to the Danish case, where cooperation like this has been far more extensive and commonplace for decades.

Nevertheless, these organizations still have to perform a delicate dance. Despite their interests in cooperation they want to advance their own policy agendas. So although cooperation has increased there is still plenty of ideological competition among them. This is why participating in cooperative

[151]Interviews with senior official, PPI; senior official, CBPP.
[152]We recognize that annual reports may suffer from selective reporting of interorganizational activities and are therefore not definitive sources. Nevertheless, a quick review is instructive. For example, the AEI 2007 annual report listed six AEI-Brookings collaborations plus others; the Brookings 2007 annual report listed five collaborations with AEI as well as Heritage, Cato, and the conservative Hoover Institution. In contrast, Cato's 2007 annual report mentioned no such collaborations with organizations from different ideological positions—even though, according to the Brookings report, they engaged with Brookings in one, and their earlier reports (1999 and 1991) mention collaborations with AEI, Urban, Heritage, and Brookings. Nor were such collaborations mentioned in the annual reports of the Hudson Institute (2008), the Economic Policy Institute (2003–5), the Center for American Progress (2006), or the Center on Budget and Policy Priorities (2007). The Urban Institute (2007) and Heritage Foundation (2007) each mentioned just a few. Note, however, that some organizations that do not seem to engage in much cooperation across the ideological center do cooperate with ideological compatriots. CAP's 2006 annual report mentions a collaboration with the progressive Century Foundation and EPI's 2003–5 annual report refers to a collaboration with CBPP.
[153]Interview with Christy Hicks, Century Foundation.
[154]Interviews with Kevin Hassett, AEI; Rudolph Penner, Urban Institute; Isabel Sawhill, Brookings Institution; James Arkedis, PPI.
[155]The AEI annual reports from 2007, 1997, and 1988–89 reveal an increase in the number of times collaborations with think tanks across the ideological center are mentioned. The same is true for the Brookings Institution, the Heritage Foundation, and the Urban Institute's annual reports for 2007, 1997, and 1987.

initiatives may alienate organizations from one another who share political convictions. For example, sometimes when the Heritage Foundation's Stuart Butler has gone with a proposal for joint activities to some of the centrist research organizations they have told him, "We have problems with people on our left. We are getting flack." He explained, "They could name organizations that are very angry with them for doing this, very angry [because] they have made the decision to essentially hang out with people like me. . . . I am conscious of the need to keep this group of people protected."[156]

A few caveats are in order about the causes of the recent trend toward cooperation. First, although everyone agreed that it was driven primarily by the things we have already discussed, a few people mentioned economics. One person told us that a Brookings-Heritage initiative was triggered in part by the fact that someone was willing to give them money to do it.[157] Furthermore, people at one of the smaller organizations reported that it behooves them to cooperate with larger organizations in order to benefit from the larger ones' resources.[158] And in two other interviews people suggested that belt-tightening among organizations due to the current lean economic climate would probably lead to more collaboration among organizations. Someone else confirmed this, noting that his organization and another half dozen that tend to compete for the same pool of funds were trying to devise ways to do joint fund-raising.[159] Thus, changes in the production regime had significant effects.

Second, a few people mentioned that cooperation was also emerging due to media considerations. As the field became more crowded thanks to proliferation it became increasingly difficult for many organizations to attract the media attention they wanted. For instance, Brandon Arnold at the Cato Institute told us that his libertarian organization was talking with the progressive CAP about doing some foreign policy events together. Why? "Because from a media perspective, from a congressional staffer perspective, you don't expect those groups to be working together; you don't expect them to be on the same stage advocating the same principles. So when you do it's a little bit more newsworthy and it might encourage people to pay a little bit closer attention."

Finally, personal networks also facilitated the recent spate of cooperation. The Brookings-Heritage budget group that Penner described was organized by him and a few others who knew each other well.[160] Similarly, the Fiscal Wake-Up Tour was the brainchild of Isabel Sawhill at Brookings, Stuart Butler at Heritage, and a handful of others who already had good personal

---

[156]Interview with Stuart Butler, Heritage Foundation.
[157]Interview with Rudolph Penner, Urban Institute.
[158]Interview with senior official, CBPP.
[159]Interviews with Christy Hicks, Century Foundation; Karlyn Bowman, AEI; James Arkedis, PPI.
[160]Interview with Rudolph Penner, Urban Institute.

relationships with each other. When we asked Butler why some organizations were not involved, he explained:

> There's self-selection. It started as an informal group that I started with Isabel Sawhill. . . . The only exclusion was actually in the sense of personal chemistry. There were some people . . . who were not so comfortable sitting down and talking to somebody who they disagree with on 70% of things, and thinking about what do we have in common. . . . I mean there are some people who are very narrow and determined and say it's either my way [or the highway]. And there are others like myself, I think, who are—have a strong philosophy. We know where we want to go, but I'm more than willing to talk to people on the far left.

Indeed, there are some organizations that do not want to participate in things like this even if invited. The liberal EPI's president told us that he disagreed with the whole premise of the Fiscal Wake-Up Tour because he did not believe that there was an entitlement program crisis per se. So Washington has not become some sort of happy love fest among every research organization across the ideological spectrum. Although the crisis of partisanship has led to more cooperation there is still a very competitive marketplace of ideas at least among private policy research organizations in Washington.

Conclusion

Let us put the U.S. case into sharper perspective vis-à-vis some of the analytic arguments we made in chapter 1. We argued that the structure and practices of knowledge regimes are largely determined by the policymaking and production regimes with which they are associated. Consider the production regime. First, as the Golden Age of postwar twentieth-century capitalism came to an end and globalization emerged, conservatives questioned the ability of liberal Keynesians in Washington to make sense of the country's economic problems and mobilized private donors to finance a new generation of advocacy organizations to challenge the liberal status quo. Liberals on the left eventually responded in kind. A proliferation of private policy research organizations resulted and with it an increase in competition especially for funding, which was exacerbated when the economy faltered and donors tightened their purse strings. Second, the line between scholarly and advocacy organizations blurred as the new advocacy organizations were financed for partisan purposes and then 501(c)(3)/501(c)(4) hybrids began to emerge. Private money, then, helped fuel the crisis of partisanship in Washington by creating a new niche in the knowledge regime. All of this eventually created a credibility deficit for many private policy research organizations insofar as people doubted whether their analysis and advice were objective and unbiased. Third, development of an entirely new sector of the economy—the new media—contributed to the crisis too by encouraging aggressive and highly partisan debate. In the end, however, all of this culminated in some organizations cultivating more cooperative relationships with each other across the partisan divide.

The policymaking regime also had effects. In particular, renewal of the congressional whipping system as well as gerrymandering election districts in a winner-take-all electoral system exacerbated the crisis of partisanship, which contributed to the proliferation of advocacy oriented private policy research organizations. And exemptions in the tax code for giving to 501(c)(3) organizations, which had been in place for years, provided an especially attractive opportunity for rich donors to establish and then support these often partisan organizations. We shall see in later chapters that this is one reason why the size of the knowledge regime's private sector was much larger than in our European countries. We will see as well that partisanship was less extreme and vicious in the European proportional representation systems.

Things were surprisingly different among state research organizations, which did not change much but where the policymaking regime still had effects. First, although in a few cases, notably the GAO and CBO, politicians grew suspicious that state research organizations were operating in partisan ways, the structure and practices of these organizations changed very little because their activities were defined by legislative mandates requiring among other things that they serve members of both parties. Second, there was much less competition among them and in some cases more formal coordination and cooperation than among private research organizations. This surprised us insofar as one might expect that the constitutional separation of powers and system of checks and balances would have led to a duplication of research tasks by organizations in different branches of the government and therefore competition between them. However, institutional factors including a legislatively mandated division of labor and various administrative coordination mechanisms, such as the National Economic Council, organized economic policy research in quite orderly ways. Of course, we were surprised by the fact that there were well-resourced and analytically sophisticated policy research organizations in the legislative and executive branches as well as the Federal Reserve and NRC, although in hindsight this made sense insofar the U.S. state is not nearly as noninterventionist or bureaucratically weak in some policy areas as is often assumed.[161]

[161]Block 2008; Campbell and Lindberg 1990; Campbell et al. 1991.

Another way to think about all of this is from the perspective of institutional complementarity. We have shown that in effect people perceived that the institutional complementarity between the knowledge regime and the policymaking and production regimes broke down as circumstances changed with the end of the Golden Age and the rise of globalization. People felt that the private side of the knowledge regime had become dysfunctional insofar as it no longer provided analysis and advice that could help make sense of and solve the economy's problems and that it suffered a credibility deficit. People responded in two ways, both intended to rejuvenate complementarity. First, to better connect the knowledge regime's ideas with the policymaking regime they created a new knowledge regime niche populated by aggressive advocacy research organizations. Some of the scholarly research organizations began to develop somewhat more aggressive advocacy tactics too. Second, to shore up the credibility deficit so that policymakers and others would take their work seriously knowledge regime leaders began later on to cooperate with each other. In this sense perceptions of a breakdown of institutional complementarity triggered a paradoxical transformation on the private side of the knowledge regime—one that involved more competition as well as more cooperation. This was, of course, not the result of some sort of clearly articulated central plan. Instead it was a decentralized and largely ad hoc set of initiatives undertaken by a variety of people with the hope—although certainly not with any guarantees—that things would get better as a result.

Nor is this to say that the structure and practices of the knowledge regime were determined entirely by the production and policymaking regimes. Despite the obvious potential for moneyed interests to bias or otherwise determine the activities of private policy research organizations there was evidence at least among some of the scholarly organizations that they did not necessarily kowtow to their benefactors' interests. AEI, for instance, refused to accept funding with ideological strings attached in the 1970s. We learned as well that other scholarly research organizations refused money from time to time when it was offered because management worried that it would influence their research programs.[162] We were also told that at places like AEI and Brookings scholars were hired and then left alone to do their research with little meddling from management or funders. And when the wealthy Koch brothers tried to get the Cato Institute to do their political bidding the organization refused and was sued as a result. Of course, the influence of private money on advocacy organizations was clearer insofar as they were started with political goals in mind and in some cases were accused during our interviews of fitting the research to their political and ideological agendas. The point is twofold. First,

[162]Interview with Robert Reischauer, Urban Institute.

as Thomas Medvetz has argued, many of these private organizations have had increasingly to walk a fine line balancing between objective, quality analysis, which is necessary to maintain their credibility, and policy recommendations that will not alienate their financial benefactors.[163] Second, in the private sector where the possibility for organizations to succumb to pressure from moneyed interests is great there were at least some instances where organizations exercised independence.

Organizational independence seems to have been more uniform among the state research organizations where private money was irrelevant. And despite whatever political pressures they may have faced to tailor their research to certain political interests, there was evidence that this did not happen much. We learned, for instance, that CBO's directors had spoken up against the favored policies of both powerful Republicans and Democrats. Several state research organizations had rigorous internal vetting systems to ensure that their research was politically unbiased. And some, notably CBO, GAO, and CRS, went to great lengths to instill in their staff a culture of professionalism and prohibit their researchers from engaging in anything that might be construed as partisan. Indeed, all of the state research organizations we visited stipulated that their job was to provide unbiased research regardless of the political persuasion of those in government making the request. To that end GAO asked that all research requests from Congress come from both a Democrat and a Republican.

Things were much different in France, where thanks to very different policymaking and production regimes the state dominated the knowledge regime and private policy research organizations remained few and far between. Private money played a much more limited role. So in many ways France represents the sharpest contrast to the United States.

---

[163] Medvetz 2012.

3

The Decline of *Dirigisme* in France

The American and French knowledge regimes could not be more different. A competitive marketplace of ideas has long operated in the United States but has emerged only recently in France. But the most striking difference is that while there have long been an ample number of private as well as state policy research organizations in the United States, state research organizations have dominated France's knowledge regime and private ones have been very scarce. We expected to find this because France is a country where *dirigisme*—central state-led economic development—prevailed for several decades after the Second World War.[1] It surprised us, then, to learn that beginning in the 1980s a more diverse set of policy research organizations started to emerge in civil society—often at the behest of the state. This was triggered by what some people described to us in effect as a *crisis of ideas* inside the state whereby policymakers perceived that the state's own policy research organizations failed to provide analysis and advice useful for making sense of and resolving stagflation and other problems that stemmed from the end of

[1]Dobbin 1994; Eichengreen 2008; Judt 2006; Levy 1999; Shonfield 1965.

the Golden Age of postwar capitalism and the rise of globalization. As a result, they sought fresh thinking from new sources. Put differently, they perceived a breakdown in the knowledge regime's institutional complementarity vis-à-vis the rest of the political economy and took steps to rejuvenate it. Our surprise was compounded when we learned that in the early 2000s despite this trend away from dirigisme in the knowledge regime the state started to restore some of the control it had relinquished by better coordinating and in some cases recentralizing some knowledge regime activities.

We begin by briefly reviewing key elements of the French political economy that affected its knowledge regime. Then we map the structure of the knowledge regime as we found it in 2008. Finally, we discuss how changes in the political-economic landscape associated with the end of the Golden Age and the onset of globalization sparked a crisis of ideas and a move away from and then back toward dirigisme in France's knowledge regime.

The Political-Economic Environment

Whereas the United States and Germany are typically described as liberal and coordinated economies, respectively, the French production regime is more ambiguous.[2] On the one hand, during the Golden Age French unions were poorly organized.[3] By 1980 only 18% of the labor force was unionized, which was even less than the U.S. labor force.[4] Although unions could mount crippling strikes for a few days at a time, especially in the public sector, overall they were unable to take a united stand on most policy issues because the five labor confederations engaged in bitter ideological rivalries and most unions lacked close ties to political parties.[5] Nor were employers well organized. There was one major employer confederation, the National Council of French Employers (CNPF), but employer associations were often unable to coordinate actions among members and were prone to conflict between large and small firms. Thanks to the lack of organizational unity among employers and unions French corporatism was more limited than in Germany and Denmark.[6]

[2]Hall and Soskice 2001a, pp. 19–21; Prasad 2005, p. 360. Culpepper (2006, p. 46) argues that France never fit neatly into the coordinated market economy category but notes that "France is emphatically not a liberal market economy." In our view, France lies closer to the coordinated market economy type insofar as economic actors have relied heavily on nonmarket institutions—specifically the state—for information with which to make decisions.

[3]Culpepper 2006, pp. 32–33; Levy 1999, p. 32.

[4]However, thanks to the so-called extension procedures, 85% of workers were covered by sector-level collective bargaining agreements (Lallement 2006; Visser 2009).

[5]Culpepper 2006; Hall 2006b, 1986, p. 244; Prasad 2005, p. 372.

[6]Culpepper 2001, 2006; Hall 2006b; Palier 2006, p. 108; Shonfield 1965. French corporatism was more evident in the administration of social benefits than in labor-management bargaining (Palier 2006).

On the other hand, there was much state intervention into the economy because after the Second World War the central government led economic rebuilding and modernization. The Ministry of Finance supervised and regulated price setting. The central administration targeted certain firms to be national champions with a variety of state subsidies and credit.[7] The state also nationalized the gas, electricity, and coal industries. And in order to guide economic development it pursued indicative planning based on formal consultations and information sharing with the unions, industry, ministries, and outside experts. This was orchestrated by the state's Planning Commissariat (Commissariat Général du Plan), which was established in 1946 and led by Jean Monnet to guide the modernization process with a series of five-year plans. Corporatist interests participated in the planning process, but the state had the last word.[8] Indeed, the commissariat was a force to be reckoned with that vested power in the hands of a few farsighted bureaucrats insulating policy from political influence.[9] For these reasons people have described France during the immediate postwar period as one of the most "statist" of all advanced capitalist economies.[10]

In the policymaking regime a system of proportional representation involved a dozen or more political parties in the National Assembly. This was a bipolar system with power vacillating between two dominant blocs. On the left were the Socialist and Communist Parties and a few others, with the Communists being particularly strong until the 1970s and the Socialists after that. On the right were the Gaullists, organized in various parties over the years, including the Rally for the Republic (RPR) in the mid-1970s.[11] Other parties on the right included the Union for French Democracy (UDF), which represented free-marketers, moderates, Christian Democrats, and centrists. Parties were more disciplined in France than the United States because they financed political campaigns and therefore better controlled their members.[12] And, of course, the ideological range from left to right was much wider in France than in the United States as it was in our other European countries.

France's presidential system of government conferred power on the executive branch to a degree unheard of in most other capitalist democracies

[7]Zysman 1983.
[8]Shonfield 1965, pp. 231–32.
[9]Eichengreen 2008, p. 106. In contrast to Soviet-style planning, the French set production targets and relied on information sharing to hit them, while the Soviets set production quotas and relied on state directives to meet them (Judt 2006, p. 71; Shonfield 1965, chaps. 5, 7).
[10]Culpepper 2006; Hancké et al. 2007b; Schmidt 2002; Shonfield 1965, chaps. 5, 7; Zysman 1983.
[11]Grunberg 2006. Gaullism refers to President Charles de Gaulle's curious blend of French nationalism, populism, and anticommunism with a strong central state dominated by an elite technocracy, weak political parties, and weak parliament. It also entailed a commitment to the free market albeit embedded in indicative planning. As it evolved the RPR became a neo-Gaullist party adopting a pro-European and more neoliberal position.
[12]Prasad 2005, p. 363, 2006, p. 244.

and provided the foundation for dirigisme. Power was—and still is—shared by the president and a prime minister appointed by him.[13] Unlike in the United States, there were few checks and balances.[14] Central state power was augmented further by a sprawling permanent civil service run by an administrative elite who graduated mostly from the École Nationale d'Administration (ENA) and École Polytechnique—two postsecondary schools that are part of the prestigious Grandes Écoles system, which trains the country's managerial, administrative, and technocratic elite. Both schools imbue the elite with legitimacy based on an ideology of neutrality and independence from both political and social influence, a sense of esprit de corps, and utter confidence in their ability to manage the economy. Unlike in the United States where many civil service positions are filled with political appointees and turn over when a new administration comes to power, in France they are filled with technocrats and only the heads of ministries and cabinet members leave.[15] All of this affords interest groups fewer opportunities to penetrate the policymaking process than they enjoy in America. According to historian Tony Judt, "The Fifth Republic had accentuated the longstanding French habit of concentrating power in one place and a handful of institutions. France was run, and was seen to be run, by a tiny Parisian elite: socially exclusive, culturally privileged, haughty, hierarchical and unapproachable."[16]

However, things changed as the Golden Age of postwar capitalism faded. In the policymaking regime beginning in the late 1970s the old party system succumbed to strain and rebalancing as the Gaullists and Communists lost steam in part because they lacked solutions for the country's recent economic malaise.[17] Furthermore, the traditional left-wing and right-wing coalitions were challenged from within their own ranks over issues like immigration, European integration, and neoliberalism. The Socialist Party grew in stature, came to power in 1981 under President François Mitterrand, but was confronted in the 1990s by the Green Party. The xenophobic National Front (FN) opposed the RPR/UDF coalition. And defections from the Gaullist RPR and center-right UDF parties led to the creation in 2002 of the now powerful Union for a Popular Movement (UMP).[18] As a result,

[13]Boyer 1997, p. 97.
[14]Prasad 2006, p. 258.
[15]Fourcade 2009, pp. 51–57; Hall 1986, pp. 243–44; Prasad 2005, p. 363.
[16]Judt 2006, p. 411. Suleiman (1987) notes correctly that the degree of state power and centralization in France varies by sector. But as many have shown this model held for economic policymaking.
[17]After the war, the Gaullists' strength stemmed in part from their promise to ensure the population's safety from violence stemming from the French colonial independence movements, notably Algeria's. Thus, resolution of the colonial question contributed to the Gaullists' fall from grace. It did the same for the Communist Party, which had an anticolonialism platform.
[18]Grunberg 2006.

the government was ruled frequently by cohabitation—a power-sharing arrangement where the president was from a party on the left and the prime minister was from a party on the right, or vice versa.[19] Politics became more fragmented and pluralist.

In the production regime Mitterrand's socialist government tried to quell stagflation with several bold moves including the nationalization of 49 firms and banks between 1981 and 1983.[20] But the experiment failed, so his government reversed course and began reprivatizing assets in 1986 including 36 banks—again with little success.[21] As the state lost its ability to control firms and provide credit through the banking system French firms became more dependent on foreign equity markets, foreign ownership of French firms increased, and the economy became more exposed to global economic forces.[22] Unionization rates dropped to 8% of the labor force by 2007.[23] Membership in employer associations dropped too. During the 1990s CNPF, the peak association, suffered more disputes among its members. Its name was changed to the Movement of French Enterprises (MEDEF) in 1998—a move that reflected the triumph of its neoliberal wing.[24]

The old *dirigiste* system began to teeter. Pressure against dirigisme first appeared in the May 1968 protests against de Gaulle's centralized semi-authoritarian rule. But it began in earnest with Mitterrand's socialist government and continued through the early 2000s with a variety of legal, constitutional, and administrative reforms.[25] In particular, postwar economic planning came to an end as the five-year plans failed to deliver strong economic performance and groups who felt increasingly shut out of the planning process opposed it.[26] During the mid-1990s Prime Minister Alain Juppé restructured the Planning Commissariat.[27] By the early 2000s it was a shadow of its former self, and in 2005 the Chirac government abolished it.[28] In addition, the powerful Ministry of Finance was weakened as the banking sector was privatized, the Bank of France became independent in 1993, and control over monetary policy shifted

---

[19]Guyomarch 1999, p. 182.
[20]Boyer 1997; Hall 1986, chap. 6.
[21]Hall 1986; Levy 1999, chap. 1.
[22]Culpepper 2006; Goyer 2006; Palier and Thelen 2012.
[23]However, 95% of workers were still covered by sector-level labor agreements (Lallement 2006; Visser 2009).
[24]Culpepper 2010, chap. 3; Lallement 2006.
[25]Guyomarch 1999; Judt 2006, pp. 547–56; Le Galès 2006.
[26]Cohen 1977, pp. 258–79; Hall 1986, chap. 7.
[27]Fourcade 2009, pp. 52–59, 208–11; Guyomarch 1999, p. 175.
[28]Pressure against dirigisme surely emanated as well from Brussels, where various EU directives led to the establishment of new independent regulatory authorities in France (Duina 1999, chap. 2) as well as squabbling among French ministries over how to best influence EU policy (Smith 2006; Thatcher 2007; Wilsford 2001).

to the European Central Bank in 1999.[29] Nevertheless, France remains a statist political economy compared to our other countries, although the state's capacities have shifted from planning and industrial policy toward defining rules, procedures, and regulations.[30]

We will show that all of this affected the knowledge regime in many ways. For instance, the dirigiste tradition meant that the knowledge regime was dominated by state policy research organizations more than in our other countries. Reflecting the production regime's corporatist legacy, some of these organizations represented business and labor. But the presence of a permanent technocratic civil service limited the opportunity for private policy research organizations to develop. Moreover, the end of the Golden Age and the advent of globalization entailed challenges to and changes in both the policymaking and production regimes that triggered transformations in the knowledge regime. The state created semi-public policy research organizations, and a few private research organizations cropped up too. In other words, people recognized that the old state-centered knowledge regime had become dysfunctional and no longer complemented the rest of the political economy so they tried to improve the situation by cultivating sources of policy analysis and advice outside the state. This was a much more statist and centralized approach to restoring the knowledge regime's complementarity than the one people took in the United States where the emphasis was instead on spawning a new generation of private and often advocacy-oriented policy research organizations in a more ad hoc decentralized manner.

Mapping the Field: The Knowledge Regime Today

In contrast to those in the United States, few people we interviewed in Paris had a good sense of the entire composition of their knowledge regime. We did not run into this in our other countries. So as our interviews progressed we began drawing schematic pictures of our interpretation of the knowledge regime's topography, showing them to the people we interviewed and asking if we had identified all the important types of organizations in the field. Several people said that they had never considered the entire regime before.[31] One senior state official said, "Your drawing is interesting. I never thought in terms of that kind."[32] Nevertheless, it was impossible to miss how dominant the state research organizations were in France's knowledge regime. Everyone we spoke

---

[29]Nevertheless, by some accounts the French Ministry of Finance is the most powerful finance ministry in the European Union (Marier 2002).
[30]Culpepper 2006; Howell 2009; Lallement 2006; Le Galès 2006; Palier and Thelen 2012.
[31]Interviews with René Sève, CAS; senior official, Enterprise and Progress.
[32]Interview with senior official, DGTPE.

with recognized this, so they were at least aware of this part of the knowledge regime as well as their own particular niche. We discuss the state policy research organizations first and then their cousins, the semi-public scholarly organizations. Together they constitute the heart of this case.

The Dominance of State Research Organizations

Much of France's policy research and analysis is conducted by four clusters of state research organizations.[33] This is due to the fact that the highly centralized French state has long dominated the French political economy in ways that policymakers in our other countries can only dream of. These clusters consist of a number of national statistical agencies, ministerial research departments, research organizations oriented around the prime minister's office, and a number of ministerial *conseils*.

First consider the public statistical system, which is run by the National Institutes for Statistics and Economic Studies (INSEE). It was established in 1946 to collect data from the ministries, develop a national account database, and help the Planning Commissariat with macroeconomic modeling.[34] Today INSEE also organizes the national census, compiles the main indicators for the national economy, runs various national surveys, and manages a number of additional databases that it uses for statistical analysis including economic and demographic forecasting. INSEE has an enormous concentration of statisticians and economists, essentially monopolizes the production of economic data, and is a central location for economic analysis.[35] It also operates the secretariat for the National Council for Statistical Information (CNIS), which oversees government statistical offices. In particular, CNIS is a gatekeeper that reviews all applications to INSEE and other public bodies for confidential data to ensure that the methodology is alright, that the identities of individuals represented in the data are protected, and that the quality of the work proposed is acceptable.[36] Furthermore, INSEE runs the Center for Research in Economics and Statistics (CREST). INSEE is a huge operation with a 2007 budget of about $570 million and a staff of about 6,100 people, including 24 regional offices.[37]

---

[33] Fourcade (2009, p. 217) agrees that there is a "nearly absolute monopoly of governmental organizations and their unique breed of 'economist-statisticians' over the construction of economic diagnostics, forecasts, and the production of policy-relevant economic information."

[34] Interview with senior official, DARES. See also Fourcade (2009, pp. 205–6) and Hall (1986, p. 140, 2006b, p. 5).

[35] Fourcade 2009, pp. 53, chap. 4.

[36] We thank Cornelia Woll for this observation. Details on CNIS responsibilities are available at http://www.cnis.fr/cms/Accueil/activites/Textes_de_reference. Accessed January 2012.

[37] INSEE annual report 2007 (http://www.insee.fr/en/insee-statistique-publique/connaitre/rae /rae07.pdf) and United Nations, Department of Economic and Social Affairs, Country Profile of France 2011 (http://unstats.un.org/unsd/dnss/docViewer.aspx?docID=579). Both accessed June 2011.

The second cluster includes the ministerial research departments, which conduct technical data analysis. Although they do not all have the same level of analytic capabilities, when we asked one senior ministerial official whether they were the most important organizations in the French knowledge regime in terms of analytic clout, she said, "In terms of analytical capacity, I've little doubt."[38] Compared to most others, however, the Ministry of Finance has "a huge capacity for economic analysis."[39] Notably, the Ministry's General Directorate of the Treasury and Economic Policy (DGTPE) has dozens of economists that produce complex macroeconomic analyses, including economic forecasts of both national and international scope as well as policy evaluation research used for budget planning in the prime minister's office.[40] Some of the ministerial research units, such as the Directorate for Research, Studies, Evaluation and Statistics (DREES) and the Directorate for the Coordination of Research, Studies and Statistics (DARES), are affiliated with more than one ministry. DARES, for example, works on labor market issues for two ministries. It collects labor market data from unions and employers as well as its own national surveys and funnels them to INSEE and other organizations. It does in-house statistical modeling and estimates the effects of current and proposed policies but outsources some work to other research institutes like the Center for Economic Research (OFCE) at Sciences Po (Institut d'Études Politiques), one of the French Grandes Écoles in Paris.[41]

A third cluster of state research organizations is organized around the prime minister's office. One is the Council of Economic Analysis (CAE), which provides policy analysis and advice to the prime minister. It has six regular members, picked by the prime minister, and a staff of about 30. Virtually all are professionally trained economists like Christian de Boissieu, its chair, who has a PhD in economics and held postdoctoral fellowships at Northwestern and Harvard Universities in the United States. Most come from universities but some from business and government.[42] The prime minister appoints members from across the political spectrum, not just those close to his viewpoint as happens in the United States when the president selects his Council of Economic Advisers. And its reports, which are often shorter and more narrowly focused than the U.S. CEA's, are written typically by a CAE member in collaboration with outside scholars from the academy or semi-public research organizations in order to ensure sufficient expertise in the subject at hand. The CAE picks these outsiders from divergent intellectual camps, including neoliberalism,

[38]Interview with senior official, DGTPE. See also Marier 2002.
[39]Interview with senior official, DARES.
[40]Interview with senior official, DGTPE.
[41]Interview with senior official, DARES.
[42]http://www.cae.gouv.fr/spip.php?article134. Accessed October 2011.

Keynesianism, and the quasi-Marxist French regulation school. As a result, its reports reflect a level of political and intellectual pluralism and political independence not seen in those of its American counterpart.[43]

The CAE has somewhat overlapping analytic responsibilities with two other state research organizations. First is the Economic and Social Council (CES), established in 1958. Its 230 members come primarily from major organizations, such as the union confederations, employer associations, mutual benefit societies, private and state-owned enterprises, and professional associations, so that its composition is a reflection of French corporatism. The government is required to consult with it on all matters concerning public expenditure. Its policy recommendations are based on information gathered from many sources including hearings with experts and must be approved by a majority vote of its members.[44]

Second is the Center for Strategic Analysis (CAS), which the prime minister established in 2006 to replace the Planning Commissariat. It was fitting, then, that when we interviewed its director general, René Sève, in his office we sat at a conference table once used by Jean Monnet himself. CAS has more analytic capacities than CAE and coordinates the activities of other research organizations on behalf of ministries and policymakers.[45] Its working groups include experts on the topic at hand, notably those from the unions, employers, universities, and other interested organizations like the conseils, discussed below. CAS does not prepare legislation but predicts the effects that it will have and helps prepare research reports to that effect, including various economic studies.[46] In short, whereas ministerial research units do narrowly focused analysis CAS helps put it all into broader perspective by synthesizing information gathered from many places. In Sève's words, "It is collective work with all the ministries, the politicians' staff, and so on."

The final cluster of state policy research organizations is the conseils. Each is located within a ministerial *cabinet*, which is the group of non-civil-service aides appointed by a minister to help him or her manage the dual responsibilities of running an administrative department and dealing with politics. The conseils are an important source of economic and political advice for ministers. Each has a secretariat—a group of research analysts—that does policy

[43]Interview with Christian de Boissieu, CAE. See also the discussion of CAE reports in chapter 7. The Commission Économique de la Nation also represents a wide spectrum of political perspectives and is made up mainly of economic specialists, although it advises the minister of finance not the prime minister and does not write reports (Fourcade 2009, p. 225; email correspondence with senior official, CEPII).

[44]Interview with Christian de Boissieu, CAE.

[45]Email correspondence with senior official, CEPII.

[46]http://www.strategie.gouv.fr/les-rapports and http://www.strategie.gouv.fr/economie-finances. Both accessed January 2012.

research for it.[47] They are similar to Danish ad hoc commissions discussed in chapter 5 except that the conseils are permanent.[48] Conseils usually consist of tripartite representation from the unions, business associations, *cabinet* members, and perhaps a few relevant experts. Their members represent a broad range of views from across the political spectrum because their purpose historically has been to generate consensus among their members and settle political and social conflicts under the supervision of administrative authorities. They often develop policy recommendations based on public hearings and meetings with experts as well as their own analysis for ministers and their *cabinets*. They specialize in particular policy areas. For example, the Employment Advisory Council (COE) and Retirement Advisory Council (COR), which are among the most important, do this for the prime minister for employment and pension policy, respectively.[49] The prime minister appoints the presidents of the conseils and CAS funds some of them, including COE and COR, but they retain considerable organizational autonomy because they are not linked directly to the prime minister's office, CAS has no authority over them, and their presidents are well known and thus demand independence.[50] We heard little about them during our interviews except for CAE, discussed earlier, which also advises the prime minister but is different from the rest insofar as it is composed largely of university economists rather than the social partners.[51]

Semi-public Scholarly Research Organizations

The French state has also created a number of scholarly nonprofit research organizations upon which it relies for expert analysis. These are semi-public organizations insofar as they are supposed to be independent from the state even though they are often funded by it either directly or indirectly. Especially prominent among these are the OFCE, The Center for Economic Research and Applications (CEPREMAP), the Center for Economic Observation and Research for the Expansion of Economy and Enterprise Development

[47]We thank Bruno Palier for this information. See also De Lamothe (1965) and Fourcade (2009, pp. 223–24). *Cabinets* are linchpins connecting political ideas and their application. They are best viewed as an interface between the knowledge regime and policymaking regime. Many organizations we spoke with in Paris viewed them as political targets that they try to influence—a point that is consistent with other research (e.g., Desmoulins 2000, p. 154; Fieschi and Gaffney 2004, 1998; Gaffney 1991; Guyomarch 1999; Searls 1978).

[48]The French government also regularly appoints temporary commissions to investigate specific topics. They too consist of people with a wide range of viewpoints and are designed to settle political and social conflicts rather than do policy research per se (Fourcade 2009, p. 224). They are unimportant in terms of producing policy analysis. We thank Bruno Palier and Patrick Le Galès for this observation.

[49]Interview with senior official, DARES.

[50]Interview with René Sève, CAS. See also Marier (2002).

[51]Interview with Xavier Timbeau, OFCE.

(Coe-Rexecode), the Institute for Economic and Social Research (IRES), the Center for International Prospective Studies (CEPII) and the French Institute of International Relations (IFRI).

According to our interviews, these organizations use data from INSEE and various other sources. Sometimes they collect the data themselves. But all of them engage in extensive and sophisticated data analysis. For example, Coe-Rexecode tracks trends with time-series analysis and makes forecasts utilizing a database with about 10,000 variables that they have built using public data as well as data that they collect from French firms. Their intent is not so much to suggest policy solutions but rather to identify problems through data analysis and, as we were told, "ring the bell" to alert policymakers to them. They also meet frequently with CAE to discuss economic problems that they have discovered.[52] Similarly, CEPII has elaborate statistical models to show the impact of trade policies on every country in the world.[53] And OFCE and CEPREMAP perform all sorts of econometric analyses.[54]

Several things stand out about these organizations. To begin with, some of them reflect France's postwar corporatist heritage. IRES and Coe-Rexecode were created in order to get input reflecting the concerns of labor and business, respectively. Coe-Rexecode conducts an annual analysis of the competitiveness of the French economy and is in frequent contact with MEDEF, the employer confederation, and other corporate supporters as well as state research organizations.[55] IRES performs similar functions for the labor movement.[56]

The funding streams of these organizations vary. Often it comes directly from the state as is true for CEPII, which was funded initially by the prime minister's office through the Planning Commissariat but now through one of the prime minister's other strategic units. Roughly 90% of CEPII's funding comes from the state.[57] But sometimes funding comes from the private sector as well. An example is Coe-Rexecode, which gets about 30% of its funding from the Chamber of Commerce, itself a beneficiary of state funding, 30%

---

[52]Interview with senior official, Coe-Rexecode.
[53]Interview with senior official, CEPII.
[54]Interview with Xavier Timbeau, OFCE.
[55]Interview with senior official, Coe-Rexecode. Among its membership it lists the state's CAS and DARES (http://www.coe-rexecode.fr/public/Qui-sommes-nous/Nos-adherents. Accessed July 2013).
[56]The boards of Coe-Rexecode, IRES, CEPII, and IFRI all include representatives from the state (Coe-Rexecode annual report 2009; CEPII annual report 2007; IFRI annual report 2006; and http://www.turi-network.eu/Members/Full-members/Institut-de-Recherches-Economiques-et-Sociales-IRES-Institute-for-Economic-and-Social-Research. Accessed June 2011.) Reflecting the dominance of state policy research organizations, IRES and Coe-Rexecode are much smaller in size and visibility than their German counterparts, DIW and Ifo, on which they are modeled, respectively (Fourcade 2009, p. 229).
[57]Interview with senior official, CEPII.

from roughly 70 corporate members, 20% from employer associations, and 20% from contract work for various state and business organizations, including CAS and MEDEF.[58] In contrast, IRES's funding comes largely from the unions but with money they receive from the state.[59] And OFCE's funding comes from the prime minister's office, but only indirectly because OFCE is housed at Sciences Po, which receives state funding and then uses it to finance OFCE.[60] IFRI gets about 65% of its funding from private sources, mainly corporations, and the rest from a subvention from the prime minister's office.[61]

These are not large operations compared to INSEE and some other state policy research organizations. IRES, for instance, has about 30 staff, including 20 researchers, half of whom are economists.[62] IFRI has about 80 people, half of whom hold PhDs. OFCE has about 90 staff, two-thirds of whom hold PhDs. Coe-Rexecode has 27 staff. By comparison, the state's CAS has 127 people on staff. And whereas CAS spent $36.8 million in 2008, Coe-Rexecode and IFRI spent only $5.7 million and $7 million, respectively.[63]

Despite the fact that all of these are scholarly organizations, some have certain ideological tendencies. For instance, one senior official at OFCE told us that his organization has a mild leftist and Keynesian bias because its early leaders were inclined in that direction and subsequent hiring has favored people with similar training. A senior official at Coe-Rexecode agreed, adding that his own organization had a more free market orientation. CEPII tends to favor free trade, except for agriculture. As we shall see shortly, however, some of the other organizations we visited are much more likely to wear their ideology on their sleeves.

Advocacy Policy Research Organizations

Recall that the U.S. knowledge regime had many private advocacy organizations like the Heritage Foundation and the Progressive Policy Institute. There are only a handful of these in France.[64] Most are quite new. Institute

---

[58]Coe-Rexecode was born in 2006 from the merger of three other organizations—Epicode, Rexecode, and the Center for Economic Observation, which was part of the Chamber of Commerce, a publicly funded organization financed by corporate tax revenues. Epicode's funding came initially from a few large state-owned and private corporations, the employer confederation (MEDEF), and the French stock market, among others. Corporations also funded Rexecode (interview with senior official, Coe-Rexecode).

[59]Interview with senior official, Coe-Rexecode.

[60]Interview with Xavier Timbeau, OFCE.

[61]Interview with Dominique David, IFRI; and IFRI annual report 2006.

[62]http://www.turi-network.eu/Members/Full-members/Institut-de-Recherches-Economiques-et-Sociales-IRES-Institute-for-Economic-and-Social-Research. Accessed June 2011.

[63]Except for IRES, all data are from organizational annual reports: CAS 2008, Coe-Rexecode 2007, OFCE 2009, IFRI 2006. Staffing and budget data were difficult to get from the French organizations due to the frequent unavailability of annual reports. Even if reports were available, these things were often not mentioned.

[64]Desmoulins 2000, pp. 149–50.

Montaigne, for example, opened in 2000 as a think tank with a clear ideological mission—to advocate policies oriented toward free markets, international economic competitiveness, and modernizing the public sector. It has a reputation for being neoliberal but according to its general director, Philippe Manière, despite its free-market ideology the organization is nonpartisan. It has people on its board from the political left and right. However, it rarely engages either the unions or employer associations because it wants to avoid the appearance of bias and because its target audience is the political system anyway.

Institute Montaigne has nine people on staff and an annual budget of about $4 million. It publishes reader-friendly reports with clear policy recommendations intended for civil servants, *cabinet* members, parliamentarians, ministries, and the media. Montaigne typically commissions task forces to write these reports, which are often syntheses of research done elsewhere rather than original policy research, although it also writes some reports in-house.[65] This is not a shop interested in doing statistical analysis. Task forces have about a dozen people, mostly civil servants and business people but always a journalist who knows how to write for nonexperts. They never include politicians and only very rarely academics. When we asked Manière why they avoided academics he echoed sentiments we heard in Washington a few months earlier: "They live on another planet!" And Montaigne is aggressive in their messaging. For example, they produce short television ads advocating certain policies and have a regular radio spot.

One of the first advocacy organizations in France was the French Institute for Research on Public Administration (IFRAP), established in 1985 by businessman Bernard Zimmern. IFRAP has a staff of 12 people. Its aim is to push public discourse more to the right. Zimmern was clear during our interview that IFRAP advocates a very conservative agenda even further to the right than Institute Montaigne. Both organizations told us that they are financed privately and would refuse public money even if it were available. Zimmern described IFRAP as a publishing operation that produces a magazine, short reports that it sells to tens of thousands of subscribers, and books written typically by Zimmern. IFRAP has an in-house research staff that produces much of this material relying heavily on national statistics, INSEE reports, and the like. Their publications do not involve sophisticated statistical analysis, but they do contain data-based graphs and charts. When we compared IFRAP to Institute Montaigne Zimmern insisted that IFRAP was a proper research organization whereas Montaigne was not because they outsourced their work. He had little respect for their publications and told us, for example, that "[t]here

[65]Interview with senior official, CEPII.

was a report in Montaigne. . . . And I was very surprised by the conclusion. And when I called the president of the group [that wrote it] and said this is a piece of shit. . . . I could hear the president tell me, 'What we published is a piece of shit which has been written in fact by a civil servant from the Minister of Finance.'"[66]

Recall from chapter 2 that the legal line in the United States between the activities of advocacy organizations and lobbyists is quite clear. Things are blurrier in France. Although there are only a few professional lobbying firms in Paris, some people we interviewed charged that IFRAP, Institute Montaigne, and some business clubs, which we discuss later, were actually lobbying operations.[67] However, what passes for lobbying in France is different from that in the United States. First, advocacy organizations like Institute Montaigne and IFRAP admit to lobbying but not according to the U.S. definition.[68] IFRAP's president, for example, frequently participates in breakfast meetings at clubs where he argues for certain policies in front of people from the ministries. For him this is an exercise in lobbying—but one where he advocates for the business community's general interests not those of a particular paying client as is the case in American lobbying. Others agreed that lobbying typically occurs at breakfasts and similar events and that it is about advocating the interests of large swaths of society.[69] Second, French lobbying targets the executive branch not the legislature because the ministries propose legislation.[70] Third, French lobbying rarely involves drafting legislative language. Institute Montaigne's Philippe Manière knew the difference between 501(c)(3) and 501(c)(4) organizations in the United States and that lobbyists in America often help write legislative language for politicians. He insisted that his organization never did this. Nor did it press politicians to vote a particular way on a piece of legislation. When he said that Institute Montaigne lobbies he meant something like what the Heritage Foundation or Brookings Institution does. In his organization:

[66]In email correspondence, Philippe Manière objected to Zimmern's characterization of Montaigne explaining that even the work they outsourced was done by qualified people, including those with official positions in other research bodies, such as CNRS. And he said that the quality of Montaigne's work was never disputed even if it was outsourced and that some of their projects took a year or two to complete, thus indicating the work's seriousness.

[67]Interview with senior official, Coe-Rexecode. François Massardier, Croissance Plus, used to lobby in Paris for Canal Plus, a television station. He told us that American-style lobbying is much less common in France than in the United States. He said that while there are thousands of professional lobbyists in Washington there are only about 25 lobbying firms in Paris, although it is hard to know precisely because this is a new phenomenon in French politics with little supervision or regulation. He said that 15 years ago there were only five such firms in Paris.

[68]Institute Montaigne notes on its website that its publications and proposals "are the basis for lobbying initiatives" (http://www.institutmontaigne.org. Accessed May 2009).

[69]Interviews with Michel Rousseau, Foundation Concorde; Frédéric Allemand, Foundation for Political Innovation.

[70]Interview with senior official, Enterprise and Progress.

Lobbying is about promoting our report, having it read by the right people so that they can use it. So it's not about writing amendments for the legislation. It's about knowing who is in charge of it at the L'Elysèe [the president's office], at the Parliament, at the Center Matignon [the prime minister's office] . . . and have meetings with them. And tell them look, we just published that. . . . It's more about promoting our ideas, our suggestions, our proposals. We never tell them you should vote that or that. We don't represent private interest.

Political Foundations

France has several political foundations often affiliated loosely with a major political party. Germany does too, but in France they are much younger, smaller, and poorer financially.[71] In the overall scheme of things the foundations play a much less important role in the French knowledge regime than they do in the German one. In France these include the Foundation Gabriel Peri and Foundation Jean Jaurès, which are affiliated with the Communist and Socialist Parties, respectively. The Foundation for Political Innovation has had ties historically to the center-right UMP. Foundation Concorde was founded by Jerome Monod, a close advisor to Jacques Chirac and the Gaullist RPR before it was absorbed into the UMP. Finally, Foundation Robert Schuman leans toward the center-right UDF.[72] All of these organizations were established in either the 1990s or early 2000s and are a reflection of the political party system in France's policymaking regime. Since the late 1990s each one had developed a think tank.

Rather than doing sophisticated economic analysis these think tanks produce synthetic distillations of other people's research or simply opinions from a particular political point of view.[73] Jean Jaurés and Gabriel Peri also archive their party's papers and documents. When they focus on public policy issues they do so by convening conferences, seminars, and working groups to discuss an issue rather than conducting data-based research.[74] All of them do this sort of work, which often yields books, reports, pamphlets, or short policy briefs for the general public, politicians, or ministries. To the extent that they do

[71]Interview with Michael Mazo, Foundation Gabriel Peri. Mazo noted that the French political foundations are Davids compared to the German Goliaths like the Friedrich Ebert Foundation.
[72]Interview with research fellow, Foundation for Political Innovation.
[73]According to email correspondence from Philippe Manière, Institute Montaigne, since the Foundation for Political Innovation reduced its ties to UMP it has improved its analytic capacities relative to the rest of the political foundations.
[74]Interviews with Michel Mazo, Foundation Gabriel Peri; Gilles Finchelstein, Foundation Jean Jaurès.

data-based research at all they tend to outsource it. Even the Foundation for Political Innovation, which claims to produce "academic studies" that require approval by its scientific council, outsources much of its research. For instance, the foundation hired a Swedish firm to conduct an eight-country survey of young people's attitudes toward globalization. This appeared to be the most research oriented of all the political foundations, but staff members explained that their reports are not technical and do not include much statistical analysis because their small staff does not have the capacity to do it.[75]

Most foundations rely on state funding, often from the prime minister's office but also the Ministry of Foreign Affairs in the case of the Schuman foundation or parliament in the case of Gabriel Peri. The exception is Foundation Concorde, which began with support from the prime minister's office but now depends entirely on corporate and individual contributions.[76] These organizations are small. The Foundation for Political Innovation, for example, has an annual budget of about $4 million and a staff of 10. Foundation Jean Jaurés has a $3 million budget and a staff of 15.[77] Gabriel Peri works with only about $2.4 million.[78]

Clubs

Distinctive to France are several prominent clubs that generate policy ideas. We found several in Paris. They are funded almost entirely by their members—firms and business people. One is Enterprise and Progress, which began in 1970. Another is the employer confederation's Institute for Enterprise (IDEP), established in 1975. Enterprise and Progress claims to be more progressive with a strong interest in promoting corporate social responsibility, whereas IDEP is more conservative.[79] Croissance Plus is a third business club founded in 1997. Its membership was initially Internet start-up companies but now consists of firms from all sectors of the economy. Its concern is with changing policy in order to facilitate entrepreneurialism as well as corporate social responsibility.

The research practices of these clubs are unique and usually not very scholarly. They hold frequent meetings for members, often over breakfast, to discuss issues of concern to the membership—including public policy issues. Sometimes they invite politicians, top-level state bureaucrats, and academics to participate. Croissance Plus also organizes working groups with 15 to 20 members to brainstorm topics. So the research of these clubs simply involves

[75]Interviews with Frédéric Allemand and a research fellow, Foundation for Political Innovation.
[76]Interview with Michel Rousseau, Foundation Concorde.
[77]Foundation for Political Innovation annual report 2007 and Foundation Jean Jaurés annual report 2008.
[78]Interview with Michael Mazo, Foundation Gabriel Peri.
[79]See also http://www.institut-entreprise.fr/index.php?id=146. Accessed June 2011.

learning from the members what their ideas are for policymakers and then disseminating them to ministries and *cabinets* through short nonacademic reports or informal conversations.[80]

Institute Choiseul is another business club but with a more academic twist. It too holds brainstorming sessions over meals with business, political, and administrative elites as well as academics and journalists. But it also has a publishing house, Choiseul Editions, which publishes several academic-style journals each dedicated to a different region of the world and covering a variety of political and economic topics. According to Paul de Fombelle, the director of Choiseul Editions, they rely on a network of about 700 researchers and authors whom they ask to write for the journals. Many of these people are academics but some are from business and politics. Journal topics often stem from ideas discussed at the club's meetings. Funding comes entirely from private sources including club membership fees and journal subscriptions.[81]

Clubs are not always just the province of the business community. For instance, CEPII, an important semi-public scholarly research organization, is affiliated with a club dedicated to making CEPII's research accessible to the business community through a variety of seminars, conferences, and breakfast meetings for corporate leaders. Although CEPII relies heavily on state funding, its club is financed by company members. The club itself is a private non-profit association.[82]

The clubs are smaller than most other organizations in the French knowledge regime. Enterprise and Progress has a staff of three while Croissance Plus has four. CEPII's club has two staffers.[83] And clubs were the organizations we visited that came closest to lobbying. The people we interviewed at them told us that they lobbied by disseminating their ideas to policymakers and civil servants at breakfast meetings and other events. A senior official of one club explained that once they develop a policy proposal they meet with officials from the relevant ministry or *cabinet* in a roundtable setting with all the relevant interests represented and discuss the issue. If the ministry supports the group's sentiments, then he approaches the ministry to offer help drafting legislative language, which may end up in the law. He said that this was a "very typical" process.[84] Someone at another club said that they do much the same thing, al-

<hr>

[80]Interviews with François Massardier, Croissance Plus; senior officials, Enterprise and Progress. Club meetings resemble informal policy discussion groups found in the United States (Domhoff 2010, chap. 4).
[81]Interview with Paul de Fombelle, Institute Choiseul.
[82]Interview with senior official, CEPII.
[83]Enterprise and Progress annual report 2009, Croissance Plus annual report 2009, and interview with senior official, CEPII.
[84]Interview with François Massardier, Croissance Plus.

though he refused to call it lobbying.[85] He mentioned as well in an email that at least insofar as the business clubs are concerned their political influence stems less from their ideas per se and more from the fact that they represent a cohesive group of many corporations. But, like the people at Montaigne and IFRAP, these people insisted that this is not done to promote the narrow interests of a particular client, as it is in the United States, but rather for those of their whole group. One told us, "The difference is that we are an association and we lobby only for members on topics about firms and society—of business in general, specifically for growing firms." He said that the breakfast and roundtable meetings they convene are something "between networking and lobbying" and are merely a starting place for French-style lobbying.[86]

Universities, Intellectuals, and Grand Ideas

The universities do not play a major role in the French knowledge regime, but the more prestigious Grandes Écoles do because they train the state's political and technocratic elite.[87] And they have very close connections with some of the most important policy research organizations, such as INSEE, for which ENSAE (École Nationale de la Statistique et de l'Administration Economique) trains many of its economists and statisticians, and OFCE, which is affiliated with Sciences Po. This is all uniquely French.[88]

Intellectuals, including professors, writers, and others, also have a unique position in the French knowledge regime that we did not find much in our other countries. France has a long tradition of intellectuals informing public policy debate. Their commentary about economic matters is considered legitimate.[89]

---

[85]Interview with senior official, Enterprise and Progress. Despite this denial, this club's website lists various strategy sheets indicating that the organization was ramping up political lobbying activities during the 1980s and 1990s (http://www.entreprise-progres.net/. Accessed May 2009).

[86]Interview with François Massardier, Croissance Plus. Clubs and advocacy organizations are the only ones we encountered that admitted to lobbying of any sort. Semi-public scholarly research organizations refrain from lobbying. A senior official at Coe-Rexecode explained that they have no expertise in drafting legislation and prefer to only identify problems and suggest possible solutions for policymakers. If anything, it is the politicians and bureaucrats who approach Coe-Rexecode for advice on preparing legislation, not the other way around. Similarly, Xavier Timbeau at OFCE insisted that his organization does not lobby. At most they do an analysis, derive its policy implications, and then disseminate this information as widely as possible. He emphasized that if anyone meets with the ministries or *cabinets* to discuss policy, "We do it very, very lightly." Similarly, we heard in interviews at Foundation Gabriel Peri and Foundation Jean Jaurès that the political foundations do not lobby.

[87]Both universities and the Grandes Écoles are publicly funded. But unlike the universities the Grandes Écoles do not educate the masses for normal jobs in French society. They are highly selective, and considered the very best, and generally train the future elites.

[88]Fourcade 2009, chap. 4; Prasad 2006, chap. 4. We thank Robert Boyer for his insights on these issues.

[89]Fourcade (2009, p. 233) explains that this legitimacy stems from the rather general training that many economists receive at places like ENA.

This is not a discourse informed by applied economics or data analysis so much as it is by moral philosophy, political theory, and other intellectual perspectives. In France the intellectual undercurrent of academic-style discourse is used to frame ideas and diffuse them throughout society. The old Saint Simon Society together with other organizations used to organize some of this. But it was replaced in 2002 by the République des Idées (Republic of Ideas) led by the well-known sociologist Pierre Rosanvallon. The organization arranges seminars, academic colloquia, and every few years a major conference for about 10,000 people on a particular theme, such as democracy, the topic for the upcoming conference when we visited their offices. It also publishes books, journals, and pamphlets focused on what can be called the grand ideas (*Grandes Idées*) of society like equality, liberty, and democracy and also big problems like ecological degradation and social justice. Those involved in République des Idées are mainly university professors, authors, and public intellectuals.[90]

According to its secretary general, Florent Guénard, République des Idées's mission is to bring the big ideas of intellectuals to the public. He considers it a "club of reflection" that stimulates public debate rather than devises policy ideas. It represents an underlying network of intellectuals that are part of what he called France's "grand intellectual debate." As far as we were told in Paris it was the only organization of its kind in France. In contrast to some of the clubs, which pursue a direct strategy of bringing ideas to policymakers themselves, République des Idées takes an indirect approach by trying to influence public debate. This is why they invite intellectuals, experts, and journalists to their events more than politicians, civil servants, or people from the political parties.

Intellectuals with big ideas were also evident elsewhere. Recall that Institute Choiseul recruited intellectuals to contribute to its journals. And some of the political foundations engaged the grand ideas as well. When we interviewed Michael Mazo at Foundation Gabriel Peri, for instance, he told us that they were preparing next year's program, which would focus on energy issues among other things and that would include presentations from sociologists, anthropologists, scientists, and even philosophers. When we asked him why they would invite philosophers to discuss policy issues he said that they will "tell the truth." Much like République des Idées, according to Mazo, Foundation Gabriel Peri wanted to help connect scholars and the public debate on big social issues in the hope of renewing and reinvigorating that debate. Intellectuals also provide a critical voice regarding policy issues by appearing in the media, publishing, and speaking at the clubs' meetings.

[90]Interview with Florent Guénard, République des Idées.

A Network of Networks

A final important feature of the French knowledge regime is the array of informal personal networks that connect many of the organizations we have discussed. For example, Pascal Lorot, who founded Institute Choiseul, developed a wide network over his career with people in politics, business, the political foundations, clubs, and the universities, and used it strategically to build the institute.[91] Of particular importance are networks that connect policy research organizations and members of parliament, the ministries, and their *cabinets*—connections that many people were proud to reveal in our interviews. We heard much more about these networks in France than in our other countries.

Connections such as these are cultivated in many ways. First, several people we interviewed started building their networks during their school days at the Grandes Écoles.[92] One person explained that "[y]ou get to know people who come from the same school, from the same university, and it's easier with them than with others." He added that this is "a good key" for opening doors to civil servants and politicians. Indeed, most members in his organization graduated from the Grandes Écoles.[93] Second, virtually everyone we interviewed had stories about developing networks through working groups, breakfast meetings and other gatherings hosted by clubs, political foundations, and other organizations. For instance, the director of Institute Choiseul's publishing arm said that "Choiseul is two things. It is to [help] people meet together and to see what they are speaking about, and to [help] them give solutions." Third, interlocking membership on organizational boards and advisory committees also help forge networks.

When we raised the issue with René Sève from CAS he emphasized, "You must not consider the institution; you must consider the persons." He added later that "[e]verybody has his own network. So you have a network of networks." And lots of policy ideas and other information are conveyed through these networks. In Sève's words, people in these networks "sit in different places and then they carry the information to the next place and that is the model for distributing ideas and knowledge."[94] The fact that personal networks are so important in France may be why the people we talked to in Paris had not thought about their knowledge regime much before we showed up—their attention was focused on personal networks rather than relationships among organizations.

[91] Interview with Paul de Fombelle, Institute Choiseul.
[92] Interviews with Florent Guénard, République des Idées; Bernard Zimmern, IFRAP; senior official, Enterprise and Progress; Dominique David, IFRI.
[93] Interview with senior official, Enterprise and Progress.
[94] People at Enterprise and Progress, IFRAP, and the Foundation for Political Innovation suggested that the media were also conduits through which policy ideas could flow among knowledge regime organizations.

In a sense, then, these networks constitute a kind of connective tissue linking various organizations in complex ways and, as we shall see in chapter 7, providing in some cases access to important policymakers. Similarly, the public intellectuals we mentioned earlier form another layer of connective tissue transmitting some of the ideas generated by policy research organizations as well as academics and others to the public. There seemed to be much more of this in France than our other countries.

Let us pause and put all of this into a more analytic perspective with respect to the effects that the policymaking and production regimes have had on the French knowledge regime. Consider the policymaking regime first because its effects are more pronounced in what we have presented so far. To begin with, the dominance of state research organizations is a manifestation of the dirigisme tradition. This is reinforced by the fact that most of the best economists and statisticians are trained at one of the Grandes Écoles—ENSAE. Not only is ENSAE the preeminent source of France's econometricians and statisticians, but it is the primary feeder school for INSEE and the ministerial statistical and research departments.[95] And the fact that the state and semi-public policy research organizations are oriented around the executive rather than legislative branch is because in France's presidential system legislation emanates from the ministries and the National Assembly is comparatively weak.

The flip side of this is that private policy research organizations are few and far between, thanks again to the policymaking regime. First, in contrast to the United States where there are dozens of congressional committees and subcommittees seeking outside policy expertise and providing channels of access for private policy research organizations to engage policymakers, these are largely absent in France. Second, the expansive and permanent French civil service elite rarely seeks the assistance of outside organizations because it is confident in its abilities and has considerable in-house expertise of its own. Third, there has been a long-standing distrust in France of intermediate associations in civil society, which surely contributes to the state's reluctance to turn to private research organizations.[96] Fourth, because the state is held responsible for protecting the welfare of its citizens and subsidizes many nonprofit organizations the private philanthropy that might otherwise support private research organizations as it does in the United States is absent.[97] Nor does the French

[95]We thank Robert Boyer for this observation. See also Fourcade (2009, pp. 206–17). We learned, however, in email correspondence with a senior official at CEPII that CAE depends primarily on economists from universities.

[96]Levy 1999, p. 10.

[97]For further discussion, see Desmoulins (2000) and Fieschi and Gaffney (2004, 1998). The nonprofit sector grew initially during the 1960s and 1970s but experienced renewed expansion beginning in the early 1980s as the government shifted away from dirigisme (United Nations 2006, p. 10).

tax code encourage such philanthropy. This is one reason, for example, why Bernard Zimmern found it nearly impossible to start IFRAP, which he wanted to model on the 501(c)(3) Heritage Foundation in America. In the end, he set up charitable foundations in the United States to finance IFRAP! Moreover, he needed permission from two or three government ministries, which was hard to get because civil servants are taught at ENA that the appropriate place for generating public policy ideas is in the state administration not civil society. As he put it, "Public policies [were] the monopoly of top civil servants." So it can take years to receive the necessary permissions. The point is that the size of this part of the French knowledge regime is tiny compared to that in the United States because of these political-institutional obstacles.[98] Others agreed.[99]

The policymaking regime had other effects too. For one thing, the multiparty system was reflected in the fact that several political parties had their own foundations with think tanks. For another thing, the business clubs we visited were derived from an old political club tradition stretching back to the Revolution. Traditional political clubs coalesce temporarily around a political figure to provide political council and strategic advice and are loosely affiliated with a party. For instance, Club 89 formed around Jacques Chirac and Démocratie 2000 and Clysthène formed around Jacques Delors.[100] But the clubs with which we are concerned are much more recent and permanent, composed of business people, not affiliated with political parties, and interested in developing policy ideas not strategically advising a single politician.[101]

The production regime also had effects although more circumscribed than in the United States insofar as private money played a smaller role in France. Although neither labor nor business peak associations were as well organized and influential as in Germany or Denmark they did have a knowledge regime presence. Business associations and firms financed the clubs. And France's corporatist heritage was evident too. For instance, the conseils (e.g., COE, COR, CES) had a certain corporatist composition to them. And the

[98]Interview with Bernard Zimmern, IFRAP. According to the IFRAP website, in 2009 he received approval from the government to set up Foundation IFRAP. The fact that the tax deduction for charitable contributions to such an organization was raised significantly in 2003 surely helped his cause (http://www.ifrap.org. Accessed June 2011).

[99]Interview with Dominique David, IFRI. Indeed, the whole idea of an American-style think tank has been foreign to French political culture. Paul de Fombelle, Institute Choiseul, said, "It is difficult to be a think tank in France. . . . Think tank is not a French idea. It is not something very French." Frédéric Allemand, Foundation for Political Innovation, said that "the enemy" of think tanks is "French culture" because France does not have the habit of relying on other organizations much beyond the state for policy ideas. Philippe Manière, Institute Montaigne, attributed this to "our very Jacobin culture and history."

[100]Desmoulins 2000, p. 154; Fieschi and Gaffney 2004 and email correspondence with Philippe Manière, Institute Montaigne.

[101]Interviews with senior officials, Enterprise and Progress.

semi-public research organizations Coe-Rexecode and IRES represented the interests of business and labor, respectively.

The configuration of France's knowledge regime that we have just described stemmed in part from the state's response to political-economic problems that emerged following the end of the Golden Age and the rise of globalization. Policymakers and others gradually realized that the old knowledge regime, based heavily on the state's own analytic capacities, was no longer producing analysis and advice adequate for dealing with these problems. Put differently, they perceived a crisis of ideas, which reflected a serious deterioration in the knowledge regime's complementary relationship with the rest of the political economy. What followed was a series of moves designed to create fresh thinking often outside the state.

Proliferation, the Crisis of Ideas, and Externalization

One of the most notable changes in the French knowledge regime since the 1980s, as in the United States, was a proliferation of new policy research organizations, many of which were in civil society. But two things distinguish the French from the American experience in this regard. First, the state—not private actors—spawned many of the new research organizations in France. Second, the creation of new organizations in France was not associated with a dramatic increase in competition or political partisanship as it was in the United States.

The story began in the production regime with the end of the Golden Age, the rise of globalization, and with it all during the 1970s and 1980s new challenges to the French political economy. Unemployment averaged 2% annually from 1960 to 1973 but skyrocketed to 9% during the 1980s, while annual productivity growth dropped from 4.7% to 2.1%. Over the same period, government budget deficits jumped from 0.3% to 3.8% of GDP and inflation escalated from 4.6% to 7.3%.[102] Several people told us that elites in both the public and private sectors started worrying that what could be called a crisis of ideas had developed—that is, they perceived that state policy research organizations were not providing analysis and advice good enough to help policymakers resolve these economic problems. In effect they suspected that the institutional complementarity between the knowledge regime and the rest of the political economy had broken down. As a result, people began to search in new ways for better ideas to make sense of this unprecedented set of challenges. The state led the way.

The crisis of ideas began in the wake of the May 1968 protests, which raised serious questions about the economy, how the country was being run,

---

[102]Kenworthy 1997, tables 3 and 7.

and what course it was taking. It accelerated thereafter. Stagflation hit and the government failed to resolve it even after the Mitterrand government's policy flip-flops in the 1980s. Adding fuel to the fire, Keynesianism now seemed incapable of making sense of France's economic malaise. The crisis continued to gather momentum during the late 1980s and 1990s during several cohabiting governments as the production regime was increasingly exposed to international competition and policymakers struggled to balance the more open economy with adequate social protections.[103] Xavier Timbeau at OFCE explained that stagflation raised serious questions about the legitimacy of Keynesianism but that economic globalization had "put this model to its knees." According to one interview, there was "a sense that government has had a bad influence on the generation of new ideas and the possibility of reform."[104] Others agreed that growing disenchantment with the state's capacity for creative thinking was serious.[105] Indeed, this was a time when intellectuals and others argued that virtually all the new social and political ideas, such as those concerning feminism and environmentalism, were coming from outside the state.[106] To cope with the crisis of ideas, political elites sought policy analysis and recommendations from new semi-public and party policy research organizations as well as new ministerial research units.[107]

Many people told us that since the early 1970s one of the biggest changes in the French knowledge regime was the appearance of new policy research organizations in civil society. Much of this was a manifestation of what Jonah Levy called "Tocqueville's revenge"—an effort to reduce central state control over economic regulation and encourage more organizations in civil society to assume some of this responsibility. The problem, it seemed, was that dirigisme had cut the state off from valuable feedback from civil society thereby hobbling the ability of policymakers to make sense of and devise economic policy that could effectively tackle the problems stemming from the end of the Golden Age. In particular, the increasing international exposure of the French economy made conventional economic prediction and indicative planning extremely difficult. So policymakers decided to emulate certain aspects of what Levy called German "associational liberalism" where the state was more connected to civil society. Associational liberalism, or corporatism, was an approach located between neoliberalism and dirigisme. An important part of this involved encouraging the development of new organizations in civil society that could provide

[103]Interview with senior official, DGTPE, and Xavier Timbeau, OFCE.
[104]Interview with senior official, Enterprise and Progress.
[105]Interview with Xavier Timbeau, OFCE.
[106]Levy 1999, p. 75.
[107]Interviews with Michel Rousseau, Foundation Concorde; Frédéric Allemand, Foundation for Political Innovation.

the state with the information it had been missing. France did not adopt associational liberalism in toto but did take a few lessons from that model.[108]

To begin with, in the late 1970s and 1980s, Raymond Barre, the conservative prime minister from 1976 to 1981, created several new semi-public scholarly research organizations, such as Epicode (now Coe-Rexecode) and IRES, to solicit input from business and labor, respectively. Sensing that globalization was afoot, he also established CEPII to help policymakers better understand the effects of the oil crisis and economic globalization.[109] He worried as well that France's expertise in forecasting and macroeconomic analysis was too concentrated in the state and that new research capacities were needed in civil society to introduce a bit more intellectual pluralism into the system to make better sense of the economic situation. So he set up OFCE to stimulate public debate and produce independent economic forecasts to compete with those from INSEE.[110] This was part of what the director general at CAS described as the "externalization" of analytic capacities from the state to semi-public organizations. It also involved moving already existing semi-public organizations like CEPREMAP and OFCE away from the Planning Commissariat, which funded them.[111] As he explained:

> OFCE, okay, was at the beginning created and financed by the Plan,
> and now it is financed by Sciences Po and other organizations. . . .
> Many think tanks were at the beginning within the Plan, or close to
> the Plan. . . . Now, it is different. They are independent I think. . . .
> The capacity of prediction, provisions, calculus, economic modeling
> and so on was concentrated in the Plan or around the Plan, close
> to the Plan. Now it is disseminated in many, many [independent
> organizations].

This initial experiment with externalization resulted in a rather fragmented field of semi-public research organizations each more or less occupying its own niche and working in isolation from the rest. Xavier Timbeau at OFCE, for example, told us that OFCE was "quite alone" in the field during its

---

[108] Levy 1999. See also Prasad (2005, 2006, chap. 4).
[109] Interview with senior official, CEPII, and CEPII's 30th anniversary newsletter 2008 (p. 1).
[110] Interviews with senior official, Coe-Rexecode; Xavier Timbeau, OFCE; research fellow and Frédéric Allemand, Foundation for Political Innovation; senior official, CEPII. See also Fourcade (2009, pp. 219–20).
[111] See also Fourcade (2009, pp. 52–59, 208–11) and Guyomarch (1999, p. 175). According to Fourcade, CEPREMAP, for instance, lost some of its applied focus and became more academic in orientation as one of France's leading research centers in economics. Other organizations were closed and their personnel transferred to places like CNRS.

early years. But he said that things changed somewhat since then as the number of organizations that do analytic work increased slowly.

Lionel Jospin, the socialist prime minister, decided in 1997 to expand the externalization initiative in a second direction by financing five political foundations each associated with a major political party and urging them to establish think tanks. Two foundations already existed, but three new ones were established, and all five set up think tanks in response to Jospin's initiative.[112] According to Frédéric Allemand from the Foundation for Political Innovation, "The initial aim was to give new ideas to the political parties."

The state's efforts to promote fresh thinking were not restricted to civil society during this period. It also created new research organizations of its own. One was CAE, which Jospin established in 1997 because he felt the need for advice from independent professional economists. The problem was that most top policymakers, advisors, and civil servants came from ENA, one of the Grandes Écoles, where they received broad training in law, economics, sociology, and political science. In contrast to the technically sophisticated economics graduates of ENSAE, many people from ENA called themselves economists but had not received an education focused on a comprehensive economics curriculum including mathematical economics.[113] As the president of the CAE explained, "We are a country of lawyers rather than a country of economists." Even today, for instance, some of the Treasury Department's (DGTPE) many staff economists still receive much of their training on the job more than through formal education.[114]

The conseils became another part of the externalization strategy. The idea was to bring experts and academics together with representatives from the state, business, and unions to generate new and hopefully consensus-based policy ideas. The unions were particularly supportive of the idea as a way to reinvigorate their sagging influence, and university professors supported the idea as a way to gain some formal political influence. Crucially, the prime minister wanted them as an alternative source of ideas from the traditional state policy research organizations. Especially important in this regard were COR

---

[112]Interview with Gilles Finchelstein, Foundation Jean Jaurès. Finchelstein explained that some parties, notably the xenophobic National Front, did not have a government financed political foundation and think tank because funding was provided at the discretion of the prime minister.

[113]We heard at Coe-Rexecode that another part of the externalization program involved setting up new PhD-granting universities that provided professional training for economists. These included the Paris School of Economics and the Toulouse School of Economics. Half of the Toulouse program's funding came initially from the state. Fourcade (2009, chap. 4) discusses the lackluster training of economists in France prior to the 1960s, which shifted with the next generation who were much better trained, especially those from ENSAE, and who were part of the international scientific community. We thank Robert Boyer for this observation.

[114]Interview with senior official, DGTPE.

established in 2000 by Jospin from the Socialist Party and COE established in 2005 by Prime Minister Dominique de Villepin from the UMP.[115]

There was also a proliferation of state policy research organizations in ministries beyond the prime minister's office. As policymakers became more interested in using data analysis and statistics to help guide policymaking, the ministries began to develop their own specialized data collection and analytic capacities. In 1993, for instance, the Labor Ministry set up DARES to provide the ministry with analytic expertise in its policy niche and coordinate ministerial work. The minister "decided that it would be a good thing to create one department that would be in charge of producing all the statistics; all the studies for the whole ministry." But there was another reason he did this too—to provide tools for competing against other ministries.[116] We will return to this point later.

Indeed, policymakers had recognized that they needed the expertise of organizations like OFCE, CEPII, and others in civil society as well as new ones inside the state more than they once did.[117] The most striking illustration of this open-mindedness was from Xavier Timbeau at OFCE who told us that shortly after Nicolas Sarkozy was elected president in 2007, his prime minister's office asked OFCE to do an analysis of a particular issue. This was because Sarkozy said, "I don't trust my administration. I want a second view on this question. And I want you to give the second view. Do what you want; say what you want. I want a second view."

When we asked a senior official at CEPII whether civil servants had become more open to ideas from her organization and others outside the state, she quickly agreed that they had.[118] She explained that this was because the state needs more external expertise than it did 20 years ago. Why? In her words, "There are more and more international issues to tackle." Thus, as the French economy became more exposed to international economic pressures after the Golden Age, part of the search for new ideas involved reorienting the work of many policy research organizations in cross-national directions. CEPII's research has always been oriented this way.[119] But since the late 1970s other organizations, such as OFCE, began to embrace cross-national research too.[120]

[115]We thank Bruno Palier and Patrick Le Galès for this observation. See also http://www.cor -retraites.fr/article62.html and http://www.coe.gouv.fr/Presentation.html?id_article=491. Both accessed July 2012.

[116]Interview with senior official, DARES.

[117]Interview with senior official, CEPII.

[118]This is not to say that the state never sought outside input previously. Coe-Rexecode, for instance, consulted informally with the prime minister's offices (email correspondence, senior official, Coe-Rexecode).

[119]Interview with senior official, CEPII.

[120]Interview with Xavier Timbeau, OFCE.

Similarly, we learned at the Treasury Department (DGTPE) that as France lost some of its macroeconomic policy tools thanks to globalization and joining the euro zone, policymakers have required a more international view. As a result, the agency does more cross-national research. This is also why in 2004 research on European affairs became linked with macroeconomic research at DGTPE.[121] Others emphasized as well that globalization and creation of the euro undermined the utility of conventional Keynesian macroeconomic models.[122]

Political elites were not the only ones trying to promote fresh ideas. Private actors did too by creating new clubs and advocacy research organizations. Consider the clubs first. Enterprise and Progress was set up in 1970 by a group of corporate CEOs in response to the May 1968 conflicts, which stemmed in large measure from the socioeconomic complaints of workers, shopkeepers and farmers. Referring to de Gaulle's tight-fisted rule and dirigisme, which many protestors blamed for their plight, we were told in one interview that "[n]obody wanted to follow 'the King' anymore." Moreover, several members of the business community suspected that the employers' confederation was either unable or unwilling to deal with these problems and complaints. As a result, they set up Enterprise and Progress to advocate more socially responsible corporate behavior and prevent a repeat of the events of 1968.[123] IDEP came along a few years later as a conservative response by business leaders. Croissance Plus emerged in 1997 to represent the ideas of fledgling Internet firms and other start-up companies that populated brand-new sectors of the economy.

The desire to cultivate new thinking for policymakers about how to make sense of and cope with the increasingly international economic environment was also behind the establishment of the advocacy think tanks, which began to appear in the 1980s. The most famous is Institute Montaigne. Its founder was Claude Bebéar, a wealthy insurance magnate and staunch neoliberal who led a successful movement to open up the economy to international markets. His purpose for establishing Montaigne was to facilitate public debate in France, which was "too often monopolized by political parties and administration, leaving aside the civil society."[124]

The emergence of Institute Montaigne and a few other advocacy research organizations was something that we heard a lot about in our interviews. Philippe Manière from Institute Montaigne told us that 10 or 15 years ago in France, "There was basically no think tank." IFRAP started in 1985. Institute Montaigne opened shop in 2000. Although the number of self-proclaimed

---

[121] Interview with senior official, DGTPE.
[122] Email correspondence, senior official, Coe-Rexecode.
[123] Interview with senior official, Enterprise and Progress. See also http://www.entreprise-progres.com/presentation/un-peu-dhistoire/. Accessed July 2013.
[124] http://www.institutmontaigne.org/. Accessed July 2011.

think tanks in the private sector has grown, this part of the field still consists of small organizations that are fragmented as a whole and mostly occupy their own specialized niches. Nothing in France begins to compare with the large full-service advocacy and scholarly research organizations in the United States.[125] A few like Institute Montaigne and IFRAP developed a high and respectable profile, but most of the rest seem to be fly-by-night operations often consisting of only a few people, a computer, and Internet access churning out blogs and other website postings and calling themselves think tanks.[126]

This was also a time of corporate privatizations and mergers, especially with firms in other countries, which eventually augmented the flow of private money into the knowledge regime and contributed to the development of advocacy organizations like Institute Montaigne and IFRAP.[127] Institute Montaigne, for example, is now financed by contributions from dozens of firms including several well-known foreign ones, such as the Boston Consulting Group, Barclays Private Equity, KPMG, Microsoft, and McKinsey & Company.[128]

However, in addition to the challenges and changes occurring in the French production regime, changes in the policymaking regime also helped foster new policy research organizations in civil society. One involved the tax code. As part of the state's move toward cultivating new ideas in civil society, officials became more accepting of private foundations.[129] This, coupled with pressure from people like IFRAP's Bernard Zimmern, led the government in 2003 to raise the tax deduction allowed for contributions to private foundations and advocacy organizations. Suddenly there were significantly greater financial incentives for corporations and individuals to give money to these organizations. These incentives were further amplified by the increasing willingness of corporations and individuals to finance advocacy organizations due to their growing disenchantment with information they got from the government and their own desire to transform civil society in ways that would generate new policy ideas and public debate.[130]

Another important change in the policymaking regime contributed to the crisis of ideas and in turn changes in the knowledge regime. This was the collapse of France's traditional political party structure, where the Gaullist and leftist parties began in the late 1970s to decline in stature. The results were

[125]Interviews with senior official, Enterprise and Progress; François Massardier, Croissance Plus; Bernard Zimmern, IFRAP.
[126]Interviews with Philippe Manière, Institute Montaigne; Gilles Finchelstein, Foundation Jean Jaurés.
[127]Interview with Bernard Zimmern, IFRAP.
[128]http://www.institutmontaigne.org/. Accessed August 2011.
[129]Interview with Gilles Finchelstein, Foundation Jean Jaurés.
[130]Interviews with Bernard Zimmern, IFRAP; Gilles Finchelstein, Foundation Jean Jaurés; Michel Rousseau, Foundation Concorde.

twofold. First, according to Michael Mazo, director and founder of Foundation Gabriel Peri, until the early 1980s both political blocs favored dirigisme, modernization, and social protections but fought over how best to achieve these goals. However, as the party system rebalanced during the 1980s there was what he called a "collapse of diversity," that is, less political disagreement over basic policy ideas and, therefore, a paucity of fresh thinking. As a result, Jospin set up the five political party foundations to compensate for this political realignment and promote ideational pluralism. And the foundations have tried to accommodate his wishes by establishing a new set of policy research organizations—their think tanks—to stimulate political and public debate and new thinking about the long-term issues confronting France. Second, from the late 1980s, again thanks to the decline of the traditional ideological juxtaposition between left and right, intellectuals became disillusioned with conventional politics. Many had been involved with the political parties until then but lost confidence in them after the party system began to rebalance. The result was that many intellectuals defected from the parties and began to voice their opinions by other means, such as through the political foundations and République des Idées.[131]

In sum, many forces pushed France's knowledge regime in new directions. In the production regime, for instance, the end of the Golden Age and the rise of globalization created problems and challenges that led policymakers to pursue fresh thinking through their externalization strategy in the first place. Economic problems also helped spark the May 1968 protests, which led to the establishment of the first business clubs. The emergence of a new high-tech economic sector had a similar effect later. People also established private advocacy organizations to generate fresh thinking in response to production regime problems. And as globalization led to the internationalization of French firms foreign money became available to support some of these advocacy organizations. In the policymaking regime changes in the tax code helped facilitate such philanthropy too. The realignment of the political parties led to a collapse of ideational diversity that caused policymakers to encourage the development of political foundations and their think tanks. Overall, all of these changes reflected widespread disenchantment with dirigisme as well as the crisis of ideas that concerned Raymond Barre, Lionel Jospin, and others. According to one senior ministerial official:

> We have moved also from a universe 40 years ago, 50 years ago . . .
> the economy was more closed. There were clear goals after the war,
> and that was easier. We've moved to a universe, I think, which is

[131]Interviews with Michael Mazo, Foundation Gabriel Peri; Florent Guénard, République des Idées.

slightly more complicated, and where it's difficult for a single body, be it CAS or anybody else to have expertise on everybody and to have the legitimacy to act as a central player.[132]

In effect, then, people realized that the knowledge regime was no longer operating in ways that functionally complemented the rest of the political economy. They came to believe that the analyses and ideas its policy research organizations were producing were stale and ineffective for coping with the new problems France faced as it tried to compete successfully in an increasingly global economy. All of the moves to reform the knowledge regime were in this sense designed to improve its complementarity with the rest of the political economy.

As a result, the French knowledge regime became relatively more open and fragmented, especially in civil society. Furthermore, as semi-public and private policy research organizations materialized not only did the size of the field grow but it added some separation between the policymaking and knowledge regimes insofar as the new organizations were not part of the state. But we do not want to overstate this last point. State policy research organizations still dominate the landscape. In particular, INSEE remains very important, the conseils have grown in stature and number, and DGTPE is a powerful central actor.[133] In short, the story we have described is not about the abandonment but rather the modernization of dirigisme as a result of a variety of problems and challenges associated with the end of the Golden Age in France and the rise of globalization.

The Absence of Competition and Cooperation in Civil Society

In the United States the proliferation of private policy research organizations was associated with an escalation in competition and eventually cooperation. To our surprise, then, the rise of policy research organizations in French civil society precipitated comparatively little of either. For instance, when we asked French advocacy organizations whether there was much competition among them they said no. Bernard Zimmern from IFRAP explained that his main competitor had been Institute Montaigne until IFRAP developed its own

[132]Interview with senior official, DGTPE.
[133]DGTPE is in permanent contact with the Ministry of Finance. It is an organization for which recruitment is extremely competitive and whose members are among the most skilled economists in the country. It is a well-known stepping stone for promotion to other public and private organizations. And it provides at least one analysis for virtually every public decision on economic matters. Few nonstate policy research organizations have such a strong position. We thank Robert Boyer for this observation.

research staff and began to do serious research. And Institute Montaigne's director told us that there was not much competition for his organization because in his view no other French think tank was as pragmatic, politically nonpartisan, and reliant exclusively on private money as his. Nor did we hear much about competition among the clubs. Croissance Plus said that their primary competitors were the trade unions, not clubs or advocacy organizations.[134] We were told much the same thing at Enterprise and Progress. When we suggested during this interview that IDEP, a more conservative club formed in reaction to Enterprise and Progress, might be a competitor, they said, "No, we don't compete," even for money because many firms now belonged and contributed to both clubs.[135] And people at most of the political foundations said that competition among them was virtually nil and would be self-defeating because they shared the same goal: rejuvenate political debate.[136] One foundation president insisted that "[t]here is no competition. It would be ridiculous to consider going against the foundations."[137] Finally, representatives from République des Idées and Institute Choiseul agreed that even though they both published academically oriented material they did not compete with each other.

This is not to say that competition was completely absent in France. People at CEPII and OFCE agreed that they sometimes competed with each other.[138] The deputy director of the Foundation for Political Innovation said that "[t]here is still a competition between the think tanks in France," which is based on different political ideologies. When we pressed for specifics he said that his organization's major competitors were Foundation Robert Schuman in the area of European affairs and Institute Montaigne in the areas of economic and social issues. Similarly, Gilles Finchelstein from Foundation Jean Jaurès, who initially denied any competition among the foundations, later identified "other Social Democratic think tanks," such as Terra Nova, a very new organization in France and République des Idées as competitors. And on a couple of occasions people told us that the state was an important competitor. At IFRAP, for instance, Bernard Zimmern reminded us, as had others, that the top civil

---

[134]Interview with François Massardier, Croissance Plus.

[135]Interviews with senior officials, Enterprise and Progress.

[136]Interviews with Michael Mazo, Foundation Gabriel Peri; Gilles Finchelstein, Foundation Jean Jaurès.

[137]Interview with Michel Rousseau, Foundation Concorde.

[138]Interviews with senior official, CEPII; Xavier Timbeau, OFCE. When we interviewed people at semi-public research organizations with an international focus—that is, CEPII and IFRI—they said that their competitors were foreign organizations. In IFRI's case, for instance, we learned that "[t]here is no competition between different centers in France. . . . It's a competition with our counterparts in foreign countries. So this is the level of our competition. We are [competing] as individuals with academics. . . . But as an institution we don't have a competition in France. Our competition is with Brookings, with Stiftung Wissenschaft und Politik in Germany, with Chatham House in London."

servants were taught at ENA to monopolize policy thinking. They did so initially, he said, by labeling IFRAP as an extreme right-wing operation not to be taken seriously, although he added that things had since changed and IFRAP was now considered more mainstream and had contacts with the Sarkozy administration. Xavier Timbeau at OFCE identified the Ministry of Economy, Finance and Employment's DGTPE as an important competitor and that OFCE often does analysis that raises questions about that done by DGTPE and vice versa. It is worth remembering as well that OFCE was established initially to provide alternative analyses to INSEE's. Nevertheless, examples of competition in France were few and far between.

We learned that there were several reasons why proliferation did not generate much competition among French policy research organizations. To begin with, there is little need to compete much for resources because the state funds most of them.[139] Even OFCE, which some government officials would have preferred to disappear given its habit of speaking truth to power, expressed little concern over losing its funding when we interviewed there.[140] Furthermore, many of the policy research organizations we visited are fairly new. So in many cases competitive cleavages have not yet had a chance to develop. The director of one political foundation explained that competition among the five foundations might develop as they got older but that so far it had not.[141]

However, the reason we heard most frequently for the absence of competition was that most policy research organizations in France occupied specialized niches with few if any other occupants.[142] Foundation Concorde focused on a few concrete policy issues, such as nuclear power, while others pursued different issues and still others tackled subjects of more theoretical or even philosophical importance.[143] Echoing this view, a senior official at Foundation Robert Schuman, which specializes in European affairs, said, "We are quite alone" in the field. They do not even compete against IFRI because IFRI's focus is on

[139]Interviews with Giles Finchelstein, Foundation Jean Jaurés; Michel Rousseau, Foundation Concorde. We heard as well almost nothing about competing for funding from private organizations like IFRAP, Institute Montaigne, or the clubs. The only time we heard much about this was when we talked with members of some semi-public research organizations who spoke of competing with universities, foreign organizations, and some state organizations like CAS for research contracts (interviews with senior official, Coe-Rexecode; Xavier Timbeau, OFCE; senior official, CEPII).

[140]Interview with Xavier Timbeau, OFCE. Timbeau did, however, complain of OFCE being level-funded for the past few years. Moreover, OFCE's budget was reduced during the first right-wing cohabitation government of 1986–88 due to the perception that OFCE was favorable to the Socialist Party (Fourcade 2009, p. 221).

[141]Interview with Michael Mazo, Foundation Gabriel Peri.

[142]The lack of competition among private organizations also stemmed from a resource-lean environment that forced many of them to position themselves alone in idiosyncratic niches in the first place. Email correspondence with senior official, Enterprise and Progress.

[143]Interview with Michel Rousseau, Foundation Concorde.

international relations in general not just Europe.[144] Indeed, IFRI's executive vice president agreed that his organization's scope was much broader than most others, which tend to focus on fewer issues and geographical regions.[145] Similarly, a senior official at CEPII said that her organization was the only one in France doing high-powered econometric simulations of international economic trends. When we asked her whether we were correct in understanding that the absence of competition in France among policy research organizations was due to an elaborate division of labor, she responded quickly saying, "Yes, that's right, that's right." Our contact at Coe-Rexecode said that their most obvious competitor would have been OFCE except that Coe-Rexecode is less Keynesian, does more micro-analytic analysis, and has more data gathered from companies.[146] The reason why République des Idées and Institute Choiseul do not compete is that the former focuses on France while the latter focuses on regional issues around the world.[147] According to Paul de Fombelle at Institute Choiseul, "We have specificity, which is, I think, very important. We are the only one." We heard the same thing from Philippe Manière at Institute Montaigne, who said, "We have a niche," with no other serious competitors.

Cooperation among policy research organizations in civil society was limited for reasons similar to those that limited competition—many of them operated in relatively new and sparsely populated niches. For instance, in response to our question whether IFRAP worked with other organizations Bernard Zimmern answered, "Not really because the other think tanks, there are not many." We heard a similar story at the club Enterprise and Progress with a specific comparison to the United States:

> There is nothing comparable to the think tanks in the U.S., and we are still, you know, small guys moving in—having problems getting together; having problems working together. We can do that. We do that from time to time. But at the same time . . . it's more of the idea of fragmentation rather than concentration.[148]

[144]Interview with senior official, Foundation Robert Schuman and Foundation Robert Schuman annual report 2007 (pp. 26–27).
[145]Interview with Dominique David, IFRI.
[146]Interview with senior official, Coe-Rexecode.
[147]Interviews with Florent Guénard, République des Idées; Paul de Fombelle, Institute Choiseul.
[148]Interview with senior official, Enterprise and Progress. He did mention one instance of cooperation. His organization worked with others, such as employer associations, on a joint petition protesting the leftist tendencies of certain economics school teachers whose mouthpiece is a newspaper from ATTAC, an aggressive anticapitalism social movement organization. Nevertheless, their website did mention one cooperative venture with IDEP, the business club established in response to Enterprise and Progress's founding (http://www.entreprise-progres.net/. Accessed May 2009).

The semi-public research organizations also told us that they did not cooperate much with each other because they tend to be the only ones in their substantive research niches. When we asked a senior official at CEPII whether her organization worked with others in France on international economics, their specialty, she replied, "No. We are the only one in France. This is very different from Germany where you have several institutions working on the same [thing]." We heard much the same at IFRI, which does not cooperate much with other French policy research organizations other than occasionally inviting them to a conference or seminar.[149] And when we asked Xavier Timbeau whether his organization, OFCE, collaborated with other semi-public organizations or think tanks he said, "It happens very rarely," usually when they assemble a committee of outside economists, some of whom may come from semi-public research organizations and other places, to review their biannual forecasts.[150]

In some cases lack of cooperation stemmed from ideological differences.[151] IFRAP's Bernard Zimmern told us that he was rarely invited to breakfasts, seminars, and the like because IFRAP's conservative views were often at odds with most other organizations, including right-wing ones like Institute Montaigne. There is also little cooperation among the political foundations.[152] Michel Rousseau from the center-right Foundation Concorde also attributed this to ideological differences, saying that they are never invited by their left-wing counterparts to participate in events. And even if invited, he said that Concorde would refuse because "[t]here is no interest for us. We don't agree with them. There's no ambition to understand them." And, "It's too difficult to work with others because the positions are different." The notable exception in this regard was the communist Foundation Gabriel Peri, which was willing to participate in any forum regardless of who sponsored it as long as it might help create new political ideas. They even invited the neoliberal Institute Montaigne to one of their conferences.[153] Ironically, cooperation among organizations with different political-ideological points of view was more prevalent in the United States, even though political partisanship and competition over the past 20 years had become much more extreme than in France.

[149]Interview with Dominique David, IFRI.

[150]OFCE developed its Ingénue forecasting model with CEPREMAP and CEPII.

[151]Our concern here is with cooperation regarding policy research. Some organizations that were not involved in such cooperative efforts still worked with other organizations for other reasons. République des Ideés, for example, lists a half dozen "partners" on its website that seem to be publishers, magazines, and newspapers including Le Monde (http://www.repid.com/. Accessed October 2011). Institute Choiseul also lists dozens of "partners" on its website, including companies, travel agencies, and private foundations, which are surely funders rather than research collaborators (http://choiseul-editions.com/partenaires.html. Accessed October 2011).

[152]Interviews with Michel Mazo, Foundation Gabriel Peri; Michel Rousseau, Foundation Concorde.

[153]Interview with Michel Mazo, Foundation Gabriel Peri.

Two caveats are in order. First, cooperation was more common when it came to European issues. Foundation Robert Schuman has worked with Institute Choiseul on these things.[154] And the Foundation for Political Innovation, which also focuses on international issues, has worked with the small handful of French think tanks that are concerned with Europe. Even so the possibilities for cooperation there were limited because "[t]here are not so many people dealing with European issues in Paris."[155] Again, niche constraints were at work. Second, several organizations, including OFCE, IFRI, Institute Montaigne, and several political foundations, reported collaborating with *foreign* counterparts.[156] CEPII worked more and more over the past decade or so with the World Bank and other international research organizations with which it is connected through its memberships in international research consortia. CEPII does this because as a small operation international cooperation provides the staff an opportunity for honing its technical skills, and because the European Commission requires international collaboration as a condition for funding certain research projects in which CEPII is interested.[157]

Competition, Coordination, Cooperation, and the State

In the United States there was not much competition among state policy research organizations due to a legislatively mandated division of labor as well as some coordinating mechanisms like the president's National Economic Council. The same was true in France. But because part of the move away from dirigisme involved cultivating new state policy, research organizations that fragmented France's knowledge regime some competition resulted among them. Recall, for example, that one reason why the Minister of Labor created DARES in 1993 was to provide a basis from which to compete with the powerful Ministry of Finance:

> The idea was to try to create a new department that would be able in the future to provide, I would say, challenging analysis or challenging duels with the analyses that are provided in the Ministry of Finance.

[154]Interview with Paul de Fombelle, Institute Choiseul.
[155]Interview with Frédéric Allemand, Foundation for Political Innovation.
[156]Interviews with Xavier Timbeau, OFCE; Dominique David, IFRI; Philippe Manière, Institute Montaigne; Michel Mazo, Foundation Gabriel Peri; Gilles Finchelstein, Foundation Jean Jaurés; senior official, Foundation Robert Schuman. According to its "Goals 2008–2012" (2008, p. 4) report, Foundation Jean Jaurés works with foundations, think tanks, associations, and political parties in 113 countries. Foundation Robert Schuman's annual report (2007, p. 6) also lists several international collaborators. And the Foundation for Political Innovation's annual report (2007, p. 49) lists more than two dozen foreign partners.
[157]Interview with senior official, CEPII.

The Ministry of Finance, I think, at the time and still now, has huge capacity for economic analysis. So the idea was to try to put together a new department that would at least be able to challenge somewhat the thinking developed in the Ministry of Finance.[158]

However, we discovered several more recent efforts to coordinate the activities of state policy research organizations, thereby largely neutralizing tendencies toward competition that might otherwise have surfaced. These included orchestrating a division of labor among some of the conseils, recentralizing some ministerial research capacities, subjecting some organizations to supervision and coordination by national umbrella organizations like INSEE and the newly created CAS, and initiating various informal efforts to coordinate interorganizational activity. We address each in turn.

To begin with, some of the new organizations were designed as part of a division of analytic labor. Some of the new conseils, such as COE and COR, were created to specialize in different policy areas. Similarly, René Sève at CAS explained that although CAS and some of the conseils "could be working on the same topics, we are not working the same way, with the same time or reason, and with the same intention. And further, we are rather complementary." When we asked him to clarify whether CAS and the others occupy unique niches, his response was, "I think so. This is my view."

Second, the state increased its coordination of policy research by recentralizing some of its ministerial research capacities. Again, DARES, is a case in point. It was initially part of the Ministry for Work, Solidarity and Civil Service, doing statistical labor market analyses, but was later assigned as well to the Ministry of Economy and Employment. Once it began serving two masters it discovered that there was some overlap in what researchers were doing in both organizations. They tried to fix this by establishing a new division of labor with some doing ex ante and others doing ex post policy analysis.[159] DGTPE in the Ministry of Economy, Finance and Employment is another example. The prime minister's office created DGTPE in 2004 by merging three other ministerial research units. The idea was to reduce the duplication of efforts by its three predecessors and improve the analytic capacity of the Treasury by putting macroeconomic expertise together with work being done elsewhere on various subjects of concern to the ministries—particularly issues of European and international affairs.[160]

Third, as new ministerial research units were created INSEE and CNIS began to coordinate their activities. As a result, "Those statistical units [have]

---

[158]Interview with senior official, DARES.
[159]Interview with senior official, DARES.
[160]Interview with senior official, DGTPE.

very close links with the national institutes."[161] DARES illustrates the point insofar as its statistics production activities are now under CNIS supervision. For example, CNIS recently persuaded DARES to initiate surveys focusing on the situation of people looking for work.[162]

Perhaps the most striking example of coordination is CAS. By the time the Planning Commissariat was abolished externalization of some of the state's analytic capacities had been in full swing for years. Then, however, the prime minister established CAS to help coordinate groups of researchers from the ministries, conseils, and sometimes semi-public scholarly research organizations that were working on the same topic, such as retirement systems or labor market reforms.[163] Under CAS's supervision these groups may meet as often as once or twice a month to exchange ideas, information, and analyses and cooperate in other ways. Moreover, CAS finances some of the conseils and helps them coordinate various projects. René Sève, the general director, offered two examples of how CAS coordinates policy research. One was a report on the transportation of goods, which included information gathered from various interested organizations including some of the unions. In this sense he said it was a "polysectoral" effort resulting in a report for the Ministry of Transportation that was written primarily at CAS. The other much more ambitious example was a report that involved coordinating several working groups composed of hundreds of experts from various organizations in order to develop several economic, demographic, and other forecasts. He explained that the final report will represent a "recentralization of all this expertise which is disseminated today" across many organizations.[164] In his view CAS gathers information from a much wider range of sources than the Planning Commissariat did in order to "build new bridges" among scattered organizations. In our view this is not so much about recentralization per se as it is about network building and coordination among organizations. After all, Sève insisted that "[i]t's not . . . a military organization," by which he meant the old dirigiste system. And because it is not, CAS has little direct authority over the organizations it helps coordinate and often needs to be more diplomatic in doing so than the Planning Commissariat. In his words, CAS needs to use a little "French nuance" to synchronize

[161] Interview with senior official, DARES.

[162] DARES strategic plans for 2006 and 2008 (http://www.travail-solidarite.gouv.fr/etudes-recherche-statistiques-dares/. Accessed May 2009.)

[163] CAS replaced the Planning Commissariat's Groupe d'Etudes Prospectives Internationales (GEPI) in 2006. Its budgetary framework is part of the Coordination of Government Work program (http://www.strategie.gouv.fr/. Accessed May 2009).

[164] This is the "France 2025" report. The group was composed of 350 people from specialized CAS working groups (http://www.strategie.gouv.fr/Le_programme_de_travail_2008. Accessed January 2012). It was commissioned by Prime Minister Villepin but killed by Nicolas Sarkozy when he became president. As a result, CAS never published a full report on the 2025 project—only a PowerPoint presentation. We thank Bruno Palier for this observation.

activities, adjudicate differences among organizations, and produce reports that synthesize information from various organizational points of view.[165]

Sometimes state research organizations cooperate with each other without an external coordinator like CAS. DARES is again a good illustration. Like other ministerial research departments it publishes its work program at the beginning of each year. The plan is based initially on conversations they have with most of the departments of their two ministers and some other ministries to learn what everyone believes are the most pressing issues in the coming year. DARES also meets with the unions and employers federation to solicit their input. Then it submits the plan to its scientific council, which includes academics and people from various ministries to ensure among other things that the work is not being done by another ministerial research unit. Finally, the revised plan goes to the relevant *cabinets* and ministries for further comment before final internal approval.[166] In these and other matters DARES also consults with INSEE and CNIS to make sure that the work it does meets certain methodological standards and is integrated with that being done by other state research units. Summarizing things, our contact at DARES said, "We cooperate, of course, very much with [INSEE] and with some other departments involved in economic analysis, such as [DGTPE] in the Minister of the Economy. We have working relationships with some other institutes [and conseils]." Others told us that this sort of cooperation has become more commonplace among state research organizations over the past 20 years.[167]

The state also facilitates cooperation among its agencies as well as the social partners through the conseils. On one occasion we heard that COR was formed in order to "help to build some consensus on what we had to do in the field of pension reform," by mustering data, statistics, and analysis to make everyone aware of the issues.[168] Beyond that, the various conseils are helpful to CAE because when it works with the prime minister's *cabinet* to prepare a report or work program, it reviews what the other conseils as well as other research institutes inside and outside of the state are doing.[169]

Coordination and cooperation extend from the state to one important set of organizations in civil society—the semi-public research organizations.

---

[165]Interview with René Sève, CAS. CAS is not as central to policy analysis as the Planning Commissariat was. Nor is it involved directly in policymaking like its predecessor. But CAS's lack of centrality makes sense insofar as the world is far more complex today than it was during the Planning Commissariat's heyday. As noted earlier, one senior official at DGTPE remarked that in contrast to the old days no single organization today could have enough expertise on everything to operate legitimately as a central player, which, of course, is why the state underwent its externalization process in the first place.

[166]Interview with senior official, DARES.

[167]Interview with senior official, DGTPE.

[168]Interview with senior official, DARES.

[169]Interview with Christian de Boissieu, CAE.

Although these organizations tend not to cooperate much with each other, they do with state research organizations. For instance, OFCE often does work for various conseils as well as CAS. When they are preparing a report for these organizations OFCE staff typically organize groups of people working on the subject with various experts and people from the administration to solicit input, share ideas, and provide updates on what they are doing. And like other semi-public research organizations OFCE frequently gets data from state research organizations, such as DARES and INSEE.[170] Similarly, CEPII often works for the prime minister, whose cabinet frequently asks it for reports and information. CEPII also works with CAS and occasionally DGTPE.[171] CEPREMAP, another semi-public scholarly research organization, works with various government agencies, including CAS, DGTPE, CAE, INSEE, DARES, DREES and others.[172] Finally, CAE often has research centers like CEPII and sometimes academics work for them on various projects.[173]

According to the old folk tale, it is impossible to put the genie back into the bottle. In France, despite the state's efforts to coordinate policy analysis as it sought in effect to restore the knowledge regimes' institutional complementarity with the rest of the political economy, it is very unlikely that things will return to the hierarchically centralized model of the postwar Golden Age. Nor is it clear that this is what policymakers and other state officials want anyway. In short, we doubt that France's knowledge regime will see a return to the old form of dirigisme anytime soon. Nevertheless, to review briefly, the policymaking regime continued to have a major influence on the knowledge regime. By helping to establish and finance the party foundation think tanks and semi-public research organizations in ways that created a fragmented niche structure, neither competition nor cooperation had much chance to develop among research organizations in civil society. Competition was also scarce among most state policy research organizations thanks to the division of analytic labor that the state spawned, such as among CES, COE, COR, CAE, and the other conseils. However, through the efforts of CAS and INSEE the state coordinated the activities of many of the new state and semi-public research organizations. It did so as well by recentralizing some research capacities in organizations like DARES and DGTPE.

Conclusion

To conclude and sum up, we return to some of our broader analytic arguments. In terms of the production regime's effects, the end of the Golden Age

---

[170]Interview with Xavier Timbeau, OFCE.
[171]Interviews with senior official, CEPII; René Sève, CAS; senior official, DGTPE.
[172]http://www.cepremap.fr/en/presentation/. Accessed August 2011.
[173]Email correspondence with senior official, CEPII.

and rise of globalization created the initial impetus for change in the knowledge regime. Stagflation and increased international economic challenges led to policy experiments, including a wave of nationalizations and then privatizations that were largely unsuccessful in resolving the problems at hand. A crisis of ideas followed and led to the establishment of various business clubs and more recently advocacy organizations, financed increasingly by firms with international profiles and from newly emergent economic sectors—two more effects of the French economy's internationalization. Finally, corporatist echoes were evident in the composition of some new policy research organizations, notably the conseils.

The policymaking regime had significant effects too. The crisis of ideas, fueled in part by a rebalancing of the party system as well as the decline of indicative planning, caused state officials to pivot away from dirigisme in order to cultivate new policy ideas by financing and sometimes establishing policy research organizations outside the state, including semi-public research organizations and party foundation think tanks. Policymakers also established new policy research organizations within the state. This was consistent with French policymaking tradition insofar as the state orchestrated it from above. All of this proliferation resulted in a more fragmented field with many new organizations more or less monopolizing their own niches, which meant that neither competition nor cooperation was particularly evident.

To the extent that new organizations emerged in civil society, the separation between the knowledge and policymaking regimes, which had been virtually nil in the immediate postwar era, began to increase. More recently, however, the policymaking regime's effects appeared again as state officials took steps to recentralize and better coordinate some of the activities of the state and semi-public policy research organizations, notably through CAS and INSEE. Although this was by no means a return to the old heavy-handed dirigiste system, the state's dominance remained the hallmark of this knowledge regime.

Several observers of modern French political economy have argued that the decline of dirigisme has meant that when the state seeks to promote certain types of activity in society it can no longer do so by directing people to follow its wishes. Instead it can now provide only opportunities and encouragement for them to do so. In this sense the state has morphed from a director into a facilitator.[174] There is evidence of this in France's knowledge regime. The state, for example, provided funds to encourage the formation of the political foundations and their think tanks. But it did not force political parties to create them. It also eventually reformed the tax code in order to create incentives for philanthropists and others to establish private advocacy research organizations.

[174]Culpepper 2006; Howell 2009; Lallement 2006; Levy 1999; Palier and Thelen 2012.

But, again, it did not force them to do so. On the other hand, however, the state established and funded all the semi-public scholarly research organizations. It also posed until recently certain administrative and fiscal hurdles that made it difficult to establish advocacy organizations. Indeed, the path away from dirigisme and toward a new set of policy research organizations in civil society was inconsistent and uneven. Sometimes the state was a director, sometimes it was a facilitator, and sometimes it was simply an obstacle.

Observers of the French scene have also argued that the decline of dirigisme was less successful than people had hoped as France's political economic performance continued to lag many of its chief competitors. And so pressures for renewed state intervention into the economy began to surface in the 1990s. As a result, the state's initial withdrawal from the economy was followed by a partial restoration of the old statist ways but in a softer form.[175] This happened as well in the French knowledge regime as some ministerial research units were merged into new ones, as others took responsibility for more than one ministry, and as the prime minister created CAS to better coordinate the activities of all sorts of state and semi-public research organizations. The point is that challenges to and changes in the French political economy have had many significant effects on its knowledge regime.

Let us return to the notion of the knowledge regime's institutional complementarity vis-à-vis the rest of the political economy. First, people in France came to perceive that the knowledge regime's complementarity had deteriorated especially in terms of the ability of policy research organizations to help restore France's international economic competitiveness. This is evident in light of the fact that one of the first and most prominent semi-public research organizations that the state inaugurated as part of its externalization strategy was CEPII, which specialized in international issues. Moreover, other new policy research organizations, such as OFCE, turned increasingly toward international datasets and cross-national comparisons in their work. Clearly, then, perceptions of the breakdown in the knowledge regime's complementarity were cast in terms of the challenges and problems France faced in navigating turbulent international economic waters. As we shall see, concerns about international economic competitiveness also figured prominently in the German and Danish cases.

Second, compared to the United States, it took a long time for most policymakers to perceive that their knowledge regime had become dysfunctional and no longer complemented the rest of the political economy. After all, it was only in the late 1990s that many of the knowledge regime changes we have described began to happen. Institutional and ideational inertias were

[175]Levy 1999, chap. 7.

substantial. Eventually, of course, people began to realize that a crisis of ideas had developed—that is, that complementarity had broken down. And once policymakers embarked on their externalization strategy in search of new ideational inspiration they acknowledged in effect that complementarity had to be restored and that they intended to do just that. All of this reinforces our argument that perceptions of a breakdown of complementarity do not automatically trigger efforts to rebuild it.

Nor were these efforts guaranteed to be successful. Despite the fact that political leaders initially engendered the formation of new policy research organizations and hoped that they would provide better analysis and advice—that is, improve the knowledge regime's institutional complementarity—once these organizations were in place they were left more or less to their own devices. Whether they would fulfill the hopes of policymakers was still very much up for grabs. In this sense when all was said and done this was as much an ad hoc trial-and-error response as it was a centrally planned one. And neither central planning nor decentralized experimentation necessarily ensures success.

There is another important difference between the American and French cases. In the United States private money played a big role in transforming the knowledge regime. This was a sensitive issue in some Washington interviews where people insisted that their organizations were independent from *private* moneyed interests. In France, however, the sensitive issue was whether their organizations were independent from the *state*. Institute Montaigne and IFRAP claimed independence by virtue of the fact that they did not receive any public funding.[176] When we asked the Institute Montaigne's Philippe Manière whether this might change, he said proudly, "I'd rather die because we want to be independent!" Yet we were struck by how frequently people insisted that their organizations were independent from the state and political influence even though they depended heavily on the state for financing. In this regard, someone at Coe-Rexecode exclaimed facetiously, "Nobody is independent and everybody is independent!" People tended to defend their assertions of independence in two ways. First, some claimed independence insofar as in their view they did high-quality scholarly work.[177] Second, others claimed

---

[176]Interviews with Philippe Manière, Institute Montaigne; Bernard Zimmern, IFRAP; Michel Rousseau, Foundation Concorde; Florent Guénard, République des Idées. During our interview at Foundation Jean Jaurés we were told that most people did not worry about relying on state money because a part of French culture stretching back to the ideas of Voltaire, Montesquieu, and the Revolution is that the state rather than the private sector operates in the best interests of society. Indeed, people at both Foundation Jean Jaurés and Foundation Gabriel Peri said that receiving funding from the prime minister's office helps *ensure* their independence from political interference, as does a 1998 law mandating their independence from the political parties with which they are affiliated.

[177]Interviews with Dominique David, IFRI; senior official, Coe-Rexecode; René Sève, CAS; senior official, DARES.

independence because their organizations spoke their mind and published what they wanted regardless of the political climate.[178] Xavier Timbeau said that independent publication was so important at OFCE that they explained during research contract negotiations, "Whatever you think about what we have done, we are going to publish it." Why? In his view, "What they are paying for is an independent study." We do not find these defenses terribly compelling.

Two organizations, however, provided more convincing arguments that they were independent despite receiving state money. One was an organization where we were told off the record that politicians had tried to influence some of its analytic conclusions but that the director refused to bend to political pressure. The other was at OFCE, which was doing an analysis of income inequality for parliament based on the state's data. The French statistics system, presumably INSEE, said it did not have income data for anyone earning over about $1.3 million (€1 million). OFCE suspected otherwise. So it published its analysis provoking a government response that revealed that more complete data were available after all. Our contact at OFCE also said that their independence was clear given that OFCE has "had frictions with all kinds of governments, whatever they are, because every kind of government has a temptation to interpret, to . . . 'put some sugar' on the data." Moreover, he said that since OFCE was a thorn in the government's side for so many years many politicians wanted to get rid of OFCE but could not due to its high public profile and reputation for excellent research.

But beyond this we suspect that many of the French organizations we visited did in fact enjoy a degree of independence from the state due to institutional factors. First, the semi-public research organizations like OFCE as well as some state organizations like CAE were established in the first place to provide alternative analysis and advice to that typically provided by the state's own research shops. In some cases, notably CAE, people are appointed from across the political spectrum—not just from the viewpoint of the prime minister who chooses them. This is much different from the case in the United States where appointments to the Council of Economic Advisers are typically close to the president's ideological persuasion. And, as we will explain in chapter 7, CAE routinely consults academics from a wide range of intellectual positions as it prepares its reports. Second, insofar as state policy research organizations are run and staffed by technocrats, one might presume that they enjoy a certain degree of independence. After all, these people are often trained at the Grandes Écoles where they develop a particular esprit de corps and professional neutrality regardless of which parties are in power. They also hold permanent positions that are surely more immune from political meddling than temporary positions, which are more common in the United States. The broader point, however, is that the degree of independence

[178]Interviews with senior official, CEPII; senior official, DARES; Xavier Timbeau, OFCE.

enjoyed by policy research organizations is determined by nationally specific parameters and is, therefore, variable across place and time.

Much of what we found in France was different from what we found in Germany. Whereas a strong centralized state marked the French knowledge regime, a decentralized state did so in Germany. Corporatism had an especially important effect in Germany too. And dedication to rigorous state-of-the-art policy analysis was encouraged in impressive ways that we did not find elsewhere.

4

Coordination and Compromise in Germany

In contrast to the U.S. knowledge regime with its competitive marketplace of ideas and the French knowledge regime with its statist tradition, the chief characteristic of the German knowledge regime is coordination among its policy research organizations. We expected as much given Germany's corporatist heritage. After all, in modern corporatist systems the state confers formal status and resources on well-organized interest groups, such as unions and employer associations, grants them formal admission to the policymaking process, and off-loads formal responsibility to them for coordinating the behavior of their members and each other in order to facilitate compromise and advise policymakers.[1]

With this in mind, we found two surprises during our interviews in Germany. First, the manner in which policy research organizations were coordinated was not always as formal as we expected. After all, the focus in much of the comparative political economy literature has been on Germany's formal corporatist systems and how during the late 1990s and early 2000s their

---

[1] Offe 1981; Lehmbruch 1979; Schmitter 1979.

rigidities compromised German economic competitiveness.[2] Often coordination in the knowledge regime was achieved informally by softer and more tacit means. Second, as the Golden Age of postwar capitalism ended and globalization emerged, economic challenges and problems mounted and a *crisis of corporatism* developed whereby some people became disillusioned with traditional corporatist channels of coordination and influence and tried to side step them. This led to the rise of advocacy policy research organizations, although nothing as extensive as what we found in the United States. These challenges and problems also led to coordinated efforts to boost the quality of policy analysis. Both responses stemmed from perceptions that the knowledge regime was becoming dysfunctional—that is, no longer a source of institutional complementarity for the rest of the political economy.

We begin with a brief description of the political-economic environment within which Germany's knowledge regime is embedded. Then we examine the knowledge regime's structure and practices as we found them during our interviews. Finally, we explain the important changes that we discovered.

The Political-Economic Environment

Germany is often described as a coordinated market economy.[3] It is based on the idea of corporatism where the state depends on certain interest groups in civil society to help make sense of and solve the country's economic problems. These groups play important roles coordinating political-economic activity.[4] For instance, during the first three decades since the Second World War the production regime was coordinated formally by tripartite corporatist bargaining among representatives from the state, unions, and employer associations in a number of policy areas.[5] Toward this end the business community was organized in three peak associations: the Federation of German Industry (BDI), the Federation of German Employer Associations (BDA), and the Diet of German Industry and Commerce.[6] Labor was well organized compared to in the United States and France. Even though unionization rates fell a bit from the early 1980s about 23% of German employees still belonged to a union in 2003, whereas the comparable figure was about 12% for the United States and 8%

---

[2]Culpepper 2001; Katzenstein 1987; Palier and Thelen 2012; Thelen 2000, 2004.
[3]Hall and Soskice 2001a; Soskice 1999; Thelen 2004.
[4]Weiss (1998, chap. 5) calls it private sector coordination. Streeck and Schmitter (1985) call it private interest government.
[5]Albert 1993; Shonfield 1965, chaps. 11, 12.
[6]Katzenstein 1987, chap. 1; Streeck 1997b. Business coordination has also been facilitated by cross-shareholdings among German firms and a financial system based on centralized bank credit (Goyer 2006; Zysman 1983).

for France.[7] Most unions belonged to the Federation of German Trade Unions (DGB). The unions acted independently of the DGB in collective bargaining, but the DGB played a major role in articulating labor's interests in politics just as the BDI did for business.[8] Other corporatist institutions included firm-level works councils and codetermination laws.[9] In sum, Germany's production regime involved what Wolfgang Streeck called "widespread organized cooperation among competitors and bargaining between organized groups, conducted through publicly enabled associations."[10]

It is important to note, however, that German corporatism is less encompassing than corporatism is in some countries including Denmark. For one thing in Germany there is a constitutional provision (*Tarifautonomie*) that prohibits the state from direct involvement in wage negotiations. This prevents the state from extracting the kind of binding agreements we discuss later in chapter 5 for Denmark. Furthermore, German corporatism is less centralized than it is in Denmark and lacks the sort of national level labor-management agreements found there.

Germany's policymaking regime involved six well-disciplined political parties. Since the war the Social Democratic Party (SPD) has been a center-left party pragmatically representing the working class as well as a segment of the professional class and favoring Keynesianism. Also on the left is the Green Party, born from the environmental movement of the 1970s, and the Left Party (Die Linke), the reformed successor to the old East German communist ruling party. The center-right Christian Democratic Union (CDU) is a catchall party consisting of conservatives, nationalists, Catholics, social reformers, workers, Protestants, and entrepreneurs. Its labor wing is close to the trade unions, and its business wing speaks for business and financial interests. The smaller Christian Social Union (CSU) is a conservative party that often works with the CDU as a joint parliamentary party. The Free Democratic Party (FDP) is a liberal party that vacillates between the orientations of the CDU/CSU and SPD.[11]

This system lends itself to coalition governments, centrist politics, moderation, and incremental change more than either the United States or France. First, thanks to a mixed-member proportional representation electoral system where half the seats in the legislature are assigned to parties depending on

[7]However, in 2000 about 63% of German employees were covered by collective bargaining agreements regardless of whether they belonged to a union. The comparable figure was about 14% for the United States and 95% for France (Visser 2006; OECD 2004, chart 3.4).

[8]Katzenstein 1987, chaps. 1, 3.

[9]Mueller-Jentsch 1995. Works councils negotiate workplace practices (e.g., hiring, firing, schedules, etc.) but not wages and benefits with management. Codetermination law affords workers representation on corporate boards.

[10]Streeck 1997b, p. 39.

[11]"Liberal" here has the classic European meaning—pro–free market.

their share of the vote, the parties must often form coalition governments and need to compromise to do so.[12] Second, the main parties—the SPD and CDU/CSU—have strong internal factions that prevent much movement away from the center. Third, the smaller FDP's survival depends on maintaining a centrist profile. Fourth, like the U.S. system of checks and balances, the German parliament has considerable authority vis-à-vis the executive branch. Fifth, legislation is invariably drafted in the ministries in consultation with the peak associations before it is submitted to the legislative branch. The Bundestag, the upper house of parliament, is organized so that its work is conducted by committees that correspond to the ministerial structure. As a result, parliamentarians develop some degree of policy expertise much like ministerial technocrats—expertise that, unlike in the United States, tends to mitigate the partisan politicization of issues and, unlike in France, prevents ministerial technocrats from monopolizing policy expertise. Finally, committee work in parliament is based on informal norms of unanimous consent.[13]

Contributing further to centrist politics is the fragmented, decentralized, federalist structure of the state. Germany is divided into 16 Länder, each with its own legislature. Each one elects representatives to the Bundesrat, the lower house of parliament, which must approve most legislation emanating from the Bundestag. This gives the Bundesrat considerable power. So in order to get legislation passed the government often negotiates and compromises with the Länder. This is unheard of in France where state power is centralized in the executive branch. Furthermore, the German state bureaucracy is fragmented and decentralized. The chancellor is permitted to form her or his cabinet with as many ministries as she or he wants. Once formed, however, each one has considerable autonomy from her or his office. Ministries are typically smaller and have less administrative expertise than is the case in other countries. Their influence is limited further by the fact that policy implementation is often delegated to the Länder, which therefore frequently have at least as much expertise and administrative capacity as the ministries. This also facilitates compromise, centrism, and incremental policy change. In the United States state governments do not typically have these capacities. Nor do they approve congressional legislation or necessarily have responsibility for implementing national policy. So federalism is more inclined toward compromise in Germany than is the case in America.[14]

---

[12]Put simply, in Germany each voter casts two ballots in Bundestag elections. The first vote is cast for a candidate running to represent a district. The candidate winning the plurality of votes is elected. The second vote is cast for a political party. The second votes determine each party's share of the popular vote. Half the Bundestag members are elected directly from the districts while the rest are elected through proportional representation.

[13]Katzenstein 1987, chap. 1; Prasad 2006, chap. 3; Streeck 1997b.

[14]Dyson 1982, p. 42; Katzenstein 1987, chap. 1; Weiss 1998, chap. 5.

This is not to say, of course, that conflict is absent in Germany. Different corporatist groups as well as different political parties fight for the interests of their members. The point is that they do so within constraints that keeps things from getting out of hand. Corporatist labor and employer associations, for instance, are formally empowered by the state to represent their members' interests, but in exchange for this status they are expected to behave responsibly, such as by not raising issues that are nonnegotiable at the bargaining table, and accept that one of their functions is to help diffuse conflict and facilitate consensus making.[15]

Consistent with corporatism, postwar Germany relied heavily on semi-public organizations that were enabled under public law and bridged the gap between public and private worlds. They did so frequently by marshaling the knowledge of private experts under the auspices of the state administration, such as through state financed expert commissions that compensated for the federal ministries' limited technocratic expertise by providing analysis and advice to policymakers.[16] They also served as political shock absorbers further encouraging incremental centrist policymaking.[17] Hence, Germany's consensus-oriented policymaking was based not just on corporatist interest group bargaining but also on expertise, which ensured that the dialogue among these groups remained rational and objective.[18]

A final reason why German politics have been rather centrist during the postwar years is that the political parties subscribed in varying degree to the notion of the "social market economy"—an ideology that advocates preserving the market economy, mitigating social conflicts, and ensuring stability and growth through competition. This entails combining the efficiency of markets with social fairness, joining economic freedom with social security, and safeguarding markets while mitigating negative externalities with state regulation. The concept has a conservative etiology stemming in part from German ordoliberalism, which calls for a strong state to facilitate free and competitive markets, guard against monopoly, and maintain economic security for society as a whole by accepting a welfare state. The social market economy is a postwar strategy for steering between socialism and planning on one side and laissez-faire on the other side.[19]

The end of the Golden Age and rise of globalization exposed the German economy to increasing international competition and other challenges.

[15] Offe 1981; Schmitter 1979; Lehmbruch 1979.
[16] Katzenstein 1987; Thunert 2000, 2004; Weiss 1998.
[17] Katzenstein 1987, chap. 1.
[18] Dyson 1982, p. 35.
[19] See Ptak (2009) and Stedman Jones (2012, pp. 121–26) for discussions of the development of the social market economy's ordoliberal roots. Importantly, corporatism is anathema to ordoliberals who put their faith not in organized interest groups but rather the honorable officers of the state who dedicate themselves to a well-functioning market.

As a result, from the late 1980s Germany shifted toward a relatively less well-organized form of capitalism. In particular, the collective organizational capacities of business and labor declined. Participation rates in business associations and trade unions fell. Independent unions and small groups of professional and skilled workers emerged aggressively representing their members' interests outside established channels and in opposition to the DGB. Similarly, bargaining coverage declined as did the number of workplaces with works councils. There were also attempts by some firms in the BDI to undermine codetermination and push for other neoliberal reforms. Furthermore, firms began turning away from bank credit toward domestic and international equity markets for financing.[20] Overall, then, the production regime became more fragmented and internationally oriented. One might argue that this signaled a crisis of corporatism. But the German political economy remains largely a coordinated one.[21]

We will show that Germany's policymaking and production regimes significantly affected its knowledge regime. For example, many policy research organizations are semi-public operations organized and funded by the Länder and sometimes the federal government. This is a manifestation of the policymaking regime's federalism and the small size and limited administrative capacities of the federal ministries. It is also a reflection of corporatism insofar as the state off-loads analytic responsibilities to these organizations, solicits input from them in coordinated ways, and confers special status and resources on them particularly if they do especially high-quality work. Furthermore, mirroring multiparty proportional representation, the major German political parties each have a foundation containing a think tank whose funding from the state is contingent on the number of seats their party holds in the Bundestag. All of this has long facilitated coordination and compromise in policy analysis and advising. We will show as well that when policymakers began to realize that the knowledge regime was not providing good enough analysis and advice to help them cope with the problems of globalization they initiated changes that elevated the quality and sophistication of the analysis that policy research organizations produced. Recall that this was a trend we also found in France and to a lesser degree in the United States. It was especially pronounced in Germany and as we shall see in Denmark. Similarly, as the crisis of corporatism emerged people became dissatisfied with the organization of the knowledge regime and began to set up advocacy research organizations, which introduced an element of competition into the knowledge regime. In a sense both of these moves derived from perceptions that the knowledge regime's complementary relationship to the rest of the political

---

[20] Goyer 2006.
[21] Streeck 2009; Thelen and Kume 1999.

economy had broken down and needed to be restored in order to better make sense of and solve Germany's economic problems.

Mapping the Field: The Knowledge Regime Today

In the early 2000s, Germany's knowledge regime was dominated by over 100 scholarly policy research organizations, including those affiliated with universities, churches, and other nonprofit organizations. Many were created by the government after the war and received most of their funding from it.[22] When we visited Germany, the core of its knowledge regime consisted of several semi-public scholarly policy research organizations as well as a few state policy research organizations.

Semi-public Scholarly Research Organizations

Everyone we interviewed agreed that among the most prominent of Germany's policy research organizations were about 30 scholarly economic research institutes. These include, for instance, the Center for European Economic Research (ZEW), the Institute for Economic Research at the University of Munich (Ifo), the Economic and Social Research Institute (WSI), and the Institute for Macroeconomic Forecasting (IMK). Also notable are the German Institute for Economic Research (DIW), the Kiel Institute for the World Economy (IfW), the Rhine-Westphalia Institute for Economic Research (RWI), and the Halle Institute for Economic Research (IWH). Some of these are quite old, such as IfW, which was established in 1914, but some are newer like ZEW, which was founded in 1990.

These organizations are different from scholarly policy research organizations in the United States and France. First, unlike in the United States many tend to be semi-public organizations that rely heavily on government funding, in return for which they provide independent analysis and advice to policymakers. And unlike in France, they are more plentiful, older, and well established. Indeed, Germany has a long-standing tradition of state-sponsored academic research especially in economics that dates to imperial times.[23]

---

[22]Thunert 2000, 2004. See Braml (2004, chap. 9) for a survey of German think tanks. We learned in a couple of interviews that churches, social insurance funds, and other nonprofit organizations conduct policy research into issues regarding families, the elderly, the poor, children, immigrants, and other groups. We are not concerned with these organizations because they are not interested in economic policy per se. When we compiled our sample of German economic policy research organizations none of the experts we surveyed suggested that we meet with these organizations, which indicates that omitting them from our sample did not blind us to something important about German economic policy analysis.

[23]Weilemann 2000, p. 169.

In contrast to France as well, where the central state funds the semi-public research organizations, in Germany the Länder governments do so, although in a few special cases the federal government does too.[24] Several also depend on research contracts from various ministries.[25] DIW and Ifo, for example, have contracts like this to do tax analysis.[26] Researchers in some organizations receive prestigious grants from the German National Science Council (DFG).[27] A few get financing from other semi-public organizations, such as the Institute for Employment Research (IAB), which depends on funding from the Federal Employment Agency as well as the Ministry of Social Affairs.[28]

Not all of these scholarly research institutes are financed by the state. The Cologne Institute for Economic Research (IW) is supported by the employer and industrial associations as well as several large corporations in order to "shape both public opinion and government policy in a pro-business way . . . [and] generate public support for a free market economy."[29] IMK and WSI operate under the umbrella of the Hans Böckler Foundation of the DGB, the German trade union federation. Most of their funding comes from the foundation, which is funded by contributions paid by trade union representatives sitting on corporate supervisory boards—contributions roughly equivalent to the extra income they receive from sitting on these boards. However, IMK and WSI also receive 15% to 20% of their funding from various research contracts.[30]

These research institutes are very scholarly. Most have staff that publish in academic journals and attend academic conferences. DIW, for example, claims to have the highest publication rate of all German economic research institutes since 2004 in journals listed in the Social Science Citation Index.[31] These institutes also have substantial analytic capacities. DIW's president told us that his organization built one of the best household socioeconomic panel datasets

[24]The special cases are members of the Leibniz Association, discussed later, which in 2011 included ZEW, Ifo, DIW, IfW, RWI, and IWH (http://www.leibniz-gemeinschaft.de. Accessed April 2011).
[25]Interview with Dieter Plehwe, WZB.
[26]Interviews with Klaus Zimmermann, DIW; senior official, Ifo.
[27]Email correspondence with Rolf Langhammer, IfW.
[28]Interviews and email correspondence with Martin Dietz and Ulrich Walwei, IAB. The Federal Employment Agency is also a semi-public organization. It is a self-governing corporation established by law to administer labor market policy. It is supervised by the Ministry of Labor and Social Affairs, financed by member contributions and state subsidies, and governed by a president and tripartite board consisting of representatives from labor, business, and the state. It does not cover the full range of economic research that other economic research institutes do but focuses mostly on labor market and social policy issues.
[29]IW's "An Employer's Body for Promoting the Market Economy" (2002, pp. 1–2) and http://www.iwkoeln.de. Accessed April 2011.
[30]HBS Yearbook 2007 and http://www.boeckler.de. Accessed April 2011.
[31]DIW annual report 2007, p. 5.

in the world and uses some of the most sophisticated econometric models.[32] IMK and WSI use data they collect through annual surveys of works council members as well as OECD and IMF data, socioeconomic panel data from the DIW, and more.[33] IW maintains a large statistical archive and the largest private economic and social science library in Germany.[34] Several do econometric modeling and forecasting. ZEW pioneered the use of microeconomic methods that are now used at several other German research institutes and uses large panel data on firms, start-ups, and individual households to that end.[35] IAB has its own statistical methods department, maintains a data center for itself and other research institutes, and collects data from various sources including its own surveys.[36] Ifo also collects data and maintains a renowned business climate index.[37]

Some private organizations have scholarly research organizations on a par with these economic research institutes. Big German banks have long had economic research capacities and in some cases have moved into the area of economic forecasting. Deutsche Bank, for example, has a think tank called DB Research that does this.[38] Yet we did not find that the banks provided analysis or advice specifically for policymakers.

Three things are worth noting about the overall size of these scholarly organizations. First, in our sample the largest of these organizations tend to be smaller than the largest private think tanks in the United States.[39] The largest U.S. private think tanks we interviewed, the Brookings Institution and the Urban Institute, spent about $62 million and $70 million each year, respectively, at the time of our interviews. The largest German organizations, ZEW and Ifo,

[32]Interviews with Klaus Zimmermann, DIW; senior official, KAS; senior official, MPIfG. See also Thunert 2000.

[33]Interview with Claus Schäfer, WSI; and interview and email correspondence with Rudolf Zwiener, IMK. Sometimes some of these organizations have not been so scholarly. For instance, in off-the-record email correspondence we learned that WSI was a leading economic research institute after the war but beginning in the 1970s slowly changed when the unions used it for patronage of union ideologues. In the 1990s the advisory board urged a reorganization to elevate the quality and respectability of its research. Under the direction of a new director these suggestions were pushed through successfully.

[34]http://www.iwkoeln.de. Accessed April 2011.

[35]ZEW Yearbook 2000.

[36]Interview with Martin Dietz, IAB.

[37]Email correspondence with Meinhard Knoche, Ifo. According to a senior official at Ifo, one such survey involves sending questionnaires to 7,000 businesses each month to track business cycle developments.

[38]Interviews with senior official, KAS; senior official, MPIfG. See also Thunert 2000.

[39]Braml (2004, chap. 6) reports that German think tanks are larger on average than U.S. think tanks. But he includes German political party foundations and private foundations in his calculations, which are large in terms of budgets and personnel. The appropriate comparison for us is between the semi-public scholarly research institutes in Germany and the private nonprofit research organizations in the United States.

each spent about $19.5 million.[40] Second, there is more parity among the German organizations than among the U.S. think tanks. Spending in the United States ranged from $70 million at Urban to about $6 million at the Economic Policy Institute (EPI) and the National Center for Policy Analysis. In Germany the range was from about $19.5 million at ZEW and Ifo to about $11 million at IW and IAB. Similarly the size of staff ranged from 408 people at the Urban Institute to 63 people at EPI in America but was narrower in Germany, ranging from 300 people at IW to 145 people at IfW.[41] Third, the U.S. organizations rely heavily on private funding, while the German organizations rely much more on public funding. It is possible, then, that other things being equal state financing might help ensure a degree of parity among organizations that private financing does not.

These organizations pride themselves on their reputations for scholarly research, which they have not wanted to jeopardize by excessive partisan advocacy work.[42] Nevertheless, they do have ideological tendencies. Virtually alone on the Keynesian side are IMK and WSI, both under the aegis of the Hans Böckler Foundation, which puts them on the political left relative to others.[43] The rest of the big research institutes tend to cluster around more conservative and supply-side viewpoints.[44] Indeed, the director of one of these institutes said, "The big institutes like Ifo and DIW or the Kiel Institute and the Essen Institute, I think, they are all now more or less the same."[45] Finally, probably somewhere in the middle is the Federal Employment Agency's

[40]Recent budget data for DIW were not available to us, but according to its annual report expenditures for 1997 were $22.1 million.

[41]German data are from the following annual reports: IAB 2007, ZEW 2006, IfW 2010, Ifo 2007, DIW 1997, IW 2002. U.S. data are from the following annual reports: Brookings Institution 2007, Urban Institute 2007, Economic Policy Institute 2003–5, National Center for Policy Analysis 2007. In email correspondence, Rolf Langhammer, IfW, insisted that his organization was actually smaller than our staffing numbers suggested—fewer than 100 full-time equivalent positions.

[42]Thunert 2000. Many flaunt their scholarly credentials. ZEW, for instance, reports doing research for the European Commission, federal ministries, firms, other private organizations, and the German Science Foundation ("Aims and Research Activities" booklet 2006, p. 3). The Kiel Institute does so for the World Bank, IMF, and OECD (http://www.ifw-kiel.de. Accessed May 2009). Others tout their membership in the prestigious Leibniz Association (DIW annual report 1997, p. 4; ZEW "Aims and Research Activities" booklet 2006), their strong external evaluations for research quality (IAB Yearbook 2007, p. ii), their selection to prestigious forecasting groups (Ifo annual report 2007, p. 9), and the number of academic prizes they garner (WZB Bericht 2006/2007, p. 6).

[43]Interviews with Rudolf Zwiener, IMK; Claus Schäfer, WSI; Wolfgang Franz, ZEW.

[44]Interview with senior researcher, IfW.

[45]Interview with Rolf Kroker, IW. His characterization was echoed in interviews with a senior official, Ifo, Rolf Langhammer, IfW, Claus Schäfer, WSI, and Rudolf Zwiener, IMK. Several times we were told that DIW was the institute that had changed most since the 1970s, shifting dramatically from Keynesianism toward neoliberalism.

research institute, IAB, which has a mix of Keynesian, institutional, and neo-classical economists but is gradually shifting toward a more conservative—or at least a more pragmatic—perspective as the old guard Keynesians are retiring.[46]

Despite their differences these organizations hardly challenge mainstream economic thinking in the German context.[47] First, virtually all of them accept the social market economy idea in one form or another. Second, the heads of the more conservative organizations including IW, ZEW, and RWI are or were recently headed by labor economists.[48] The president of DIW joked, "The labor market economist mafia is running the institutes." Generally speaking, given their proclivity for hard-nosed empirical research rather than mathematical modeling and theorizing, labor economists tend to be less ideological than other economists in Germany.[49] Third, reflecting Germany's tripartite corporatist traditions, some of the boards of directors of these organizations include people from businesses, unions, and the ministries as well as universities.[50] The point is that all of these things tend to temper the ideological dispositions of many of these organizations.

Two scholarly semi-public policy research organizations are particularly prominent in Germany. One is the Council of Economic Experts (CEE). Echoing many of our respondents, a senior researcher at the Kiel Institute described the CEE as "very important." In particular, this was because it issues a massive 500-page report each year for the government that contains all sorts of economic forecasts as well as very detailed analyses of economic policy to which the government is required to respond publicly.[51] By law the CEE report must address four main policy objectives: price stability, full employment, the external balance of payments, and economic growth.[52] Its five members are appointed by the minister of economic affairs in close consultation with the minister of finance and the chancellor's office. However, unlike its counterpart in the United States, the Council of Economic Advisors, which is part of the government's executive branch, the CEE is not part of the government. It is independent from it. CEE members elect their own chair rather than the chancellor or government appointing the chair. And the government cannot

[46]Interview and email correspondence with Martin Dietz, IAB.

[47]Weilemann 2000, p. 173.

[48]Interview with Klaus Zimmermann, DIW.

[49]Interview with Rolf Kroker, IW. He explained that the rising prominence of labor economists in these institutes is one reason why there is less ideological diversity among economists in them than there was 20 years ago.

[50]Interview with senior official, Ifo.

[51]Interviews with senior researcher and Rolf Langhammer, IfW.

[52]Katzenstein 1987, p. 91. The law is the Stability and Growth Act of 1967 (Gesetz zur Förderung der Stabilität und des Wachstums der Wirtschaft).

appoint someone to the CEE who has a political affiliation or is affiliated with the unions, employers, or firms.[53]

The second prominent semi-public economic policy research organization is the Bundesbank—the German central bank—whose responsibility among other things is to advise the federal government on matters of monetary policy. Since 1999 it has been part of the European Monetary Union system sharing responsibility for the euro. The Bundesbank is reputed to have more economic expertise and analytic capacity than all the federal ministries combined. Although half of the six-member executive board is appointed by the federal government and the other half by the Bundesrat, the Bundesbank is independent of instructions from the government and is politically nonpartisan.[54]

The CEE and Bundesbank help to neutralize a policy sector that the Germans think requires "a particularly high degree of substantive knowledge uncontaminated by partisan politics."[55] However, they have long been associated with conservative economic policy views, at least within the context of the German social market economy. Since the 1970s the CEE has favored self-regulating markets, distrusted Keynesian aggregate demand management, and believed that high wages cause unemployment. Nevertheless, the CEE has remained politically neutral. It has not hesitated to criticize governments in power regardless of whether they were run by the SPD, CDU/CSU, or both.[56] The Bundesbank has long been committed to strict monetary policy—a position that emerged full-blown in the mid-1970s in response to a Keynesian public sector wage hike in 1968–69 that contributed to a serious bout of inflation.[57]

Ministerial Research Units

There are several state research organizations in Germany. As is typical of our other European countries, the federal ministries have their own policy research capacities. In the United States, many of the state research organizations that we visited and heard about were not part of a particular cabinet department.

[53]Interview and email correspondence with Wolfgang Franz, CEE. In off-the-record email correspondence with someone else we learned that nobody with strong leftist tendencies would have a chance of being appointed.

[54]Its analytic capacities were augmented by the founding in 2000 of the Bundesbank's Research Center, whose advisory boards include 12 people with PhDs, all but one of whom hold university appointments. It has a research staff of about 60 PhDs (http://www.bundesbank.de/index. en.php. Accessed October 2011). The Bundesbank is said to be more independent from the government and interest groups than central banks in most other advanced industrial countries due to Germany's disastrous experiences with inflation (Katzenstein 1987, pp. 60–64, 116).

[55]Katzenstein 1987, p. 59.

[56]Katzenstein 1987, p. 63.

[57]Streeck 2009, p. 57. According to Claus Schäfer, WSI, this was a turning point for German economic policy analysis because this "[i]n practical politics was the beginning of the neoliberal wave in Germany." Before this, however, the Central Bank Law of 1957 required that the Bundesbank's foremost objective was maintaining monetary stability.

But virtually every ministry in Germany has at least one research unit and some have more than one, bringing the total number to about 50 such units. These organizations do serious social science research, including surveys and other forms of data collection as well as sophisticated quantitative analyses.[58] Beginning in 2004 they were evaluated periodically by the German Council of Science and Humanities (Wissenschaftsrat) to ensure high standards of scientific research. This is the same organization that evaluates the universities. Ministerial research units enjoy some discretion in setting their own research agendas, although, of course, they also do work requested of them by their ministries. In some cases they help universities train researchers in degree-granting academic programs, which is further testament to the rigorous nature of their research capabilities.[59]

For our purposes one of the most important state research organizations is in the Ministry of Economics and Technology, which issues a high-profile annual forecast of the German economy and consults during its preparation with other ministries as well as CEE. The ministry's analytic capacities are said to be as good as those found in these other organizations.[60] However, it also commissions an elite group of the semi-public scholarly research institutes to issue additional forecasts—the Joint Economic Reports.[61] We will have more to say about this later. Relying on work done by semi-public scholarly research organizations is something that other ministries do too at both the federal and Länder levels.[62]

Party Foundations

Affiliated with each of the main political parties is a party foundation, most of which were set up after the Second World War by public decree.[63] There is nothing like this in the United States or in Denmark. In France the party foundations are substantially less developed and younger than those in Germany. The Social Democrats have the Friedrich Ebert Foundation, the Christian Democrats have the Konrad Adenauer Foundation, the CSU has the Hanns Seidel Foundation, and the FDP has the Friedrich Naumann Foundation. The Green Party has the Heinrich Böll Foundation, and the Left Party has the Rosa

[58]Some cabinet departments in the United States have research capacities too, such as the Treasury. In America, however, there are also research organizations, such as the Congressional Budget Office, that provide research capacities for any politician in Congress, so one does not need to go through a particular cabinet to get research. There is virtually nothing like this in our European countries, where such requests are directed to the appropriate ministry, vetted, and either approved or not.
[59]Interview with senior official, SOWI.
[60]Interview with senior official, BMWI.
[61]Day 2000; Gellner 1998.
[62]Weilemann 2000, p. 174.
[63]Weilemann 2000, p. 174.

Luxemburg Foundation. Most of the foundations were established initially to promote civic and political education, conflict resolution, the party system, democracy, and freedom.[64] Each one espouses its party's ideals at home and abroad. Each one has an in-house policy research capacity, sometimes referred to as a think tank.[65]

As in France, much party foundation think tank work is dedicated to big, programmatic ideas rather than technical analysis and forecasting like the more scholarly economic research institutes do. Some do public opinion polling, voting behavior studies, and research on other aspects of political culture. But economic research is not a large part of their portfolios.[66] When we asked what the relationship was between the foundation think tanks and the political parties we learned that the foundations "try to offer ideas which might not find their way into the daily political work."[67] The emphasis on big ideas was especially clear when we discussed these things at the Konrad Adenauer Foundation (KAS) where people complained that the Friedrich Ebert Foundation (FES) was trying to appropriate the concept of the social market economy from them and meld it with social democratic discourse. This was a contest over one of the biggest ideas guiding German policymakers since the 1950s. And, according to a senior official from KAS, "This is really what the foundations can do. . . . We can really put our finger on the basic principles. We can do that basic work."[68] The focus on big ideas was emphasized by Peter Donaiski at FES when he insisted that although they meet with ministers and politicians it was not to lobby for a client's narrow interests but to advocate big ideas for solving basic social problems like saving social security systems.

The relationship between the foundations and their parties is ambiguous. First, their funding comes not from the party but from the state.[69] Yet

[64]The Friedrich Ebert Foundation was established in 1925, later disbanded by the Nazis, and reconstituted in 1947. Founding dates for the rest are as follows: Friedrich Naumann Foundation (1958), Konrad Adenauer Foundation (1964), Hanns Seidel Foundation (1967), Heinrich Böll Foundation (1989), and Rosa Luxemburg Foundation (1996).

[65]Interview with Peter Donaiski, FES.

[66]Weilemann 2000, pp. 179–82. Much of their energy, instead, goes toward organizing conferences, seminars, and discussion groups. KAS claims to sponsor 2,500 such events with 145,000 participants per year (http://www.kas.de. Accessed May 2009) while Hanns Seidel notes that over 1 million people have participated in its events in Germany alone over the past 40 years (HSS annual report 2007). The Friedrich Ebert Foundation reports that 150,000 people visited its 3,000 events in 2006 (FES annual report 2007, p. 17).

[67]Interview with Peter Donaiski, FES.

[68]Dieter Plehwe, WZB, confirmed that that the Social Democratic Party had moved to appropriate the Christian Democrats' notion of the social market economy but in a way that was supposed to lead to the "social democratization of the social market economy." Rolf Kroker, IW, and a senior official, INSM, agreed.

[69]Interview with Peter Donaiski, FES. He explained that according to a long-standing informal agreement the party requests finical support for its foundation from parliament. Then a group of parliamentarians determines how much money each party gets. Most of the money is distributed

the amount of money each foundation receives is roughly proportional to the number of seats its party holds in the Bundestag. Hence, in 2007 FES and KAS spent $166 million and $138 million, respectively, while the Heinrich Böll Foundation spent only about $60.4 million.[70] Second, the constitutional court ruled that the foundations cannot take specific orders or requests from party leaders or otherwise do their party's bidding because they are supported by public money and, therefore, ought to operate in the country's interests as a whole.[71] Yet the foundations have party members on their boards. KAS, for example, which is affiliated with the CDU, has had two CDU chancellors, Angela Merkel and Helmut Kohl, on its board.[72] Moreover, KAS is well aware of the party's interests because the board reviews and approves the KAS annual plan—a process that often involves negotiation between the board and KAS administrators. Moreover, according to the Heinrich Böll Foundation's Andreas Poltermann, the parties try to "use the foundation as a platform for public statements of their party politicians. . . . So the foundations see themselves as megaphones, as platforms, instruments of public dissemination of political or party information." Particularly when a party falls out of power it encourages its foundation to take a more aggressive role in public debate to help the party compensate for its loss of access to ministerial capacities and for its diminished voice in the policymaking process.[73] Summing things up, our contact at KAS said, "We are near to the party. The party people know us very well. We know the party very well. We are partisan. But we don't do work directly for the party, so we set up our own agenda."

Advocacy Research Organizations

Germany does not have an extensive tradition of privately funded advocacy policy research organizations like the United States. This is because the party foundations have a well-funded political mandate to develop policy analysis and advice and provide public education, because there are relatively few private foundations so financing for private research organizations is limited, and

---

to the foundations through the Ministry of the Interior, but occasionally other ministries depending on the nature of the party's request.

[70] Data are from annual reports from FES 2007, KAS 2007, and HBS 2007. See also Braml (2004, chap. 4). Because the foundation budgets pay for much more than just their think tank activities, including maintaining offices abroad, it is difficult to gauge how well funded their think tank operations are, but we suspect that it is small. One source told us off the record that one of the major party foundations spent only about 3% of its budget on its think tank.

[71] Interview with Peter Donaiski, FES. A senior official from KAS, which is close to the Christian Democratic Union, explained, "If I would get a letter from Angela Merkel [CDU Chancellor] in which she would write 'Please give me some good hints for my speech for the next campaign,' I would have to say 'No' because this would be a crime that I would commit . . . and this is prohibited."

[72] Its 2007 annual report notes that of KAS's 22 board of directors members 17 are party members.

[73] Interview with senior official, KAS.

because the state funds most of the economic policy research institutes anyway.[74] Nevertheless, there is a small set of private advocacy policy research organizations. Prominent among them are a few public relations firms, such as the Initiative New Social Market Economy (INSM), which was established in 1999 with about $11.7 million (€9 million) per year by Gesamtmetall, the metal working industry's trade association.[75] INSM specializes in cultivating favorable media coverage for neoliberal policies and has what it calls a think tank that often outsources research especially to IW and then disseminates the results through the media.[76] As such INSM's emphasis is clearly on public relations and marketing ideas rather than producing them itself. There are only a few other organizations like INSM. Their intent is to influence not policymakers directly but the public discourse to which they believe policymakers pay close attention.[77]

There are also advocacy research organizations associated with private foundations like the Bertelsmann Foundation and the Quandt Foundation, which are largely family owned and have their own think tanks.[78] The Bertelsmann Foundation, for instance, was established in 1977 by Reinhard Mohn, whose family owns 23% of Bertelsmann AG, the publishing conglomerate. It is the largest private nonprofit foundation in Germany. It funds itself through its majority ownership of Bertelsmann AG and describes itself as "both a think tank and an agent for social change" that runs projects on federalism, democracy, European integration, globalization, corporate social responsibility, and more. Its operating budget in 2005 was roughly $68 million.[79] Some business foundations, such as the Vodafone Foundation, also have advocacy think tanks. Despite their advocacy orientation people told us that some of them do scholarly research. In some cases, respected economists advise them on research, such as Rolf Langhammer from the Kiel Institute who sits on advisory boards of the Bertelsmann's Transformation Index and Sustainable Government Index.[80] In contrast to INSM, the foundations have much more money

[74]Braml 2004, chaps. 4, 9; Gellner 1998; Weilemann 2000, p. 169.
[75]http://www.insm.de. Accessed April 2011; Streeck 2009, pp. 50, 84–85.
[76]Interviews with Rolf Kroker, IW, and senior official, INSM. INSM and IW work so closely together that they refer to each other on their websites and have offices in the same building. Both share a deep belief in the need for a renaissance of the more conservative elements of the social market economy model. Hence, INSM's name refers to the *new* social market economy.
[77]Interviews with Rudolf Zwiener, IMK; Dieter Plehwe, WZB; Peter Donaiski, FES.
[78]Braml 2004, p. 60. Party foundations are financed by the state, while private foundations are self-financed. Hence, they constitute different legal entities in Germany (Weilemann 2000, p. 174).
[79]http://www.bertelsmann-stiftung.org. Accessed April 2011.
[80]Email correspondence with Rolf Langhammer, IfW.

and in-house research capacity.[81] They also confer directly with policymakers. And they are more open about their ideological positions whereas, INSM tries to, "hide who they really are."[82]

Another advocacy organization to which people often referred that tries to push big ideas on to the policy agenda is the Foundation Market Economy (SM). It is located in central Berlin near parliament so that its staff can easily maintain personal contacts with parliamentarians, learn what issues are important for them, and then respond to these issues quickly with short policy briefs. Like INSM, SM is a small organization with only about a half dozen people on staff, so it outsources much of its research. It too is primarily focused on marketing rather than producing ideas. But it also convenes working groups and seminars with professors and people from business to gather data and generate policy ideas, such as a commission it organized to study tax reform. Like other advocacy research organizations, SM relies entirely on private funding.[83]

Recall that the party foundations do not lobby in the narrow sense of the term. It is important as well to distinguish all of these advocacy research organizations from lobbyists, which press politicians for narrow changes in the law as they do in the United States. INSM's managing director, for example, insisted that his organization was more interested in pushing big agenda-setting ideas because the firms nowadays do their own lobbying. So there is a division of labor between the broad public relations work that his and other advocacy research organizations do and the more narrow special interest lobbying that firms do. In his words:

> We are not a lobby. For instance, we don't talk to politicians and say well, please change part of 273A in this way and this word we need. That's not our business. . . . Our business is to make agendas I think for topics we really need and owners [of firms] want.

Similarly, although SM's modus operandi is to meet personally with members of parliament and the ministries to advocate various policy positions, their intent is not to press for narrow changes in the law on behalf of a particular client, but to advance large policy ideas, such as their big tax reform plan, that are shared by most German firms. According to an SM senior official, "We are lobbyists lobbying for an idea, not for interests, special interests, but for an idea. And our idea is to have a little bit more market liberty, of market

---

[81] Interview with senior official, INSM.
[82] Interview with Peter Donaiski, FES. Neither Bertelsmann nor INSM wanted to grant us interviews. We got one at INSM only when we spotted one of its officials in an elevator that we happened to share while we were going to another interview. We had lunch with him later.
[83] Interview with senior official, SM.

economy in Germany. So this is something we're fighting for." To underscore the point he emphasized, "We don't lobby for companies and for special interests." So, as in France where we heard much the same thing from clubs and advocacy organizations, the term "lobbyist" has several meanings and does not carry a strict legal definition as it does in the United States.[84]

Universities

In keeping with Germany's tradition of policy dialogue informed by rational and objective expertise, universities are more involved in the German knowledge regime than they are in France or the United States because many of the scholarly research institutes are closely affiliated with them.[85] Some, such as WSI, IMK, and ZEW, have university professors on their boards of advisors and in top managerial positions. Their staff lectures at universities. They provide fellowships for training PhD candidates, whose advisors sit in universities, and they hire people working on postdoctoral habilitation degrees.[86] Some research institutes have formal cooperation agreements with universities.[87] According to Wolfgang Franz, ZEW's president, this sort of relationship has become increasingly common over the past 20 years at ZEW and similar institutes including Kiel, Ifo, and DIW. For instance, Ifo signed formal cooperation agreements with the University of Munich and a few others to expand doctoral training and appoint professors to head all Ifo departments. Ifo also established the LMU-Ifo Economics and Business Data Center with the Ludwig Maximilian University in Munich—a joint venture designed to be a hub for applied policy research and scholarship.[88] So, in contrast to places like Brookings and the American Enterprise Institute in the United States, whose staff have informal and ad hoc relationships with people in universities, many of the best German economic research institutes have more formal associations with universities that transcend individual collaborations and specific research projects. The party foundations and some ministerial research units also have contacts with university academics to whom they outsource work or collaborate in other ways.[89]

[84]Interview with senior official, SM.

[85]Braml 2004, p. 58.

[86]Interviews with Claus Schäfer, WSI; Rudolf Zwiener, IMK. The German university system awards a PhD and a habilitation, which is equivalent to a second PhD.

[87]Braml 2004, chap 6. Ifo cooperates with universities in Munich, Dresden, Konstanz, and elsewhere (Ifo annual reports 2007, pp. 7–8, 2006, p. 2). Kiel runs an annual workshop with the Massachusetts Institute of Technology (IfW annual report 1997, p. 61). IAB cooperates with universities in Bocconi, Nottingham, Warsaw, Konstanz, and more (IAB Yearbook 2007, p. 196).

[88]Email correspondence with Meinhard Knoche, Ifo, interview with senior official, Ifo, and Ifo annual report 2007 (pp. 7–8).

[89]Interview with senior official, KAS. SOWI cooperates with the University of Potsdam among various German universities (SOWI Yearbook 2007, pp. 29–31).

Universities also affect the knowledge regime by providing top managerial talent for many of the best scholarly policy research organizations. Klaus Zimmermann who runs DIW explained:

> Most of the people who are now presidents of these institutes in Germany have been either at the same university on the same faculty or have been close in other ways. Just to give you an example, both Hans-Werner Sinn [Ifo president] and I were with Wolfgang Franz [ZEW president] once sitting all on the same floor at the University of Mannheim.

There is certainly much career mobility and networking among these organizations as there is in our other countries.[90] Importantly, however, in contrast to the United States, where there was a lot of mobility between private and government organizations, we found little of this in Germany. After all, Germany like France has a well-established career civil service at high levels in the state, so the sort of revolving door that swings between public and private organizations in America is largely absent in Germany. If there is a revolving door in Germany it is between semi-public policy research organizations and universities.[91]

Despite their close connections with universities, the work that most semi-public policy research organizations do differs from traditional university social science research as it does in our other countries. Their work is applied. In the words of the Kiel Institute's vice president, "We are doing applied research so we are sticking always to problems, actual problems. We are not doing state of the art, let's say for the art itself but we are trying to solve problems."

But in this regard two other research organizations are worth mentioning briefly even though they do not do much applied research. One is the Max Planck Institute for the Study of Societies (MPIfG) in Cologne, which does research in the area of comparative political economy and economic sociology. Its funding comes from the Max Planck Society, an umbrella organization supporting German research institutes mostly in the natural sciences. Because the society's funding comes from the Länder and federal government, MPIfG is another semi-public organization. So is the Berlin Social Science Research Center (WZB), which gets roughly 75% of its funding from the federal government and 25% from the Berlin state.[92] MPIfG belongs to a summer school consortium with Northwestern University, Sciences Po, and the European University institute, and has a joint doctoral training program with Sciences Po. WZB has joint programs with the University of Toronto, Humboldt University,

90 Interviews with senior officials, BMWI and SOWI.
91 See also Braml (2004, chaps. 3, 6) and Weilemann (2000, pp. 174, 180).
92 Email correspondence with Dieter Plehwe, WZB.

and Harvard.[93] We mention them because despite their strong emphasis on basic rather than applied social science research they have felt pressure to contribute to the applied policy-related debates in the media and elsewhere. At MPIfG the pressure came from one of its supervisory boards while at WZB it was greater and came from a new president, Jutta Allmendinger.[94] Occasionally, researchers from both organizations provide advice and information to public officials, but this is not a routine practice and both organizations have shied away from an explicit political or ideological agenda.[95]

To review, the specificity of Germany's political economy infused its knowledge regime with several features not seen in our other countries. Consider the policymaking regime's effects. The party foundations were established by public decree. Their funding—and by extension their think tanks' funding—is a function of the distribution of seats among parties in the Bundestag. And the constitutional court ensured that the foundations have a modicum of independence from the parties. Furthermore, German federalism affected the arrangement of the semi-public scholarly policy research organizations, which were spread among and often established and financed by the Länder states. Of course, all of this reflected German corporatism insofar as the public authorities frequently off-loaded important policy advising functions to organizations in civil society upon which they conferred status and resources. The fact that ministries solicited work from these policy research organizations, such as by commissioning the Joint Economic Reports and consulting with CEE, is another corporatist echo. For all these reasons semi-public policy research organizations were far more central to the German knowledge regime than they were in either the United States or France.

The production regime also had effects, and again corporatism was important. First, the fact that labor and employer associations are expected to participate in tripartite corporatist policy discussions means that they recognize the benefits of having their own sources of policy analysis and ideas, which is why they support their own policy research organizations. Notably, labor has IMK and WSI while business has IW.[96] Second, advocacy research organizations are a newly emergent and still marginal phenomenon in Germany's knowledge regime. They have not been particularly necessary due to state funding for party foundations and the various semi-public research or-

[93]Interview with Jutta Allmendinger, WZB.
[94]She explained to us that this was not easy and she had to enlist the aid of an internationally renowned WZB researcher—Ralf Dahrendorf—to help coax department heads on her behalf. We were told off the record by someone else outside the organization that the staff she inherited has been reluctant to follow her back toward applied policy research, so she has had to settle for them doing a bit of public relations.
[95]Interviews with Jutta Allmendinger and Dagmar Simon, WZB; senior official, MPIfG.
[96]Interviews with senior official, KAS; senior official, MPIfG. See also Thunert (2000).

ganizations. But thanks to the recent sponsorship of corporations and private foundations that, as we shall see later, sought new ways to influence policy-making, advocacy research organizations have started to appear.

The emergence of these advocacy organizations was a response by those people who believed in effect that the knowledge regime's complementary relationship to the rest of the political economy had slipped badly—perceptions based on the premise that German corporatism was in crisis and no longer able to manage the problems associated with the end of the Golden Age and the rise of globalization. But before we get to this story we need to discuss the comparatively high level of coordination and compromise we found in the German knowledge regime.

Coordination and Compromise in Economic Policy Analysis

Germany is famous for the corporatist and other formal institutions by which political-economic activity is coordinated and compromise achieved. Not surprisingly then, we found in Germany's knowledge regime formal mechanisms that coordinate policy analysis and advising in ways that facilitate compromise among the experts. But there were informal mechanisms too. Coordination in the interest of compromise was especially evident in the case of the three major economic forecasts that have informed policymaking for many decades: the Joint Economic Report, the Ministry of Economics and Technology's report, and CEE's report. But it was also apparent in other annual deliberations.

The Joint Economic Report

Since the 1950s the state has commissioned the Joint Economic Report (*Gemeinschaft Diagnose*).[97] Every three years the Ministry of Economics and Technology hires four or five scholarly policy research organizations to collaborate and develop a set of economic forecasts and policy recommendations. Twice a year this group produces a 50- to 100-page Joint Economic Report to that effect. The ministry uses it to verify its own forecasts and help make sense of the economic situation.

Organizations want this job not only because the ministry pays but because being part of the forecasting group is a status marker for doing high-quality work. Selection is based on an organization's scientific prowess.[98] Rudolf

---

[97]Interview with Wolfgang Franz, ZEW.
[98]Interviews with senior officials, BMWI and Ifo; Rolf Langhammer, IfW. Historically, members of the Joint Economic Report group were from the Leibniz Association and its predecessor the Blue List—prestigious scientific associations that include only research organizations whose work is of the highest caliber.

Zwiener from IMK said that in order to be selected, "You have to prove that you have the experience and the staff to be able to do the proper work." Politics, in his view, is not so important—something of which he is confident because IMK, a left-leaning organization associated with the unions, was picked recently for the job by a conservative government. However, Klaus Zimmermann, president of DIW, was less sanguine. DIW was dropped recently from the group after having been a member for years. Zimmermann said that the official reason was that they were "too expensive." But he suspected that it was really politics.[99]

Once the ministry picks the group each of the participating institutes generates its own forecast. Then the institutes meet behind closed doors to resolve their differences and try to reach a compromise. DIW's Zimmermann explained that everybody shows up with their own forecasts, models, and analytic assumptions. The forecasts may differ. But because the government demands consensus on the forecast they all negotiate until they reach a compromise. In the end, he said, "It's like a policy process." This is an example of formal coordination leading to compromise. But informal mechanisms are also involved.

The first involves anticipation of the process itself. Because the ministry insists that the report is based on agreement, each research institute tends to temper the forecasts and policy recommendations it brings into the process in the first place. The idea is to avoid taking extreme positions unless you are absolutely convinced that you are right. IMK's Rudolf Zwiener explained that the result of this kind of informal strategic game is an agreement that is "not a very deep one in a way" because most participants tend to avoid the issues that might undermine it. A representative from Ifo surmised that the recent introduction of teams of forecasting organizations into the process rather than just individual organizations, which we discuss later, amplified this tendency for compromise insofar as team members must reach agreement internally before meeting with the other organizations to negotiate the Joint Economic Report.[100]

A second informal mechanism by which coordination and compromise has become more likely involves the evolution of professional economics. We have more to say about this later too, but for now what is important is that we were told that German economists have resolved many of their basic differences over the past 20 years. One person explained, "The whole profession, I think,

---

[99]Interview with Klaus Zimmermann, DIW. Others we spoke with suspected off the record that DIW was dropped because Zimmermann fired the head of his forecasting department, Gustav Horn, a die-hard Keynesian who appeared often on television and may have been fired because he was a public nuisance for Zimmermann. Ironically, after Horn left he set up IMK, which became a member of the Joint Economic Report group.
[100]Interview with senior official, Ifo.

has moved away a bit from the big controversies to a more synthetic view."[101] Another said that this involved monetarists gradually eclipsing Keynesians in many ways—at least until the 2008 financial crisis—such that the big differences among research institutes have largely dissipated and in turn compromise within the Joint Economic Report has been easier to achieve.[102]

However, despite these changes and compromises some disagreements persist. In particular, there are still disputes over the meaning of the social market economy and especially the need for egalitarian redistribution and welfare state spending.[103] But disagreements among participants in the process now tend to be about policy recommendations rather than forecasts. IMK's Rudolf Zwiener spoke about this noting, "It's easy as long as it is a forecasting part. But it's very difficult as soon as you have to agree on the policy part. . . . In the policy part you have differences and cannot agree." This is especially true, he said, for labor market policy. Notably, IMK, one of the last bastions of Keynesianism, has found it difficult to find common ground with the others involved, such as the Kiel Institute. Nevertheless, some sort of compromise is usually reached in the end and has become more common over the past 20 years. Indeed, there are fewer dissenting minority reports attached to the Joint Economic Report than there used to be.[104] The broad point, however, is that preparation of the report involves formal and informal means of coordination that facilitate compromise.[105]

The Ministry Forecast

The Ministry of Economics and Technology also prepares major economic forecasts and policy recommendations (*Jahrlische Wirtschaftsberichte*) on a regular basis. As noted earlier, the Joint Economic Report provides a touchstone for the ministry. One ministry official said, "The forecasting done by the institutes is more or less a point of departure for our own forecast." And he continued, "We want to do a credible forecast of our own and for that purpose it is very helpful to be quite close to forecasts done by, well, the experts in a number of institutes."[106] There are a couple of informal coordination mechanisms that help align the two reports.

[101] Interview with senior research, IfW.
[102] Interview with Rolf Kroker, IW. Not all German economists are in such agreement. Several dozen economists signed an open letter, reported in the *Frankfurter Allgemeine Zeitung* newspaper, calling for an overhaul of the German economics curriculum in light of the 2008 financial crisis—an initiative we were told at IfW that was linked to the University of Cologne, whose economics department had long been heterodox in orientation.
[103] Ptak 2009, pp. 125–26.
[104] Interviews with senior official, Ifo; Rolf Langhammer, IfW; senior researcher, IfW.
[105] Interview with Rolf Langhammer, Kiel Institute.
[106] Interview with senior official, BMWI.

The first involves a "silent observer." This person is from the ministry's forecasting department and is an expert in statistical analysis, data, and forecasting. The observer attends various meetings of the Joint Economic Report group in order to keep the ministry apprised of what is going on but does not contribute to the group's discussion or try to influence its proceedings. As such, the ministry gains a sense of the Joint Economic Report before it is released. Not only does this information help the ministry bring its own forecasts more into line with the Joint Economic Report in the first place, but it provides the ministry with methodological information that can be very helpful if it has to explain serious discrepancies between the two reports should they arise.[107] Not surprisingly, however, such discrepancies have become rare.[108]

The second mechanism by which the two reports are coordinated and major discrepancies are avoided involves informal personal networks. Economic forecasters tend to know each other professionally. This facilitates a certain amount of informal back-channel communication between the forecasters from the ministry and from the Joint Economic Report group about how they are conducting their work, if not what their results might be.[109] Overall, then, these two informal coordinating mechanisms facilitate tacit compromise between the two groups and the two reports tend to align with each other.

The Council of Economic Experts Report

CEE also prepares an extensive economic forecast for the government each year. It is several hundred pages long and contains far more analysis of economic policies than the Joint Economic Reports.[110] Its preparation involves several informal coordination mechanisms that facilitate compromise and moderation.

Two mechanisms involve the selection of CEE members. First, in a soft echo of German corporatism, the appointment of one of its five members is subject to the informal approval of the trade unions while a second appointment is subject to the informal approval of the employer associations.[111] The remaining three seats are simply filled with an eye toward assembling a wide range of competencies and fields of expertise among the members. Second, the norm is to appoint people who are moderate in their thinking and thus open to compromise. Wolfgang Franz, who was in his third term on the CEE and the chairman when we interviewed him, was a classic example of such a person.

---

[107]Interview with senior official, BMWI.

[108] Interview with Rolf Langhammer, IfW.

[109]Interview with senior official, BMWI.

[110]Interview with senior official, BMWI.

[111]In email correspondence Dieter Plehwe, WZB, pointed out that having a single labor-sensitive member on CEE was not enough for the trade union movement, which established a Memorandum Group, which shadows the official CEE reports with counter-expertise.

The unions had blessed his first stint on the council, while the employers had done so for his second and third stints.[112] All of this lends credence to the notion that the CEE is an "honest broker" seeking to moderate differences of opinion and facilitate compromise among the social partners.[113]

A third mechanism that enables compromise is a number of informal meetings and back-channel consultations with other experts often facilitated by personal networks. CEE staff meet frequently with staff from the research institutes preparing the Joint Economic Report and others to discuss econometric modeling and how to improve the methods that they all use. In Wolfgang Franz's words:

> The people from the staff of the Council frequently meet with one or another persons of the research institutes . . . exchanging ideas about modeling. For example, we have a huge macroeconometric model and the institutes, of course, have a similar model. And they exchange ideas about the problems and how to improve these models and the like. . . . They are in frequent contact by meeting personally or by telephoning or making calls and the like.

In addition, the CEE meets at least once a year with the heads of these research institutes to discuss and make sense of the current economic situation. They get a good idea of what each other's forecasts will look like.[114] Communication like this makes compromise and occasionally consensus more likely insofar as people tend to learn from each other and therefore adopt similar analytic strategies. This tendency, of course, is augmented by the transformation of the economics profession noted earlier insofar as members of the council as well as other economists agree increasingly on basic economic and methodological principles. According to Wolfgang Franz, for this reason and because researchers increasingly use the same data most forecasts from the CEE, Joint Economic Report group and the Ministry of Economics and Technology have grown rather similar over the past 20 years.

The January Meeting and ARGE

Informal communication between scholarly policy research organizations and ministries is common in Germany.[115] The most encompassing of these is an informal meeting that the Ministry of Economics and Technology convenes behind closed doors each January. Representatives from the major economic

[112]Interview and email correspondence with Wolfgang Franz, CEE.
[113]Katzenstein 1987, p. 73.
[114]See also Katzenstein (1987, pp. 63–64).
[115]Interview with Martin Dietz, IAB.

research institutes and ministries as well as other experts are invited. Usually 50 to 60 people attend. In an effort to prevent politicizing the conversation too much people from the labor unions and employer associations are not invited. Nor are representatives from CEE. The Bundesbank is represented but not other financial institutions.[116]

The purpose of the meeting is to help everyone make sense of the economic situation for the coming year and to solicit views on timely topics, such as the international financial crisis when we visited Germany. The discussion is confidential. Nothing is published from the meeting. It is designed simply as a time for information sharing among the experts and government. Hence, the meeting is an informally coordinated gathering. Whether this helps facilitate compromise among those in the room on analytic or policy issues is unclear from our interviews. But maintaining ongoing dialogue like this has often helped forge compromise in other areas in postwar Germany.[117]

Two similar events are organized annually by the German Consortium of Economic Research Institutes (ARGE). Consistent with the German corporatism, ARGE is a formal association representing the economic research institutes including those in universities and a few other organizations.[118] ARGE meetings enable members to discuss common interests and coordinate some activities. More important, ARGE convenes two meetings each year to present analysis and discuss economic policy issues with representatives from the ministries. One meeting is broadly focused while the other attends to a special topic, such as the financial crisis, which was on tap for the 2010 meeting. As with the January meeting, the government uses these gatherings to hear what the other institutes think about the state of the economy as it tries to make sense of the situation.[119]

Let us pause and put all of this into analytic perspective. Several mechanisms help coordinate economic forecasting and policy advising among the most prominent scholarly policy research organizations and the state, and in ways that tend to enhance the possibilities for compromise. Some are formal and stem from the policymaking regime, such as the official mandate that the Joint Economic Report group reach a consensus on its forecasts and policy recommendations. But many are informal, including the Ministry of Economics and Technology's January meeting, its silent observer, and back-channel communications among experts in various research organizations, including

[116]Interview with senior official, BMWI.

[117]For discussions of how continued dialogue has helped facilitate compromise in Germany, see Shonfield (1965, chap. 9) and Streeck (1997a). For more general discussion of how continuing dialogue can facilitate political compromise, see Piore (1995), Sabel (1993), and Sabel et al. (2000).

[118]http://www.arge-institute.de. Accessed April 2011. ARGE stands for Arbeitsgemeinschaft Deutscher Wirtschaftswissenschaftlicher Forschungsinstitute.

[119]Interviews with senior official, BMWI; Klaus Zimmermann, DIW; Wolfgang Franz, ZEW.

those that facilitate agreement on research and forecasting methods. Other mechanisms reflect the production regime's corporatism, such as the informal consultation with business and labor over appointments to CEE. Certainly corporatism's influence is evident in all of these examples but especially insofar as the state seeks input from well-organized groups of experts in civil society, such as the Joint Economic Report group and ARGE, many of which it convenes and finances. Most of these mechanisms of coordination and consultation are long-standing, which means that compared to our other countries Germany's knowledge regime has remained rather stable over the past 20 years or so.

One curiosity about our German interviews was that almost nobody mentioned the role of commissions as coordinating mechanisms. Yet commissions are common in Germany. The Bundestag can establish commissions that involve members of different political parties and outside experts to investigate important economic, social, and other issues. They prepare a consensus report for parliament, which requires resolving political and ideological differences among members.[120] Ministries can also convene commissions consisting of experts and representatives from different interest groups to investigate problems defined by the ministry. These are far more common than the Bundestag commissions.[121] For example, the famous Hartz Commission, established in 2002 by Chancellor Gerhard Schröder, examined possibilities for labor market reform.[122] Both types of commissions are formal organizations that are designed to facilitate compromise and consensus on various policy issues.

We do not view the German case as a Panglossian world. First, the tendencies for compromise among policy research organizations should not be exaggerated. After all, Keynesian, neoliberal, and other views are still represented among them.[123] Second, conformity within the economics profession can sometimes lead it astray. Soon after the 2008 financial crisis it became clear that conformism had led to forecasts that were largely incorrect. Moreover, subsequent forecasts varied more widely because new information was constantly becoming available and the economic situation was very uncertain.[124] But we were still impressed by how often we found evidence about compromise when it came to forecasting and policy advising.

---

[120]http://www.bundestag.de/bundestag/ausschuesse17/gremien/enquete/index.jsp. Accessed January 2012.

[121]Tiefken 2007. In 1990 there were 189 ministerial commissions, and in 1998 there were 127.

[122]The Hartz Commission was not as tripartite as most. It was composed of 15 experts—2 academics and 13 members from trade unions, management consultancies, company managing boards, and political and economic circles. The two most important employer and business associations—BDA and BDI—did not participate.

[123]Interviews with Wolfgang Franz, ZEW; Klaus Zimmermann, DIW; Rolf Kroker, IW.

[124]Interview with Wolfgang Franz, CEE and email correspondence with senior official, MPIfG.

Coordination and Economic Science

As noted earlier, one factor that facilitated better coordination and more compromise was that economists in the ministries and semi-public policy research organizations came to see things more eye to eye than they had previously. This stemmed partly from policymakers' demands for better scientific advice with which to understand the complexities of globalization. But it also stemmed from the state's efforts to elevate through accreditation the quality of work done by the research institutes in the wake of a monumental shift in the German political economy—the unification of East and West Germany.

Demands for Scientific Policy Advice

We were told frequently that over the past couple of decades policymakers had demanded more scientific policy analysis.[125] Martin Dietz, who studies labor market policy for IAB, explained why:

> I think here in Germany during the last, I don't know, ten years perhaps the role of scientific research changed very much in the political process. Before that nobody was interested in what research was saying and especially in labor market policy. But then they started to think, okay, we are spending so much money to deal with labor market problems and we don't really know . . . if the money is spent in the right way.

Rolf Kroker from IW was most explicit in connecting more sophisticated analysis with political demands. Referring to the need for presenting the best analysis possible he explained, "If you don't have numbers and figures . . . you will not reach the politicians." Ministry officials confirmed the greater demand for scientific analysis. One told us that it was related as well to the more complex nature of the problems policymakers faced after the Golden Age and during the rise of globalization:

> One of the biggest changes is that ministries rely more on this scientific expertise than they relied in the time before because in today's world to make political decisions, the decisions are more complex than they were decades ago, and you need more and more scientific expertise to make the right decisions. I think this is the general trend in politics.[126]

[125]Interviews with senior official, MPIfG; Wolfgang Franz, ZEW; Rolf Kroker, IW; Ulrich Walwei, IAB.
[126]Interview with senior official, SOWI.

As a result of the increased demand for scientific policy analysis to make sense of a more complex world, the quality of that analysis improved. According to Meinhard Knoche from Ifo, "In terms of methodology there has been a process of change in the past 15 years in the direction of stronger scientific underpinnings, which has affected the economic research institutes." The IW's Rolf Kroker agreed: "Empirically oriented research has increased dramatically . . . not only in our institute but in other institutes too." The chairman of CEE gave a very specific example. Twenty years ago, he said, the CEE annual report contained virtually no econometric analysis. In his words, "In former times it was more that general or more plausible economic arguments [were made] where they presented good arguments, of course, but by and large without numbers." Nowadays, however, the CEE reports contain numerous equations, data, and methodological appendixes.[127]

All of this involved a more open dialogue among different branches of the economics profession, which paved the way for a degree of analytic consensus among them. Business cycle models, for instance, now take into consideration structural changes that may affect economic performance. Similarly, economists agreed more on what constituted appropriate methodology and data—both of which have become increasingly sophisticated.[128] Notably, most research institutes now accept the need for microeconomic as well as macroeconomic modeling. Finally, most German economists now recognize that they must consider the impact of economic globalization in their analyses.[129] All of these adjustments and compromises occurred as economists tried to make sense of an increasingly complex, difficult, and uncertain economic environment following the end of the Golden Age. Of course, more convergent analytic thinking was facilitated as well by advances in computing power and the availability of better data, particularly open-source data from the OECD, IMF, Eurostat, and other statistical offices.[130]

The point is that the shift toward more sophisticated scientific policy analysis dampened policy disagreements among analysts.[131] IW's Rolf Kroker told us that there have been tendencies toward "a convergence in thinking . . . because it is necessary today that you use the state-of-the-art and the other methods." He continued saying, "Twenty years [ago] I think it was more an ideological competition and at the moment we don't have such ideological competition." Polarized policy debates diminished, although they certainly did

[127]Interview with Wolfgang Franz, CEE.
[128]Interview with Martin Dietz, IAB.
[129]Interviews with Rolf Langhammer and senior researcher, IfW.
[130]Interviews with Rolf Kroker, IW; Wolfgang Franz, ZEW.
[131]Interviews with Martin Dietz, IAB; Wolfgang Franz, CEE.

not disappear, and compromise became more likely due to the scientific turn in policy analysis.[132]

The Leibniz Accreditation Process

Another important reason for the improvement in analytic capacities and therefore possibilities for compromise among analysts is the Leibniz Association, formerly known as the Blue List. The Blue List was a small group of esteemed scholarly research institutes, established in 1977, that received special funding because of the national importance of their work.[133] Research institutes became part of the Blue List if they periodically passed an evaluation process by the German Council of Science and Humanities (Wissenschaftsrat), which was designed to ensure excellence in research. Only the very best research organizations were put on the Blue List. With German unification the size of the list nearly doubled and it was renamed the Leibniz Association whose senate since 2000 did the evaluations.[134] The Wissenschaftsrat and Leibniz Association coordinated research activities by establishing standards of excellence to which the economic research institutes aspired and by making recommendations to the federal and Länder governments about funding for these institutes.[135]

Several people told us that research organizations elevated the quality of their work striving for state-of-the-art methods to try to meet the demands of the Leibniz evaluation.[136] This was because the Leibniz Association offered two benefits for members: status and money. Consider status first. Leibniz membership constitutes a stamp of excellence. The association evaluates each scholarly research institute on seven-year intervals paying close attention to three things: (1) the quality of research, which must be as good as university research as indicated by numbers of refereed journal publications, quality of methods and data used, number of researchers on staff, and so on; (2) whether the institute's work is of national importance; and (3) whether the institute serves the public interest by contributing to public debate. By all accounts research quality is the most important criteria.[137] For instance, when we asked the Kiel Institute's vice

---

[132]The fact that Gustav Horn was forced out of DIW when it took an anti-Keynesian turn and the trade unions built their own research institute for him at WSI suggests that not everyone is in agreement on basic economic policy issues. So does the fact that IW often works closely with INSM, a conservative advocacy organization. We thank Dieter Plehwe for this insight.
[133]The name Blue List arose because the list was initially printed on blue paper.
[134]http://www.leibniz-gemeinschaft.de. Accessed April 2011. See also Braml (2004, p. 26).
[135]For further discussion of the coordinating functions of these two organizations, see Stucke (2011) and Wagner (2011).
[136]Interviews with Ulrich Walwei, IAB; senior official, Ifo; Wolfgang Franz, ZEW; Rolf Langhammer, IfW.
[137]Interviews with Wolfgang Franz, ZEW; Rolf Langhammer, IfW; senior official, SOWI.

president about this he insisted that research excellence "is number one," and mentioned ZEW, which received Leibniz membership because "[t]hat institute is academically first class." Leibniz membership improves an organization's reputation by affirming the high quality of its research.[138]

But money is also at stake. Whereas most research institutes are financed primarily by the Länder in which they reside, those that belong to the Leibniz Association receive special federal funding as well. The Kiel Institute, for example, gets about half of its funding from the Länder and half from the federal government thanks to its Leibniz membership. Loss of Leibniz accreditation can be devastating. When the Hamburg Institute for International Economics Archive (HWWA) lost its accreditation it eventually closed. Similarly, when Ifo lost its Blue List accreditation in 1996 due to subpar research and forecasting it was downgraded from a Leibniz-funded research institute to a Leibniz-funded service institute with less money and less funding from the hosting state, Bavaria. Its budget was cut by 30% and its staff was slashed by nearly half. After that Ifo hired more academic quality researchers and undertook more sophisticated econometric modeling. As a result, it was reinstated as a Leibniz research institute in 2010.[139]

By affirming an organization's reputation for high-quality research Leibniz membership also improves an organization's chances for garnering grants and contracts. Ulrich Walwei, vice director of IAB, explained, "Excellent research is more or less the basis for consultancy work." If you do not have top-quality research, he added, as indicated, for instance, by Leibniz membership, then your reputation in the market for other funding suffers. Wolfgang Franz from ZEW concurred, remarking that "[m]any people know that to be a Leibniz institute that you are meeting high academic standards, so that helps us. It helps us, it helps give the reputation . . . [and] it helps to get good projects."

The Leibniz criteria were beefed up after unification to weed out weak East German research institutes that continued to receive state funding regardless of the poor quality of their work. The new criteria were applied to the institutes in the west as well.[140] This facilitated not only higher quality research but a degree of methodological convergence. For example, when we asked Ulrich Walwei at IAB whether all of this caused important changes in scholarly research organizations like his, he said that it had "pushed the process," whereby research organizations monitored each other to ensure that they were using the best methods and data. This included keeping tabs on

[138]Interviews with Ulrich Walwei, IAB; Wolfgang Franz, ZEW.
[139]Interviews with Rolf Langhammer, IfW; Wolfgang Franz, ZEW; senior official, Ifo; and email correspondence from Meinhard Knoche, Ifo; Rolf Langhammer, IfW.
[140]Interview with senior official, Ifo.

each other's Leibniz evaluations.[141] And when we asked him whether this had led to a degree of methodological convergence among these organizations he replied, "Absolutely right!"[142] The Wissenschaftsrat recently began conducting evaluations similar to Leibniz reviews for the ministerial research units, which will presumably have similar effects on them.[143]

In order to satisfy the Leibniz criteria research organizations often hired high-profile university professors to run them—another mechanism that facilitated methodological convergence. The president of DIW told us that his appointment to run DIW was a response to the organization's Leibniz evaluation. Referring to university professors who run a couple of other important policy research institutes, he said, "We share the same ideology about how to do this job," by which he meant ensuring that their organizations subscribe to the best scientific practices.

In sum, the demand by policymakers and the Leibniz Association for better research was stimulated by the more complex economic problems associated with globalization and concerns about the quality of work done by some policy research institutes after unification. This demand led to improved research quality among the scholarly policy research institutes.[144] Especially insofar as the Leibniz process was concerned, this was a mechanism of coordination that facilitated a degree of tacit agreement among research organizations as to the appropriate analytic techniques for economic forecasting and policy analysis. In turn, this enhanced the possibilities for compromise in places like CEE and the Joint Economic Report group.[145] We found nothing like the Leibniz process in our other countries. In a sense, then, policymakers began to question whether the knowledge regime was complementing the policymaking regime as well as it might in view of the new economic circumstances stemming from

[141] Interviews with Ulrich Walwei, IAB; Klaus Zimmermann, DIW.

[142] See Wagner (2011) and Stucke (2011, pp. 168–69) for further discussion of how the Wissenschaftsrat and then Leibniz evaluation processes identified weakness in the quality of German economic research at the major economic research institutes and moved to improve it by elevating standards. Wagner (2011) argues, as well, that this led to a general improvement in the quality of the research after the 1980s across these institutes. DIW, for instance, was criticized in one of its reviews and subsequently required that its staff publish in peer-reviewed journals listed in the standard citation indexes.

[143] Interview with senior official, SOWI. The ministerial research units have already coordinated their recommendations regarding the criteria by which the Wissenschaftsrat evaluates their work.

[144] Competition for Leibniz acceptance has grown even tougher since we finished our interviews and in one case caused an institute president to resign after two consecutive disappointing Leibniz reviews (email correspondence, Rolf Langhammer, IfW).

[145] The contrast is especially sharp with the United States where economics is split fiercely between "fresh water" economists in the Midwest, who subscribe to a highly formal brand of economics based on assumptions about perfect markets, and "salt water" economists on the coasts, whose work is based more on empirical research and different assumptions (Stiglitz 2009, chap. 2).

the end of the Golden Age and the rise of globalization. Their demands for better policy analysis were tantamount to a call for recalibrating the knowledge regime to improve its institutional complementarity with the rest of the political economy.

The Crisis of Corporatism and the Escalation of Competition

People warned us in Germany not to confuse coordination and compromise with a lack of competition. One knowledge regime veteran responded to our questioning as follows:

> Your implication is that by coordination you will have less competition. I would not see it that way. It is accepted that there is competition between, let's say, employers and the trade unions, whatever or other institutions. But coordination means to me that you try to solve this conflict in a way that the whole society or the whole economy benefits.[146]

There was certainly competition in Germany. Indeed, the biggest change in Germany's comparatively stable knowledge regime was an increase in competition among policy research organizations over the past 20 years. The story starts with the end of the Golden Age, the rise of globalization, and what could be called a crisis of corporatism. Wolfgang Streeck has argued that since the 1980s Germany has been moving beyond corporatism to more pluralist and competitive interorganizational relations and politics.[147] Others including Bruno Palier and Kathleen Thelen reject the postcorporatism argument and say that Germany is simply developing a dual political economy. On the one hand, traditional corporatist institutions persist in the core manufacturing industries and are defended by labor unions and employer associations. On the other hand, an alternative set of institutions, such as nonstandard work contracts, has emerged elsewhere in response to increasing international economic competition and a shift toward more service sector employment.[148] Regardless of the correct interpretation, German corporatism faced serious challenges in response to globalization and other problems associated with it. Notably, unemployment averaged 0.8% annually from 1960 to 1973 but ballooned to 6.8% during the 1980s. Annual productivity growth dropped from

---

[146] Interview with Rudolf Zwiener, IMK.
[147] Streeck 2009, chaps. 2–4. See also Albert (1993) and Lash and Urry (1987).
[148] Palier and Thelen 2012, 2010. Dualism might also be a stepping stone toward postcorporatism.

4.1% to 1.4% during this period. Government budgets, which averaged a surplus of 0.1% of GDP from 1960 to 1973, fell into deficits averaging 2.7% of GDP during the 1980s. Inflation, which was a more serious problem in other countries, averaged 3.4% annually from 1960 to 1973, hit 4.7% during the late 1970s, and receded to 2.9% during the 1980s.[149]

We showed earlier that the government sought more scientific policy analysis and advice to help make sense of and solve these problems.[150] But policymakers and others took additional steps to cope with the situation and improve the knowledge regime's capacity to provide analysis and advice commensurate to the problems at hand. These steps were intended in effect to rejuvenate Germany's economic competitiveness by improving the knowledge regime's complementarity vis-à-vis the rest of the political economy. In doing so they also facilitated more competition in the knowledge regime.

To begin with, the state opened up membership in the Joint Economic Report group to competitive bidding. This included bids from teams of policy research organizations, including teams with foreign members. Chancellor Gerhard Schröder's office initiated competitive bidding in 2007 because it was dissatisfied with the policy advice that it was getting from the research institutes under the old system. Much like France in the mid-1990s when Prime Minister Jospin sought fresh policy ideas by funding new policy research organizations, there was a sense in the German government and elsewhere that the Joint Economic Report group had become an exclusive cabal of like-minded institutes and that it would be good to introduce new perspectives into the group.[151] According to the IfW's vice president, the idea was

> to have fresh air in the group. . . . Forecasting is really a very special animal and these guys [the traditional group of forecasting institutes] are very much experienced. They have done the job for many years. . . . Why not bring some new outsiders in? The outsiders complained [that] this is a cartel monopoly of these institutes that share the same view . . . so why not bring competitive pressure into it.

This made sense given the increasingly volatile and difficult economic environment that dogged Germany after the Golden Age. Fresh ideas might facilitate more effective economic policymaking in this tougher environment. As a result, the Joint Economic Report group from 2007 to 2010 included four

---

[149]Kenworthy 1997, tables 3 and 7.
[150]Interviews with Rolf Kroker, IW; senior official, MPIfG. The requirement that applicants for EU research funds team up with researchers in other countries amplified the trend.
[151]Interview with senior official, BMWI.

members: (1) IfW; (2) a team including Ifo and the Swiss Institute for Business Cycle Research in Zurich; (3) a team including IWH, IMK, and the Austrian Institute for Economic Research in Vienna; and (4) a team including RWI and the Institute for Advanced Studies in Vienna.

Teams with foreign organizations were now involved because assembling a team could increase the areas of expertise on offer and thus improve one's competitive edge. A senior official at Ifo told us that this helped them in the most recent competition: "The idea was when we made our bid to participate in the project that . . . if we had the know-how of the Swiss Institute for Business Cycle Research, which is quite well respected, that it would add to our credentials. And obviously it did help." In sum, the traditional way of offloading analytic functions in corporatist fashion from the state to the same old organizations was brought into question and the process was opened up and made more competitive.

The end of the Golden Age also increased competition in the knowledge regime in another way—one that stemmed even more directly from the crisis of corporatism. Firms began turning away from traditional corporatist channels of influence toward advocacy research organizations operating outside that system. Globalization and the internationalization of business increasingly put the interests of big multinational firms at odds with small and medium size firms thus making it difficult for employer associations to represent all of their interests.[152] This is why, for instance, the metal working trade association agreed in 1999 to appease members coveting neoliberalism by creating INSM.[153] A senior official at SM, another upstart advocacy policy research organization, explained that the problem with corporatism, and one reason why SM and groups like it were founded, was that it took too long for the employer association members to analyze and compromise on pressing policy issues. This was part of a more extensive trend toward special interest lobbying. He explained:

> Ten or fifteen years ago, there was one organization, big organization of all employers and of all companies. And now, companies have so many different interests. They saw that they are not very well represented in the big employers' organization. So they have their own [public affairs] bureaus here in Berlin. Every big German company has its own bureau, makes its own publications . . . invites [ministerial] deputies for talks, and so on. So, there is much more competition.[154]

[152]Streeck 2009, pp. 84–85; Thelen 2000; Thelen and Kume 1999.
[153]Interview with senior official, INSM.
[154]The advent of lobbying, he explained, also included corporations hiring firms like KPMG and Ernst & Young.

He continued with a specific example:

> BDI, for example, they have so many interests in them . . . they have
> the chemical industry, pharmaceutical industry, they have steel. . . .
> They represent everything. And they need weeks or months to find
> a common interest, to communicate it to the Chancellor. And in the
> time of Internet and BlackBerry you don't have weeks or months;
> you don't have even an hour. You need minutes. . . . And so the
> ThyssenKrupp AG just on the other side of the street, they are much
> faster. They need two minutes to, and they have a personal network
> to get in there.[155]

To be clear, his point was that corporatist lethargy in an increasingly fast-paced
global economy led to (1) the emergence of advocacy research organizations
like his that were independent of the employer associations and that did policy
analysis and pushed big policy ideas and (2) the development of lobbyists that
did little of this but pressed politicians on behalf of the narrow interests of
corporate clients. Both facilitated more competition. But what matters for us
is not so much the rise of lobbying but the rise of the advocacy research organizations. As we explained in chapter 1, this sort of lobbying is not integral to
knowledge regimes because it does not involve policy analysis or broad policy
recommendations. In Germany, while lobbyists have increased substantially in
number the advent of advocacy policy research organizations has been more
limited although, as our contact at SM explained, it has still contributed to
more competition in policy analysis circles.[156]

Three additional changes in the policymaking and production regimes exacerbated the crisis of corporatism and in turn competition in the knowledge
regime. First was German unification, which surely aggravated the sluggish-
ness with which the labor and employer associations operated in the political
sphere insofar as their constituencies grew with the addition of East German
members whose interests were not always consonant with their West German counterparts. Second was moving the federal government from Bonn to
Berlin in 1999 as a result of unification. This created new political opportunities for advocacy research organizations and others to enter the field and

---

[155]He was clear that advances in communications technology were partly to blame insofar as organizations had to move faster and faster vis-à-vis the policymaking process.
[156]There are many American-style lobbying firms in Germany. Their number has grown much
during the past decade. There may be as many as 2,500 to 5,000 lobbyists in Berlin today, although it is difficult to be sure given the lack of transparency and the fact that business associations, unions, church groups, and social insurance funds lobby too. (Interviews with Andreas
Poltermann, HBS, and Dieter Plehwe, WZB. See also http://www.lobbycontrol.de. Accessed April
2011.)

compete—opportunities associated with the creation of a bigger state infra-structure in the policymaking regime.[157] We heard, for example, that

> [t]he situation in Berlin changed the way that political think tanks are working a lot because the competition is really dense in Berlin. You have a lot of think tanks. You have a lot of lobby groups. You have a lot of institutions doing events, publishing things. . . . Some-times you really invite 10,000 people and you could be happy if 80 of them really address the conference even if you have a Nobel Prize winner on the board. It's really very, very difficult in Berlin because you have such a lot of offers and such a lot of special events in the political field.[158]

Finally, in the early 2000s the laws governing private foundations—including those involved with policy research—were changed to increase the tax breaks for those who contributed to them. This created incentives for people to create advocacy organizations, private foundations and the like in order to capitalize on the new political opportunities that had emerged when the government moved to Berlin. In some cases the tax breaks were 10 times larger than before and worth up to about $1.3 million (€1 million).[159]

The ensuing competition revolved in part around resources. For example, in some cases funding grew harder to get. On the demand side there were more policy research organizations seeking it. This is one reason, we were told, why some party foundations began collaborating with private foundations on certain projects—that is, to take advantage of the private partner's finan-cial and other resources.[160] On the supply side, funding possibilities shrank thanks to a global economic recession and other problems afflicting the Ger-man economy thanks to the end of the Golden Age. Moreover, unification was expensive, put pressure on federal and Länder budgets and therefore further limited the amount of money available for research organizations including party foundations and semi-public scholarly research institutes.[161] And the state began to encourage more competition for funding. In addition to open-ing up bidding for the Joint Economic Report group the ministries began to solicit competitive bids for policy research grants and contracts. Whereas 20 years ago a single research institute might have approached a ministry with an

---

[157]Interview with senior official, SM. See also Braml (2004, p. 93).
[158]Interview with senior official, KAS.
[159]Interviews with senior officials, SM and KAS.
[160]Interview with senior official, KAS.
[161]Interviews with senior officials, Ifo and KAS; Wolfgang Franz, ZEW. See also Braml (2004, p. 27) and Weilemann (2000, p. 176).

idea for a project nowadays the ministry solicits bids and receives perhaps as many as 30 or 40 to choose from.[162]

Competition for research staff also grew. Given the increase in policy research organizations and tight funding, winning grants and contracts required increasingly top-notch researchers. The catch was that being able to recruit these people required that organizations offer them prestigious projects with big budgets in the first place.[163] The Leibniz process further amplified the demand for quality researchers by raising the bar to perform at the highest scientific level.[164] The president of one research institute said that, as a result, his organization and others like it had to compete not just against each other but also against universities. Competition for well-trained researchers, he said, is "much higher than it [was] 15 or 20 years ago."[165] Others confirmed this.

Competition was often niche specific. For instance, KAS and the Heinrich Böll Foundation both listed the party foundations as their primary competitors.[166] Similarly, almost all of the scholarly research institutes with whom we spoke listed each other as primary competitors.[167] Rolf Kroker, for example, at IW, pointed to others in his niche: "The most important competitors are the other big institutes . . . like Ifo and DIW or the Kiel Institute and the Essen Institute." Competition for advocacy organizations is also niche specific. When we interviewed a senior official from INSM he admitted that his competitors were the private companies and their public relations departments.

Sometimes, however, competition transcended niches. For instance, IMK viewed the commercial banks as competitors because they also specialized in

[162]Interview with senior official, Ifo. See also Braml (2004, p. 160).
[163]Interviews with senior official, Ifo; Wolfgang Franz, ZEW.
[164]Interview with Klaus Zimmermann, DIW.
[165]Interview with Wolfgang Franz, ZEW. According to Jutta Allmendinger, WZB, the ability of semi-public research institutes to compete with universities for the best researchers was made more difficult by the government's recent decision to create centers of excellence in universities that can offer researchers generous resources as well as a five-year leave from all teaching responsibilities. In email correspondence with Rolf Langhammer, IfW, we learned as well that the emergence of the excellence cluster initiatives brought research institutes like IfW and Ifo closer to the universities; the number of joint professorships is rising; and the proximity of research institutes to universities even gets close to mergers. As such, universities can exercise more leverage over the research institutes and push them more toward academically excellent research, which may compromise their policy advising mission and thus create more distance between the institutes and ministries. It may also create splits among staff within the institutes, some of whom are inclined toward academic research and some of whom are inclined toward policy advising.
[166]Interviews with senior official, KAS; Andreas Poltermann, HBS; Peter Donaiski, FES. They reported, however, that the foundations still coordinated a variety of efforts with each other, such as conducting joint research projects and working together to garner media attention and government funding.
[167]Interviews with Klaus Zimmermann, DIW; Ulrich Walwei, IAB.

macroeconomic forecasting.[168] Furthermore, when we spoke with a senior official at SM he worried about WZB, which surprised us because it is a very scholarly research organization quite unlike his own public relations and lobbying oriented operation. As strange as this may sound, it might make sense at least insofar as WZB's president, Jutta Allmendinger, was trying to elevate her organization's public profile. In this regard, for small organizations like SM, WZB may pose a competitive threat especially because it has much more staff, better research capacities and an impressive research reputation.[169]

Overall, then, challenges to and changes in Germany's political economy, which were often associated with the end of the Golden Age and the rise of globalization, led to the emergence of new policy research organizations and more competition in the knowledge regime. Changes in the production regime—notably the crisis of corporatism—figured prominently in this. But changes in the policymaking regime did too, such as revisions in the tax code governing foundations, the development of the Leibniz process, and German unification. Let us be clear, however, that the emergence of new advocacy organizations and competition did not overwhelm the knowledge regime. In contrast to the situation in the United States, the advocacy organizations remained few and far between. And the advent of more competition did not mean that coordination and compromise were diminishing. This has not been a zero-sum situation. Old mechanisms and patterns of coordination and compromise persisted even as new organizations began to appear and competition increased.

Conclusion

As in the United States and France, Germany's knowledge regime was shaped by its surrounding political-economic environment. Insofar as the production regime's effects were concerned, corporatist traditions were reflected in the fact that unions and employer associations financed some of the prominent policy research organizations, including IMK, WSI, IW, and INSM. Reflections of corporatism were also evident in tripartite board membership at some of these organizations and in the informal vetting by labor and business of some appointments to CEE. Moreover, long-standing corporatist institutions meant that until recently there was little need for advocacy policy research organizations or private foundation think tanks. After all, if economic interests were well organized and capable of influencing policymaking through labor and employer associations with their own policy research organizations, then there was little need for American-style advocacy organizations.

---

[168]Interview with Rudolf Zwiener, IMK.
[169]Interview with senior official, SM.

The policymaking regime's effects were also significant. Federalism as well as corporatist legacies led to the development decades ago of several semi-public scholarly policy research organizations that the state uses for expert policy analysis and advice. Another manifestation of the state's use of semi-public policy research is its support of the party foundations whose funding depends on the balance of parliamentary power in an electoral system based partly on proportional representation. Much of this stemmed as well from policymakers' desire to cultivate independent voices to which they could listen in an effort to make sense the country's economic problems.

Although the state plays an important role in the German knowledge regime it should not be confused with the French case. First, in statist France the state's own policy research organizations dominate much of the knowledge regime, notably INSEE, the conseils, and the ministerial research units, which do much analytic work. But in corporatist Germany the state has long off-loaded much of this work to semi-public organizations, such as the scholarly research institutes, CEE, and the Joint Economic Report group, and set up the Leibniz process to ensure a certain level of quality control. This is entirely consistent with corporatist—not statist—practices insofar as in corporatism the state confers formal status and resources on groups in civil society in exchange for their advice and help in policymaking. Second, thanks to its federalist structure the German state is far more decentralized than the French state, which is why German policy research organizations are sprinkled all over the country and not typically beholden to the federal government.

What most set the German case apart, however, from the French as well as the U.S. cases was the greater degree of coordination among German policy research organizations. In several important cases, such as the Joint Economic Report, this led to compromise over policy analysis and advice. Sometimes an even deeper meeting of the minds occurred. Such was the case where, thanks to the Leibniz process and the government's demand for better scientific policy analysis in order to make sense of a more complex global economy, most research institutes began gradually to coalesce around ever more sophisticated methodological principles. The surprise for us was the considerable amount of informal coordination there was throughout the knowledge regime because the comparative political economy literature emphasized formal not informal coordination in Germany.

Although Germany's knowledge regime has been more stable since the 1980s than either the U.S. or French knowledge regimes there were still some important changes. The end of the Golden Age and the rise of globalization led to a crisis of corporatism in the production regime, which in turn spawned new advocacy policy research organizations and private foundation think tanks outside traditional corporatist channels. Competition in the knowledge regime increased accordingly. Changes in the policymaking regime exacerbated this. Notably, unification and with it the federal government's move from Bonn to Berlin created opportunities for private advocacy research organizations and therefore a more competitive knowledge regime. Unification also contributed to the development of the Leibniz process, which raised the bar for quality research and serendipitously facilitated competition for qualified researchers. The government's desire for fresh analysis and policy recommendations in order to make better sense of the country's new economic problems also stimulated competition in the knowledge regime by opening up bidding for state contracts as well as membership in the Joint Economic Report group.

To put all of this in the analytic terms of chapter 1, much of the search for fresh thinking and with it various changes to the knowledge regime were responses to the perceptions of policymakers and others that the knowledge regime was no longer functioning as it should for the political economy. In other words, people recognized that the institutional complementarity between the knowledge regime and the rest of the political economy had started to break down and no longer provided the analysis and other ideas necessary to make sense of Germany's problems and enable the country to remain competitive in an increasingly global economy. Importantly, many of the changes that resulted were done in ways largely consistent with already existing institutional arrangements. That is, the emphasis remained primarily on semi-public scholarly policy research organizations and key state research organizations as had long been the case. This was different from France where efforts to restore the knowledge regime's complementarity remained considerably more statist than in Germany. It was also different from the United States where attempts to restore the knowledge regime's complementarity emphasized much more than in Germany the creation of private advocacy research organizations to promote a competitive marketplace of ideas and where semi-public policy research organizations were virtually nonexistent. In other words, the German response was a mixed bag. It involved state-led coordination, such as beefing up the Leibniz accreditation criteria for semi-public policy research organizations and encouraging more competition among those who wanted invitations into the Joint Economic Report group. It involved off-loading analytic and advisory responsibilities to all of these organizations in a decentralized fashion. And it involved the decentralized, haphazard emergence of various private advocacy organizations. Of course, there were no assurances that any of these efforts would necessarily reinvigorate the knowledge regime's institutional complementarity with the rest of the political economy, although this was certainly what people wished.

A hallmark of German corporatism is the deal cut between the state and corporatist organizations like unions and employer associations. The state confers status and resources on these organizations in exchange for which they agree to shoulder certain responsibilities on behalf of the state, such as managing conflict and facilitating compromise in civil society and providing policymakers with input and advice. As part of this deal these organizations enjoy a modicum of independence from their members and the state. Independence from the membership stems from the fact that they do not depend on the members' financial support. Independence from the state stems from the fact that they are granted immunity from political interference.[170]

Rarely did the issue of independence come up during our German interviews. This was not the case in either the United States or France where people made a bigger fuss trying to convince us of their organization's independence from either private or public influence, respectively. Nevertheless, some people we interviewed in Germany did talk about the independence of their organizations. For instance, as noted earlier, we learned that the constitutional court ruled that the political parties must grant their foundations some autonomy. Apparently the foundations took this seriously. One person told us off the record that his or her foundation was preparing a policy proposal that contradicted the party's position and would not sit well with the party elite. Moreover, we learned that the foundations agreed informally with each other to refrain from doing anything during the three months prior to an election that might be construed as supporting a particular candidate or party's position on issues. Nor do they get involved with political campaigns or work too closely with people in parliament. Doing so might jeopardize their funding, which is why when someone from a party foundation wants to participate in a political campaign they must take a leave of absence from the foundation.[171] After all, the foundations ostensibly serve a general public interest not the narrow interests of the party, which is why they receive government funding in the first place.

Consider as well the semi-public research institutes. Although they depend on state financing they are able to conduct their work with impunity from political interference.[172] The following story helps explain why. In the mid-1970s when the Bretton Woods system of fixed exchange rates collapsed one important semi-public research institute published a memorandum detailing how Germany should respond. The document so enraged the finance minister that he threatened to cut off the institute's funding. But the public outcry was so loud that he backed off. We were told that something like this "never happened again" because people insisted that policy research organizations must be free to operate independently from the state.[173] Moreover, everyone

---

[170]See, for example, Offe (1981, pp. 137–138).
[171]Interviews with Andreas Poltermann, HBS; Peter Donaiski, FES. In terms of coordination, party foundation representatives also meet four times a year to coordinate their efforts in negotiating with the ministries that finance them about the rules and procedures under which they operate.
[172]Braml 2004, chap. 5.
[173]Interview with Rolf Langhammer, IfW.

remembers how the Nazis and then in East Germany the communists manipulated scientific knowledge for political purposes. Nobody wants to repeat those mistakes. Hence, today the state subsidizes most scholarly research institutes to ensure that their work is of the highest quality but refrains from political interference.[174]

Finally, we were assured that there is no ministerial interference with the preparation of the Joint Economic Report. It remains confidential until it is released officially to the ministry and the press. Rolf Langhammer from one of the institutes involved underscored the point: "The joint forecast is top secret and you would be really killed or punished . . . by the Ministry of Economics if . . . these papers were to be circulated outside the group." And according to a ministry official, "There's no chance to influence the result of that report."[175]

The point is that the party foundations and semi-public policy research organizations we visited in Germany seemed to enjoy a degree of independence from both the state, upon which they depend for status and resources, and certain influences in civil society that might seek to influence their activities. This independence is not absolute in every case. For example, the party foundations, as we have seen, have an ambiguous relationship with the parties. And the federal government can influence the scientific practices of the semi-public scholarly research institutes via the Leibniz process. But for institutional reasons specific to the German political economy many of the policy research organizations we visited seem to enjoy a healthy amount of independence. Put differently, there has long been a significant—yet far from total—separation between important parts of the knowledge regime, on the one hand, and the policymaking and production regimes, on the other hand. This separation was more pronounced in some ways than in France where the state dominated the knowledge regime. And it was less pronounced in some ways than in the United States where there were almost no semi-public research organizations bridging the gap between the policymaking and knowledge regimes and where a large part of the knowledge regime was populated by private policy research organizations that had no formal connection with the policymaking regime. In short, independence was contingent on the national institutional context.

In many respects Germany's knowledge regime is more similar to Denmark's than it is to either the United States' or France's in particular because both have long-standing corporatist traditions. Yet, as we are about to see, Denmark also differs in some important ways from Germany as well as our other countries. And we uncovered some surprises there too.

[174]Thunert 2004.
[175]Interview with senior official, BMWI.

5

The Nature of Negotiation in Denmark

Denmark's knowledge regime is a blend of key elements found in the German and French cases. It resembles Germany's insofar as both have been heavily influenced by tripartite corporatist traditions.[1] But there are important differences too. As we expected, because Denmark is a small country there are far fewer policy research organizations than in Germany. Moreover, because the Danish state is not federalist its knowledge regime is more centralized than Germany's. Virtually all the important policy research organizations are located in Copenhagen. Finally, Danish policy research organizations are oriented toward compromise and consensus more than they are in Germany. This stems from a variety of institutionalized negotiations involving the state, the social partners—that is, business and labor—and others. These institutions are reinforced by a taken-for-granted understanding of how society should work to which almost everyone subscribes—a consensus view that favors balancing economic growth and socioeconomic equality. Denmark's size matters here too. Small advanced countries are notoriously

[1] Campbell et al. 2006; Katzenstein 1985; Lehmbruch 1979; Pedersen 2006a.

vulnerable to international political and economic threats and challenges. To cope with their vulnerability small countries, especially culturally homogeneous ones like Denmark, often develop centralized interest groups; well-organized bargaining among them and state officials; and an ideology of solidarity and social partnership—all of which unite the nation and facilitate consensus making.[2]

The Danish knowledge regime, however, also resembles France's to the extent that the central state does a lot of important economic analysis and helps coordinate the activities of policy research organizations. And, as in France, this responsibility falls to the ministries rather than parliament. We expected this too insofar as the Danish state has absolutist and imperial roots stretching back several centuries.[3] The big difference is that the state's role in the knowledge regime increased in Denmark after the Golden Age of postwar capitalism whereas the state pulled back a bit in France.

There were some surprises for us too in Denmark. First, relative to our other countries the separation of Denmark's policymaking, production and knowledge regimes was minimal in the sense that some organizations either operated in all three regimes simultaneously or provided sites where representatives from all three regimes met. Second, however, the demise of the Golden Age and the rise of globalization presented challenges to and changes in the political economy that sparked a *crisis of ideology*, particularly among the political parties, by which traditional left-right ideological differences diminished due to a concern that they did not provide solutions to the unprecedented problems at hand. This in turn increased the knowledge regime's separation from the other regimes. Specifically, its tripartite corporatist moorings loosened and experts and organizations beyond the traditional social partners became more involved in policy analysis and advising. The turn toward more expertise and better scientific policy analysis was similar to trends we found in other countries, especially Germany. Third, at the same time, the state assumed more control over the knowledge regime, especially as the gatekeeper selecting who participated in these activities. Finally, although Denmark has not had a competitive marketplace of ideas like the United States, a few embryonic advocacy organizations emerged to challenge consensus politics and force a more confrontational discussion of policy ideas. All of these changes stemmed from perceptions that the ideas policy research organizations were producing were no longer helping Denmark compete effectively in the global economy or cope with some of its other problems. In other words, people realized that the knowledge regime had become dysfunctional and that its once complementary relationship with the rest of the political economy had deteriorated.

[2]Campbell and Hall 2006, 2009; Katzenstein 1985, chap. 1; Schwartz 1994, 2001.
[3]Østergård 2006.

We begin by sketching the essential features of Denmark's political economy that have influenced its knowledge regime. Next we move to a description of the knowledge regime's structure and practices as we found them during our interviews. Finally, we examine the knowledge regime's important changes.

The Political-Economic Environment

Denmark is often described as a coordinated market economy like Germany.[4] However, after the Second World War the Danish political economy was more mixed than Germany's as it blended elements of corporatist, statist, and liberal types.[5] Denmark relied heavily on corporatist decision making and often delegated authority to private and semi-public organizations and commissions to provide policy advice and help craft and implement legislation.[6] However, it had a large public sector and very generous welfare state. Finally, there was not much state regulation of industrial development or labor markets, little state ownership, and substantial reliance on private credit markets.[7] Because Denmark was a small country and thus especially vulnerable to international political-economic challenges everyone learned by the mid-twentieth century the value of cooperation and flexibility in an open market environment.[8]

Denmark's postwar production regime was—and still is—highly organized. Nearly 79% of workers belonged to unions in 1980—one of the highest rates in the world.[9] And the unions belonged to peak associations—umbrella organizations that represented the interests of the various unions that belonged to them. The biggest today is the Danish Confederation of Trade Unions (LO). Others include the Confederation of Professionals (FTF), the Danish Confederation of Professional Associations (AC), and two other small associations.[10] In addition, there is a peak association called Local Government Denmark (LGDK), representing all 98 municipal governments, and another one called Danish Regions (DR), representing the five regional authorities.[11] There are five business peak associations too. The most prominent are the Confederation of Danish Employers (DA), which coordinates collective bargaining for 13

[4]Hall 2006a; Hall and Soskice 2001a; Soskice 1999, 2007.
[5]Campbell and Pedersen 2007b; Kenworthy 2006; Kjær and Pedersen 2001.
[6]This stemmed from Danish absolutism where the crown consulted frequently with the elites and institutionalized class compromise and cooperation in the Basic Agreement of 1899 (Esping-Andersen 1985; Pedersen 2006a).
[7]Iversen 1999, pp. 121–25. Among the advanced industrial countries in 2004, Denmark was among those that regulated business the least and protected private property rights the most (International Bank for Reconstruction and Development/World Bank 2004, p. 89).
[8]Campbell and Hall 2006, 2009; Katzenstein 1984, 1985, 2003; Senghass 1985.
[9]Visser 2009.
[10]Due et al. 2010, p. 173.
[11]Pedersen 2011, chap. 4.

employer associations, and the Confederation of Danish Industry (DI), which represents its members' policy interests.[12] There are also the Danish Chamber of Commerce (Dansk Erhverv) and the Danish Federation of Small and Medium Sized Enterprises (Håndværksrådet).

In the policymaking regime for decades virtually all important policy decisions were made collectively through organized deliberations involving the state, employer associations, and unions. Hence, Denmark was often called a "negotiated" economy, which indicated how little separation there was between the policymaking and production regimes thanks to Danish corporatism.[13] Notably, until the late 1980s general labor market agreements were set at the national level through negotiations among the labor and employer peak associations. Furthermore, from the 1950s through the mid-1980s the state convened about 440 permanent tripartite committees where it delegated formal authority to the unions and employer associations to advise ministers and help coordinate policy implementation in collaboration with civil servants and party representatives.[14] During this period the state also convened about 300 ad hoc commissions per year involving the social partners and others to draft legislation for parliament.

For more than a century the main political parties were linked tightly to labor market associations, which further deepened the interpenetration of policymaking and production regimes. The Social Democratic Party was established by unions and operated as their political wing. Similarly, the Liberal Party and Social Liberal Party were closely affiliated with agricultural interests while the Conservative Party represented business interests. This, then, led to an electoral system based on proportional representation that was inclined toward centrist politics, compromise and consensus making. First, the parties needed to compromise in order to form coalition governments. Since 1925 only rarely has a party formed a government without at least one coalition partner. Second, three of the main parties—Social Democratic, Liberal, and Conservative—had strong internal factions that prevented movement too far away from the center. Third, as in Germany's Bundestag, the Danish Parliament was organized so that its work was conducted largely by committees that corresponded to the ministerial structure. Hence, parliamentarians developed policy expertise much like government technocrats, which tended to mitigate the politicization of issues.

Another reason why Danish politics have been consensus oriented during the postwar era was that since at least the 1930s the political parties, interest associations, and virtually everyone else subscribed to the notion of social

[12]http://www.da.dk/. Accessed June 2010. DI annual report 2007/2008, p. 58.
[13]Pedersen 2006a.
[14]Pedersen 2006b.

partnership.[15] In economic policy, this involved the gradual development beginning in the 1960s of a taken-for-granted view of socioeconomic balance that blended liberal and social democratic principles. It was liberal in the sense that it respected the autonomy of private economic actors and organized interests, it preferred negotiated settlements rather than state intervention into the economy, and it recognized that because Denmark's small economy was open and exposed to international competition it needed to be flexible to be competitive. It was social democratic in the sense that it portrayed the national economy as a community of fate in which all social groups should share economic benefits and burdens. All of this was an artifact of Denmark's history as a small vulnerable country.[16]

But some things changed after the mid-1970s in the policymaking regime thanks to problems associated with the end of the Golden Age and the advent of globalization and Europeanization. First, the tight links between interest associations and parties slackened. Political parties have come and gone over the years, but today there are nine major parties. The traditional Social Democratic, Liberal, Social Liberal, and Conservative Parties remain, although their ties to their union or employer association allies have worn thin. The five other parties are relative newcomers established mostly in the 1970s and 1980s. They have few if any ties to the interest associations. Some are protest parties, notably the anti-immigration Danish People's Party. One is a libertarian party, the Liberal Alliance. Others are leftist parties including the Red-Green Alliance (Enhedslisten), which is a new version of the old Communist Party, and the Socialist People's Party, which is older, having split from the Communist Party in 1959. Since the 1990s the party system has become divided into two political blocs: a center-left bloc, consisting of the Social Democrats, Socialist People's Party, and the Red-Green Alliance; and a center-right bloc including the Liberal, Conservative, Liberal Alliance, and Danish People's Parties. The Social Liberals forge coalitions with parties from both blocs.

Second, the system of tripartite permanent committees and ad hoc commissions also became more disconnected from the social partners. Beginning

---

[15]Kjær and Pedersen 2001; Pedersen 2006b.

[16]Østergård 2006; Pedersen 2006b. The normative underpinnings of the notions of social partnership and a community of fate, which appear to be substantially stronger than in Germany, extend back to the mid-nineteenth century when Denmark embarked on a remarkably explicit program of nation building. This was triggered in part by Denmark's military defeat by Prussia in 1864, which served as a national awakening among the elites that Denmark was in fact a small vulnerable country. The efforts of Nikolai Grundtvig and his followers were instrumental in institutionalizing the notion of social partnership and solidarity by building among other things a system of Danish People's High Schools where students took residential six-month general courses to learn about Danish social, political, and cultural history. It has been said that until a generation ago every Danish government contained a core of ministers who had experienced a spiritual and national "awakening" by attending such a school (Øhrgaard 2012).

in the 1980s the government opened them up to a broader array of people beyond the social partners. Many of the traditional tripartite committees remain, but they have lost much of their authority. And the number of ad hoc commissions diminished. The social partners are still influential in negotiations with government but less through commissions than before.[17]

The production regime also changed after the Golden Age. Corporatist labor market negotiation persists. But some of it was decentralized to the regional and firm levels in order to infuse the system with more flexibility that better fit the needs of firms trying to cope with globalization.[18] This has not meant movement toward a less organized postcorporatist or dual economy model as it has in Germany. While participation rates in trade unions and business associations fell somewhat from the early 1980s, 68% of workers in 2007 still belonged to unions, 82% were covered by bargaining agreements, and 58% of employers belonged to employer associations.[19] A few small independent unions emerged in opposition to the LO, but they posed no real threat to the traditional unions' influence. The number of sector-level employer associations declined but as a result of mergers designed to strengthen bargaining power in the newly decentralized negotiation system.[20]

Hence, institutionalized negotiation remains the heart and soul of the Danish political economy. Today Denmark has an extensive and binding system of negotiations. First, each year the Ministry of Finance negotiates the state budget with the other ministries in order to prepare the government's budget proposal for parliamentary approval. Once approved, the ministry negotiates with the local authority peak organizations DR and LGDK how much money the regions and municipalities get from the national budget. Then it is up to authorities in the regions and municipalities to negotiate individual budgets with their various constituents. In each case, higher level agreements set the parameters within which lower level agreements are negotiated. Second, every other year LO and DA negotiate national wage agreements that set the terms within which subsequent labor market negotiations play out at the sector and firm levels. This happens too for public sector wage negotiations, but with the Ministry of Finance serving as the peak organization for public employers at the national, regional, and county levels. The point is that Denmark's production and policymaking regimes are still linked through a system of hierarchically organized but now decentralized negotiations involving the Ministry of Finance. Hence, corporatist negotiations are more extensive and often state coordinated than in

---

[17]Pedersen 2011, chap. 5.

[18]Iversen 1999, chap. 5; Kristensen and Zeitlin 2005; Martin 2006; Wilthagen and Tros 2004.

[19]Visser 2009; http://www.eurofound.europa.eu/eiro/country/denmark_1.htm. Accessed February 2012.

[20]Iversen 1999, pp. 149–50.

Germany.[21] Importantly, everyone still strives for consensus as they try to make sense of and cope with the nation's economic troubles.

In the next section we show that the organization of the production and policymaking regimes had significant effects on its knowledge regime. For instance, thanks to Denmark's corporatist heritage there are few policy research organizations other than those supported by business, labor, or the state. And the state casts a particularly long shadow over the knowledge regime. The Ministry of Finance has formidable analytic capacities and supports a variety of semi-public research organizations upon which policymakers rely. In subsequent sections we will show that as challenges to and changes in the policymaking and production regimes developed after the Golden Age people began to suspect in effect that the knowledge regime's institutional complementarity with the rest of the political economy had broken down. To restore it they initiated several changes designed to move away from ideologically oriented to analytically oriented policy advice and sense making. As a result, the dynamic was different than in our other countries. In Germany change was associated with a crisis of corporatism, in France with a crisis of state ideas, and in the United States with a crisis of partisanship. In Denmark it involved a crisis of political ideology.

Mapping the Field: The Knowledge Regime Today

There are three ways in which the Danish knowledge regime differs from the rest. First, there is more variety. It includes state policy research organizations, three types of semi-public policy research organizations, university-based policy research organizations, peak association policy research organizations, and conventional scholarly and advocacy policy research organizations. Second, it is more closely integrated with the policymaking and production regimes than elsewhere. Third, it is more consensus oriented.

State Research Organizations

Much of Denmark's policy research and analysis is conducted, organized, and financed by the state. The Ministry of Finance is especially prominent because it conducts much economic analysis. About one-third of its 1,100 employees have degrees in economics, and they are generally regarded as being among the best in the country.[22] A senior official at DA explained:

> My standards [as an economist] are that our analytical people and
> my economists working as political consultants . . . should be of the

---

[21]Mansbridge 1992; Pedersen 2011, chaps. 4, 5.
[22]http://www.djoef.dk/blade/djoefbladet.aspx. Accessed October 2009.

same standard, for instance, as the staff of the Danish Economic Council [DØR] or the civil servants in the Ministry of Finance. . . . And I'm sure that the labor market organizations' economists think the same way. I mean if we are not . . . then we're not up to the standards which we should be up to.

Three times a year the ministry publishes the most comprehensive forecasts and overviews of the Danish economy—the Economic Survey (*Økonomisk Redegørelse*) and the Budget Overlook (*Budgetredegørelse*)—as well as policy proposals, policy evaluations, and methodological papers.[23] It has several analytic units that construct and maintain econometric models and databases that are used throughout the knowledge regime. One such unit is the Macroeconomic Policy Center, which does econometric modeling and devises economic policy strategies. It relies on the state's sophisticated DREAM, ADAM, and Law econometric models. The DREAM model, for instance, is a four-part dynamic computable general equilibrium model employing more than 100 million equations.[24] The ministry uses it to prepare the Economic Survey. The model is now maintained by the DREAM Group, an independent organization affiliated with the ministry and financed partly by it.[25]

Statistics Denmark also figures prominently in the Danish knowledge regime. Like INSEE in France, it is a repository for a vast amount of data on all aspects of Danish society. It was founded in 1850 and now operates under the supervision of the Ministry of Economics and the Interior.[26] By law its mission is to compile and provide statistical information for public use on social and economic trends in society. Most of its data come from various administrative registries, but it also conducts surveys and gets data from the labor market organizations, including the peak associations. This is a large organization with five departments, 24 divisions, and about 545 employees.[27]

The state also finances several applied policy research and forecasting units beyond the Ministry of Finance. In 2008 it spent about $193 million on

[23]http://uk.fm.dk/. Accessed July 2011. Since the change of government in October 2011, the Economic Survey has been produced and published by the Ministry of Economics and the Interior.
[24]Interview with Lars Haagen Pedersen, DØR. See also http://www.djoef.dk/blade/djoefbladet. aspx. Accessed October 2009. DREAM stands for the Danish Rational Economic Agent Model; ADAM stands for the Annual Danish Aggregate Model; SMEC stands for Simulation Model of the Economic Councils; Law Model stands for Lovmodellen. SMEC and ADAM are macroeconomic models developed in the 1960s and 1970s. DREAM and Law are microeconomic models developed since the early 1990s.
[25]Interview with Lars Haagen Pedersen, DØR. The DREAM Group is a set of top-flight econometricians, modelers, and forecasters.
[26]The Ministry of Economics and the Interior was previously the Ministry of Economic and Business Affairs.
[27]http://www.dst.dk/pukora/epub/upload/15295/profi.pdf. Accessed February 2012.

state research organizations positioned within or under the supervision of various ministries.[28] But it also supported many types of semi-public policy research organizations.

Semi-public Policy Research Organizations

There are three types of semi-public policy research organizations in Denmark. All are organized and financed by the state but are not part of the state apparatus per se. They include permanent scholarly research organizations, ad hoc expert commissions, and knowledge councils.

Permanent Scholarly Organizations

Like Germany, Denmark has a number of permanent semi-public scholarly research organizations upon which the state relies for policy analysis and advice. In 2008 the state outsourced $212 million worth of work to them.[29] Consider the Danish National Center for Social Research (SFI) that was established in 1958 and conducts research in the area of welfare state policies.[30] It falls under the aegis of the Ministry of Social Affairs. SFI has a research budget of about $13.5 million and a staff of about 180, of whom one-third are academics, many with PhDs. Jørgen Søndergaard, an economist, is the general director. Its executive board includes several university professors, two representatives from the ministry, and two from the municipalities. Roughly half of its budget comes from the ministries and half from various research councils. Indicative of its scholarly orientation, SFI helps mentor PhD students, has cooperative agreements with five Danish universities, and often works with universities on its projects. Most of these projects have an advisory board composed of academics and in keeping with Denmark's corporatist tradition people from the ministries and social partners. SFI distributes its work through academic-style working papers and peer-reviewed journals as well as press releases and its own quarterly magazine and monthly electronic newsletter. It also convenes conferences and seminars.[31]

The Danish Center for Governmental Research (AKF) is another permanent semi-public scholarly research organization. It was established in 1975, is headed by Mette Wier, an economist, and is under the Ministry of Interior and Health's jurisdiction. It has partnerships with several universities.[32] Until 2010 AKF was financed in part by a special fund managed by the regional

---

[28]Ministry of Finance, *Statsligt Forskningsbudget 2007* (http://www.fm.dk. Accessed July 2011). A number of these organizations were later transferred to universities.
[29]Ministry of Finance, *Statsligt Forskningsbudget 2007* (http://www.fm.dk. Accessed July 2011).
[30]http://www.sfi.dk/english-2631.aspx. Accessed July 2011.
[31]SFI annual report 2008, p. 18.
[32]AKF annual report 2007, p. 47.

and municipal authority peak associations.[33] In 2009 its budget was about $9.3 million, about one-third each from the ministry, from research councils and other funds, and from contract work done for the ministries, local authorities, private companies, and others. Its board includes managing directors of the two peak associations, four ministerial representatives, and two professors. In any year it typically runs about 100 research projects often in collaboration with universities and other research organizations. Much of its work is for government, regional, and municipal agencies. It disseminates its work in ways similar to SFI.[34]

The Danish Economic Council (DØR), established in 1962, plays an especially important role in the knowledge regime.[35] It is funded by the government under the Ministry of Economics and the Interior and generates some of the key economic forecasts and policy analyses for the state. It consists of two parts: the council per se and the so-called Wise Men, a special group of economists that chairs the council. The council has 26 members representing unions, employers, the central bank, the government, and independent experts.[36] Its secretariat—that is, its administrative bureaucracy and research apparatus—is staffed by 35 people, about 20 of whom are economists, whose responsibilities include monitoring the economy, doing forecasts, and scanning the economics literature to stay abreast of current theoretical, empirical, and methodological trends. It uses DREAM, SMEC, and other models.[37] It also maintains large databases in order to study business cycles, long-term structural trends in the economy, and other economic issues. The scientific quality of this work is high. Its secretariat is headed by Lars Haagen Pedersen, who led the team that developed the DREAM model. And the secretariat presents research reports at professional meetings and publishes in peer-reviewed journals.[38]

DØR's council members are appointed for three year terms by the minister of economic and business affairs on the recommendations of the ministries, social partners, and others.[39] DØR exemplifies Danish political-economic

---

[33]In 2010 this fund—the Momsfonden, worth $46 million—was taken over by the Ministry of Finance. In 2012 AKF was merged into KORA (Det Nationale Institut for Kommuners og Regioners Analyse og Forskning) together with the Danish Institute for Health Services Research (DSI) and the Danish Evaluation Institute for Local Government (KREVI) and integrated into the Ministry of Economy and Interior as an "independent institute."

[34]AKF annual report 2010.

[35]Since 2007 the Council has consisted of two councils, one for economics and one for the environment.

[36]DØR annual report 2007. See also http://www.dors.dk/sw403.asp. Accessed June 2010.

[37]The additional models DØR uses include MUSE (Multi-Sector Model of the Economic Council), MILASMEC (Micro-Data Labor Supply Model of the Economic Council), and DSGE (Dynamic Stochastic General Equilibrium).

[38]Interview with Lars Haagen Pedersen, DØR.

[39]Interviews with Peter Birch Sørensen, Wise Men; Lars Haagen Pedersen, DØR.

tradition insofar as it was designed to facilitate corporatist consensus making. By law DØR's work is intended to "contribute to the coordination of different economic interests."[40] As one insider told us:

> The intention was to create a forum for debate among the social partners, as we call them—the trade unions, employers' associations, all the big business organizations—also including some independent experts. . . . [It] was to be chaired by three university professors in economics [the Wise Men] who were supposed to deliver reports for discussion in this Council. And the idea was, apparently, that by getting the social partners together and sort of forcing them to react to these reports from experts who were supposed to be independent it would help to improve the chances of creating a consensus on economic policy. So, it was—you might say it was probably sort of a corporatist idea. But it was certainly explicitly stated at the time that the goal was to create a consensus on sound economic policies.[41]

In contrast to the U.S. Council of Economic Advisors, DØR is neither part of the government nor a mouthpiece for it. It is a semi-public organization like the German Council of Economic Experts, but is not required by law to address particular issues like price stability and unemployment in its reports. And unlike the French Council of Economic Analysis, which is not obliged to do economic forecasting and rarely does, this is part of DØR's core mission.

DØR's Wise Men are four university economists appointed by the minister of economic and business affairs for staggered six-year terms on the recommendation of the Wise Men themselves. They are in fact usually men, hence the name used repeatedly by people we interviewed. Three times a year they present the council with detailed reports on the Danish economy based on analysis they request from the DØR secretariat, which outsources some of the work to the DREAM group.[42] These reports touch on a variety of economic matters that are selected by the Wise Men in consultation with the DØR secretariat.[43] According to Peter Birch Sørensen, Wise Men chair when we interviewed him, the reports are occasionally "quite controversial" and trigger debates within DØR that are "quite frank" and may meet with "fairly heavy criticism." He explained that this is because DØR members "have their well-defined interests [that] they are supposed to defend." As a result, the Wise Men

---

[40] Law no. 574 of June 6, 2007.
[41] Interview with Peter Birch Sørensen, Wise Men.
[42] These reports include two each year on economics in general and one each year on environmental economics.
[43] Interviews with Peter Birch Sørensen, Wise Men; Lars Haagen Pedersen, DØR.

submit these reports two weeks prior to their meeting with the council so that its members can prepare for the discussion. Following the meeting the reports are sent to the government with an appendix containing whatever dissenting opinions there may be from council members. The Wise Men also hold a press conference to present the main findings to the public.

Ad Hoc Expert Commissions

The government also relies heavily on temporary ad hoc expert commissions. These are a type of semi-public research organization that we did not hear much about in our other countries. They have several important features. First, the government—typically the prime minister's office—sets them up, funds them, and gives them a broad mandate to analyze a particular policy issue and offer policy recommendations. It also appoints commission members and civil servants to run the secretariat, and specifies how the commission will interface with the labor and employer peak associations.[44] Second, commission members are all either experts in the policy field in question or people with special knowledge of it. In this way they are different from the older tripartite commissions we mentioned earlier that were less expert-oriented.[45] Nevertheless, the social partners often sit on the commission boards. The government solicits input from the social partners as well as other ministries, the political parties and others when it establishes a commission and appoints its members.[46] Third, the Ministry of Finance looms large here insofar as it often houses the commissions' secretariats, does analysis that the commissions request, and produces data and other information for them.

The commissions are an especially clear knowledge regime manifestation of the general Danish negotiated economy model.[47] In particular, they are in close contact with the social partners sharing information, discussing policy views and conferring on how to proceed with the analytic work.[48] On several occasions, for example, the Welfare Commission and the Labor Market Commission, which ran from 2007 to 2009, invited the social partners to come and discuss analyses, documentation and other matters.[49] Jørn Neergaard Larsen from DA confirmed that they were in "very, very close contact with

[44]Interview with Jørgen Søndergaard, Labor Market Commission. In the case of the Welfare Commission civil servants were not running the secretariat but at the beginning had the right to take part in meetings.
[45]Both the older tripartite and newer ad hoc commissions had policy experts involved. In the former many came from the labor and employer associations. In the latter many were independent.
[46]Interviews with Jørgen Søndergaard, Labor Market Commission; Torben M. Andersen, Welfare Commission.
[47]Pedersen 2006a.
[48]Interview with Niels Trampe, DA.
[49]Interviews with Torben M. Andersen, Welfare Commission; Jørgen Søndergaard, Labor Market Commission.

the secretariat [of the Labor Market Commission] . . . sharing everything with them," by which he meant data, technical information, methodological advice, and more. The same was true for the Welfare Commission. A senior official from DA told us that

> [t]he charter of a commission like this is that they should talk to social partners. . . . It's inherent in the way we work. . . . We have lots of meetings with the secretariat . . . and if they didn't phone us, we would phone them. Right? And that's—I mean, that's part of the Danish model.

Knowledge Councils

Prime Minister Anders Fogh Rasmussen introduced the third and newest type of semi-public policy research organization in 2005—the knowledge council. Although the knowledge council is less scholarly than the other semi-public policy research organizations, its purpose is to advise the government on socioeconomic matters and facilitate negotiations with the political parties, social partners, and others. He established the Globalization Council and then his successor, Lars Løkke Rasmussen, established the Growth Forum.[50] Each included the prime minister, the minister of finance, and representatives from other ministries, the social partners, local authorities, financial institutions, universities, and members of expert commissions. Both councils held many meetings. Some were public and some were private, but they often included conversations with external experts.[51] They were another manifestation of the negotiated economy model. Indeed, according to its summary report the Globalization Council was guided by the idea that "Denmark should be a country where everyone participates in the renewal process" and does so "through an open and transparent process incorporating broad groups in society."[52] Discussions in the Globalization Council morphed into several new expert commissions on important topics that the council identified.[53]

Knowledge councils were not entirely without precedent. In 1989, a well-known journalist and editor, Erik Rasmussen, established Monday Morning—a privately funded for-profit company—as a vehicle for generating new policy

---

[50]The Globalization Council and Growth Forum ran from 2005 to 2007 and from 2009 to 2010, respectively.

[51]The Globalization Council heard from 13 international experts and 35 Danish experts, and held discussions with 111 representatives from organizations (http://www.globalisation.dk. Accessed November 2011.)

[52]Danish Government, *Progress, Innovation and Cohesion* 2006, p. 4. (http://www.globalisation .dk. Accessed November 2011.)

[53]Interview with senior official, SFI. See also Pedersen (2011, chap. 9).

ideas and influencing the political agenda. It still operates. One of its core missions is to organize meetings, seminars, and conferences where government officials discuss policy issues with business leaders and academics. One example in the 1990s was Monday Morning's Competence Council, which focused on Denmark's international competitiveness and foreshadowed the Globalization Council. Rasmussen told us that the purpose of these meetings was not only to generate new ideas but also to "try out ideas" on the participants to see what might foster consensus.[54]

Also foreshadowing the Globalization Council was businessman Anders Knutsen's Think Tank for Future Growth (TFV), established in 2003 at the request of the Ministry of Trade and Industry. It lasted two years. Like Monday Morning it received no government funding. It assembled people primarily from business but also a few from labor and academia to discuss issues related to globalization. When we asked Knutsen why he included a diverse array of people he said that it was a "Danish phenomenon" and quite "natural" to do so. People from TFV, the Ministry of Trade and Industry, the Danish Council of Trade and Industry, and Monday Morning did the research. The goal was to achieve a consensus report. To that end, and to avoid posturing for organizational interests, people were invited as individuals, not as representatives from their organizations.[55] Monday Morning's Competence Council and Knutsen's TFV resemble the business clubs we visited in Paris but with a strong emphasis on consensus making.

Peak Association Analytic Units

In contrast to our other countries, we heard a lot in Copenhagen about the in-house analytic capacities of the union and employer peak associations. Notably, LO, DA, and DI all do serious economic analysis. Occasionally they outsource some projects, particularly DI, which, according to a senior official, does not do as much sophisticated research as the others. As noted earlier, these organizations aspire to have economists that are as good as those in the Ministry of Finance and DØR. They need solid empirical research to participate effectively in policy and labor market negotiations.

They all regularly publish analytical reports. The LO, for instance, prepares economic forecasts and annual labor market reports based on simulations using the ADAM and SMEC models. LO staff also prepares reports on a variety of other economic issues and disseminates the essence of this work in a weekly newsletter called *Ugebrevet A4* as well as an online newspaper called *Avisen.dk*.[56] Similarly, DA frequently appoints small task forces to write reports

---

[54]Interview with Erik Rasmussen, Monday Morning.
[55]Interview with Anders Knutsen, TFV.
[56]Interviews with Jan Kæraa Rasmussen, LO; senior official, *Ugebrevet A4*.

on selected themes, produces the annual *Labor Market Report*, and publishes a newsletter and several information sheets including *Statistical News* and *DA Statistics*. Much of this work utilizes labor market data that DA has collected over the years and that now constitutes one of the most comprehensive databases on Danish labor market issues, which DA shares with LO, DI, and the government.[57] DI also produces statistical reports, notably its annual report on globalization, which benchmarks the international competitiveness of the Danish economy, and publishes news sheets, an online weekly, a newsletter, and a number of small reports on special policy issues.[58] The regional and municipal authority peak associations also have special units responsible for economic analysis and publish annual reports of various sorts.

Closely associated with the LO is the Economic Council of the Labor Movement (AE), which was established in 1936 through the initiative of Thorvald Stauning, the first social democratic prime minister, and funded and managed by the unions. AE does research for LO and helps the Social Democratic Party on some occasions. Specifically, it does modeling and data analysis on economic topics.[59] It has a staff of 18, mostly economists, and a board chaired by an economics professor. It uses its own econometric models, inspired by or otherwise derived from others mentioned earlier, and data from the usual public sources. It consults with the unions and Social Democratic Party in preparing its four-year research plans. AE was involved as well in negotiations with the government regarding welfare reform.[60] In short, AE is a mixture of scholarly, party, and advocacy research organizations operating on behalf of the labor movement and Social Democratic Party.

Conventional Scholarly and Advocacy Research Organizations

There are very few policy research organizations in Denmark that are funded by wealthy individuals, private foundations, or individual corporations as there are in the United States. According to the director of DA, they are scarce in Denmark because the peak associations, which have their own analytic capacities, have in effect crowded them out of the field:

> One of the differences between the States and here probably has something to do with the Danish model. . . . Whereas in the States you say you have lots of think tanks and independent research organizations, Brookings Institute and all these organizations, probably there hasn't been room or demand for those kind of think tanks in

[57]Interview with senior official, DA.
[58]Interview with senior official, DI.
[59]AE annual report 2006/2007, p. 4, 1997, pp. 2–4.
[60]Interview with Lars Andersen, AE.

Denmark because an organization like this [DA] or Danish Industry [DI] or the Council of Agriculture, they have produced much of the thinking.

Nevertheless, Denmark has a few of these private research shops. One is the Rockwool Foundation's research unit, which was set up in 1981 and takes a scholarly approach with little inclination for advocacy work.[61] According to its website, it assumes that, "The preparation of objective analyses related to specific social issues can both improve the basis for decision making among politicians and facilitate more informed public debate."[62] Torben Tranæs, the research director, elaborated, saying that "[i]f you sort of give the right and the correct information to this political process . . . then they will simply do better." This is a philosophy much like that of some scholarly think tanks in America prior to the 1970s, which believed that advocacy work was unnecessary because good policy analysis could speak for itself.[63]

Indeed, Rockwool's commitment to scholarly standards is clear. For example, when they discovered an important statistical error in one of their new books they immediately alerted the newspapers and published a corrected second edition that they gave for free to everyone who had bought the first edition. Moreover, a scientific committee of university professors advises the Rockwool board on research issues. And although the board includes high ranking politicians, former top civil servants, a former CEO from DI, and members of the family that established the foundation, Rockwool is self-financing and nonpartisan. Its mission, according to Tranæs, is simply "to strike a practical balance between equality and growth in the Danish tradition." That Rockwool's vision is the same as the taken-for-granted consensus view of how Danish economic policy ought to be balanced is not surprising because the organizations' vision was forged when Rockwool was being set up by the funding family with help from Erik Ib Schmidt, who played a key role in cultivating the Danish welfare state and consensus politics after the Second World War.[64]

Privately funded advocacy research organizations are also scarce in Denmark. Only one received much mention during our interviews—the Center for Political Studies (CEPOS), an independent think tank established in 2004 to promote "a society based on freedom, responsibility, private initiative and limited government."[65] It has a staff of 11 people with six working full-time on analytical projects. It sometimes does research in collaboration with university

---

[61] The Rockwool Foundation also funds research by other organizations as well as doing its own research (Rockwool Foundation annual report 2007, p. 24).
[62] http://www.rockwoolfonden.dk. Accessed July 2011.
[63] Ricci 1993; Smith 1991.
[64] Interview with Torben Tranæs, Rockwool Foundation.
[65] http://www.cepos.dk. Accessed June 2010.

researchers, research staff at consultancy firms, and freelancers. It outsources a small number of projects to university professors or consultancy firms and to people who have worked in the government, often in the Ministry of Finance, as well as people at the employer associations. They invite civil servants and academics to discuss and comment on their research reports, which are generally based on data from Statistics Denmark, OECD, the Ministry of Finance, and other sources. In 2010, CEPOS published five books, nearly four dozen policy papers, but only three peer-reviewed journal articles.[66] Martin Ågerup, the director, explained that CEPOS is in frequent contact with politicians and civil servants but does not lobby in the American sense of advocating for narrow special interests. As such, they are like the advocacy research organizations we found in our other European countries. They are also in routine contact with the employer associations but rarely talk to the unions.

According to Ågerup, the organization is a member of the international "free market community" that includes the Cato Institute and Heritage Foundation in America, with which CEPOS maintains close ties. In his view, CEPOS is "up against virtually everyone else" in the Danish knowledge regime because it opposes the consensus orientation of Danish politics. It was financed initially with $3 million from various private foundations, corporations, and anonymous donors. CEPOS neither accepts money from the state, nor applies for it from the Danish research councils or the European Union.

In addition to being crowded out of the field by the peak associations, advocacy research organizations like this are scarce because attempts to start them often failed due to their involvement with ivory tower academics. In Ågerup's words:

> There have been several other attempts at starting free market think tanks in Denmark, but they haven't been successful, and I think the reason why . . . is that when you get some academics who decide they want to run a think tank, they don't necessarily speak the language that business talks, and . . . the way they talk about it sounds like a lot of hot air. Sorry![67]

Only a few other advocacy research organizations are around. These are also small and include the Copenhagen Institute, established in 2003 as an independent think tank working for personal freedom and a free market economy.[68]

[66] http://www.cepos.dk. Accessed July 2011.
[67] Ironically, several of CEPOS's founders are university academics; its nine-member board of directors includes one professor; and its Center Council, which according to its website is its "highest authority," consists of 61 people, of whom 11 are university academics (http://www.cepos.dk. Accessed July 2011).
[68] http://www.coin.dk. Accessed November 2011.

And on the center-left is the Center-Left-Academy (CEVEA), an advocacy think tank financed mainly by the trade unions and opened in 2008 in reaction to CEPOS to advocate for freedom, equality, and community.[69]

Universities

Universities are more significant in the Danish knowledge regime than in our other countries. Not only do they train economists, but they have scholarly policy research organizations. For example, the Employment Relations Research Center (FAOS) is affiliated with the Department of Sociology at Copenhagen University. It was established in 1999 by a circle of academics there to do applied research on labor markets, industry, and employment relations.[70] FAOS is a relatively small operation with 13 on staff, including full-time professors and PhD students. It publishes academic books and peer-reviewed journal articles as well as analytical papers and reports. It also organizes public seminars and sometimes international academic conferences.[71] It is a nonprofit organization funded more or less equally by the trade unions, employer associations, and the Ministry of Employment. A senior official explained that FAOS does "dialogue based research," meaning that it conducts its research in close contact with the ministry and social partners, including meeting with them annually to discuss its research findings. It also communicates with its funders about ongoing projects and ideas for future research. This is much in line with Denmark's traditions of corporatism and negotiation. Nevertheless, he told us that FAOS walks on "two legs." One involves dialogue with its stakeholders, but the other involves doing objective scholarly research. FAOS solicits comments on its ongoing work from its stakeholders and sometimes incorporates their ideas into final reports.[72]

Another university-based policy research organization is the Center for Labor Market Research at Aalborg University (CARMA). All of CARMA's approximately 15 staff members are professors, postdoctoral fellows, and students from the university. Some are close to the trade unions and Social Democratic Party. Since its inception in 1989, its work has been funded by the unions, employer associations, the Ministry of Employment, other ministries, and municipalities—another vestige of corporatism. However, CARMA members also seek their own research funding from the European Union and other Danish sources. In this sense a senior official said that CARMA is not really a formal research center per se but a research network—that is, "a fancy name for a well-established group of university researchers." Like FAOS, people at CARMA do

[69]http://www.cevea.dk. Accessed November 2011.
[70]FAOS annual report 2007.
[71]http://faos.ku.dk/english/. Accessed February 2012.
[72]Interview with senior official, FAOS.

not use the big simulation and forecasting models. But they do empirical analysis with data from Statistics Denmark, Eurostat, the OECD, and other places. They publish their work in peer-reviewed journals, books, academic edited volumes, the CARMA Research Papers series, newspaper columns, and the like. Members occasionally meet with the social partners, ministries, and expert commissions and their secretariats to discuss each other's work.[73]

Similar to CARMA is the Center for Alternative Social Analysis (CASA), which was founded in 1987 by academics from Copenhagen and Roskilde Universities. It is supported by research contracts from unions, ministries, municipalities, and private organizations. Some of their projects are self-financed by profits earned from the contract work. The board is composed entirely of academics. It is a scholarly operation whose modus operandi is to do the analysis, lay out the policy options that follow from it, and then leave it up to the people who hired them to make the policy recommendations. Their work is very empirical and occasionally involves some forecasting. They outsource much of it to academics and other organizations. But they say that they maintain a high level of quality control because their credibility depends on it.[74]

Personal Networks

We noted in the French case that dense personal networks were especially important. The same is true in Denmark although for somewhat different reasons. In Denmark we learned that these networks span policy research organizations as well as firms, unions, and the state. They are often used to help assemble commissions, knowledge councils, and the like. For instance, Monday Morning's Erik Rasmussen noted that for more than 20 years he has used his networks in Denmark to gather policymakers, civil servants, corporate leaders, and academics to discuss pressing socioeconomic issues.

But two things distinguish the Danish networks from France's. First, they stem in part from Denmark being a small country. Second, and more important, these networks serve as a crucible for building trust. As Niels Trampe from DA explained, "I mean, it is a small country, so people who are in these circles, they often know each other and they trust each other, because if you can't trust each other, you know, you can't work in this environment." We heard nothing like this in our other countries.

A high level of trust is a well-known feature of small, homogeneous countries like Denmark. It was far more evident in our interviews there than in the

---

[73]CARMA *Annual Labor Market Research Review* 2004, and interview with senior official, CARMA.
[74]Interview with Finn Kenneth Hansen, CASA. See also http://www.casa-analyse.dk. Accessed November 2011.

other countries we visited because it is part of the deeply ingrained consensus about the importance of social partnership and socioeconomic balance that we mentioned earlier.[75] This was reflected, for example, in a remark by Jan Kæraa Rasmussen at LO, who explained that the scope for disagreement between the employer and labor peak associations was rather narrow. This is because

> [i]n Denmark we all start by recognizing our counterpart's legiti-
> macy. . . . It's taken for granted that employer organizations, what
> they're really trying to do is to give a good framework for Danish
> business to perform well . . . and I think that's okay to have that goal.
> We respect that. And they know that we want our affiliates' mem-
> bers to have a job, and a good job.

As Torben Tranæs told us at the Rockwool Foundation, this sort of common taken-for-granted vision is "the Danish tradition." Not only does this breed trust, but it also expedites compromise and consensus making.

To review, Denmark's policymaking regime has shaped its knowledge regime in many ways. The state has formidable analytic and forecasting operations, organizes the country's primary database through Statistics Denmark, and produces some of the most important economic reports through the Ministry of Finance. It has also established a slew of semi-public scholarly research organizations, ad hoc commissions, and knowledge councils, which reflect Denmark's corporatist heritage of negotiated policymaking. But the production regime's influence is also apparent. Corporatism and the general system of negotiations mean that the peak associations are prominent players in the knowledge regime.[76] They have their own research units, which they need in order to operate effectively in negotiations, they participate in various semi-public research organizations, and they tend to crowd out private scholarly and advocacy research organizations. Many policy research organizations have supervisory boards with representatives from the state and the social partners. The knowledge councils have tripartite representation on them too. The ad hoc commissions interface regularly with the social partners. And by incorporating the social partners as well as state officials into the knowledge regime in so many ways, it is more intertwined with the policymaking and production regimes than it is in our other countries.

This last point warrants further explanation as the intersection of knowledge, policymaking, and production regimes occurs in two ways. First, some

---

[75]The level of social trust toward fellow citizens and public confidence in representative democratic institutions in Denmark is among the highest and most stable in the world (Katzenstein 2003; Zak and Knack 2001, p. 306).
[76]Pedersen, 2006a.

organizations operate in all three regimes. For instance, in addition to the Ministry of Finance's analytic capacities as a member of the knowledge regime it also negotiates labor market agreements as a peak organization for public employers and heads budgetary negotiations with organizations representing regional and municipal authorities. People from the ministry also sit on various commissions. It helps craft legislation and often has responsibility for policy implementation.[77] Hence, the ministry operates in the knowledge, policymaking, and production regimes and therefore connects all three. Similarly, the peak associations, which have their own analytic capacities, engage frequently in policy and labor market negotiations with the government and each other, thus providing additional linkages among the three regimes. Second, some policy research organizations provide sites where representatives from all three regimes meet to analyze, discuss, and negotiate economic policy. Given the tripartite composition of its membership and reliance on the Wise Men's analyses, DØR is one such site.[78] So are the ad hoc expert commissions, which are organized by the state, engage the social partners, and draw on expertise from the universities and elsewhere. Knowledge councils are also a place where people from the policymaking and production regimes confer with experts from the knowledge regime in an effort to set the policymaking agenda. Finally, the university-based research organizations assemble experts and people from the state and the social partners on their boards and in negotiations over their research agendas. Tight coupling among the three regimes is important because it points to the foundations for widespread negotiation and consensus making in the Danish knowledge regime.

Negotiation and Consensus in Economic Policy Analysis

In Germany, institutional mechanisms coordinate policy research organizations in ways that sometimes produce compromise in analysis, forecasts, and policy recommendations. Often this stems from the state's inducements and demands, such as its mandate that the Joint Economic Report group compromise on a single forecast or the Leibniz Association's demand for state-of-the-art analysis before it rewards research organizations with membership. In Denmark, however, most policy research organizations simply *assume* that they ought to cooperate and compromise. They also assume that their reports and analyses—not to mention their data and methodologies—are like public goods to be shared freely among all participants in the knowledge regime, often even before publication. As noted earlier, people told us several times

[77]Due et al. 2010; Pedersen 2011, chap. 4.
[78]Interviews with Peter Birch Sørensen, Wise Men; Lars Haagen Pedersen, DØR.

that this is a taken-for-granted part of the Danish negotiated economy model. And it is amplified by the fact that there is a strong sense of social partnership and solidarity among many policy research organizations as well as a fundamental consensus on the core principles of socioeconomic balance. As a result, cooperation, compromise, and consensus emerge more naturally and organically in Denmark's knowledge regime.

Consensus-oriented cooperation and compromise occur on three levels. They happen within individual policy research organizations; across policy research organizations; and thanks to the bridging effects of some policy research organizations, across organizations operating in knowledge, policy-making, and production regimes.

DØR provides an especially good example of organic consensus-oriented cooperation and compromise *within* a policy research organization. In fact, the Social Liberals—a party constantly seeking consensus—convinced other parties to establish DØR by law as a vehicle for consensus making in the first place. Yet, as we have seen, controversy and disagreement occur within the council over some of the reports it receives from the Wise Men. This is not surprising. According to Peter Birch Sørensen, the Wise Men chair, within a year of the council's founding, "[i]t became clear that it isn't enough to just have some university professors prepare a report on how they see problems. That doesn't guarantee that there will be a consensus automatically emerging on what to do about the problems." Part of the difficulty at the time was that some people worried that the Wise Men's reports were being influenced by the social partners on the council. As a result, the Wise Men decided not to take council input into consideration while they prepared their reports. Nor did they change them if they received criticism from the council when the reports were discussed. In short, they distanced themselves from the council. However, the Wise Men do take the criticisms seriously and consider whether they should change things in subsequent reports in order to improve the chances for consensus next time. Sørensen was clear about this:

> If we are faced with fairly heavy criticism from a broad range of
> council members, of course that makes an impression on us. We
> sometimes ask ourselves, well . . . the criticism that we received, was
> it justified? Or to what extent would there be any reason for us to,
> for instance, in some future report approach the same problem from
> a different angle?

A senior official from DI, which is represented on DØR, confirmed this and said that when the Wise Men receive criticism from the council this may "inspire them" to pursue new topics or think about things differently later. Over time, consensus can emerge from these negotiations and compromises.

In order to accommodate everyone's interests the Wise Men are careful in selecting the topics they analyze in the first place. They pick topics not only because they are interesting to economists and the Wise Men themselves but because they are of concern to the social partners on the council—and in fairly equal measure. That is, they try not to pick topics that are consistently in the interest of one side or the other. But the Wise Men make the final selection and do so by consensus—a self-imposed professional code.[79] If the four members "do not have consensus, then the issue is not taken up."[80] Furthermore, even though the Wise Men frequently suggest policies that are met with criticism from either the government or social partners they try to present policy recommendations that have the possibility of being accepted by both. To do so, said Sørensen, "[We] put ourselves in their place," in order to try to anticipate everyone's reactions. So through the selection of research topics as well as the crafting of policy recommendations the Wise Men strive as best they can to establish conditions for consensus making even if their primary goal is to present recommendations based on factual analysis.

There are additional examples of consensus making within policy research organizations. As we have seen, ad hoc expert commissions strive to produce ideas that will be well received by everyone involved. Indeed, we were told that "[t]hey are used by the government to create politically acceptable proposals."[81] Monday Morning's seminars and working groups are also designed to generate consensus among a wide range of participants. And at FAOS the staff is in dialogue with the ministries, social partners, and other funders in determining the organization's research agenda.

But cooperation, negotiation, and consensus making are also ubiquitous *across* policy research organizations. Examples abound. The Wise Men share data and analytic expertise with the commissions, which can help foster consensus.[82] Furthermore, once DØR releases a report it goes to other organizations that sometimes try to replicate the analysis. As a result, research organizations learn from each other and make methodological adjustments accordingly.[83] In situations like these agreements about methods are usually forthcoming, which surely expedites consensus making on more substantive matters later.[84]

A particularly interesting example of interorganizational cooperation and consensus making involves DA and LO, which often work together on research projects. In one case, they ran a joint research program on inequalities in the labor market and used the results to amend their general labor market

[79]Interview with Peter Birch Sørensen, Wise Men.
[80]Interview with Lars Haagen Pedersen, DØR.
[81]Interview with Jørn Neergaard Larsen, DA.
[82]Interviews with Peter Birch Sørensen, Wise Men; Lars Haagen Pedersen, DØR.
[83]Interview with Lars Haagen Pedersen, DØR.
[84]Interview with Lars Andersen, AE.

agreement.[85] And we learned during our interviews that they were presently collaborating on a research project studying the sickness leave system where they hoped to reach consensus on policy recommendations and then together lobby the government for legislative reforms. A senior DA official told us that this is not unusual and that DA and LO shared information with each other "all the time." He noted as well that there are well-known points of disagreement between them. But these do not usually cause trouble:

> It's a very peaceful process where things—consciously or unconsciously—are kept separated. These are the areas where we compete; these are areas where we can collaborate. . . . We don't even have to have a meeting because we know each other so well. . . . I mean we talk together all the time.

In short, they have developed over many decades a taken-for-granted understanding that they should work together as much as possible. It is all quite natural now. Indeed, when we left LO headquarters after interviews one day we passed a seminar room where DA's administrative director was addressing a group of trade unionists—an event that was not especially unusual. The head of LO and DA meet monthly to share information and coordinate their activities. DI also works with the unions preparing research reports and policy recommendations.[86] This is remarkable from an American perspective, where labor and business are generally at each other's throats.[87]

Of course, there is also competition in this world as we will discuss later. But several people told us that even when policy research organizations compete for funding, staff, or influence it is with mutual respect and collegiality. The relationship between LO and DA, just described, is one of many illustrations. Another is the relationship between CARMA and FAOS. They compete for funding but also cooperate on research projects. A senior official at CARMA described FAOS like this: "They are what we call competitor colleagues." Mutual respect like this was less evident in the United States where people made several disparaging remarks about competing organizations. Nobody made remarks like this to us in Denmark.

---

[85]Interview with Jørn Neergaard Larsen, DA. DA was engaged in cooperation with unions on several projects at least as early as the early 1980s (DA annual report 1983/1984, pp. 28, 32).
[86]Interview with Finn Larsen, LO. He noted, as well, that LO requires routine training of its staff in how to collaborate with people from DA, DI, and other peak associations. In his words, "One of the main tasks of my job is to work and teach the new people how to deal with people in DA."
[87]In Denmark business-labor cooperation is deeply rooted in mutual respect for each other's interests. The LO's Finn Larsen explained his strategy in business-labor negotiations: "There's always two sides of a problem. . . . You should not bring up a deal and an agreement with your counterparts . . . if you don't think that it creates positive results backwards [for both sides]."

Policy research organizations also facilitate cooperation and consensus making throughout the Danish political economy by providing *bridges* connecting the knowledge, policymaking, and production regimes. Consider the Wise Men again. They connect frequently with the policymaking regime by giving briefings to civil servants and various parliamentary committees, and with the production regime by conferring with the social partners not only within DØR but also as members of boards, commissions, and the like where they sit together.[88] When we asked the Wise Men's chair whether these activities help connect the three regimes he said, "Yeah, to some extent you'll be a bridge. That's true." Thanks to bridges like these people in different parts of the political economy interact frequently with one another, learn about each other's problems and ideas, and thus have opportunities to reach agreement on a wide variety of policy issues. Similarly, we heard from the director of research at LO that through their research unit's frequent communication with ministries, commissions, political parties, and employer associations during the course of their research, much sharing of information occurs in ways that reduce the chances for surprise and disagreement when final reports are issued. As a result, he explained, "In four out of five times there would be no real news."

A senior official from CARMA gave us a nice example of how his policy research organization helped facilitate consensus in the policymaking and production regimes. Through CARMA's research he and some others introduced the term "flexicurity" to describe Denmark's labor market policies. Flexicurity is a set of policies, including low levels of employment protection so that employers can hire and fire virtually at will; generous welfare programs for those who lose their jobs; and substantial job retraining and relocation programs to ease the unemployed back into the work force. Their research showed how this policy package helped improve Danish labor market performance in ways that benefited both workers and employers.[89] According to our contact at CARMA, both social partners latched on to the term and now advocate it publicly both in Denmark and abroad as "a wonderful model . . . based on this give and take model of negotiations." In other words, developing the flexicurity concept helped crystallize understanding and enthusiasm between the social partners for these policies. Upon hearing this we asked him whether CARMA in this context was part of the Danish "consensus making machine." He replied without hesitation, "And there the answer will be yes sir! I think we are."

Overall, then, policy research organizations try to make sense of the nation's economic situation in consensus-oriented ways that feature much

[88]Interviews with Peter Birch Sørensen, Wise Men; Lars Haagen Pedersen, DØR.
[89]For example, see Madsen (2006).

dialogue and negotiation with the social partners, policymakers, and experts within and across policy research organizations. In this sense, the Danish knowledge regime is a collective and solidaristic enterprise seeking to promote socioeconomic balance in the interests of everyone. This is facilitated further by consensus among Danish economists.

Consensus Making and the Brotherhood of Economists

There is considerable agreement among Danish economists about the appropriate econometric models that should be used for modeling the economy and making forecasts about it. Whereas much of the agreement on methods that we found in Germany was the result of external forces, notably the Leibniz process of accrediting policy research organizations, the like-mindedness among Danish economists was more organic.[90]

To begin with, Denmark is a small country with only a handful of university economics departments. And according to the LO's director of research, most economists in policy research organizations receive their training at either of just two Danish universities—Copenhagen and Aarhus—which are reputed to have the best economics departments and use the same economic models. As he put it, "It's still considered that there are only two real economic [departments] in Denmark. It's Copenhagen and Aarhus. . . . You need to come from these two."[91] As a result, economists in the peak associations, ministries, and elsewhere tend to think alike.

Second, Lars Andersen at AE told us that economists from different policy research organizations confer with each other to work out mutually agreeable methodological and modeling approaches. As one economist explained, "In a small country like this one, of course, most people in the economics profession know each other. And they talk—they can't avoid meeting each other and they talk, so there's a lot of informal exchange of ideas."[92] Economists at AE, for instance, talk with economists at the Ministry of Finance and DØR. Andersen said that "technical negotiations" like this are "normal" and often resolve "analytical conflicts." Similarly, as noted earlier, when economists try to replicate an analysis from DØR they often confer with DØR's economists in ways that facilitate methodological cross-fertilization and thus methodological convergence. We heard the same thing from people at other

---

[90] As in Germany, this is rather different from the United States, where deep divisions persist within the economics profession (e.g., Skidelsky 2009, pp. 30–31).

[91] He said that if someone was trained at another Danish economics department, he would not hire them!

[92] Interview with Peter Birch Sørensen, Wise Men.

organizations who, for example, sometimes even share computer programs with each other toward this end.[93] Indeed, people want to avoid methodological arguments wherever possible. As a result, organizations such as AE and the Ministry of Finance also monitor each other to keep abreast of what they are doing methodologically, which is also why the entire field has become more sophisticated scientifically.[94]

Third, almost everyone uses the same data, generally assembled and provided by Statistics Denmark.[95] DA also produces a variety of data about the labor market that it shares widely. And the basic econometric models, ADAM, SMEC, and DREAM, are public goods available to everyone.[96] The Ministry of Finance, AE, DØR including the Wise Men, and other policy research organizations tend to rely on these models and share information with each other about how to use and improve them. This is indicative of an underlying consensus that these are the analytic tools and by implication the theoretical assumptions that everyone should share. Hence, agreements about methods are usually forthcoming.[97] According to the LO's research director, "You have to confess to the same statistics and the same models. That's the framework, the world we are discussing." Others concurred.[98]

Finally, consensus among policy research organizations on methodological matters stems as well from the considerable occupational mobility of economists among these organizations and the diffusion of methods that accompanies it. The AE's Lars Andersen said, for instance, that one of their economists came from the ministry and that this is one reason why AE adopted some of the ministry's analytic techniques.

All of this has given rise to what the LO's Jan Kæraa Rasmussen called an extremely tight-knit "brotherhood of economists" among policy research organizations in Denmark that agrees on the basic econometric and analytical approaches.[99] For reasons we discuss shortly, the brotherhood of economists has become more important over the past couple of decades. There are more economists doing this sort of work now than there used to be in the peak associations, universities, ministries, regional and municipal authorities, and banks because it is no longer the case that political muscle is the key policy

[93]Interview with Lars Haagen Pedersen, DØR. He mentioned too that the development of the DREAM model was itself a collaborative effort between economists at the Ministry of Finance and Ministry of Business.

[94]Interview with Finn Kenneth Hansen, CASA.

[95]Interviews with Jan Kæraa Rasmussen, LO; Lars Andersen, AE; Lars Haagen Pedersen, DØR.

[96]The Law Model, however, is used mainly by the Ministry of Finance.

[97]Interview with Lars Andersen, AE.

[98]Interview with Lars Andersen, AE.

[99]Whether he was factually correct in implying by the term "brotherhood" that most of these economists were men is unclear. But we use the term here because it was one that people used during our interviews.

determinant. As Rasmussen put it, political muscle is now "the last thing you try." Many people we interviewed agreed.[100] Today, he said, you need sound argument and analysis to carry the day—and in this environment good economists have become particularly valuable because they have reached agreement on basic analytic principles and therefore can do analysis that helps "smooth the process" of reaching consensus. Put differently, the consensus on methods, forecasting, data, and the like among Danish economists has increased their credibility and influence such that if the brotherhood is in agreement, then it is very difficult for anyone to criticize their view.[101] This surely expedites compromise and consensus on policy later. We found nothing quite like this in our other countries.[102]

In sum, an important reason why policy analysis involves so much consensus making is that the brotherhood of economists does much of the work. And the brotherhood itself has reached consensus on most important matters as a result of their common training and their willingness to negotiate methodological differences and otherwise work together. This, of course, is another echo of the small Danish negotiated political economy.

But why did the brotherhood of economists and sophisticated policy analysis become more important in Denmark? And why is it that political muscle is the "last thing you try" nowadays to influence Danish policymaking? The answer is that beginning in the late 1970s people began to perceive that the knowledge regime had become dysfunctional in the sense that analysis and advice long based on ideology was no longer seen as useful for policymakers and others in coping with the problems wrought by the end of the Golden Age and the rise of globalization. They recognized in effect that the knowledge regime's complementary relationship with the rest of the political economy had broken down. This requires explanation because it also accounts for other knowledge regime changes.

Change and the Crisis of Ideology

Thanks to the end of the Golden Age the 1970s and 1980s were difficult times for Denmark. Unemployment averaged 1.3% annually from 1960 to 1973 but jumped to 8% during the 1980s as annual productivity growth slipped from 3.0% to 1.2%. Importantly, between 1960 and 1973 the government enjoyed budget surpluses averaging 1.6% of GDP but during the 1980s suffered deficits

[100]Interviews with Niels Trampe, Jørn Neergaard Larsen, and a senior official, DA; senior officials at FAOS, SFI, and *Ugebrevet A4*.
[101]Interview with Lars Andersen, AE.
[102]Peter Birch Sørensen, Wise Men, said that the economics profession was more tightly knit in Denmark than in any other country. This is presumably also an artifact of the country's small size.

averaging 3.4% of GDP. Annual inflation averaged 6.2% during the 1960s and early 1970s, jumped to 10.8% in the late 1970s, and slipped back to 6.9% during the 1980s.[103] Many people believed that inflation was driven by public and private sector wage growth and began to doubt whether traditional corporatist institutions could still moderate wage demands as they had during the Golden Age. They also wondered whether Keynesian demand management policies to which everyone had agreed since the 1950s worked anymore, especially insofar as public sector spending seemed to be unsustainable in the tough post–Golden Age economy.[104]

The government moved on several fronts to resolve these problems. In 1982 it pegged the Danish currency to the West German mark and increased its control over municipal budgets. A conservative government struck a deal with the social partners in 1987 to restrain wages. And welfare reforms were undertaken to help curb public spending. None of this happened quickly but rather involved the efforts of four consecutive governments and exhaustive negotiations with the political parties, ministries, social partners, and others.[105] Furthermore, in an effort to infuse the economy with more flexibility the old system of centralized tripartite corporatist negotiations was replaced by today's hierarchical and decentralized general system of negotiations that is coordinated by the Ministry of Finance and accessible to a wider array of participants than before.

The important point for us, however, is that Denmark's political-economic problems triggered a crisis of ideology and a search for new ways to make sense of the country's economic situation. Beginning in the mid-1970s both left- and right-wing governments began to realize more so than their counterparts in our other countries that their ideologies could no longer make sense of what was happening in the economy or how to handle it.[106] As a result, new political parties began to emerge that did not subscribe to the conventional left- or right-wing political ideologies. During the so-called landslide election of 1973 the traditional Danish party system was upended as the number of parties in parliament doubled from five to ten, of which three were brand-new. Furthermore, in 1978, for the first time since the war, the Social Democratic and Liberal Parties formed a left-right coalition government although one that lasted only about a year. Summarizing things a few years later Prime Minister Poul Schlüter declared famously that "all ideology was rubbish."[107]

[103]Kenworthy 1997, tables 3 and 7.
[104]Iversen 1999, chap. 5.
[105]These governments were led by the Social Democratic Party (1975–82 and 1993–2011), the Conservative Party (1982–93), and the Liberal Party (2001–11).
[106]Interviews with Jørn Neergaard Larsen and Niels Trampe, DA.
[107]Lees-Marshment 2009, p. 230.

According to Niels Trampe at DA, the crisis of ideology was amplified by the European Union single market project, which further exposed Denmark's already open economy to even more international competition. The upshot of all this, he explained, was that "[w]e can't base Danish policymaking on old, local ideological thinking. And in the EU system you can't use the left- and right-wing political views." More pragmatic and less ideological sense making was required. He exaggerated a bit when he told us that "[i]deology in Denmark is gone. I mean, you don't—15, 20 years ago you were a liberal or you were socialist. That is gone now." But others agreed that the influence of ideology had diminished significantly since the 1970s.[108]

The crisis of ideology had far-reaching consequences for the knowledge regime. In particular it led to (1) an increased reliance on economic expertise in policy analysis and advising, (2) more state control in organizing knowledge regime activities, and (3) an escalation in competition, advocacy work, and lobbying.

The Rise of Economic Expertise

The crisis of ideology led to the rise of expert economic analysis as the cornerstone for policy advising. This was part of an increasing tendency for the state to intervene into economic affairs traditionally left to the social partners and corporatist institutions. For instance, in the old days DA and LO retreated behind closed doors, made decisions about wages, working conditions, and other labor market issues, and everyone accepted the outcome. But after the Golden Age politicians and civil servants felt that these matters were too important and complex to leave to the social partners and that the state needed to play a greater role. And as the state became more involved it increasingly demanded ideologically neutral, evidence-based policy analysis from DA, LO, and other organizations in order to make sense of the situation. In one interview someone told us, "The politicians are asking for more evidence in the political process," so if organizations want to have influence, then they need to base their arguments on good data and analysis.[109] Others agreed that the demand for scientific policy analysis had grown significantly.[110] A senior official from the university-based FAOS said, "There is a demand for research-based knowledge that [is] much more clear or solid now, I would say, than 10 years ago." He noted that this is why you will find a lot more academics working in these organizations nowadays. This is one reason, he added, why the state, unions, and employers are all willing to fund a policy research organization like his.

---

[108]Interview with Per Schultz Jørgensen, Alternative Welfare Commission.
[109]Interview with senior official, SFI.
[110]Interviews with Lars Andersen, AE; senior official, DA; Finn Kenneth Hansen, CASA; and Jan Kæraa Rasmussen, LO.

Further evidence of the push for better economic research lies in the fact that many policy research organizations now encourage their staff to publish more of their research than they used to in scholarly journals.[111] Moreover, the move toward more evidence-based argument spilled over into the media. One journalist told us that the media now report more surveys and other sorts of data than they did 20 years ago. Why? Because the interest organizations that the media cover realize that they can no longer just express their ideological views. Now they need to make their arguments in evidence-based ways that will help shape how everyone understands the economic situation.[112]

The rise of expert policy analysis also stemmed from the weakening of ties between the peak associations and the political parties. According to a senior official at DA, this was "one of the reasons why this organization and other organizations changed from this ideological approach to a more analytical approach." Others at DA and elsewhere concurred.[113]

The crisis of ideology and the trend toward more expert policy analysis also affected the state's research capacities. Beginning in the 1980s the state began cultivating more analytic capabilities. In particular, the Ministry of Finance began working on the ADAM model to include supply-side effects. Later in the 1990s the DREAM model was developed to do long-term forecasting of how demographic and other changes would affect welfare expenditures and thus the state's fiscal problems. The Law Model, which was similar in purpose, was developed at the same time but used exclusively by the Ministry of Finance. The Ministry of Business began devising another model to evaluate the effects of economic policies on economic performance, but the DREAM model was eventually used instead. And Statistics Denmark began building a massive database for microeconomic analysis. The impetus behind it all was twofold. First, thanks to the end of the Golden Age, in the early 1980s the government faced serious problems, notably mounting budget deficits, which stymied conventional Keynesian thinking, so new econometric models were required.[114] Second, thanks to the crisis of ideology, the state wanted to become less dependent on ideologically biased analysis from outside organizations like the peak associations. A senior official at DA explained:

> They [politicians and civil servants] wanted to be better prepared
> and have advice on more than just an ideological basis. . . . Generally
> you could say that the politicians in the 1970s in this country were
> at the mercy of organizations like this [DA]. I mean he [a politician]

[111]Interview with senior official, SFI.
[112]Interview with senior official, *Ugebrevet A4.*
[113]Interviews with senior official and Niels Trampe, DA; Lars Andersen, AE.
[114]Interview with Lars Haagen Pedersen, DØR.

had no—perhaps he shared a secretary with five other members of parliament. But he had—I mean he could get a paper from an organization and he would have nobody to give it to and ask, "Could you look through this? Is it true that this is a problem? And the remedies they propose, are they relevant?" And the politicians couldn't do that before the mid-1980s.

This was also why in the mid-1980s the state began to replace the traditional tripartite commissions with ad hoc expert commissions to provide policy analysis and recommendations on an array of economic issues. The idea was to rely less on input from the traditional social partners and more on input from experts and other interested groups.[115] Torben M. Andersen, chair of the Welfare Commission, explained that the move toward commissions with more expertise was "because [of a] desire for non-ideological and open discussion." Expert commissions were especially prominent after the 1990s. Since then, there have been at least seven high-profile commissions advising the government on major reforms in taxation, welfare, public administration, and more. The shift from tripartite to expert commissions was also a reflection of an opening up of traditional corporatist institutions.[116]

To be sure, the causes behind the ascendance of expert policy analysis in Denmark's knowledge regime were complex. The diminishing importance of political ideology was perhaps the most proximate cause, but it was not alone. Post–Golden Age challenges confronting the production regime, including more intense international competition due to globalization and the European Union single market project, also had effects. Making sense of these new challenges was increasingly difficult within conventional ideological frameworks. The policymaking regime was also confronted with unique challenges stemming from the end of the Golden Age—in particular a fiscal crisis of the state—which gave rise to new econometric tools, such as the DREAM and Law Models, and databases to help make better sense of the economy. Peter Birch Sørensen, Wise Men chair, summed it up saying that major changes in analytic thinking, modeling, and the policy reforms that followed "were forced through during [these] times of crisis."[117]

Of course, the growing importance of expert analysis does not mean that everyone has developed comparable analytic capacities. We were told in one

[115]This was a direct challenge to the power of the LO and DA insofar as the tripartite commissions had previously drafted much legislation for parliament but would now serve only an advisory role (Pedersen 2011, chap. 5).

[116]Interview with Jørgen Søndergaard, Labor Market Commission.

[117]The ability to run these new and more complex models was also fostered by advances in computing technology and the availability of better data (interview with Lars Haagen Pedersen, DØR).

interview, for instance, that some private research organizations to which the state and others occasionally outsource research do not always do especially rigorous work.[118] Similarly, although forecasting models have improved substantially, not everyone has the in-house expertise to use them.

There are signs that the decline of ideology and the rise of more expert economic and policy analysis contributed to more consensus making in Denmark. Two examples illustrate the point. First, Niels Trampe from DA said that because ideological differences had diminished between DA and LO they competed less over policy analysis than they used to. Notably, when DA produces an analysis it is no longer the case that the LO will immediately produce one that shows something very different. This, he added, is because the two organizations are now "thinking very much in the same direction." Second, the LO's director of research explained how relying more on solid empirical research led the LO to change some of its long-standing policy views in favor of those favored by the employers and the state. Based on their research the LO realized the advantages of active labor market policies over open-ended unemployment benefits in terms of moving people back into the labor market. As he put it, "A combination of research and gradual reform showed that a much better way [to reduce unemployment] was to have an active labor market policy." When we asked whether this was a case of the LO changing its policy position based on its research he said that it was. He said that this is how the LO worked nowadays meaning that analysis now trumped ideology. Besides, he added, they would not be able to hire good economists if they ignored or misrepresented their own research results. One of his colleagues agreed that for all the organizations involved in negotiations over these and other matters, expert analysis had become the key to decision making.[119]

This is not to say that there were no disagreements over policy analysis and advice. But the assumption was that people would try to achieve compromise and consensus in the pursuit of the underlying principles of socio-economic balance.[120] This attitude spilled over into the analytic realm as people sought agreement on the empirical assessment of the causes and consequences of the country's economic problems. Not surprisingly, then, when Denmark's Keynesian consensus began to wobble with the passing of the Golden Age a new consensus eventually replaced it that supported tighter control over state budgets and greater labor market flexibility but in ways that still maintained an egalitarian welfare state.[121]

[118]Interview with Finn Kenneth Hansen, CASA.

[119]Interview with Finn Larsen, LO.

[120]Pedersen 2006a.

[121]Despite this shift, net welfare state transfers received by low-income households actually *increased* significantly between 1979 and 2007 (Iversen 1999, chap. 5; Kenworthy 2011, chap. 2).

The critical point, however, is that the crisis of ideology triggered perceptions that the knowledge regime had become dysfunctional for the rest of the political economy and that the situation had to be rectified. People turned toward more objective and sophisticated empirical analysis as a result. The state played an important role in this regard. But, as we are about to see, its presence was felt in other ways too.

Increased State Control of the Knowledge Regime

The advent of more expert analysis was paralleled by an increase in the state's control over the knowledge regime. In addition to developing some of the most sophisticated forecasting models and databases available, sharing them with other organizations and demanding more evidence-based analysis, the state exercised greater discretion over who was involved in economic policy analysis and advising in the first place. Rather than assuming that commissions should be staffed only by civil servants, the social partners and perhaps a few others, the state shifted away from this tripartite structure to ad hoc expert commissions thereby ensuring itself a freer hand in selecting commission members. This meant that the state had more control over the commission formation process and was less dependent on analysis from the social partners.[122] Similarly, the prime minister's office began establishing knowledge councils, which included a wider array of experts, interest groups, state officials, and others to help generate new policy ideas. In short, the state began to assert its gatekeeping authority more than before.

A particularly notable example of this shift toward more pluralistic and expert oriented policy research organizations was the expansion of DØR in 2007. In addition to the traditional tripartite structure an environmental unit was added to the council. As a result, today's DØR includes the social partners and civil servants from several ministries but now also organizations representing environmental interests. A fourth member was also added to the Wise Men—a university-trained environmental economist.

The state's expanded influence on the knowledge regime is reflected in the fact that these other policy research organizations now sometimes shadow the government's research. For example, the LO prepares economic forecasts just as the Wise Men prepare their Danish Economy reports and the Ministry of Economics and the Interior prepares its Economic Survey. AE four-year research plans are also designed in part to shadow the government's research program. For instance, it checks and sometimes challenges economic analyses from the Ministry of Finance.[123]

---

[122]Interview with Lars Andersen, AE.
[123]Interview with Lars Andersen, AE.

Shadowing is occasionally politicized. For instance, AE and the Danish Elderly Association (Ældresagen), which represents senior citizens, kept an eye on what the Welfare Commission was doing and in some cases produced research on similar topics. AE produced reports criticizing the commission in part on methodological grounds for failing to dynamically model certain labor market trends.[124] The most ardent critic of the commission was the Alternative Welfare Commission, which ran from 2004 to 2008 and was established by a diverse group of social scientists soon after the Welfare Commission was set up. It offered alternative policy analysis and recommendations to those coming from the Welfare Commission.[125] The Alternative Welfare Commission began as an advocacy organization working with priests, authors, philosophers, and others to defend the welfare state in the interests of social justice and equality but then developed a scholarly side with university professors and researchers.[126] But the important point is that the state's policy research agenda now sets a rhythm for policy research organizations like these insofar as they shadow government sponsored analysis. As a couple of people explained, there is a "season" for the release of economic forecasts and analyses by many policy research organizations.[127]

In sum, another manifestation of the crisis of ideology was the state's move to incorporate a wider array of experts and policy research organizations into the knowledge regime. And, intentionally or not, it set an agenda and cyclical rhythm for policy analysis in the knowledge regime. All of this was done to improve the utility of policy analysis and advice for policymakers and was in effect another move to improve the knowledge regime's complementary relationship vis-à-vis the rest of the political economy. But the crisis of ideology had yet another effect—it stimulated competition in the knowledge regime.

The Rise of Competition, Advocacy Organizations, and Lobbying

The increasing importance of expertise in matters of economic and policy analysis helped introduce new elements of competition into Denmark's knowledge regime. To begin with, more university-based policy research organizations, such as CARMA and FAOS, entered the field and competed for funding.[128] We heard as well that SFI experienced more competition for government contracts from new research shops at Aalborg and Aarhus Universities.[129] Even the Wise Men and the rest of DØR, which have a special legal status requiring them to provide certain forecasts and reports each year to the government, have experienced more competition from university research shops, such as

---

[124]Interview with Lars Andersen, AE.
[125]Alternative Welfare Commission report, "The Future of the Welfare Society," 2005, pp. 8–9.
[126]Interview with Per Schultz Jørgensen, Alternative Welfare Commission.
[127]Interviews with Finn Larsen and Jan Kæraa Rasmussen, LO.
[128]Interviews with senior officials, CARMA and FAOS.
[129]Interview with senior official, SFI.

the Center for Economic and Business Research at the Copenhagen Business School that started to do similar kinds of work on a contract basis for the ministries. So, although the Wise Men and DØR "still have this little bit of a monopoly position" there are now more organizations doing the same kind of analytical work.[130] And in addition to university-based research organizations a number of private consulting firms have emerged in the field over the past 15 or 20 years selling analytic services.[131]

But beyond this proliferation of new research organizations, which is modest compared to our other countries, government policy helped stimulate competition. A senior official at SFI told us that over the past two decades, "[t]here's been a policy of the government that they wanted to have more open competition for contract research." Given the state's fiscal woes and thus tighter budgetary constraints stemming from the end of the Golden Age ministries now need to muster convincing empirical evidence of the effectiveness of their programs in order to get more money for them from the government. As he explained:

> I think it's become more difficult for the Minister of Labor [for instance] to go and ask for more money . . . unless they can come up with convincing evidence that it would be a good bargain. . . . I think the request for the documentation of your request for money is increasing quite a lot.[132]

And in order to obtain the best possible evidence ministries as well as municipal governments began reaching out to a larger number of research organizations in a more competitive bidding process. Although 20 years ago it was sufficient for a government agency to call a single policy research organization and offer them a contract for some analysis, today that is no longer acceptable. And the larger the contract, the more organizations the agency needs to consider before making an award. As a result of this sort of competition, some research organizations have hired coordinators to monitor contract possibilities, calls for proposals, and the like. In one case, the director of a policy research organization told us off the record that their organization had lobbied the Ministry of Finance for more consideration in its competitive bidding process. According to another observer, all of this has been a "huge change in the field."[133] Others agreed that competition has risen due to these changes in government funding policies but added that the change was compounded in

---

[130] Interview with Peter Birch Sørensen, Wise Men.
[131] Interview with Finn Kenneth Hansen, CASA.
[132] He was emphatic that it has become "very, very hard for them [the ministries] to get new money" under the current budget constraints in Denmark.
[133] Interview with Finn Kenneth Hansen, CASA.

the early 2000s by the Liberal-Conservative government's belief in the virtues of competition.[134]

As the relevance of ideology diminished and the importance of expert analysis escalated, competition revolved increasingly around which organization's research was the best on technical grounds. In this sense AE, for instance, saw itself competing with the Ministry of Finance's DREAM Group.[135] When we asked the director of research at LO how he evaluated the LO's competitive status in the field he said that they tracked which organization's forecasts were the most accurate and which organization's policy analyses turned out to be right or wrong. As he put it, "Well, you take—usually you take maybe the foremost important variables like unemployment, GDP, inflation and current account balance or public deficit. . . . Then you will see how we fared in that forecasting." Consequently, to be competitive in this game you need to hire the best people, which he said was a second metric by which he assessed the LO's competitive position—a metric against which he felt that the LO fared rather well: "I think we recruit some of the best economists in Denmark." Fifteen years ago, he added, it was harder to recruit the best but that has changed because now the LO is recognized as a place where a lot of energy is put into research and analysis. Others agreed that recruiting people who can do the best analytic work has become more important and competitive over the years.[136]

However, there was one organization that everyone agreed was a competitive maverick. This was CEPOS. Martin Ågerup, the director, explained that CEPOS was established in response to change in the policymaking regime. Specifically, it was a reaction to the Liberal-Conservative government of Anders Fogh Rasmussen moderating its initial right-wing views and shifting toward the center of the political spectrum. It was also a response, he said, to Rasmussen's public call for a free market think tank in Denmark. The recent emergence of CEPOS and a very few other advocacy organizations reflects an increasing concern with what one official at *Ugebrevet A4*, the LO's magazine, called the "consensus society." In his view:

> No one—[not] even the politicians—have the courage to have opinions. Before they go into the public sphere, they do—they compromise with their own views, and I think that's very, very dangerous to the political culture that no one dares to say what they think. No politicians dare to say what they think. And I think that's a very, very big challenge for the political culture in the future. . . . You have this commentary tendency and it has this consensus—you have

---

[134]Interview with Mette Wier, AKF.
[135]Interview with Lars Andersen, AE.
[136]Interview with senior official, SFI.

this tendency that you have to—that you drop your opinion before entering the public sphere, and that is very dangerous, I think.

In other words, CEPOS is a backlash against the institutionalized consensus making that has been the hallmark of the Danish political economy for decades and the Liberal-Conservative government's move away from ideological argument. People told us, nevertheless, that the main influence of CEPOS on the field has only been to exacerbate the amount of competition for media attention and, in turn, to expand the range of public debate.[137] Otherwise CEPOS remains on the margins of the knowledge regime.

Perhaps indicative of this backlash as well, lobbying is on the rise in Denmark. Tripartite negotiations involving the social partners and state are still a primary mechanism for influencing policymaking. But we were told on several occasions that lobbying has become more prevalent over the past 15 years as a means of influencing the government.[138] Even some peak associations have started hiring professional lobbying companies, such as Burson-Marsteller from the United States. This reflects the move away from traditional corporatist bargaining toward a more open policymaking regime and system of negotiation. A senior official at DI said that lobbying has become one of his organizations more important means of influence. Why? He explained that as traditional tripartite corporatist institutions gave way to new more pluralist forms of negotiation "the necessity" for lobbying grew. A senior official from DA noted that over the past 10 years DA has established a group of 11 professional lobbyists. Importantly, he as well as some of his colleagues said that the lobbying and research sides of the organization have also come to work more closely together over the past decade.[139] Here, then, is another example of the tight connections among knowledge, policymaking, and production regimes.

However, this is not American-style lobbying advocating for narrow special interests. Rather, as in France and Germany, it involves pressing ideas deemed to be in the general interest of society.[140] Moreover, lobbying also involves the media. So, for example, the peak associations have established communication departments that are now working with their lobbying and research units to influence the public discourse as well as whatever negotiations they may be involved in or anticipating. The media, then, have become

[137]Interviews with senior official, DA; Lars Andersen, AE.
[138]Interviews with senior official, Niels Trampe, and Jørn Neergaard Larsen, DA; senior official, DI; Finn Larsen, LO.
[139]Interviews with senior official, Niels Trampe, and Jørn Neergaard Larsen, DA.
[140]We heard, however, in several interviews that DA, DI, and LO engage in American-style lobbying in a different sense—they sometimes prepare legislative language for politicians to use when writing new laws.

an increasingly important target for many organizations. We heard at both LO and DA that their lobbying initiatives are now often preceded by placing news stories in the media in an effort to prepare politicians, civil servants, and the public for upcoming policy debates and negotiations.[141] This too makes sense insofar as the old corporatist backroom decision making has given way to more inclusive and transparent negotiations. Indeed, many ad hoc expert commissions are now required by the state to issue not only technical reports for the government but also summary reports for the public, and to run open seminars and conferences.

Although the entrance of a few more policy research organizations and the turn toward lobbying has led to more competition, this pales in comparison to the intense competition we found in Washington. As we have seen, competition in Demark is quite collegial and friendly in most cases. Several things that we have discussed help keep competition in check. First, it is not uncommon for competitors for funding in one situation to work together on projects in another. Second, the social partners often lobby *together* for the same thing, which minimizes competition between them. We were told at LO that joint lobbying with employer associations happened almost monthly.[142] Third, because it is a small country with relatively few policy research organizations there is a degree of niche specialization that mitigates competition. Some organizations specialize in forecasting while others do policy evaluation research. Some focus on macro-level analysis while others specialize in micro-level analysis.[143] Finally, competition in Denmark is muted by the fact that policymaking is still embedded in an institutionalized and very much taken-for-granted system of consensus-oriented negotiations.

Let us be clear about the significance of all this. Increased competition was yet another manifestation of the crisis of ideology and people's subsequent efforts to restore the knowledge regime's institutional complementarity with the rest of the political economy. But in at least one case—CEPOS—competition involved a direct challenge to one of the most basic principles of the knowledge regime and for that matter the Danish political economy—the principle of consensus.

Conclusion

Denmark's knowledge regime is unique thanks to its history as a small vulnerable country, its legacy of extensive negotiations in both the political and economic spheres, its well-organized production regime, the prominence of

---

[141]Interview with Finn Larsen, LO.
[142]Interview with Finn Larsen, LO.
[143]Interviews with senior officials, CARMA and SFI.

the central state, and nearly everyone's support for the basic concepts of social partnership and socioeconomic balance. The effects that its production and policymaking regimes had on its knowledge regime were profound. The production regime's effects resembled those in Germany insofar as the demands of corporatism led business and labor organizations to establish their own policy analysis operations. But in Denmark they developed their own analytic capacities *in-house* in order to be especially well prepared for various political and economic negotiations rather than relying on independent policy research organizations as they did in Germany.[144] As one of our contacts at the LO explained, "Our whole life is about negotiations."[145] Furthermore, the formidable presence of the peak associations minimized the possibility that other private policy research organizations might be established, such as those found frequently in the United States. Corporatist echoes were also evident insofar as the social partners sometimes funded and sat on the boards of some university policy research organizations, such as FAOS and CARMA, and interfaced with semi-public research shops like the ad hoc commissions and DØR's Wise Men.

The policymaking regime's effects resembled those in France insofar as the central state played a very direct role in organizing knowledge regime activities. Today the state funds various semi-public policy research organizations, often has representatives on their boards, and sets up various ad hoc commissions. It also maintains the premiere econometric models and databases that everyone uses—many of which it produced in the first place. It produces some of the most important economic forecasts and analyses every year that other policy research organizations shadow. And in many cases it serves as a gatekeeper granting different organized groups and experts access to the processes of policy analysis, negotiation, and consensus making.

The blending of certain German and French traits was clear when problems in the production regime materialized thanks to the end of the Golden Age and the rise of globalization—problems that precipitated a crisis of ideology and subsequent response. People perceived in effect that the knowledge regime no longer provided complementary benefits for the rest of the political economy. The state led the way in trying to fix things in the knowledge regime by demanding, facilitating, and in some cases providing more expert evidence-based policy analysis and guidance, such as through the development of new analytic models and databases. The difference with France, of course, was that this was all done in ways that were in keeping with Denmark's legacy of institutionalized systems of political and economic negotiation with the social partners and to an increasing extent others—a legacy similar to but more extensive than that which we saw in Germany. And along these lines the Danish

[144]Interviews with Jan Kæraa Rasmussen, LO; senior official, DA.
[145]Interview with Finn Larsen, LO.

labor and employer peak associations ramped up their analytic capacities too. Indeed, much of the policy analysis produced in Denmark is oriented toward policy negotiations of various sorts among an array of public and private actors. Notably, economic surveys and analyses from the Ministry of Finance, the Ministry of Economics and the Interior, DØR as well as the peak associations are designed to influence negotiations on the public budget, labor market agreements, and other matters.

The importance of negotiations in Denmark requires further emphasis. The fact that much policy analysis in the knowledge regime is directed at negotiations underscores how tightly linked the knowledge, policymaking, and production regimes are in Denmark. For instance, the LO's director of research emphasized this connection when he told us that their research unit is essentially the "back office" providing analysis and information to their negotiators. The link between scholarly research and negotiations in the production and policymaking regimes is also very tight at the LO's counterpart, DA, where Jørn Neergaard Larsen told us:

> We have created during the last ten years in this organization [DA] a very clear and systematic way of handling analysis. . . . We work with strategic plans, decided by our board, for periods—for five-year periods. And inside such a five-year period, for example 2004 to 2010, we decide in our staff . . . which political labor market issues will come and be heavy issues in two years' time, year after year. And based on that we produce a labor market analysis, and that's to try to create a foundation for our political priorities and for our lobby activities.[146]

His colleague at DA, Niels Trampe, agreed, saying, "Our political lobbying and our analytical work have been integrated. And I think that's true for most other interest groups in Denmark, that you have merged these two things."

To be sure, the recalibration of Denmark's knowledge regime led to some separation between it and the policymaking and production regimes. There are now more independent policy research organizations, such as FAOS, CARMA, and CASA. CEPOS does not have tight links to either the policymaking regime or the production regime's peak associations, although it does have corporate funding. And the role of experts was elevated relative to the role of the social partners on the ad hoc commissions and elsewhere.

Yet the three-way linkage among knowledge, policymaking, and production regimes remains tighter in Denmark than in our other countries thanks

---

[146] A senior official at DI told us a very similar story.

to the nature of Denmark's political economy where most important political and economic decisions are made in consensus-oriented negotiations. These linkages are especially clear in policy research organizations like the peak associations that operate simultaneously in all three regimes. But they are also clear in policy research organizations like DØR and the ad hoc commissions that provide sites where people from all three regimes meet, analyze, discuss, negotiate, and seek compromise and consensus. Indeed, although there is a bit more competition in the Danish knowledge regime than there used to be cooperation continues to rule most of the time—even among strange bedfellows like the employer and labor peak associations.

To be sure, cooperation, negotiation, and consensus making are not a panacea. There are no guarantees that the policy analysis and decisions that flow from such a process will necessarily be effective in improving national economic performance. Put differently, resorting to consensus making does not ensure that people will always restore their knowledge regime's institutional complementarity if they perceive that it has broken down. After all, consensus making still involves trial-and-error experimentation and casting about for better analysis and policy advice—even if much of it is centrally orchestrated by the state. And the result of this process might involve people agreeing to things that turn out to be entirely wrong! The point is that there can be a downside as well as an upside to Danish-style consensus making.

One final clarification is in order. Just because the knowledge, policymaking, and production regimes remain tightly connected does not imply that policy research organizations are necessarily dominated by or subservient to economic or political interests. Consider in particular some of the semi-public scholarly research organizations like the ad hoc commissions. Although the state finances them it would be wrong to infer that it controls them in ways that bias their research. Their independence is guaranteed by law.[147] Ministries, for instance, are not allowed to give orders to the boards, managing directors, or staff of these organizations once they are up and running. And these organizations defend their independence when necessary. For instance, the government appointed civil servants from four ministries to the secretariat of its Welfare Commission, which ran from 2003 to 2005. But the commission soon became concerned about maintaining its political independence and eventually asked these people to leave.[148] Moreover, although the government gives commissions a mandate of which topics to address, they have considerable leeway in how they do so. The fact that they are obliged by law to take full responsibility for the research that they publish is another incentive to protect their independence.

[147]Law no. 326 of May 5, 2004.
[148]Interview with Torben M. Andersen, Welfare Commission.

The Wise Men also exhibit considerable independence. Peter Birch Sørensen insisted that they are independent not only from the rest of DØR but from the government too. How could he be so sure? "We usually criticize the government no matter what its political color is . . . [and] we have been willing to say quite a few unpopular things over the years." This, he added, has enhanced the Wise Men's credibility. Similarly, insofar as university-based policy research organizations are concerned they insist on publishing the results of their research regardless of what their funders or other stakeholders say about it—including the state.[149]

Even the peak associations' research units seem to enjoy a modicum of independence in doing their work. After all, as we noted earlier, the LO's research unit produced evidence that convinced the LO leadership to give up supporting open-ended unemployment benefits—one of its old sacred cows—in favor of active labor market policies, which brought the organization's position on the issue into line with the employers association and the state. Solid empirical analysis won out over whatever LO ideology or politics there might have been otherwise to stay the course.

This is not to say that the Danes we interviewed made a fuss over convincing us how independent their research operations were as they often did in the United States and France. Their remarks about the subject were only occasional asides during our interviews. Nor can we be sure that all of Denmark's policy research organizations enjoy the same degree of independence. But we suspect that the institutional context within which they operate nowadays, which puts a premium on negotiation, expertise, and rigorous empirical analysis as well as social partnership and socioeconomic balance, is at least as conducive to independence as that in any of our other three countries.

---

[149]Interviews with Finn Kenneth Hansen, CASA; senior official, FAOS.

Reprise

Initial Reflections on the National Cases

L et us pause and consider the implications of what we have presented in part I. We begin by reviewing our main findings so far about the national origins of policy ideas. Then we examine their implications for comparative political economy and for arguments about the independence of intellectual enterprises like policy analysis and advising. We conclude with a brief discussion of typologies of policy research organizations.

Main Findings

In part I we showed that each of our four knowledge regimes had a unique and nationally specific organizational and institutional topography. Then we argued that the end of the Golden Age of postwar capitalism and the rise of economic globalization triggered challenges to and changes in the policymaking and production regimes in each of our four countries that, in turn, precipitated change in the knowledge regimes. However, we also showed that the way this general story played out varied considerably across countries. First, it depended on the institutional configuration of each country's policymaking and production regimes, not to mention the initial institutional configuration of the knowledge regime entering the post–Golden Age era. Second, it depended on how people in each country viewed the situation—particularly how they perceived that their knowledge regime had become dysfunctional and in effect how its complementary relationship with the rest of the political economy had broken down. By dysfunctional and breakdown we mean that people believed that their knowledge regimes no longer helped them make sense of their particular situations. This involved perceptions of nationally specific crises—a crisis of partisanship in the United States, a crisis of state ideas in France, a crisis of corporatism in Germany, and a crisis of political ideology in Denmark. The result was that each knowledge regime ended up with a modified but still nationally specific character.

Table R.1 summarizes the key characteristics of each knowledge regime as we reported them in part I. This includes the unique mix of different types of policy research organizations operating at the time of our interviews (2008–9) as well as the most important changes.

The United States was the most *competitive* knowledge regime. As table R.1 indicates, its private sector was dominated by several scholarly and advocacy research organizations. Indeed, this knowledge regime had the most well-developed private sector of all of our countries. It also had strong state research capacities in both the executive and legislative branches of the state. There were virtually no semi-public research organizations, which meant that the public and private sectors in this knowledge regime were separated more clearly than in our other countries. Nor were there any research organizations affiliated formally with the political parties. Finally, the universities did not play a particularly significant policy research role. There was considerable competition for resources among the private organizations, which increased as they proliferated. Proliferation was initially a response to an emergent crisis of political partisanship but eventually contributed to it as well. Paradoxically, the crisis grew so intense that it finally led some private policy research organizations to try cooperating with each other across partisan lines in order to transcend political differences and seek common ground upon which they might develop ideas for solving the country's most pressing political-economic problems.

France was the most *statist* knowledge regime. Several prominent state research organizations operated on the executive side. The state also supported a number of permanent semi-public policy research organizations. In addition, the state financed political party foundation research operations but these were less central to the knowledge regime than these other organizations. There were virtually no private scholarly research organizations and only a few advocacy organizations. Unique to the French knowledge regime were a small handful of private business clubs. The Grandes Écoles provided a source of professional networks but had virtually no policy research organizations of

Table R.1. National Characteristics of Four Knowledge Regimes, 2008–2009

	United States (Competitive)	France (Statist)	Germany (Coordinated)	Denmark (Negotiated)
Mix of Policy Research Organizations				
Private: scholarly	***		*	***
Private: advocacy	***	*	*	*
Private: clubs		*		
Semipublic: permanent		**	***	***
Semipublic: temporary				***
State: executive branch	***	***	**	***
State: legislative branch	***			
Party		*	**	
University			*	**
Major Changes	Proliferation of private research organizations	Externalization of research from the state	Accreditation of research capacity	Rising state control over research
	Rising competition and then cooperation among private organizations	State's partial recentralization of research	Rising competition	Rising competition and expert advising

Note: ***Strong presence, **Moderate presence, *Weak presence. The absence of an asterisk indicates that this type of policy research organization was either absent or otherwise insignificant.

their own.[1] Many of the semi-public and private research organizations were founded in response to a crisis of ideas whereby people believed that the state's policy research organizations alone were no longer able to provide analysis and advice to help policymakers make sense of the country's post–Golden Age problems. The state led the way by externalizing some of these responsibili-

[1]Some might argue that OFCE is an exception insofar as it is housed in and funded through Sciences Po in Paris. But we still view OFCE as a semi-public research organization because, as we were told by a senior official there, it was established in the first place by politicians and its budget is still subject to their discretion.

ties to semi-public organizations that it founded, but others established the advocacy organizations and clubs—all in an effort to cultivate fresh thinking. This led to a more fragmented knowledge regime, part of which the state later moved to coordinate and recentralize.

Germany's knowledge regime is best characterized as *coordinated*. Often through the Länder the state funded a variety of important, permanent, semi-public scholarly economic research institutes. There were also a few privately funded scholarly shops that received support from either employer and industry associations or unions. Some of these research institutes were affiliated closely with universities through formal agreements for joint research activities. There were also some important state policy research organizations in the executive branch. And the state financed several political party foundations that operated think tanks, which were for the most part older and better resourced than their French counterparts. These were less central to the knowledge regime than the research institutes and state research organizations. The activities of several of these organizations, but especially the semi-public research institutes, were coordinated in formal and informal ways, including an accreditation process for the semi-public research institutes that was beefed up following unification. But when it became apparent to some people that there was a crisis of corporatism and that these traditional approaches to policy research and advising were either too sluggish for the fast-paced globalized world or otherwise inadequate they established a few advocacy organizations, which operated largely on the knowledge regime's margins but that introduced a bit more competition to it.

The defining feature of the Danish knowledge regime is that it involves much *negotiation*. Reflecting its corporatist tradition, it has permanent and temporary semi-public scholarly research organizations. Furthermore, the labor and employer peak associations have their own prominent private and rather scholarly research capacities but there are also a few other private scholarly research shops. Denmark also has a fair number of university-based policy research centers that interface with the state and the social partners—as do virtually all the semi-public research organizations. Reflecting its statist tradition, policymakers have formidable research capacities in the executive branch. And the state's control over the knowledge regime has increased to help overcome a crisis of ideology whereby people realized that traditional left-right political ideologies were inadequate for making sense of the country's post–Golden Age problems. This realization also led to the use of more expert-based analysis and advising as well as the establishment of a tiny handful of advocacy research organizations. Their presence plus the state's solicitation of more bids for contract research increased competition somewhat. Nevertheless, many of Denmark's policy research organizations still cooperate with each other and strive for consensus.

Implications for Comparative Political Economy

As we discussed in chapter 1, one of the great insights of the Varieties of Capitalism School for comparative political economy is that political and economic institutions sometimes complement one another in functionally synergistic ways that improve economic performance. Sometimes, as Robert Boyer argued, institutional complementarities are intentionally created but sometimes they occur by chance and are discovered only later, much as an investor spots opportunities for arbitrage. Furthermore, in Boyer's view institutional complementarities are not static; they can break down as circumstances change.[2] The analysis we have presented so far benefited greatly from these insights. However, it also provides additional lessons for comparative political economy in general and the theory of institutional complementarity in particular.

First, knowledge regimes are important. They generate much analysis and policy advice to which policymakers are exposed, and that policymakers may use to try to make sense of and resolve problems in their policymaking and production regimes. It stands to reason, then, that knowledge regimes can constitute a critical source of institutional complementarity for advanced political economies. Research in comparative political economy dwells on the institutional complementarities arising from the relationships between the policymaking and production regimes but neglects that complementarities can also involve knowledge regimes. Indeed, in each of our four cases, when people were confronted by serious problems stemming from the end of the Golden Age and the rise of globalization, they realized in effect that their knowledge regimes were no longer providing analysis and advice good enough for policymakers and others to make sense of and resolve these problems. And then they took steps to improve the situation. In other words, they perceived a breakdown in their knowledge regime's complementary relationship with the rest of the political economy and tried to fix it. Demonstrating whether the policy ideas that resulted from these reforms ultimately improved their country's political-economic performance is well beyond the scope of this book. Fortunately, as we explained in chapter 1, others have shown that these sorts of ideas have indeed affected national policymaking and performance.[3]

---

[2]Boyer 2005a, 2005b.

[3]See, for example, Blyth (2002, 2013), Campbell (2011), Peter Hall (1992, 1993), Pierson (1994), Prasad (2006), and Stiglitz (2009). A more comprehensive demonstration of the complementary relationship between a knowledge regime and the rest of the political economy would involve detailed process tracing showing not only how the organization (or reorganization) of a knowledge regime led to the production of certain ideas—a subject we explore more thoroughly in chapter 7—but also that these ideas eventually improved political-economic performance. We hope that other scholars will tackle these complex linkages, thereby tying our analysis closer to the existing literature on how ideas affect policymaking and political-economic performance.

Second, knowledge regimes and the complementarities they may engender are not static. Boyer's insights notwithstanding, much research from the Varieties of Capitalism School seems to take the stability of institutional complementarities for granted rather than seeing them as dynamic and subject to fluctuation. Indeed, several people have criticized the Varieties of Capitalism School for failing to account for change, a point to which we will return shortly. We have found in our cases that the degree to which people perceive that their knowledge regimes are functional or not in this regard is variable. Put differently, whether or not people believe that their policy research organizations help make sense of their problems is subject to fluctuation. Moreover, the art of constructing—or in our cases trying to restore—complementarities is not straightforward. It is often a trial and error process involving uneven stops and starts and sometimes partial reversals. In France, for example, policymakers initially launched an externalization strategy for cultivating fresh thinking in the knowledge regime but later realized that this led to an excessively fragmented set of policy research organizations. So policymakers took a second step by recentralizing and coordinating some knowledge regime activities. Similarly, in the United States efforts to improve the knowledge regime's complementarity for the rest of the political economy led initially to a proliferation of aggressive advocacy organizations, which had the deleterious consequence of exacerbating partisanship. In turn, a few of these organizations launched efforts to cooperate in ways intended to overcome some of the problems that excessive partisanship had caused. Indeed, establishing and restoring complementarities is likely a prolonged and complex process.

This leads to the third lesson—complementarities are not functionally guaranteed. And there is no assurance that when people try to create or restore complementarities that they will succeed. Insofar as knowledge regimes are concerned the changes people make do not always improve how well they make sense of their situations. Why? Because there is often much experimentation, puzzling, casting about and muddling through in the hope of improving policy analysis and ideas. Again the French and American cases illustrate the point insofar as in each one the initial effort to improve the knowledge regime's institutional complementarity for the rest of the political economy was eventually deemed inadequate and additional steps were taken—recentralization in France and decentralized cooperation in the United States. In this regard it is also important to remember that another reason why successful reform is not guaranteed is that it may involve conflict and struggle as is the case in most episodes of institutional change. In France, for instance, although some people wanted to foster private advocacy organizations they struggled for years with the civil service to obtain permission to establish them and then to change the tax code to make them easier to finance. In the United States although some organizations like the right-wing Heritage Foundation wanted to reach out to less conservative organizations and cooperate with them they faced opposition from partisan organizations that did not want them to do so. And in Denmark, the advocacy organization, CEPOS, set up shop in part as an act of resistance to the entire "consensus machine" as the knowledge regime was called in one of our interviews. This suggests as well that people may disagree vehemently over the best way to improve their knowledge regime's complementarity once they believe that it has broken down and no longer helps them make sense of their nation's political-economic problems.

The fact that these changes involved struggle, experimentation, muddling through, and so on regardless of how relatively centralized (i.e., France, Denmark) or decentralized (i.e., United States, Germany) it all was is fully in keeping with the sociological literature, which suggests that sense making is typically a rather dicey and haphazard affair. The Varieties of Capitalism School would benefit from paying closer attention to this literature not only because it helps safeguard against functionalist reasoning but because it may shed light on how people try to restore institutional complementarities once they suspect that they have broken down. On the other hand, sociologists interested in sense making could benefit from a comparative political economy perspective in order to infuse their arguments with a bit more national specificity. After all, we have found that the way sense making occurred and changed was nationally specific. Hence, our argument is as much about the national organization of sense making as it is about the national origins of policy ideas.

The fourth lesson for comparative political economy is that perception matters. Defining a situation in the first place as one where in effect complementarity has broken down may be up for grabs. And even when people believe that institutional complementarities have failed there is no assurance that they will take it seriously enough to initiate reforms. Although it is surely not the only explanation, this helps account for variation in the timing of change in our cases where it took longer for France and Germany to move than it took the United States and Denmark. To begin with, although the French began to see a crisis of ideas and embrace their externalization strategy in the late 1970s by establishing a few semi-public scholarly research organizations, arguably efforts to cultivate new sources of ideas did not really hit their stride until the late 1990s when the prime minister's office became so concerned about the dearth of fresh thinking that it funded the establishment of political foundation think tanks, established the Council of Economic Analysis, set up some new and important conseils, and created the Center for Strategic Analysis. It was also fairly late in the game when the new advocacy research organizations, notably Institute Montaigne, appeared. Change also came comparatively late in Germany insofar as the government did not open up the Joint Economic Report group to more competitive bidding until 2007. Although it established the Blue List accreditation process in 1977 it did not beef up the accreditation standards until founding the Leibniz Association after unification. And advocacy groups like INSM and SM did not appear in reaction to a perceived crisis of corporatism until the dawn of the twenty-first century. In contrast, at least on the private side of the knowledge regime, substantial changes in the United States began fairly early—in the late 1970s and 1980s—with the proliferation of new research organizations. The Danes were perhaps the fastest to see that their knowledge regime had become dysfunctional. After all, they acknowledged a crisis of ideology in the 1970s and by the 1980s were well on their way to devising better econometric forecasting models, replacing the traditional tripartite commissions with ad hoc expert commissions and more. The notion that perception matters may seem trite but is nonetheless important insofar as institutional theories—including those upon which the Varieties of Capitalism School is based—have been criticized for neglecting human agency and therefore being excessively deterministic.[4]

Finally, institutional complementarities may be a source of change. As noted earlier, comparative political economy and in particular the Varieties of Capitalism School has been criticized for not having a theory of change. In part this is attributed to the fact that they view institutional complementarity as a source of stability. The idea is that the interconnectedness of institutions and the complementarities or synergies that result tend to make it very difficult to change one institution because changing one implies changing others too since they are tightly coupled. And changing one could undermine the benefits resulting from institutional complementarity.[5] Our analysis points toward one way out of this dilemma. As circumstances change, in this case as problems developed in association with the end of the Golden Age and the rise of globalization, people may perceive that institutional complementarities break down, thereby undermining their ability to make sense of things. And when they do this creates incentives for them to try to restore complementarities through change. This is what happened in all of our cases. The point is that because institutional complementarities are not static but ebb and flow they may precipitate change if people perceive that they have failed. Once we take the dynamic nature of institutional complementarity seriously it can actually help us explain political-economic change rather than preventing us from doing so. Needless to say, the fact that these perceived breakdowns may involve the institutional complementarity of knowledge regimes is another reason why neglecting knowledge regimes as an integral part of modern political economies along with policymaking and production regimes is a serious oversight in comparative political economy.

Of course, all of this is nationally specific, which would come as no surprise to comparative political economists. Nor would they be surprised by

---

[4] Hirsch 1997; Hirsch and Lounsbury 1997; Thelen and Steinmo 1992.
[5] Campbell 2010; Crouch 2005, pp. 30–31.

the fact that the steps people took to improve their knowledge regime's institutional complementarity reflected past institutional arrangements and practices. In brief, the Americans developed more of what they already had—privately funded policy research organizations. This took place alongside a set of state policy research organizations many of which had been in place for several decades. The French did what they have always done by relying heavily on the state to ameliorate the situation. After all, the externalization strategy was state-led. The Germans tried to improve the manner in which they already coordinated activity among organizations, such as by beefing up the Leibniz accreditation criteria and by reaching out to more semi-public research organizations through a more open and competitive selection process for the Joint Economic Report group. And the Danes turned increasingly toward more scientific policy analysis but in ways that involved much negotiation and cooperation among organizations, which had long been key features of their political economy. In short, changes in each country unfolded in path-dependent ways—that is, knowledge regimes changed but in ways that were still consistent with the national character of their political economies.

Implications for the Independence of Policy Analysis

The degree to which policy research organizations operated independently from their supporters was not a central question for us in this project. Nevertheless, in each of the preceding empirical chapters we have offered some observations about this—although certainly not a systematic analysis. In some cases this meant independence from the state while at other times it meant independence from private actors including wealthy individuals, philanthropic foundations, corporations, employer associations, and labor unions. These observations have implications for theories concerning the nature of expert policy ideas and advice. As we explained in chapter 1, materialists stretching at least back to the writings of Marx and Gramsci maintain in one way or another that these sorts of ideas reflect the interests of powerful ruling classes or elites. In contrast, an idealist like Karl Mannheim in his writing on free-floating intellectuals argued that these sorts of ideas may come from independent intellectuals or experts who are largely immune from the influence of political and economic actors. Our evidence complicates this debate.

To begin with, the materialists are probably right that sometimes expert ideas reflect powerful class or elite interests. But they would be wrong to generalize too far. In the United States, for instance, one could argue that the analysis and advice emanating from private research organizations like the Heritage Foundation, Progressive Policy Institute, National Center for Policy Analysis, and Center for American Progress (CAP) may very well be influenced by the interests and ideological inclinations of those who support them. Indeed, Heritage was established in the first place by wealthy benefactors who wanted to push particular policy ideas into the policy discourse. So was CAP. In Germany the new advocacy organization INSM is well known for touting the neoliberal ideas of the metal industry's employer association, which established it. And in France, the research coming from IFRAP obviously reflects the thinking of Bernard Zimmern, the business entrepreneur who founded it and writes much of the material it publishes.

However, we also found evidence that some of the private research organizations in the United States were somewhat less susceptible to such influence insofar as they refused to take money on occasion because they worried that doing so would unduly affect their research programs. And state policy research organizations in the United States exhibited clear signs of independence, such as when the Congressional Budget Office's (CBO) directors told powerful Republican and Democratic politicians that according to CBO analysis the policies they favored would not deliver the results they promised. Similarly, in Denmark DØR's Wise Men often produce analysis and advice that runs counter to what the government in power favors—and does so regardless of whether it is a left- or right-wing government. In France OFCE has taken on the powers that be too. And the Danish Confederation of Trade Unions (LO) has a research unit whose analysis contradicted the LO leadership's long-standing belief in the virtues of open-ended unemployment benefits. All of this suggests that policy research organizations are not always slaves to their sponsors.

So depending on where one looks there is some truth to both the materialist and idealist arguments about the independence of policy analysis and advice. And therein lays the essential point. The degree to which experts and other idea producers are independent from powerful political or economic actors is contingent on the institutional constraints they face including their own professional norms. We address norms first and then more formal institutions.

We found some evidence that a modicum of independence was ensured among some expert analysts thanks to professional norms. State policy research organizations in the United States like the CBO, Government Accountability Office, and Congressional Research Service are well known for their fierce nonpartisan independence due in large measure to the organizational culture of professionalism shared by their leaders and staff economists.[6] So is the National Research Council. But there is other evidence as well. One economist we interviewed at the American Enterprise Institute (AEI) changed the analysis he had presented to Congress when a professional colleague at another research organization brought technical errors in the analysis to his attention.

[6]Bimber 1996, chap. 8; Joyce 2011.

Another economist at the Heritage Foundation told us that he would quit the organization if they tried to distort or misrepresent his analysis.[7] The president of the Economic Policy Institute insisted that their technical analysis must be above reproach in order to maintain their credibility. The Danish Wise Men decided early on that they needed to do their analysis and write their reports the way they wanted regardless of how the social partners and state officials on the rest of DØR felt about it. They were, after all, members of the brotherhood of economists! Professionalism mattered in all these cases. It did as well in the Danish ad hoc commissions, which are very protective of their professional independence. As we noted in chapter 5, the Danish Welfare Commission had representatives from several ministries working in its secretariat. But when the commission grew concerned that this might compromise their independence, they asked them to leave.

Insofar as more formal institutional constraints are concerned one of the best examples of how they can facilitate independence is in Germany where the court forbade the party foundations and their think tanks from doing the explicit bidding of the party thus ensuring some independence for them. In the United States enabling legislation mandated that certain congressional policy research organizations, such as the CBO, operate independently of partisan political interests.[8] Another if much more modest example of institutions ensuring a degree of independence is the U.S. tax code, which forbids 501(c)(3) organizations from lobbying on behalf of paying clients. This is not to say that the law prevents advocacy work, but it does limit how far organizations can go in advocating positions favored by their supporters. And, of course, the presence of so much private money in the U.S. knowledge regime in the first place creates comparatively greater opportunity for moneyed interests to influence the sort of ideas produced by a sizable portion of the knowledge regime. Such opportunities are much less evident in the European countries where there is less private money in play—in part for institutional reasons, such as different tax codes and different party and electoral systems, and also because European states are less fragmented, porous, and accessible to a wide variety of interest groups than is true in America.

It follows, then, that the degree to which policy research organizations operate with independence—or at least claim to do so—is institutionally and therefore nationally specific.[9] This is reminiscent of the more general

[7]Interviews with Kevin Hassett, AEI; senior fellow, Heritage Foundation.
[8]Joyce 2011.
[9]Of course, claiming legitimacy and independence does not necessarily mean that one actually has it. But the two may be positively correlated. In light of what we have already said about French professionals and their commitment to public service, it is worth noting, for instance, that some researchers have argued that health care professionals do in fact enjoy more autonomy in France than they do in other countries with different political-institutional arrangements (Leicht et al. 2009).

sociological literature on professions, which shows that how professions are organized and operate, including the professional principles to which they subscribe and the relative freedom from external constraints that they enjoy, are institutionally determined.[10] Unfortunately for us, virtually all of this literature focuses on health care providers, lawyers, and professions other than the sort of policy experts and policy research organizations with which we are concerned.[11] Furthermore, it tends to dwell on the Anglo-American countries.[12] But what we have discovered is at least consistent with one of its most important insights: professional autonomy is often based on a normative system that professionals learn during their professional socialization—a system that instills in them a commitment to high standards of work practices and autonomy from external influences.[13] Indeed, we found people in policy research organizations in all four of our countries who mentioned that their credibility as independent analysts unencumbered by political or economic interests rested in part on their ability to do unimpeachable technical analysis. In other words, their independence stemmed partly from professional norms of self-imposed standards of discipline and excellence.

Beyond this the literature on professions suggests that the institutional configuration of national political economies affects the specific norms and standards upon which professionals operate and by which they claim legitimacy and independence. American professionals, for example, often base their claims to legitimacy and independence on university credentials as indicative of technical competence. This is because compared to other countries the U.S. state left the development of the professions to actors in civil society. In contrast, French professionals often make claims to legitimacy and independence based on their commitment to pursuing objective truth on behalf of the public good—a reflection of the fact that the highly centralized French state inhibited the development of professional associations in civil society and took responsibility for educating professionals, notably in the Grandes Écoles, thereby instilling in them a particular esprit de corps by which they sought to

[10]Leicht et al. 2009; MacDonald 1995, chap. 3; Sciulli 2005.
[11]This neglect may be because some scholars believe that "professionals" and "experts" are not necessarily the same thing (e.g., Sciulli 2005, p. 937). Others disagree and tend to equate the two (e.g., Brint 1994; DeVries et al. 2009; Evetts 2006, pp. 135). In our view, the policy experts in our knowledge regimes are for the most part professionals insofar as many are professional economists with advanced university degrees and substantial professional training.
[12]Cross-national comparisons beyond the Anglo-American world began to receive attention in the early 1990s but rarely looked at academics or professors, paying most attention instead to physicians, lawyers, and professions much different from those with which we are concerned. For instance, Bourgeault et al. (2009) reported that of all the cross-national comparative studies of professionals published between 1961 and 2005, only 15 looked at academics or professors of any kind (see also Leicht and Fennell 1997).
[13]Evetts 2006; Freidson 1984.

practice their craft in the public interest and almost always within the state's ambit. German professionals make claims to legitimacy and independence with reference to their high levels of organizational self-regulation by professional associations—a result of the German state's propensity to off-load regulatory functions on to corporate groups in civil society as well as professionals being trained at Germany's strong state-supported university system. Finally, in Denmark and Scandinavia more generally claims to legitimacy and independence are often rooted in the commitment of professionals to public spirited pragmatic goals rooted in beliefs in the importance of egalitarianism and other social democratic principles broadly construed—an artifact of political systems with strong central states, strong labor movements, and corporatist-style arrangements.[14]

Whether these nationally specific patterns that have been identified for physicians, lawyers, and other professionals hold for the policy experts and policy research organizations in our knowledge regimes is hard to say with certainty. We simply do not have enough evidence at hand to be sure. But at least these patterns seem to be in tune with what we have found in our four countries. That is, the U.S. knowledge regime was populated by a sizable number of private scholarly policy research organizations; the French knowledge regime was very statist with many professionals trained at the Grandes Écoles; the German knowledge regime had many semi-public research institutes with close ties to universities; and the Danish knowledge regime was characterized by many policy research organizations that were pragmatic and dedicated to the principle of socioeconomic balance.

To sum up, it appears that nowhere today do either moneyed or partisan political interests enjoy hegemonic influence throughout a knowledge regime—not even in the United States where moneyed interests and excessive political partisanship are the most evident among our four cases. Nor, however, do free-floating intellectuals monopolize activity in our knowledge regimes. Whether the materialist or idealist views best account for the degree of independence enjoyed by policy research organizations and their experts depends on the surrounding institutional context. In this regard, Steven Brint comes close to what we have in mind when he writes that, "national contexts are preeminently important in shaping the specific relation of professionals to the political order."[15] National institutions are such that the materialist view

---

[14]On the United States, see Fourcade (2009, pp. 8–9, 128) and MacDonald (1995, chap. 3); on France, see Brint (1994, pp. 192–98) and DeVries et al. (2009); on Germany, see Kuhlmann et al. (2009) and MacDonald (1995, chap. 3); and on Denmark and Scandinavia see Brint (1994, pp. 192–98).

[15]Brint 1994, p. 176. This is entirely in sync with Andrew Abbott's (1993, 1988) view that professions should not be studied in isolation from their surrounding environments but as part of complex interacting social systems.

probably has stronger support in the American than the European countries, and that the idealist view may have stronger support in the European countries than in the United States. But even that depends on which specific organization we are talking about and its institutional relationships with the surrounding political economy at a particular point in time. Put differently, on the question of independence there is much variation *within* as well as *across* national knowledge regimes. This is why, as argued in chapter 1, we need a middle-range institutionally focused understanding of the production of policy ideas. The institutional and organizational machinery of national knowledge regimes is too variable and complicated for it to be otherwise. Of course, much more research is required into all of this. Anecdotes and examples like the ones we have offered are not conclusive. Such research would help fill a significant hole in the literature on professions.

Implications for Types of Policy Research Organizations

There is a small literature, as we noted briefly in chapter 1, which examines policy research organizations or think tanks as they are often called. It tends to focus on four ideal types of think tanks.[16] These include the following: (1) private scholarly organizations much like universities without students, (2) private advocacy organizations more interested in packaging and disseminating the work of other researchers than doing their own, (3) think tanks affiliated with political parties, and (4) state think tanks, if that is the appropriate term for them.

We initially organized our research around these four ideal types and sampled organizations in each of our countries based on this typology. But we soon discovered the shortcomings of this scheme. First, not every country had examples of each type. There were no party think tanks in the United States or Denmark. Private scholarly research organizations like Brookings or AEI were virtually nonexistent in the European countries. Instead, however, there were in Germany and Denmark private research units supported financially by or actually part of labor and employer associations that were doing rather sophisticated, that is to say scholarly, research. And advocacy organizations like the Heritage Foundation or CAP were just barely visible in any of the European countries, especially Denmark.

Second, there was often considerable blurring among these four types. In particular, everywhere except the United States semi-public policy research organizations were prevalent that blended elements of the scholarly and state

---

[16]Rich 2004; Smith 1991; Stone 2004; Weaver and McGann 2000.

types. These included temporary ad hoc commissions in Denmark and more permanent research shops like the Länder-supported economic research institutes in Germany. There were also semi-public organizations like the French Council of Economic Analysis and the German Council of Economic Experts that were set up by the state and financed by the state and whose members were appointed by the state—but that operated with a considerable degree of independence from it. And in the United States although there were no formal party think tanks, some private advocacy organizations had clear if informal connections with parties, such as the Progressive Policy Institute and the Heritage Foundation.

Third, there were some types of organizations that did not fit the fourfold typology at all. One was the business clubs we discovered in France that were derived in part from the legacy of French political clubs, but that conducted research of various sorts and lobbied members of government although in ways much different from lobbying in the United States. Another was the university-based research shops that we found in Denmark. And in Germany there was an increasing tendency for the universities to collaborate formally with some of the semi-public economic research institutes, which, if not examples of a university-based research shop, were at least examples of blurring among different types of organizations.

The point is a simple one. Much of the literature on think tanks or policy research organizations is based on studies of policy research organizations in North America and Britain that tend to fit the fourfold typology pretty well. But when one's scope is broadened to a more diverse set of countries, the utility of this typology begins to decline and additional categories are required, such as the ones we use in table R.1. It behooves researchers to take care in defining types of policy research organizations if they want to sample different types of organizations in future research and especially if they want to pay close attention to the national character of different knowledge regimes.

* * * * * * *

We turn now to a different set of issues. Instead of exploring differences in the national character of knowledge regimes we examine the possibility that these differences are eroding.

II

ISSUES OF SIMILARITY AND IMPACT

So far we have explored through detailed case studies of the United States, France, Germany, and Denmark the national character of four knowledge regimes—how they are organized, operate, and have changed since the Golden Age of postwar capitalism. The emphasis has been on their persistent and nationally specific differences. Part II shifts gears. It asks two questions. One is about whether our four knowledge regimes have become more similar to each other in important ways since the 1970s. That is, have the national origins of policy ideas started to disappear? The other is about what sort of influence knowledge regimes have on policymaking and whether this has changed since the 1970s and in particular whether the ideas they produce have become similar as well.

The first question bears directly on research in organizational and economic sociology and globalization studies. Many scholars have argued that organizations tend to adopt structures and practices that are similar to other organizations in their field and that this is especially likely during times of great uncertainty in the field. Globalization theorists have also argued that structures and practices diffuse across nations in ways that diminish their nationally unique qualities. If they are right, then we would expect to find evidence of convergence in the structures and practices of policy research organizations both within and across our four knowledge regimes since the 1970s—a time of considerable uncertainty thanks to the end of the Golden Age, the onset of stagflation and the rise of globalization. We take up these issues in chapter 6.

The second question is in some ways related to the first. It is hard not to wonder whether some policy research organizations have more influence than others on the thinking and decision making of policymakers. And in light of much research in comparative political economy and globalization studies one might wonder as well whether the sorts of ideas that these policy research organizations produce have become more similar over time. After all, there has been much debate about the diffusion of neoliberalism across countries and the impact it has had on national policymaking. Some have argued that there has been convergence across countries on a common set of neoliberal ideas among policymakers. These issues involve the causal relationships on the right-hand side of figure 1.1. Chapter 7 addresses this.

6

Limits of Convergence

The heart and soul of comparative political economy has long been the analysis of persistent cross-national differences. But another body of research, often associated with organizational and economic sociology, suggests something quite different. As we explained in chapter 1, these scholars argue that when organizations in a field face uncertainty they gradually change in ways that lead to convergence in their structures and practices. This is a well-known and widely accepted view in sociology, so the puzzle for us is why there was not more convergence within and across our four knowledge regimes. We address that question in this chapter. Our answer involves an analysis of both the *mechanisms* that facilitated tendencies toward convergence and the *constraints* that mediated it.

Mechanisms of the sort we have in mind are causal processes through which change occurs. As Jon Elster wrote, mechanisms are the "cogs and wheels that can be used to explain quite complex social phenomena."[1] Constraints are social forces that limit change. Their effects are like throwing sand

---

[1] Elster 1989, p. 3.

into Elster's cogs and wheels—they slow down or stop the machinery. Constraints can involve many things, but for our purposes two types of constraints are especially important: resources and institutions, particularly of the sort we discussed in part I of this book. Generally speaking, constraints do not fully determine outcomes but rather limit the range of options from which people are more or less likely to choose. In other words, constraints set the probabilities that people will pick one option over others.[2]

With this in mind we make the following arguments in this chapter about convergence. First, all four of the mechanisms that theorists have identified that facilitate convergence within a field of organizations operated in our knowledge regimes and triggered movements toward convergence. We introduced these mechanisms in chapter 1 but will review them again shortly. Second, institutional and resource constraints mediated the degree to which these mechanisms ultimately resulted in convergent outcomes. This is why movements toward convergent outcomes were no more than *tendencies* in our knowledge regimes. This is also why outcomes within as well as across our knowledge regimes were much more lumpy, uneven, and partial than convergence theory would lead us to expect.[3] As a result, each knowledge regime retained much of its own unique national character despite the operation of mechanisms that might otherwise have led to convergence during the post–Golden Age era. So in this case convergence theory is right about the mechanisms but misleading about the outcomes because it tends to overlook the constraints within which these mechanisms operate.

The chapter unfolds as follows. First, we elaborate the nature of the puzzle before us—the absence of much convergence where one might expect to find it. Second, we review the convergent tendencies we found among policy research organizations in the development of the *analytic* practices by which they utilized data, methodologies, forecasting models, and the like, and the *dissemination* practices by which they distributed their research results and policy recommendations to others. Third, we report the country specific differences we discovered in the four mechanisms that facilitated these tendencies. Mechanisms occurred in somewhat nationally specific combinations that reflected the institutional structure of each country's knowledge regime and the rest of the political economy as we described them in previous chapters. Finally, we discuss the constraints that tended to inhibit convergence in each country—not only in analytic and dissemination practices but also in other aspects of our knowledge regimes, such as the proliferation of the advocacy organization model.

[2]See Campbell (2004, chap. 3) for further discussion of these issues.
[3]Convergence theory does not typically claim that *all* organizations in a field will come to exhibit the same structures and practices but rather that *most* of them will. However, the threshold by which it can be said that convergence has occurred is often ambiguous in this literature.

We focus primarily on convergent tendencies in analytic and dissemination practices for three reasons. First, we concluded each of our interviews by asking people what the two or three most important changes had been in their knowledge regimes as well as their own organizations over the past two decades or so. The vast majority mentioned these two things. Second, these are the two areas in which we detected the most movement toward convergence. Finally, analysis and dissemination are the core missions of virtually all of our policy research organizations.

The Puzzle

Many organizational and economic sociologists argue that organizations in a field look to each other in ways that tend to promote change and often convergence on a common set of structures and practices, especially in situations of high uncertainty. This occurs through several mechanisms. One is *normative* where organizations subscribe to common professional norms, such as best practices and benchmarks, and as a result end up adopting the normatively appropriate structures and practices in the field. Another is *mimetic* where organizations blindly mimic the structures and practices of others who are apparently successful. In our view, both mechanisms involve learning albeit of different sorts. In the normative mechanism, learning is much deeper and more deliberate, such as acquiring professional training from people in other organizations or formal socialization at places like business schools, universities, professional associations, and the like. In the mimetic mechanism, learning is much more superficial insofar as you learn—or at least observe— what other organizations are doing and simply copy these things but without much if any understanding as to why they are apparently effective for other organizations.[4] A third mechanism is *coercive* whereby organizations in a field are forced to subscribe to the structures and practices favored by another powerful organization, such as the state.[5] Finally, *competition* may also

---

[4]For a discussion of normative learning, see Fligstein (1990, pp. 282–87; see also Guillén 1994), who shows that common sources of professional training constitute a source of organizational convergence. For a discussion of mimetic learning, see March (2010, chap. 2), who suggests that blindly replicating one's own past practices or copying those of another organization is another form of learning—although one he calls disparagingly "low-intellect learning." Strang (2010, p. 2) refers to this as "vicarious learning."

[5]For general discussions of normative, mimetic, and coercive mechanisms, see DiMaggio and Powell (1983) and Mizruchi and Fein (1999). For discussions of organizations coping with uncertainty and sense making, see especially March (2010), but also Weick (1995), Westphal et al. (1997, pp. 369–70), Edelman (1992), Davis et al. (1994), and Kalev et al. (2006). These mechanisms often involve problems of bounded rationality (Cyert and March 1963). And insofar as normative learning and mimetic learning are concerned, the information involved often flows through organizational or interpersonal networks (Gulati 2007; Haas 1992).

lead to convergence by weeding out structures and practices that are relatively inefficient.[6]

Insofar as the field consists of organizations in different countries that confront a common set of transnational problems one might expect convergence not only within but also across countries on a certain set of organizational structures and practices as a result of these four mechanisms.[7] The puzzle, then, is why policy research organizations in our four knowledge regimes did not converge on a common set of structures and practices more than they did when they were coping with the severe uncertainties associated with the end of the Golden Age and the rise of globalization.

Resolution of this puzzle requires an analysis of the mechanisms by which fields change but also the constraints within which they operate. Much of the sociological literature on organizational fields has long assumed that fields evolve in convergent ways and that the mechanisms involved tend not to involve much conflict. For many years scholars argued that normative and mimetic mechanisms were the ones largely responsible for convergence among organizations within a field; coercion and competition were much less evident.[8] Consequently, as Neil Fligstein and Doug McAdam observed, much of this research "greatly underestimates the role of power in the structuring of fields."[9] Sociologists, notably those who have incorporated insights from social movements theory into organizational analysis and who study fields, have recently started to appreciate that the transformation of fields often involves conflicts and struggles over resources, power, status and other things—conflicts and struggles that have long been recognized as being at the heart of comparative political economy.[10] But to our knowledge few have argued that the interplay

[6]Mizruchi and Fein (1999) argued that organizational theorists tend to address only normative, mimetic, and coercive mechanisms, not competition—a surprising oversight insofar as the article by DiMaggio and Powell (1983) that introduced normative, mimetic, and coercive mechanisms also discussed how competition was a fourth isomorphic mechanism. Recently competition has been reintroduced into some analyses. But as Dobbin et al. (2007, p. 459) point out, diffusion studies focusing on competition typically neglect these other mechanisms. So errors of omission cut in both directions.

[7]Bartley 2007; Boli and Thomas 1999; Djelic and Sahlin-Andersson 2006; Djelic and Quack 2010; Meyer et al. 1997a, 1997b; Thomas et al. 1987. In addition to field studies, there is a literature on the homogenizing effects that globalization might have on nation-states and national policy (e.g., Campbell 2004, chap. 5; Dobbin et al. 2007; Doremus et al. 1998; Guillén 2001b; Jacoby 2005; Simmons et al. 2008; Swank 2002). It should not be assumed, as much of this literature does, that organizations necessarily converge within or across nations on functionally "good" or "best" practices. Sometimes convergence may occur around functionally "bad" ones too (Schrad 2010).

[8]See Mizruchi and Fein's (1999) review of this literature.

[9]Fligstein and McAdam 2012, p. 29.

[10]Davis et al. 2005; Dobbin 2004, 2005; Fligstein and McAdam 2012. See Campbell et al. (1991) for an early statement of the importance of power, conflict, and struggle in the evolution of economic sectors—an important type of field.

of these things actually inhibits convergence despite the fact that normative, mimetic, coercive, and competitive mechanisms of change are operating in an organizational field.

Notably, two recent reviews of the convergence literature say virtually nothing about constraints that might obstruct convergence.[11] This is ironic insofar as coercion is one of the four convergence mechanisms discussed in the literature. After all, coercion implies that the process of change involves the exercise of power and may be contested and resisted in ways that prevent convergence. Along these lines one can imagine a variety of constraints. Powerful actors with vested interests in the status quo may mobilize their *resources* in order to block change that might otherwise lead to convergence.[12] And *political* and *economic institutions* may limit the range of changes that people pursue.[13] Recognizing this is crucial for solving our puzzle because it alerts us to the possibility that forces may be in play that counteract to some degree whatever tendencies there might otherwise be for convergence. As such our argument brings research on political economy together with research on organizational and economic sociology in ways that shed fresh light not only on knowledge regimes but organizational fields in general.

Convergence studies are open to two additional criticisms. First, much of the work on convergence has been based on quantitative analysis identifying trends in large populations of organizations. It has been criticized for theoretically positing but neither empirically demonstrating the causal mechanisms involved nor carefully differentiating the effects of one mechanism from another. Frank Dobbin and his colleagues are clear on this: "Too often, they [researchers] test only their own theory or simply show evidence of diffusion and impute that their favored mechanism is at work." The worst case scenario in their view is the practice of champions of one theory or another simply taking evidence of convergence as proof that their preferred mechanism is right.[14] Others have shown that one way to avoid these problems is through the detailed qualitative analysis of change processes.[15] This is our approach.

Second, the early literature on convergence often ignored the possibility that mechanisms may operate in combination with each other. In a few of these studies researchers found that coercive mechanisms initiated convergence in a field of organizations but that once the process had started normative or mimetic mechanisms took over—the point being that one mechanism was

[11] Dobbin et al. 2007; Strang 2010, chap. 1.
[12] This is the logical extension of theories of coercive feedback (e.g., Pierson 2000b).
[13] Campbell 2004, chap. 5; Campbell and Lindberg 1990; Dobbin 1994; Duina 2003, 1999; Guillén 2001b; Hall 2010; Swank 2002.
[14] Dobbin et al. 2007, pp. 462–63. See also Mizruchi and Fein (1999) and Strang (2010, chap. 1).
[15] Bartley 2007; Halliday and Carruthers 2010; Schneiberg and Clemens 2006; Strang 2010.

followed by another, not operating in *tandem* or *interacting*.[16] Lately research-ers have been more attentive to the possibility that combinations of mecha-nisms may be at work and that some combinations may be more prevalent in certain institutional environments than others.[17] As far as we know, however, this possibility has rarely been explored in a cross-national context.[18] But it fol-lows from this recent work that certain combinations may be more common in some political economies than others given the cross-national variation in their institutions. Recognizing this helps us resolve our puzzle too insofar as it provides a better understanding of the mechanisms that trigger movement toward convergence in the first place.

Of course, the tension between convergent forces and resilience due to various mediating factors has been addressed by others—but not as system-atically as we would like. For example, some studies focused on some but not other convergence mechanisms. Marie-Laure Djelic's *Exporting the American Model* showed how normative and coercive mechanisms led to the diffusion in varying degree of the American corporate economic model to European countries after the Second World War but did not examine whether mimetic or competitive mechanisms were operating too.[19] David Strang showed how normative and mimetic but not coercive mechanisms led to the diffusion of certain corporate practices into an international financial services company.[20] Beth Simmons and her colleagues are among the very few to empirically ex-amine all four of the mechanisms with which we are concerned, but they pay relatively little attention to the factors that might mediate, mute, or otherwise derail convergence once these mechanisms are operating.[21]

Most studies that consider the factors that mediate the possible effects of convergence mechanisms have a limited view of what those constraints might be. Djelic emphasized national institutions but neglected how organizational resources may have had mediating effects. Conversely, Strang considered the mediating effects of organizational resources but not broader field-level insti-tutions. Mark Roe's analysis of the diffusion of corporate governance models focused on the mediating effects of national political-legal institutions—but not other institutions or resources.[22]

---

[16]Tolbert and Zucker 1983.
[17]An excellent example of research that does consider the coincident effects of multiple mecha-nisms in different institutional contexts is Anthony et al. (2012). For meta-analyses of institutional research that laments the fact that there is still not enough attention paid to coincident effects, see Heugens and Lander (2009) and Dobbin et al. (2007).
[18]Cross-national studies that do this include Bartley (2007), Halliday and Carruthers (2007, 2010), and Simmons et al. (2008).
[19]Djelic 1998.
[20]Strang 2010.
[21]Simmons et al. 2008.
[22]Roe 2003.

Finally, a small handful of studies considered the full range of convergence mechanisms as well as a variety of resource and institutional constraints that mediated their effects, such as Terry Halliday and Bruce Carruthers's excellent analysis of the transnational diffusion of bankruptcy guidelines and Francesco Duina's research on the transposition and implementation of European Union directives by EU member countries.[23] Others have found that thanks to national institutions globalization did not precipitate convergence on common economic practices or fiscal and social policies despite the operation of multiple convergence mechanisms.[24] Despite their insights, however, none of these studies discussed how the four convergence mechanisms noted above tend to cluster in nationally specific ways. They did not recognize that institutions affect the initial starting up of convergence mechanisms as well as the eventual outcomes those mechanisms may produce. Nor did they attend to the forces for and against convergence both within and across national fields.

This chapter extends this literature in more systematic and encompassing ways than has been the case previously by showing that convergence mechanisms tend to operate in nationally specific combinations due to the institutionally unique character of each political economy, and by showing that the effects of these mechanisms are heavily mediated by nationally specific resource and institutional constraints. The next two sections focus on how tendencies toward convergence played out in terms of analytic and dissemination practices in our four knowledge regimes. In the first section we describe these tendencies and in the second section we identify the mechanisms that precipitated them. We found that in the United States there was much competitively inspired mimicry and partisan coercion, which triggered movement toward convergence on analytic and dissemination practices. France was characterized by state coercion and international mimetic and normative learning. In Germany there was lots of coordinated mimetic and normative learning. And in Denmark consensus-oriented normative learning and state coercion were especially evident.

Remember two things. First, we are describing tendencies and identifying mechanisms and constraints. As noted earlier, more attention is required to empirically identify the mechanisms and constraints by which convergence does or does not occur. Qualitative analysis can help here. So what follows contains much description of processes as they unfolded in each knowledge regime. Some of this description is based on evidence presented in earlier chapters, so we dispense with footnotes to interviews and other sources unless we introduce material not presented previously. The important point is that our approach is closer to small-N case study research than it is to large-N

<hr>

[23]Duina 1999; Halliday and Carruthers 2010.
[24]Campbell 2004; Guillén 2001b; Swank 2002.

quantitative analysis because we are most interested in identifying the mechanisms at work.

Second, the tendencies we found among policy research organizations occurred at two levels. During our interviews these tendencies were most evident *within* knowledge regimes but occasionally we found evidence of convergent tendencies *across* knowledge regimes too. Indeed, policy research organizations live in two worlds. Their primary world is the field of organizations that constitute their national knowledge regime where the target of their activity is ultimately national decision makers. But they also operate albeit to a lesser degree within a broader, more international field of organizations. Put differently, our four national knowledge regimes are linked such that practices may diffuse among them. As we will see, organizations sometimes interact with each other across national boundaries in ways that may facilitate a modicum of convergence thanks to some of the mechanisms we have discussed. They do so by participating in formal international organizations and informal personal, professional, and organizational networks. Nevertheless, the pressures to conform are certainly much stronger within knowledge regimes than across them if only because policy research organizations are not trying to influence a common international target as they are at the national level.[25]

Tendencies toward Convergence

In part I we showed that in the 1980s our four knowledge regimes were populated in varying degrees by an array of several types of policy research organizations, all of which were trying to influence policymakers albeit in different ways. For example, some, like the Urban Institute, the Brookings Institute, INSEE, the German semi-public research institutes, and DØR, emphasized doing technical economic policy analysis. In contrast, others, like the Heritage Foundation, NCPA, IFRAP, the French business clubs, and a bit later Institute

[25]Defining an organizational field is tricky because there are many definitions from which to choose. For example, some say that fields consist of organizations of similar size and producing similar products that recognize their interdependence and sense of legitimate action (Fligstein 1990, pp. 5–6; Fligstein and McAdam 2012, p. 9). Some say that fields include a wider variety of much more dissimilar organizations including key suppliers, producers, consumers, regulatory agencies, and other organizations that produce similar services and products (DiMaggio and Powell 1983, p. 147). Some say that organizations—both similar and dissimilar—in a field have local as well as distant connections, both horizontal and vertical in nature (Scott and Davis 2007, p. 118). Our view of knowledge regimes as fields accepts that (1) policy research organizations produce similar products (policy analysis and recommendations), (2) knowledge regimes involve several different types of organizations (scholarly, advocacy, party, state, etc.), and (3) these organizations are linked horizontally within the national knowledge regime and vertically through formal international organizations and informal networks with policy research organizations in other countries—that is, they operate in a national as well as an international field.

Montaigne, INSM, and CEPOS, were much less interested in doing technical analysis and much more interested in aggressively disseminating and advocating their policy preferences to decision makers. However, we discovered through our interviews that in all of our knowledge regimes there had been tendencies since the 1980s toward convergence on more sophisticated technical economic policy analysis as well as a common set of more aggressive dissemination practices.[26]

Economic Policy Analysis

Some policy research organizations in the United States that have always done technical policy analysis adopted more common and sophisticated analytic practices. For example, the Congressional Budget Office's (CBO) Douglas Hamilton explained that CBO and other organizations have moved increasingly to more extended forecasts. In CBO's case they moved from the traditional 10-year forecasting window in some cases to a 50-year window. He also said that it has become increasingly common for organizations to use more elaborate databases and do cross-national analysis. Thanks to technological advances this sort of data has become readily available—often online—from international organizations like the OECD, European Central Bank, International Monetary Fund, and World Bank. Others agreed.[27] According to one senior government official, "Now you can just get that online. . . . It's much more easy to consult. . . . Rather than flipping through papers, it's saved as a web link, and it's very easy to look through. So, I think the availability of information has certainly increased the comparative type of [research]."[28]

Others said that improvements in the power of inexpensive desktop computing boosted the ability of more organizations to analyze these data in more sophisticated ways.[29] We were told at several interviews in Washington that organizations that had not done much technical analysis previously now do more of it.[30] Referring to the Heritage Foundation, which began with little if any sophisticated analytic capacity, Stuart Butler explained how this facilitated

---

[26]It was clear from our interviews that convergence had occurred since the 1980s. We had hoped to have additional time-series evidence to supplement the interviews in this regard, such as the number of technically competent PhDs on staff in each organization, whether the organization had a scientific advisory board, whether the organization had a communications or public relations department, how big these departments' budgets and staff were, and so on. We tried to gather these data from organizational annual reports and websites. However, as discussed in the appendix, we ran into serious missing data problems, which made it impossible to measure quantitatively how much convergence had occurred since the 1980s in each knowledge regime.

[27]Interviews with Douglas Hamilton, CBO; Gene Dodaro, GAO; Kevin Hassett, AEI.

[28]Interview with senior official, CEA.

[29]Interview with senior official, CRS.

[30]Interviews with Rudolph Penner, Urban Institute; senior officials, CBPP; Lawrence Mishel, EPI.

his organization's convergence on some of the more high-powered analytic practices of other organizations:

> The greater and greater emphasis on computerized data [and] statistical work has certainly increased, and that's partly because of the technological revolution. *We are now able to do things that only universities and the government were able to do.* . . . We can get vast amounts of data now online. In the '80s and '90s it was disks and so forth, or you know, there was an openness, which now meant we could do things. So, that's changed. The web has clearly changed what we do. (our emphasis)

Some of the analytic trends we heard about in America also appeared in France. As we noted in chapter 3, as France became more integrated into the international economy some French research organizations began doing more cross-national comparisons. Furthermore, there appears to have been a trend among some organizations to converge on similar and ever more sophisticated methods of economic analysis and forecasting. For instance, at the state's Treasury Department (DGTPE), one senior official told us that like several other organizations in France, "We are developing tools all the time. And we have developed, for instance, well, one or two years ago, a dynamic stochastic general equilibrium model, I mean, *like several others.* . . . So we are not immune, I would say, to technological progress" (our emphasis). When asked for clarification that this was a general trend in the field, she agreed, saying, "It's the main evolution I've seen."[31]

Less methodologically sophisticated organizations, such as the French party foundation think tanks and business clubs, did not conform in doing this sort of high-powered analysis. But there were still spillover effects whereby the state-of-the-art work done at places like DGTPE and the Center for International Prospective Studies (CEPII) trickled down to others. A senior official at CEPII reminded us of both the unevenness with which sophisticated analytic practices were spreading as well as the spillover effects: "There are think tanks . . . that pick up economic work and then write policy briefs. . . . So, there's a difference from CEPII and—between CEPII and other places. Some places are doing really good research, but not so many." But insofar as these other places synthesize work done at top-level research shops, even the publications and reports of the less methodologically astute organizations benefit from the trend to more sophisticated analytic techniques. The same is true in the rest of our countries.

---

[31]Interview with senior official, DGTPE.

In Germany over at least the past 20 years there has been a "race to the top" toward a common set of more methodologically sophisticated analytic practices among the semi-public economic research institutes.[32] According to Rolf Kroker from the Cologne Institute for Economic Research (IW) everyone has tried increasingly to do state-of-the-art analytic methods. For example, Wolfgang Franz from the Center for European Economic Research (ZEW) explained that to an increasing extent the other institutes were using micro-econometric methods, which ZEW pioneered and to which others eventually conformed, as well as evaluation research on active labor market policies. As in other countries, there was also a trend to more cross-national analysis.[33]

Ulrich Walwei, at the Federal Employment Agency's Research Institute (IAB), reiterated what many people told us in Germany, which was that one of the most important areas of convergence in the field had been on more sophisticated scientific practices. Others agreed, noting, for example, that "I think the empirical oriented research has increased dramatically, of course, and I think not only in our institute but in other institutes too."[34] And we heard from another research organization that "[e]conometric approaches play an increasingly larger role in the empirically oriented economic research insti-tutes. This holds not only for the economic research institutes but also for the universities."[35]

Finally, Danish policy research organizations have converged on a com-mon set of sophisticated econometric models and data too—perhaps more than anywhere else. As we reported in chapter 5, the DREAM model and a few others have come to constitute the basic analytical tool kit that almost everybody uses nowadays who models the Danish economy. The director of research at the Danish Confederation of Trade Unions (LO) said that virtually all professional economists in Denmark now agree on the models and datasets that are appropriate for modeling the Danish economy. The Wise Men's Peter Birch Sørensen agreed that over the years professional economists in Denmark had settled on a new generation of dynamic models that better captured the effects of microeconomic incentives than the old Keynesian models. "So, over the years . . . there's been this trend in the profession towards greater reliance also on these other type of models." Lars Andersen at the Economic Council of the Labor Movement (AE) emphasized that "[w]e have a tradition of that

[32]Interviews with senior researcher, IfW; Rolf Kroker, IW; Martin Dietz, IAB.
[33]Interviews with Rolf Kroker, IW; Rudolf Zwiener, IMK; Claus Schäfer, WSI; Ulrich Walwei, IAB; Wolfgang Franz, ZEW. According to Claus Schäfer, WSI, the availability of socioeconomic panel data from the German Statistical Institute in Wiesbaden, large income and consumer surveys, and a large annual micro-census laid the foundation for the shift toward microeconomic analysis.
[34]Interview with Rolf Kroker, IW.
[35]Email correspondence with Meinhard Knoche, Ifo.

in Denmark" and that "[y]ou have more consensus in Denmark" on methods than you do in some other countries.

Overall, then, while the trend toward more sophisticated analytic practices was clear thanks in part to technological advancements, it was also uneven. In the United States some organizations tend to do more sophisticated policy analysis than they used to, such as the Heritage Foundation, which now says it does analysis that only universities or the government did 30 years ago. But we heard little about this at other U.S. organizations, such as, for example, the Progressive Policy Institute (PPI) or the Center for American Progress (CAP). And in one interview with a senior official at the U.S. Council of Economic Advisors (CEA), we were told that their analysts would not bother talking to people at places like Brookings or the American Enterprise Institute (AEI) about analytic issues because even though they are considered among the most scholarly private policy research organizations in the United States the technical work they did was not in the same league as the CEA's.[36] Semipublic policy research organizations in France and Germany had elevated their analytic games in similar ways. But the same was not true for the French business clubs like Enterprise and Progress or advocacy organizations like Institute Montaigne, whose research was still either outsourced or based on the much less sophisticated approaches of their own task forces, discussion groups, and the like. Nor did the German advocacy organizations, such as Initiative New Social Market Economy (INSM) and Foundation Market Economy (SM), which had comparatively miniscule in-house research capacities, indicate that they had adopted high-powered analytic techniques. This sort of unevenness may have been less pronounced in Denmark, but certainly an advocacy organization like the Center for Political Studies (CEPOS) would not have the same capacities for sophisticated analysis as the union or employer associations or some of the semi-public research organizations like the ad hoc commissions or the Wise Men. Our point is twofold. First, policy analysis has become more technically sophisticated since the 1980s. Second, some organizations have tended to converge on a common set of these more technical practices, but others have not.[37]

In light of these examples it appears that the degree to which analytic techniques diffuse evenly or not may depend in part on the state. As discussed later, the state played important roles in facilitating the relatively uniform diffusion of techniques and methodologies among state and semi-public policy research organizations in some of our countries. But when it came to the

---

[36] Interview with senior official, CEA.
[37] Of course what passes for sophisticated policy analysis may vary across countries. For example, as Marion Fourcade (2009) showed, French economics has historically been less technically sophisticated than U.S. economics.

private policy research shops where funding was more diffuse and therefore pressure to adopt state-of-the-art analytic techniques was presumably less uniform there seemed to be much more unevenness. Whether this means that the state's involvement is especially important for convergence is something we would encourage other researchers to investigate further. In any case, we found lots of evidence about the unevenness of convergence when it came to dissemination strategies too.

Dissemination

In the United States many private policy research organizations tried increasingly over the past 20 years or more to disseminate their ideas in ways that were more appealing to policymakers, the media and the general public. In this regard, many of them converged on some of the trappings of early advocacy research organizations like the Heritage Foundation, such as shifting toward shorter and more reader friendly publications like executive summaries, newsletters, policy briefs, and tear sheets for the media. Most organizations also now have at least one person whose job it is to communicate with the media. Much of this was unheard of in the early 1980s except at a few advocacy organizations.[38] The Century Foundation's vice president for public affairs, Christy Hicks, explained that people finally realized that having good ideas was not sufficient to influence policymaking and public discourse:

> People came to the realization that that's not good enough, that you really have to have a plan, and you have to promote your work, and you have to promote your people, and you have to do it aggressively . . . bringing more of sort of business marketing ideas and forms into the nonprofit in terms of communications. . . . Strategic marketing, I think, has been a huge, huge, huge sea change in organizations.

She illustrated the point by referring to the bookcase behind us during our interview, which she said represented the evolution of their dissemination strategy over the twentieth century. Its contents ranged from hefty academic books from the organization's early days on the left side to ever more recent, shorter, and edgier publications and pamphlets on the right side.

We heard similar stories at virtually every private policy research organization we visited in the United States about how everyone had conformed toward shorter pithier pieces—pioneered in the first place by a few advocacy organizations like Heritage. One organization president said that one of the biggest changes in the field over the past 20 years was better marketing and

---

[38] Interview with John Goodman, NCPA.

media outreach.[39] Even the Urban Institute and Brookings—two scholarly behemoths in the field—have been moving in this direction for the past 20 years producing shorter pieces but based on longer studies that are still available to those interested.[40] Smaller organizations like PPI and the Economic Policy Institute (EPI) publish more short pieces nowadays too. EPI did so from the start but especially since the mid-1990s after the Gingrich revolution in Congress.[41]

State policy research organizations in America are not immune from the so-called marketing trend. Several that we visited have communications departments or liaisons that interface with the media. CBO, for example, which used to do very little of this sort of thing, jumped on the bandwagon when it ramped up its communications operation in 2000 and 2001 to get its message out more effectively to the media and public. Its communications team occasionally arranges for the director to meet with the editorial boards of the major national newspapers. CBO also has an extensive website now, as do the other state organizations.[42]

We heard similar things in France about convergence toward new dissemination strategies including the production of shorter pieces by organizations in civil society. Even some very scholarly research organizations like the French Institute of International Relations (IFRI) have moved away gradually from more academic-style books to shorter policy briefs and reports. This change conforms to the practices of some of the newest advocacy organizations in France, which opted for shorter publications all along. For instance, when we asked whether the Institute Montaigne ever published long academic-style books, its general director exclaimed, "We don't do that. Never!" He explained that shorter reader-friendly publications were more likely to resonate with the public and policymakers than long ones. Bernard Zimmern, president of the French Institute for Research on Public Administration (IFRAP), another advocacy organization, also told us that his organization was shifting toward shorter publications disseminated over the Internet. Similarly, Gilles Finchelstein explained that Foundation Jean Jaurés was going to start publishing short policy briefs and distribute them to people over the Internet.

This is not to say that French policy research organizations have all abandoned publishing books and longer reports. IFRI and even IFRAP still publish books occasionally as do Brookings, AEI, and some others in the United States. And both CEPII and IFRI continue to publish in scholarly journals.[43] In CEPII's case, they have increased—not decreased—their exposure in these

[39]Interview with John Goodman, NCPA.
[40]Interview with Rudolph Penner, Urban Institute.
[41]Interviews with senior official, PPI; Lawrence Mishel, EPI.
[42]Interview with senior official, CBO.
[43]Interviews with Bernard Zimmern, IFRAP; senior official, CEPII; Dominique David, IFRI.

journals over the past 10 years or so. République des Idées publishes books by academics but written for a general audience, not scholars. Institute Choiseul still publishes academic journals.[44] So the degree to which organizations have simply dropped one dissemination strategy and converged on the new one has been uneven.

As in the United States and France, virtually everyone we spoke with in Germany said that targeting the media in order to influence public discourse and the political agenda had become more common and important for organizations over the past 20 years. Certainly the upstart private advocacy organizations like INSM specialize in media messaging in order to influence public discourse. Indeed, when we interviewed a senior official at INSM he stressed his organization's savvy approach to publicly disseminating their ideas. Other types of organizations are well aware of this. For instance, at the Friedrich Ebert Foundation Peter Donaiski told us that new private organizations like INSM and the Bertelsmann Foundation put lots of money and intellectual effort into running media campaigns. In short, he said, "They do lots of public relations." But now even some of the more scholarly research institutes that did not do this before do so now, such as the Berlin Social Science Research Center whose president stressed that she was trying to increase the media visibility of her researchers even though they too still focus heavily on scholarly publications.[45] People at other organizations concurred that there had been a convergence in the field on disseminating their work to the media.[46]

We heard less about convergence on the new marketing strategies in Denmark than elsewhere, perhaps because there is so much inclusive negotiation so it is easier to reach the intended audiences—especially in such a small country. Nevertheless, all the organizations we visited had developed websites that disseminated much of their policy research and ideas. We also discovered that LO and the Confederation of Danish Employers (DA) had hired staff to help them better interface with the media.[47] And one of the first things that CEPOS did when it began operating was to hire a communications specialist.[48]

The adoption of new technologies was an important part of the story in every country. This involved using new media, including mass emailing, video streaming, YouTube postings, online news letters, and blogging. In America, CAP is often said to be on the forefront of these new technologies. Nevertheless, CAP's Sarah Rosen Wartell said that many of the major policy research organizations now have extensive websites and online newsletters and video.

[44]Interviews with Florent Guénard, République des Idées; Paul de Fombelle, Institute Choiseul.
[45]Interview with Jutta Allmendinger, WZB.
[46]Interviews with senior official, MPIfG; Ulrich Walwei, IAB; Rolf Kroker, IW; Dagmar Simon, WZB; and email correspondence with Meinhard Knoche, Ifo.
[47]Interview with Niels Trampe, DA.
[48]Interview with Martin Ågerup, CEPOS.

The Urban Institute's Rudolph Penner summarized the situation, saying, "It's almost useless to do hard copy stuff these days. I would say 90% of the comments I get about my work come from people reading it on the web as opposed to hard copy somewhere." Similarly, almost everyone we spoke with in France, Germany, and Denmark talked about how important this sort of thing had become for everyone over the past couple of decades. This was often so for state policy research organizations as well as semi-public and private ones.

Nevertheless, and this is the important point as it was for convergence on common analytic practices, there was much unevenness in how sophisticated organizations were in this regard. Some were clearly leading the pack. Notably, in addition to CAP, France's Institute Montaigne, which even produced television commercials to promote its policy positions, and Germany's INSM, which specialized in state-of-the-art media messaging, were among the leaders in their countries. Conversely, some organizations still published lots of books and scholarly articles. And there was also unevenness across countries as became especially clear in one interview with a German research institute where we heard that important German organizations lagged the Americans:

> With the Internet, the presidents of the [semi-public research] institutes are more oriented toward the outside, and probably have a stronger public recognition, as a result. And all of them have taken on to using the Internet as a platform for disseminating their ideas. It was slow at the beginning, and I think the German institutes, I think we're about five years behind American institutes in learning how to use the Internet.[49]

Let us be clear about the unevenness of convergence. First, we were impressed by the fact that the tendency toward convergence was more pronounced for the development of the new dissemination practices than it was for the development of sophisticated analytic practices. This stands to reason because it is easier for an organization to begin writing short policy briefs and press releases if it has never done so than it is for an organization to begin doing complicated economic forecasting if it has never done so. Second, insofar as adopting new dissemination strategies is concerned, this often involved layering new strategies on to old ones. Organizations like Brookings, AEI, the Urban Institute, IFRI, CEPII, the German semi-public economic research institutes, and others which had for decades disseminated their analysis and recommendations in very scholarly ways started to utilize the new dissemination strategies developed initially by advocacy organizations. But they did not

---

[49]Interview with senior official, Ifo. Braml (2004, p. 219) confirms this lag.

abandon their old ways. Brookings, for instance, has a bookstore in its lobby where one can still buy all sorts of scholarly books and journals published or edited by its researchers.

National Differences in Convergence Mechanisms

What were the mechanisms that facilitated these tendencies toward convergence? We noted earlier four mechanisms that researchers argue facilitate convergence: normative, mimetic, coercive, and competitive. During our interviews we heard many examples of all four mechanisms operating for both analytic and dissemination practices. They often worked in combinations. We will focus on those combinations that seemed to be more prevalent in some countries than in others. Indeed, the evidence we collected during our interviews suggests that there are some interesting patterns that make sense vis-à-vis the arguments we made in previous chapters about each country's knowledge regime. We found that the mechanisms that tended to dominate in a particular situation often reflected the institutional configuration of the knowledge regime and the rest of the political economy.

The United States: Competition, Mimicry, and Partisan Coercion

The U.S. knowledge regime was marked by a proliferation of private advocacy policy research organizations that had engaged in an increasingly competitive war of ideas since the late 1970s that was intimately connected with rising political and ideological partisanship in Washington. This established the foundation for three important mechanisms that facilitated convergence: competition, mimicry—that is, competitively inspired mimicry—and coercion, which was often associated with political or ideological partisanship.

Consider competition and mimicry first. Insofar as marketing and dissemination is concerned organizations mimicked what their competitors did in order to keep pace. Nearly everyone echoed the view of one longtime policy researcher who said, "It is a more competitive world. There are more voices out there."[50] So the convergence toward shorter publications, as the Century Foundation's Christy Hicks explained, was the result of growing concerns with standing out in an increasingly crowded and competitive field of research organizations. According to many of our interviews, it began with the Heritage Foundation, which introduced a new business model in the late 1970s that stressed aggressive marketing.[51] Others followed suit. EPI, for example, was established with an emphasis on marketing shorter pieces in part as a response

---

[50]Interview with Isabel Sawhill, Brookings Institution.
[51]Interview with Lawrence Mishel, EPI. Mishel noted that it is well known in Washington that about half of Heritage's budget is devoted to marketing its ideas.

to the development of this approach by conservative organizations. EPI also tried to top them by doing sophisticated research for these short pieces and much more quickly than traditional scholarly policy research organizations like Brookings, which had long been content to let their analysis speak more or less for itself. EPI prided itself on cranking out the research and writing a briefing paper in a couple of months. According to EPI's president, "I think our ability to analyze data, and present it—quick turn-around—is something that many people didn't have that has become more *de rigueur*."[52]

The importance of this competitively inspired mimicry is hard to over-state. One veteran from AEI, a scholarly research organization, admitted that, "The advocacy tanks have been very effective, and they've changed the way all of us do business."[53] Christy Hicks concurred and told us that, "Conservative think tanks—they have a lock on this. They figured this out." She added that the progressive, center-left organizations were just playing catch up. Others agreed.[54]

The proliferation of research organizations has forced everyone to keep abreast of the new communication technologies. Another reason why EPI began writing shorter papers and policy briefs and developed a quick turn-around time for doing and disseminating its research was that it needed to conform to the rapid-fire 24/7 news cycle as an increasingly important means of disseminating ideas. Nevertheless, EPI's president lamented that they have not yet adopted the most cutting-edge media strategies like video streaming and thus were still catching up to the competition. The diffusion of these com-munication strategies has very much been the result of imitating what other organizations were doing. For instance, although Heritage pioneered aggres-sive marketing, CAP's Sarah Rosen Wartell explained:

> We kind of leapfrogged Heritage in some ways and they copied us. . . . We started doing video of our experts and . . . within a matter of weeks, literally, Heritage started having a similar video model to the way we were approaching it, and they kind of got a little bit ahead of us in some uses of some technologies, and then we devel-oped a new outlet forum by working with some news media.[55]

[52]Interview with Lawrence Mishel, EPI.

[53]Interview with Karlyn Bowman, AEI. We also learned in this interview that Edward Feulner, who helped start the Heritage Foundation, actually copied the idea of short policy briefs from AEI, which had written them occasionally, but he amplified the practice in his new business model.

[54]Interview with senior official, CBPP.

[55]"Doing video of our experts" refers to producing short video clips of their experts being inter-viewed and sending them to TV and radio stations in order to solicit invitations for their experts to appear on the air.

Competitively inspired mimicry also affected analytic techniques. CBO competed with another government agency over long-term projections for the viability of the Social Security Program. According to one CBO analyst, in contrast to the more traditional actuarial approach, CBO relied on micro data-based modeling with different assumptions about the economy. The two agencies' long-term projections diverged markedly until their methodological assumptions and thus their forecasts began to converge. He explained how this happened:

> Over the years I think they've looked at some of the things that we've done and made some of the assumptions we looked at and thought, "I think I like what CBO has done better." We looked at some of the work they did and the more that we talked and had a conversation the more we were able to change some of our assumptions as well. The projections have converged a little bit.[56]

The relationship between CBO and the president's Office of Management and Budget (OMB) is especially interesting insofar as it was marked by competitively inspired mimicry. Congress established CBO to counter OMB's budget analyses because the legislature wanted its own numbers in order to compete with those coming from the executive branch. As a result, the two began to mimic each other's analytic techniques and gradually converged on common approaches.[57]

Coercion also facilitated tendencies toward convergence. In terms of some private policy research organizations pressure to adopt the new dissemination strategies frequently came from politically partisan funders. Stuart Butler from the Heritage Foundation, for instance, told us that CAP was able to pursue cutting-edge messaging techniques because they had resources from liberals who wanted to push that sort of activity. We heard similar stories about other organizations. CAP's Sarah Rosen Wartell explained:

> I think the idea of the emphasis on dissemination is certainly a trend. . . . I think the embrace of new media is part of the trend. I think that the funding community is trying to think differently about how they fund institutions. I wouldn't say that's been transformed yet, but I think there's evolution there.

Partisan coercion was also implicated in the spread of some analytic practices. Notably, in the late 1990s when Congress suspected CBO of partisanship

---

[56] Interview with Douglas Hamilton, CBO.
[57] Eventually the two agencies cooperated with each other from time to time recognizing that if either one's budget analyses diverged too much from the other's without very good reason, then their credibility might be questioned (Joyce 2011).

and its director feared that its budget might be slashed as a result he decided to defend the agency by making its analysis and methods more transparent. So CBO began sharing its models with other policy research organizations, including those in the private sector, to see what they thought of them.[58] Such sharing clearly facilitated some convergence. The Center on Budget and Policy Priorities, for example, obtained and used CBO models.[59]

But partisan coercion also affected the development of some of these models in the first place. In 1990 Congress ruled that any tax cut had to be budget neutral—that is, balanced by either a tax increase somewhere else or spending cuts.[60] Historically, CBO and the Congressional Joint Committee on Taxation estimated the effect of tax cuts without estimating how economic growth might eventually boost tax revenues. Congressional conservatives who advocated supply-side tax cuts argued that this static forecasting was wrong-headed and demanded that CBO devise a dynamic model that accounted for these presumed revenue effects. It was a very contentious issue, and for a while CBO's directors refused to bend to the pressure. But by the early 2000s CBO succumbed—although the analyses it generated still did not produce the results that conservatives had hoped for. And even though the congressional rule eventually expired, dynamic modeling survived.[61] According to one of their forecasters:

> If we went back to that [old] system, I'd guarantee you we'd end up back in a dynamic where the estimating agencies find themselves in the middle of a battle between the two political parties. That's essentially what it was. We were in the middle of that battle. . . . We were doing an estimate of the potential effects of cutting the capital gains tax. I think the Speaker of the House [Gingrich] called us intellectually dishonest. It was in the *Wall Street Journal* on the front page.[62]

In sum, partisan coercion, competition, and mimicry facilitated a modicum of convergence and very much reflected the political economy's institutional context. Competitively inspired mimicry was associated with the competitive relationships among private policy research organizations. Insofar as CBO and OMB forecasting models were concerned mimicry was associated with competition between the legislative and executive branches as institutionalized in the constitutional separation of powers. Among private policy research organizations partisan coercion stemmed from the prominence of

---

[58] Interview with senior official, CBO.
[59] Interviews with senior officials, CBPP.
[60] This was part of the Omnibus Budget Reconciliation Act of 1990.
[61] Joyce 2011, pp. 38–44.
[62] Interview with Douglas Hamilton, CBO.

private funding and in the CBO examples it stemmed from the fact that CBO was beholden to Congress.

Two caveats are in order. First, recall that excessive partisanship in Washington politics precipitated efforts among some private policy research organizations to cooperate in order to restore their legitimacy and press policymakers to get over their partisan feuding and work more effectively on the nation's problems. Stuart Butler explained that there were attempts on the left to adopt the Heritage business model and that he talked to people on the left about this including those from PPI and the Democratic Leadership Council with whom he shared information about the Heritage model to help them decide whether it might suit their needs. In the end, however, they went in a different direction.

Second, sometimes the interaction between competition and mimicry occurred at the interorganizational level along partisan lines. We learned from EPI's president that on the left EPI, CAP, and a few others participate in something called the Tuesday Morning Group, which he described half jokingly as "the conspiracy of the left." They meet biweekly to share information and discuss various issues. He also told us about the EARN network, which is a private Internet listserv that links different national organizations on the left in a forum where people ask questions, get help, and learn what other organizations are doing. He refused to give further details but said that these collaborations emerged because "[t]here was a sense that it was done on the other side." In other words, organizations on the left felt compelled to copy the collective practices of organizations on the right in order to compete effectively against them. Of course, this also likely facilitated mutual learning and therefore possibilities for convergence.

France: State Coercion and International Mimetic and Normative Learning

France's political economy is more statist than in many other countries but when policymakers perceived a crisis of ideas following the Golden Age they began to externalize policy analysis by facilitating the creation of new semi-public policy research organizations. This was a coercive move on the state's part that initially involved and subsequently triggered a degree of cross-national convergence thanks to much mimetic and normative learning about foreign knowledge regimes. This was often something the new French policy research organizations needed to do given that there were few to emulate at home in their sparsely populated niches, which is also why competition was not an especially prominent convergence mechanism in France.

To begin with the prime minister's office set up and financed various semi-public scholarly policy research organizations. The idea was to facilitate the development of new organizations doing sophisticated policy analysis. The state also urged the political parties to set up foundations if they did not already have one and to establish think tanks within them—and offered to finance them. But the state did not force them to do so per se. In the first case overt political and financial coercion was at work. In the second case it was more a matter of political persuasion. But in both cases policymakers were inspired by German corporatism where organizations in civil society provided valuable analysis and feedback to the state. A senior official at one of the French semi-public policy research organizations, Coe-Rexecode, explained that policymakers drew particular inspiration from the German semi-public economic research institutes but that there were other foreign models they learned from as well. For instance, IFRI was "designed along American lines" following the examples of the Carnegie Endowment for International Peace, the Brookings Institution, and the Council on Foreign Relations as well as a few think tanks in other countries.[63] So the mechanisms of state coercion and international mimetic and normative learning operated in tandem to bolster France's policy analytic capacities and otherwise stimulate fresh policy thinking. This led to some convergence between the French and German knowledge regimes.

Once this process was set in motion there was yet more mimicking and normative learning from organizations in other countries. Some of this affected the analytic practices of these French policy research organizations. For example, researchers at CEPII and DGTPE monitored research done abroad to keep up to date on their analytic techniques, including those developed by foreign academics and policy research organizations.[64] When we asked at CEPII whether they monitored foreign organizations to see what sort of topics, methodologies, models, and databases they used, and whether CEPII imitated or otherwise learned from them, a senior official explained, "We keep informed—we are very well informed with what other researchers in the world are doing in the same field as we do."[65] Indeed, over the past 20 years CEPII staff published more and more of their work in international journals, which demanded the best analytic techniques as defined by the international community of professional economists.[66] It stands to reason, then, that CEPII researchers honed their methodological skills and brought them into line with best practices as defined by their peers in other research organizations worldwide. Convergence through mimetic and normative learning like this is not uncommon in France. We heard the same thing at the Center for Economic Research (OFCE) where researchers pay close attention not only

[63]IFRI's 20th Anniversary Brochure 1999, pp. 5–7.
[64]Interviews with senior officials, DGTPE and CEPII.
[65]Absent any mention of direct didactic contact with researchers in other countries, this seems to best reflect mimetic rather than normative learning.
[66]Interview with senior official, CEPII.

to the substantive topics that their foreign counterparts study but also how they study them. OFCE still sends representatives to meet with counterparts at places like Brookings to learn from them.[67]

This sort of international learning was at work elsewhere too. The Council of Economic Analysis (CAE) meets annually with the German Council of Economic Experts (CEE) in order to exchange views on current topics of interest to both bodies, benchmark best practices, and more. According to Christian de Boissieu, CAE president, they also read each other's reports. Similarly, CAE has learned about the Danish flexicurity system—a combination of limited employment protection, active labor market policies, and generous welfare provisions for the unemployed—by engaging with their Danish counterpart, the Wise Men. He lamented that the CAE does not have regular contact with the U.S. Council of Economic Advisors and hoped that this would change someday.

We heard less about the international mimetic or normative learning of dissemination practices when we visited the semi-public research organizations in France. But we did hear about it from people in the advocacy organizations. Notably, Bernard Zimmern, founder of IFRAP, said that he had belonged to various clubs in France but they had no staff, no funding, and therefore no capacity for serious policy analysis. Then he had an epiphany:

> I discovered in the United States, think tanks. I came in 1983 across the Heritage Foundation. . . . And I said, "My Lord, you never see that in France" . . . and I discovered that most entrepreneurs in the United States [were] starting a foundation. . . . So I said, "Well, it's a very good idea." I said, "Well, I should start a foundation, the same thing in France." And that's the start of IFRAP. So, *IFRAP is a think tank that's modeled—well, on Heritage.* (our emphasis)

He was impressed with not only the analytic practices of some of these organizations but also their practices of rapid-fire dissemination of analysis and policy recommendations. So he modeled IFRAP in their image. And he explained that IFRAP still sends emissaries to various U.S. think tanks to learn about a variety of things including how best to disseminate their ideas, such as over the Internet. We heard a very similar story about Institute Montaigne, whose founder, Claude Bébéar, wanted to create the institute because he had met with think tanks in the United States, Belgium, and England, had been impressed by what they brought to public debate, and thought that something similar would be useful in France. So he sent people to visit them and see how they worked.[68] Not surprisingly, then, Montaigne's dissemination practices as

[67]Interview with Xavier Timbeau, OFCE.
[68]Interview with Philippe Manière, Institute Montaigne.

well as some of its analytic capacities resembled those of these foreign organizations, notably short policy briefs and articles that are easily understood by policymakers, journalists, and other nonexperts.

The point is that as French policymakers began to transform their knowledge regime they did so in the image of Germany's semi-public organizations and used the various coercive powers of the state to do so. Then, once opportunities for new types of policy research organizations materialized, the people who set them up and then ran them also turned frequently to their foreign counterparts to mimic or otherwise learn in greater depth about how they operated. Private entrepreneurs also mimicked and learned normatively from foreign policy research organizations. This all made sense in the French institutional context insofar as there were few similar domestic organizations to either emulate or learn from. So, once again, the mechanisms triggering movement toward convergence worked in combination and reflected the unique institutional features of the surrounding political-economic environment, particularly its dirigiste tradition.

Germany: Coordinated Normative and Mimetic Learning

Germany's political economy is known for coordinated decision making through corporatist institutions. Likewise, Germany's knowledge regime was characterized by a considerable amount of coordination among policy research organizations—some of it explicit but some of it tacit—that resulted in a modicum of convergence among policy research organizations through coordinated normative and mimetic learning.

Coordinated normative learning was especially evident in terms of economic policy analysis. For instance, recall from chapter 4 that the Ministry of Economics and Technology sends a silent observer to learn about the methodological activities of the research institutes involved in preparing the Joint Economic Reports. Information from this person is then used by the ministry in preparing its own forecasts so that its methods are more or less in sync with those of the Joint Economic Report group.[69] Moreover, as members of the Joint Economic Report group try to anticipate what everyone will bring to the table for discussion—something they need to do in order to help them coordinate forecasts once they get there—they certainly have to learn about each other's analytic practices.

Another example of the coordination of normative learning involves the CEE whose research staff meets at least once a year with their counterparts in other German research institutes to share methodological information. The CEE's chair, Wolfgang Franz, explained:

[69]Interview with senior official, BMWI.

They are exchanging ideas about modeling. For example, we have
a huge macroeconometric model and the institutes of course have
a similar model and they exchange ideas about the problems and
how to improve these models and the like . . . they are in frequent
contact by meeting personally or by telephoning or making calls
and the like.[70]

We were told that dialogue like this among different types of economists, such
as those working on business cycles or on structural aspects of the economy,
had increased and contributed to a degree of convergence in econometric
modeling across German research organizations.[71]

An important if tacit form of coordination is facilitated by the Leibniz
Association. The Leibniz evaluation process facilitates mimetic and normative
learning insofar as organizations scrutinize each other's Leibniz evaluation in
order to benchmark analytic practices that they need to adopt in order to improve their own evaluations. According to one researcher:

People [are] now much more looking at the developments in other
institutes. So for example, benchmarking. . . . Our next [Leibniz]
evaluation will be 2012 and 2013. Of course in the period from
now to then there will be a lot of evaluations of other institutes.
There also will be a lot of changes in other institutes. . . . We look at
how . . . they deal with certain problems.[72]

Following up, we asked whether over the past 20 years or so policy research
organizations involved in the Leibniz process monitored each other more in
order to elevate their scientific standards in ways that resulted in methodological convergence. He said that we were "absolutely right" and that benchmarking like this has led to a standardization of and convergence on certain
research practices. Others agreed.[73] We were told that the same thing was happening among ministerial research units now that the Wissenschaftsrat had
started evaluating them in similar fashion.[74]

Desire for Leibniz membership led sometimes to normative learning at
the international level. For instance, according to a senior official, Ifo lost its
Blue List status due to a subpar Wissenschaftsrat evaluation. Once the Leibniz

[70]Interview with Wolfgang Franz, CEE.
[71]Interview with Rolf Langhammer, IfW. This is not to say that all information is shared freely.
We heard from Klaus Zimmermann, DIW, that some of their models are a proprietary source of
competitive advantage.
[72]Interview with Ulrich Walwei, IAB.
[73]Interview with senior official, Ifo.
[74]Interview with senior official, SOWI.

Senate took over this responsibility from the Wissenschaftsrat, Ifo sought to regain its lost status through Leibniz Association membership by establishing a sister organization, CESIfo, to build up an international network of economists and organize monthly international research conferences to help Ifo learn from economists around the world.

Leibniz evaluations also facilitated some convergence on dissemination practices among the semi-public policy research institutes. Successful evaluation depended in part on demonstrating that the institute served the public interest by having its staff members write op-ed pieces in the newspapers, publish books and articles for the general public, and appear in the media. Research institutes interested in Leibniz membership built up their communication strategies and in doing so often adopted increasingly similar ones—packaging their ideas in streamlined messages that would resonate with the public. As one researcher mentioned, "I think maybe there is another [element of] convergence in terms of being part of the media. . . . That means that your results need to be relevant. That means that the projects you are doing should not be outside of what is interesting for the public."[75] Of course, news reporting used to involve fairly lengthy analysis but now features short, crisp, and clear stories and sound bites, which makes it incumbent on research organizations to tailor their message to this format.[76] Many organizations we spoke with in Germany cultivated these capacities. And occasionally they imitated media dissemination practices from abroad. In this regard, IW copied U.S. advocacy think tanks as did some others.[77]

To be sure, there is sometimes a fine line between mimetic and normative learning. When professionals confer with each other as, for example, the CEE analysts do with their counterparts at other research institutes whatever convergence might occur does so clearly through normative learning—that is, professional socialization. But when organizations monitor each other's Leibniz evaluations to determine analytic benchmarks to which they should aspire, it is harder to tell whether the convergence that results is due to this sort of learning or just relatively blind mimicry. Nevertheless, what strikes us as unique about Germany is not that there has been much normative or mimetic learning but that it is often coordinated either explicitly, as in the case of the Joint Economic Report, or tacitly, as in the case of the Leibniz evaluations. This is what one would expect given the high level of institutionalized coordination we found throughout the German political economy and knowledge regime.

[75]Interview with Ulrich Walwei, IAB.
[76]Interview with Rudolf Zwiener, IMK. See also Braml (2004, pp. 200–202).
[77]Interviews with Rolf Kroker, IW; senior official, KAS.

Denmark: Consensus-Oriented Normative Learning and State Coercion

The hallmark of the Danish political economy is its hybrid character, notably a mixture of statist influence and inclusive consensus-oriented negotiations. The same is true of its knowledge regime. So it should come as no surprise then that two of the most prevalent mechanisms facilitating convergence there were state coercion and cooperative normative learning. And because this is a small country learning often involves monitoring what is happening in other countries.

As noted earlier, because Denmark is a small country where access to policymakers is comparatively easy, we did not hear much about dissemination strategies. So we have little insight to offer about mechanisms operating in this realm. However, we heard a lot about consensus-oriented normative learning in the area of economic policy analysis. Indeed, when it comes to policy analysis such learning was a key mechanism driving convergence toward common analytic practices. The Wise Men are a good example. According to Peter Birch Sørensen, its chair at the time of our interview:

> We have this policy that we always make—I mean we document our analyses and background—technical working papers, and I mean, the models we use if somebody wants to check it out by running simulations, I mean, they can get access to that. So, we—because, I mean, we have a public service application. After all, it's the taxpayers' money, so we don't keep any secrets in that sense.

Moreover, the Wise Men and those who initially developed the DREAM model continue to work together using and refining it.[78]

Lars Andersen, director of AE, said that there is much sharing of methodological information among organizations and use of the same models because policy research organizations generally want to avoid squabbling over methods and focus instead on substantive issues and policy implications—another example of the effects of the consensus-oriented negotiated economy and the declining importance of ideology among policy research organizations since the late 1970s. As a result, he explained that AE learned some of the Ministry of Finance's methodologies and the Center for Labor Market Research (CARMA) learned from AE how best to use micro-level data.[79]

[78] Interviews with Peter Birch Sørensen, Wise Men; Lars Haagen Pedersen, DØR.
[79] Interviews with Lars Andersen, AE; senior official, CARMA.

Learning like this sometimes spans national borders. Indeed, when we asked whether economic forecasters in Denmark learned from their foreign counterparts we found that they did and that they were particularly familiar with models developed in the United States because the Americans were "kind of the front-runners for this type of model."[80] The chair of the Wise Men told us that the supply-side thinking in Denmark first emerged from the Wise Men in the late 1970s and early 1980s and that there were international influences behind it—chiefly economic theory from the United States and Britain. But even now, he said, "We are significantly influenced by what we hear and discuss at international conferences." He noted as well that by attending events organized by the OECD and European Union people in the Danish ministries as well as policymakers became aware that there needed to be a shift of emphasis toward more structural analysis after the Golden Age.

Other Danish policy research organizations keep an eye on their foreign counterparts too "to see if there [is] anything we could learn from their procedures," such as how they organize their research and what sorts of things they do to improve its quality.[81] For instance, the Employment Relations Research Center (FAOS) learned from Norwegian colleagues a respondent-driven sampling technique for interviewing illegal immigrants.[82] In addition, some Danish economists are involved in the Association of European Conjuncture Institutes, which is composed of policy research institutes whose researchers are interested in developing new techniques of business cycle forecasting. Membership enables the Danes to learn what is going on in other countries.[83]

Beyond consensus-oriented normative learning, however, there have been coercive forces at work. Specifically, as the state responded to the crisis of ideology it turned increasingly toward expert analysis and advice and took steps to homogenize some of the semi-public research organizations it relied on. For instance, a law passed in the mid-1990s (Stillingsstruktur) required certain structures and practices of all semi-public research organizations like the Danish National Center for Social Research (SFI). According to SFI's administrative director the law required that these organizations develop parallel structures to the universities in important respects. As he explained, "I think having this common framework has contributed to some kind of harmonization, not completely, of course, but there has been a contribution from that."

[80]Interview with Lars Haagen Pedersen, DØR.
[81]Interview with senior official, SFI.
[82]Interview with senior official, FAOS.
[83]Interview with Peter Birch Sørensen, Wise Men. Members of AIECE include several scholarly policy research organizations central to the knowledge regimes in our countries including in Denmark DØR; in Germany Ifo, IfW, RWI, HWWI, and DIW; and in France INSEE, OFCE, and Coe-Rexecode. The OECD, IMF, and Eurostat also belong (http://sites-test.uclouvain.be/aiece/. Accessed September 2011).

For instance, they have all adopted similar hiring criteria—emphasizing to an increasing extent PhD-trained researchers, which would presumably facilitate convergence across these organizations in analytic techniques insofar as these economists subscribe, for reasons already mentioned, to an increasingly common set of methods and models and constitute the tight-knit "brotherhood of economists" we discussed in chapter 5. Summing up, he remarked, "In those [and other] sorts of areas there has been a tendency towards more equal ways of operating."[84]

But the state facilitated convergence in other ways too. For instance, it organized and financed the initial development of the key economic models that became ubiquitous among economic policy analysts in Denmark. It did so in order to provide everyone with a common tool kit for better making sense of the Danish economy. Indeed, the DREAM model was designed for a Microsoft Windows platform so that people on the Danish Economic Council (DØR) and in other research organizations could use it.

However, in addition to providing everyone with these more sophisticated tools the state facilitated convergence on state-of-the-art analytic practices through its role as gatekeeper to policy negotiations, which encouraged much monitoring among policy research organizations. The AE's Lars Andersen told us, as did others, that the convergence on more sophisticated and technical forms of analysis had been going on for at least the past 20 years and that one important reason why was that organizations needed to be as good as the best in the business. "We have to match the Finance Ministry; we have to match the SFI; we have to match the DREAM group." We heard as well at the Center for Alternative Social Analysis (CASA) that they feel compelled to improve their expertise and analytic capacities in order to keep pace with the rest.[85] And at DA we learned that one reason they beefed up their analytic capacities was to bolster their influence politically vis-à-vis other organizations.[86] But why was everyone so intent on monitoring and keeping pace with each other in this regard? The LO's Finn Larsen told us, as did others, that monitoring and copying like this was driven at least partly by concerns among some organizations of being left out of the political conversation, which could happen if policymakers decided that an organization was in the

---

[84]This is a bit like the effect that the Leibniz evaluation process had on policy research organizations in Germany enticing them to converge on common analytic practices except that it is now a coercive requirement in Denmark, not a persuasive inducement as in Germany.

[85]Interview with Finn Kenneth Hansen, CASA.

[86]Interview with Niels Trampe, DA. Tramp and Lars Andersen, LO, told us that a related aspect of all this involved following each other's research agendas. Andersen mentioned, for instance, that the LO's weekly news magazine, *Ugebrevet A4*, prides itself on raising new issues and watching others begin studying them. Similarly, Trampe told us that DA was one of the first organizations to do serious research into the Danish labor market but that others soon followed.

dark with respect to key policy issues or was producing poor quality analysis. This concern became especially important as the state flexed its gatekeeping muscles by including more and more experts in ad hoc commissions and other forums—something that it was increasingly inclined to do in response to the crisis of ideology.

Two additional points are important here. First, there is certainly an element of competition in this but it stems largely from the increased willingness of the state to regulate who is privy to policy negotiations and advising in the first place. Concerns about being excluded from these discussions hang like the sword of Damocles ready to fall on organizations that do not live up to the state's standards. The monitoring and learning that results leads toward convergence. Second, it is again sometimes difficult to disentangle the type of learning involved here. Mimesis is at work insofar as organizations want to adopt certain analytic practices in order to be viewed as legitimate by the state. But normative learning is also present because organizations cannot use these techniques without actually understanding how they work, what the underlying assumptions are, how to manipulate the models, and so on.

Overall, then, convergence in Denmark, particularly on analytic practices, has been driven to a considerable degree by two mechanisms. One is the proclivity for consensus-oriented normative learning. The other is the state's involvement in the knowledge regime in ways that tended to push policy research organizations toward a common set of analytic practices. Both reflect the institutional structure of the Danish political economy—one marked by lots of consensus-oriented cooperation and by an increasingly strong state.

To sum up this section, three things stand out about these convergence tendencies within and across countries. First, all four of the convergence mechanisms depicted in the literature (normative, mimetic, coercive, and competitive) showed up in our knowledge regimes. Second, mechanisms often worked in combination with each other. Third, these combinations mirrored important differences in each country's knowledge regime and broader political economy. In the United States we found many examples of movement toward convergence driven by coercion and competitively inspired mimicry that reflected the broader political-economic influences of private financing and political partisanship in the knowledge regime as well as the separation of powers within the state. In France there were combinations of state coercion and international mimetic and normative learning thanks to the influence of French statism and the isolated niche structure of its knowledge regime. In Germany we found coordinated normative and mimetic learning spawned by some of the knowledge regime's many coordination mechanisms. And in Denmark, consensus-oriented normative learning and state coercion created tendencies toward convergence—both outgrowths of key institutional features of the Danish knowledge regime.

Constraints on Convergence

Resource and institutional constraints mediated convergence within and among knowledge regimes. There was considerable evidence from our interviews that this occurred in all four of our countries. And often the manner in which these constraints were organized was nationally specific.

Resources

Access to financial and staffing resources was a constraint that inhibited convergence on common dissemination and analytic practices in all four countries. Sometimes this was closely related to organizational size. This may seem banal but is nonetheless important. We heard frequently that small organizations had fewer resources and thus often found it difficult if not impossible to adopt practices they observed in large organizations. For instance, in the United States the National Center for Policy Analysis, the Century Foundation, and some other smaller policy research organizations were unable to do as much sophisticated analysis as they might have liked in-house and so outsourced it to university academics or others. Similarly, people at the relatively small Center on Budget and Policy Priorities worried that "[i]t's the Internet age. I think we're trying to even catch up with that. I mean, we don't have the same kinds of resources for communications that, for example, Heritage and some of our colleague's organizations have."[87] And in Denmark, Finn Larsen from LO complained that although LO and DA had beefed up their analytic capacities LO was at a disadvantage. Why? DA had more resources and focused largely on labor market issues whereas LO had fewer resources and had to spread them across a broader portfolio, including as well welfare and pension reform issues. So even though the LO was a large organization compared to many in our four countries, it was smaller from a resource standpoint in this regard vis-à-vis DA and thus was constrained in how much it could emulate what research DA was doing.

Size-related resource constraints limited cross-national convergence too. In France, although CEPII monitored the latest methodological techniques and data sources of their foreign counterparts, the small size of its staff limited how much it could use them. According to a senior official at CEPII, "It depends, because we are only 30 economists, so we cannot do everything." We were told the same thing at OFCE in Paris.[88] And at Institute Montaigne, the French advocacy organization, the director, Philippe Manière, said that although he visited Heritage, Cato, and other large organizations periodically, Montaigne was small compared to them and therefore incapable of doing many of the

[87] Interview with senior official, CBPP.
[88] Interviews with senior official, CEPII; Xavier Timbeau, OFCE.

things they did. In his words many of their practices "cannot happen here" due to Montaigne's small size. One person we spoke with at Enterprise and Progress, the French business club, agreed that size mattered when he said, "There is nothing comparable to the think tanks in the U.S., and we are still, you know, small guys moving in."[89] So both within and across countries convergence was uneven due to resource constraints associated with organizational size.

There was one very important country-specific difference in resource constraints. For many policy research organizations in the United States, resources came from private sources. In Europe this was much rarer because the state funded many of them. Regardless of how much money they received, state-funded organizations were assured for the most part that their resources would not change suddenly and dramatically. For example, even OFCE in France, which was often a thorn in the government's side, was never threatened with funding cuts, although it did receive level funding for some years.[90] This meant that whatever tendencies there may have been toward convergence on either common analytic or dissemination practices, it would not likely be undermined by a sudden and unexpected tightening of resource constraints.

Things were different in the United States where many organizations depended financially on the generosity of private donors or the returns of the organization's endowment. This meant that funding was potentially erratic and unpredictable because it was tied closely to the fate of the economy, especially the stock market. When the market tumbled endowments slipped and donors were less forthcoming so organizations had to tighten their belts. Sometimes this involved cutting back on analysis—something we did not hear about in Europe. Indeed, when we were in Washington the economy was softening. And we were told on several occasions that even some of the larger private organizations had turned lately toward outsourcing some of their research or synthesizing research already done by others rather than doing it in-house.[91] Insofar as convergence on common and more sophisticated analytic practices was concerned, dependence on private financing created the possibility that convergence would be a much more uneven and herky-jerky sort of process.

Dependence on private funding constrained convergence in two other ways in the United States that we did not hear about much in Europe. First,

[89]Interview with senior official, Enterprise and Progress.
[90]Interview with Xavier Timbeau, OFCE. The two European exceptions that we discovered were the German political party foundations, whose budgets depended on how many seats their party won in national elections, and the German semi-public research institutes whose funding depended partly—but not entirely—on how they fared in their Leibniz evaluations.
[91]Interviews with Christy Hicks, Century Foundation; Ted Hand, RFF; Isabel Sawhill, Brookings Institution.

sometimes funders did not want to support analytic work at all, which certainly blocked whatever hopes researchers might have had for adopting more sophisticated analytic practices. Irrespective of swings in the economy, one person told us off the record that due to pressure from funders some of the larger foundations had become less interested in paying for serious empirical analysis and pushed instead toward simply synthesizing other people's research. In the extreme cases, funders only wanted to fund slipshod research that substantiated certain foregone conclusions—an approach that certainly stymied best methodological practice. For example, we learned in one interview that "[t]here is a lot of funding there . . . to produce research or whatever, that gives you whatever conclusion the funders want, so that there's all this stuff out there that is not very good. . . . I'm not sure it should be taken seriously, and I think that's a change."[92]

Second, the partisan coloring of private funding in the United States put progressive organizations on the left at a considerable disadvantage relative to their conservative counterparts because most of the money came from conservative sources. This hobbled the ability of progressive organizations to conform to cutting-edge practices. The Century Foundation's Christy Hicks affirmed what others told us about this, especially when it came to adopting the most technologically savvy dissemination strategies:

> There's some more money over there [on the right] . . . there's lots more money, and if you look at, say, my communications team, and oh, let me pull one out of the air. . . . Heritage's communication staff is almost as big as the entire staff of the Century Foundation . . . liberal, progressive, center-left organizations are really just trying to follow suit without the financial resources to do that.

Echoing the concern about the left needing resources for effectively disseminating ideas, a senior official at the PPI, which is a small shop in this world, explained that PPI tries to compensate for this resource constraint by working with the Democratic Leadership Council, which has political and communications offices connected to a huge network of elected officials and that distributes PPI products through the network.[93] Moreover, liberal money from Silicon Valley and elsewhere has recently helped narrow the gap by supporting organizations like CAP—one of the few policy research organizations in Washington that has enough money to be able to spend 50% of it on disseminating their ideas.[94] The recent influx of liberal money into this world is

[92] Interview with senior official, CBPP.
[93] Interview with senior official, PPI.
[94] Interview with Sarah Rosen Wartell, CAP.

further evidence of the fickle nature of private funding that contributed to the tightening and loosening of financial constraints.[95]

We heard much less about the unpredictability of resource constraints in Europe. But if private policy research organizations continue to emerge in Europe then the distinctiveness of the U.S. knowledge regime in this regard may begin to fade and resource constraints may have more of these effects in the European countries. In one French interview we discovered evidence that pointed in this direction. Recall that many French policy research organizations were converging toward shorter publications intended for policymakers, nonexperts, and the public. However, we were told off the record of one case in which there was strong countervailing financial pressure to this trend. Our informant explained that a large international consulting firm had approached his organization about copublishing a series of books on economic issues. He said that if the deal was consummated his organization would suddenly be swimming against the tide by publishing more—not fewer—books because the consulting firm would pony up the resources to subsidize it. A shift in resource constraints could reverse whatever inclination this organization might have had to adopt the dissemination practices on which it and others were converging. It seems then that private resources tend to be both more erratic and come with more strings attached than public resources.

Policymaking Regimes and Political Institutions

Policymaking regimes and their political institutions constitute a second constraint on convergence in analytic and dissemination practices. But their effects on convergence were felt in other areas as well.

To begin with, the cross-national variability in resource constraints that we just discussed was partly an artifact of political institutions. The reason why so many policy research organizations in the United States were susceptible to the vagaries of private funding in the first place was that U.S. policymakers were less inclined to support policy analysis and research activity in civil society than European policymakers. In this regard the state was more laissez-faire in America than in Europe with its statist and corporatist traditions.

Political institutions also affected the degree to which policy research organizations converged on common dissemination practices. For instance, in the United States government research organizations were sometimes much less concerned than private ones with adopting the latest media savvy marketing strategies because their legislative mandates essentially forbade it. Much of the research done by the Congressional Research Service, for instance, must be kept secret because it often stems from confidential requests from members

[95]For a detailed discussion of the left's recent success in raising financing from liberal donors in Silicon Valley, Hollywood, and elsewhere, see Bai (2009).

of Congress.[96] Similarly, much of the forecasting done by the CEA is necessarily held in confidence for fear of influencing the capital markets.[97] The Government Accountability Office, CBO, and National Research Council are less constrained legally in disseminating their reports to the public. There is also cross-national variability in this regard where, for example, the German CEE and the Danish Wise Men are required to issue high-profile public reports of their general economic forecasts, which therefore attract much media attention, while their French counterpart, CAE, is required to neither produce such forecasts nor publicize the more specialized reports it does issue. Again variation in political institutional constraints explains the difference.

Tax codes were another political institution that inhibited the cross-national convergence on dissemination strategies. As we explained in chapter 2, in the United States private policy research organizations were wary of creeping too close to lobbying as a means of disseminating their analysis and recommendations because it could jeopardize their special 501(c)(3) tax statuses and therefore their financing.[98] No such constraints existed in Europe, which is why French business clubs and German advocacy organizations were more open to lobbying the government as an important dissemination strategy.

But the effects of political institutional constraints extended beyond just analytic and dissemination practices. Nationally specific tax codes are again instructive. If registered as a 501(c)(3) organization, private policy research organizations could solicit tax deductible contributions from private donors. This created an institutional opportunity for these organizations to proliferate, which they did. But tax laws were different in Europe and posed serious obstacles to the establishment of private policy research organizations when people wanted to emulate American organizations. Recall that when Bernard Zimmern initially tried to set up IFRAP he discovered that the tax deductions available in France to potential benefactors were meager. As a result, raising money in France was prohibitively difficult, which is why he established a foundation in the United States to support IFRAP. This proved to be a problem for some of the political foundations in France as well.[99] Tax obstacles had similar effects in Germany, which is one reason why private policy research organizations are largely absent there too. But since these laws were changed recently in both countries, we may eventually see more advocacy organizations emerging there. Time will tell.

---

[96] Interview with senior official, CRS. According to this source, every year or two CRS lawyers have to defend this confidentiality in court when CRS is sued for discovery.

[97] Interview with senior official, CEA.

[98] Both AEI and the Heritage Foundation had been investigated by the U.S. tax authorities to ensure that they had not crossed the 501(c)(3) line into 501(c)(4) lobbying.

[99] Interview with Michel Rousseau, Foundation Concorde.

Bureaucratic rules and procedures inhibited cross-national convergence in other ways too. In France one needed permission from various ministerial offices in order to set up a private policy research organization. It could take years to obtain the official go-ahead. Such permissions were not required in the United States. Hence, bureaucratic red tape was another political obstacle to the diffusion of the American advocacy organization model to France—and one about which IFRAP's founder, Bernard Zimmern, complained bitterly.[100]

Legislative and executive mandates are another set of political institutional constraints. The French CAE has not emulated the organizational structure and practices of its counterparts elsewhere, according to the CAE chair, "[b]ecause each organization is idiosyncratic. And it was created [legally] to be idiosyncratic." He gave an example. The German CEE members think that the CAE is not as independent from the French prime minister as the CEE is from the German chancellor in part because the Germans are appointed for longer terms than the French. His point was that institutional differences in the two policymaking regimes meant that it would be very difficult for the French CAE to copy how the German CEE operated lock, stock, and barrel. Nor was the CAE similar to the Danish Wise Men, which in his view tended to represent the views of the social partners.[101] In France with a different set of political institutions the conseils shoulder that responsibility more than the CAE.

The power of institutional constraints like these on convergence was emphasized to us in an interview with the director of the U.S. Government Accountability Office. He told us about the International Organization of Supreme Audit Institutions (INTOSAI), an international organization in which he was heavily involved and whose mission was to disseminate best practices among national accounting offices like the GAO. Their efforts often ran into institutional constraints:

> What we try to do is provide assistance, but people come to us to learn, you know, how do we do things? And then they adapt that to their government structure. . . . They're in a parliamentary type of system where we provide assistance to all committees of our Congress, so that's an entirely—we have an entirely different kind of setup. Some of them were actually created by their constitution, so they have very defined responsibilities. We were created legislatively by the Congress and we have very broad authorities into a wider range of work . . . so it's the size, the legal authorities, the culture, the history, the government structure, really are more factors shaping how they're organized.

[100]Interview with Bernard Zimmern, IFRAP.
[101]Interview with Christian de Boissieu, CAE.

Another senior GAO official explained that even if the Danish equivalent of the GAO might be tempted to adopt some of GAO's practices, "The Danish office would want to meet its mandate from the Danish Parliament . . . which would certainly constrain them from doing some of the things we would do . . . and vice versa." We heard virtually the same thing at the U.S. CBO, which often shares information with its counterparts in foreign countries about how they operate.[102] Put differently, the degree to which organizations like these converge on common structures and practices through either normative or mimetic learning is limited in varying degree by the political institutional constraints within which they operate.

Production Regimes and Economic Institutions

Economic institutions also mediated convergent tendencies in analytic and dissemination practices among others. We have already seen some examples in other contexts so we can be brief. One was the effects of policy research organizations being tied institutionally or not to the fortunes of the stock market and the economy more generally for funding. Another was the unequal distribution of financial resources that put policy research organizations on the left at a disadvantage in the United States—a disadvantage that stemmed partly from the fact that the labor movement in America was comparatively weak and that there were no corporatist institutions to bolster them. EPI was the only research shop in Washington of which we were aware that received much funding from the unions, and it was one of the smaller private research organizations we visited there.[103] Hence, much to his dismay, EPI's president told us that they have not yet managed to achieve state-of-the-art dissemination practices.

Comparisons to the European countries where labor is much better organized are instructive here too. For example, the Danish LO has substantially more resources for this sort of thing—enough in fact to publish a nationally circulated weekly newspaper, *Ugebrevet A4*, and distribute it for free! Thanks as well to its corporatist roots the well-organized German labor movement had substantial policy research capacities through the Institute for Macroeconomic Forecasting (IMK) and the Economic and Social Research Institute (WSI), both under the aegis of the Hans Böckler Foundation, not to mention the Institute for Employment Research (IAB).[104] It stands to reason that even if

---

[102]Interview with senior official, CBO. CBO often hosts visitors from their counterparts in other countries and sends staff overseas as advisors.

[103]Interview with Lawrence Mishel, EPI.

[104]IMK and WSI have a combined staff of about 60, which is comparable to EPI's staff, but IAB's staff is five times larger. Data for IMK and WSI are from http://www.boeckler.de; for IAB they are from http://www.iab.de; and for EPI they are from http://www.epi.org. All accessed August 2012.

EPI wanted to emulate the extensive dissemination and analytic capacities of these other organizations, the labor movement's weakness in America would constrain that effort.

The limits to convergence posed by economic institutions were also evident in our interviews when it came to the diffusion of particular organizational structures across countries. For instance, a senior official at FAOS in Denmark said that his organization was different from the foreign research organizations they monitored insofar as FAOS was financed by both the trade unions and employers. This, he explained, was a manifestation of the long-standing institutionalized cooperation between business and labor in Denmark. He told us that there was nothing like it even in corporatist Germany or the rest of Scandinavia. In those countries you find organizations funded by either the unions or employers but not both. In his words, "It's specifically Danish because even going to the other Nordic countries . . . you do not have the close relations between the employers and trade unions as we have here in Denmark. [It's a] much more conflictual environment [there] so it's difficult to imagine that you could have a research center like this one." So, even though FAOS worked with foreign organizations and copied some of their practices— and vice versa—at least its funding structure carried a particularly Danish stamp that would not likely be emulated in these other countries. The same is certainly true for other Danish research organizations like CARMA and CASA that receive funding from both unions and employers. It is particularly hard to imagine this structure being adopted in the United States where in the absence of corporatist institutions the relationship between business and labor is far more combative.

As we saw with political constraints, the fact that economic institutions constrain convergence is especially clear when they change. Consider people's perceptions about the value of corporatism. For decades faith in corporatist institutions helped block the possibilities for diffusion of American-style advocacy organizations to Germany. We learned in one interview that Germans were wary historically of private political consultants and American-style think tanks. The perception was that these things represented the seamy and corrupt side of politics because they involved shadowy backroom deals and "smelly" politics, as one person described them, that lacked transparency. People used to be careful not to even use the term "think tank" when referring to their research organizations because of its negative connotation. But this changed. As the economic issues confronting politicians became more complex after the Golden Age, particularly with the rise of economic globalization, the mood shifted and people began to believe that these organizations could provide useful advice to policymakers and that doing so was not necessarily so bad. This shift was amplified by perceptions of the crisis of corporatism that we discussed in chapter 4. People began to see the value of American-style advocacy think tanks as well as lobbyists. And so the American-style think tank model began to diffuse to Germany in the form of INSM, SM, the Bertelsmann Foundation, and the like.[105] A similar story may be beginning in Denmark where, as we explained in chapter 5, people said that the presence of the peak associations effectively crowded out other policy research organizations but that CEPOS and one or two other advocacy organizations have appeared recently.

The French were also averse to American-style advocacy organizations but for different political reasons. In a statist political economy where most people believed that the business and political elites could run things alone, there was no need for such organizations. Indeed, we were told on several occasions in Paris that American private think tanks were seen as antithetical to France's Jacobin heritage.[106] This is likely another reason why it took a long time for Bernard Zimmern to receive permission from the ministries to set up his IFRAP. Nevertheless, after the Golden Age as the crisis of ideas came into focus these constraints began to loosen, the French government started searching for new types of policy research organizations in civil society to help make sense of the situation, and institutional space opened up for organizations like IFRAP and Institute Montaigne to emerge.

Overall, then, resource and institutional constraints often mediated convergent tendencies in analytic and dissemination practices as well as other aspects of policy research organizations. These effects were evident both within and across our knowledge regimes. The availability of resources affected the degree to which policy research organizations could conform to state-of-the-art analytic techniques as well as cutting-edge marketing strategies. Institutional effects sometimes underpinned the availability of resources in the first place. However, institutions had other effects too. Insofar as political institutions were concerned tax codes and legislative mandates influenced whether organizations could adopt the same dissemination practices. Tax codes also affected the adoption of the advocacy organization model across borders as did certain aspects of state bureaucracy. Insofar as economic institutions were concerned differences in how organizations were connected to gyrating private capital markets and fickle donors affected their ability to emulate each other's practices. And the presence or absence of corporatism and the organizational capacity of labor affected the ability of policy research organizations on the left from keeping pace with innovations adopted by those on the right. Corporatist legacies in Germany as well as statist legacies in France stifled moves toward advocacy organizations for a long time.

[105]Interviews with Dieter Plehwe, WZB; senior officials at KAS and SM. See also Braml (2004, p. 227).
[106]Interviews with Paul de Fombelle, Institute Choiseul; Frédéric Allemand, Foundation for Political Innovation; Philippe Manière, Institute Montaigne.

What all this means is that in order to understand the constraints that influenced the degree to which policy research organizations converged or not in various ways within and across knowledge regimes one must adopt a comparative political economy approach to the problem. Without this we cannot explain the puzzle by which mechanisms of convergence do not always lead to convergent outcomes.

Conclusions

We have identified tendencies toward convergence whereby some policy research organizations, which had little in common in the 1980s, edged toward similar structures and practices by the time we visited them in 2008 and 2009. We have shown that a variety of mechanisms triggered these tendencies and that they sometimes operated in nationally specific combinations thanks to the institutional configurations of their knowledge regime and the rest of the political economy. And we have explained how resources and institutions constrained these tendencies in ways that limited convergence in varying degree within as well as across knowledge regimes. There are some important lessons in all of this for convergence theory.

To begin with, let us underscore a few points in our argument about the nature of different convergence mechanisms. Some of them are more subtle than is sometimes appreciated. For example, coercion is not just about arm twisting and brute force. Sometimes, of course, it is—as in the case of the Danish state's requirement (Stillingsstruktur) that semi-public research organizations adopt some practices typically associated with universities. But sometimes it is more about persuasion as we saw in the case of the French state not forcing but urging political parties to establish policy research organizations as part of their foundations and offering to pay for it if they did so. Arguably, the Leibniz accreditation process in Germany also involved an element of persuasion—at least insofar as it granted certain rewards to organizations that met its standards. Indeed, the exercise of power has more than one dimension.

Note as well that competition is not, strictly speaking, a matter of Darwinian survival of the fittest where organizations either adapt or die, which is the way it was presented in some formulations of convergence theory.[107] To be sure, some policy research organizations worried about competition. And if they had completely lost the competition for funding, for instance, then they would have disappeared altogether. But we heard of only two specific cases during our interviews of organizations dying at all—and these had nothing to do with competition. One was the French Planning Commissariat that was

---

[107] DiMaggio and Powell 1983.

a victim of the demise of dirigisme. The other was the U.S. Office of Technology Assessment (OTA) whose funding was eliminated for political reasons.[108] What people told us frequently was that competition was primarily about influence. For instance, some Danish policy research organizations tried to have the best analytic practices for fear of being left out of policy negotiations if they did not. And many organizations turned toward the new media to disseminate their work for the same reason. Thus competition motivated organizations to adapt in order to preserve or augment their status and influence—not because they worried about going out of business. We will return to the issue of influence in chapter 7.

This brings us to our next point. Researchers have complained that more attention was needed to differentiate the independent effects of various mechanisms from each other in order to better understand convergence.[109] This was important advice that others took to heart in subsequent research.[110] But it may have obscured something equally important for researchers. As we mentioned in the beginning of this chapter, relatively little attention has been paid to how mechanisms may operate in combination with each other. In other words, researchers have neglected the interactive effects of convergence mechanisms. We found considerable evidence for such effects, such as when competition led organizations to adopt each other's practices through either normative or mimetic learning. And in the United States among private research organizations on the left competition with those on the right led to copying certain types of cooperative interorganizational strategy sessions. Competition begat convergence through mimicry.

Furthermore, as we also mentioned earlier, not enough attention has been paid to how combinations of mechanisms may be nationally specific. This matters insofar as researchers have become interested lately in theorizing the dynamics of institutional change.[111] For instance, James Mahoney and Kathleen Thelen identified different mechanisms of change and argued that each one tends to be associated with a particular institutional context.[112] Their concern was not with convergence per se so the mechanisms they posited were different from those that we have been discussing. But their insight is still important and points in the same general direction as we have—that is, there is at least a loose association between certain mechanisms and certain institutional contexts.

But two clarifications are immediately in order. First, we found that *all* of our mechanisms operated in *several* countries—each with rather different

[108]Bimber 1996.
[109]Mizruchi and Fein 1999.
[110]See, for example, Bartley (2007), Halliday and Carruthers (2010, 2007), and Simmons et al. (2008).
[111]For a review of this literature, see Campbell (2010).
[112]Mahoney and Thelen 2010b.

institutional features. So while it may be appealing for purposes of theoretical parsimony to argue for exclusivity in terms of the association of a particular mechanism with a particular context, we find that at least for knowledge regimes the world is more complex than their theory would have led us to believe. Second, we found that certain combinations are more likely to occur in some national contexts than others. Yet these are only *tendencies*. In other words, the degree to which different convergence mechanisms are likely to be in play is constrained but not fully determined by the institutional context. Competitive pressure for convergence, for instance, operated in the United States and Denmark. But it was more common in the United States due to the proclivity for politically partisan combat and the need to secure private funding—both of which were greater in America than Denmark. In short, institutional contexts matter because they affect the possibility—not the inevitability—that different mechanisms will trigger movement toward convergence in the first place. We have only begun to scratch the surface in this regard, so much more research needs to be done.

Remember too that institutions also matter because they constrain the outcomes that may result once convergence mechanisms have started up. As we have seen, for example, efforts to introduce American-style advocacy think tanks in France and Germany through some combination of mimetic and normative processes were largely inhibited by institutional obstacles. Similarly, INTOSAI's effort to disseminate certain performance benchmarks among national audit agencies was hobbled in varying degrees by national institutions, such as legislative mandates. The operation of constraints like this is why the outcomes we have reported in this chapter were so uneven and why there was not more evidence of convergence within and across our knowledge regimes.[113]

Recognizing that the operation of convergence mechanisms is mediated by resource and institutional constraints creates significant opportunities for building bridges between comparative political economy and organizational and economic sociology in ways that improve our understanding of convergence processes. As we noted at the beginning of this chapter, sociologists who study fields have only recently started to appreciate that the transformation of fields often involves conflicts and struggles over resources, power, status, and

---

[113] As we have shown, the influence of international networks like these came up occasionally in our interviews in each country. We were surprised, however, by how little importance people attributed to them relative to domestic networks. The big exception was that people referred frequently to using databases from transnational organizations like the OECD, IMF, World Bank, and Eurostat. Nevertheless, beyond this people emphasized much more the flow of information through domestic networks. It is not clear why this was the case. And it is a bit of a mystery insofar as researchers have found international networks to be an important source of information flows among professionals (e.g., Djelic and Sahlin-Andersson 2006; Haas 1992). So this requires further investigation.

other things—conflicts and struggles that are at the heart of comparative political economy. The analytic benefits of blending these perspectives are clear. Convergence within a field may require—perhaps typically—that institutions be transformed so as not to block it. Sweeping away institutional barriers involves conflict and struggle. Bernard Zimmern's struggle to change tax laws in order to facilitate the establishment and funding of French advocacy organizations is a case in point as were his efforts to convince French bureaucrats that such organizations could be a useful source of policy analysis and advice in addition to that provided by state technocrats. Hence, insofar as institutions must be changed in order to facilitate convergence conflict is an inherent part of the process.

This understanding of the interplay among convergence mechanisms and constraints raises all sorts of interesting questions. For instance, one might wonder whether conflict over institutions is often a chronologically phased precondition for convergence. Others have suggested that it may be, and our results support that view in some cases.[114] One might wonder as well whether the stories of partial or stalled convergence that we have reported might turn out different if we waited a while longer. In other words, given more time to play out might not the normative, mimetic, coercive, and competitive mechanisms that we have identified eventually lead to more convergence? We suspect not as long as the resource and institutional constraints we found remain in place. But this, of course, depends very much on whether struggles to overcome or otherwise transform them are initiated and then are successful or not. In this regard, the concept of fields from organizational and economic sociology and the concept of conflict from comparative political economy are inseparable!

---

[114]Campbell et al. (1991) and Fligstein (1990) argued the organization of various fields and sectors in the U.S. economy often changed only after antitrust and other laws were modified.

7

Questions of Influence

What influence do knowledge regimes have? This was *not* the central question motivating this book because many others have already tried to determine how ideas affect policymaking. Instead, we wanted to understand how the analysis, recommendations, and other ideas upon which policymakers relied were produced and disseminated to them in the first place. But it is difficult to avoid the question of influence, and indeed we have been asked about it many times. So we tackle it in this chapter although very cautiously for reasons that will soon become clear.

The issue of influence actually involves two more specific questions. The first question is the most obvious: To what extent do *individual* policy research organizations in a knowledge regime actually affect the thinking of policymakers? Put differently, which organizations do policymakers pay the most attention to for analysis, advice and inspiration as they contemplate making policy? In order to answer this we turned to data from our interviews and discovered that it was difficult to know how much influence individual research organizations had on policymakers. Indeed, the organizations themselves were often unsure about how much influence they had.

This realization led us to ask the second question, which to our knowledge nobody else has asked: To what extent do knowledge regimes as *fields* of organizations influence the sorts of ideas that policy research organizations tend to produce and disseminate to policymakers in the first place? In other words, do the ideas that policymakers are exposed to vary according to the national character of the knowledge regimes that produce them? For example, are some knowledge regimes more likely to produce Keynesian, supply-side, or neoliberal ideas than others? Keynesianism, of course, favors government intervention to manage aggregate economic demand and regulate swings in the business cycles. Supply-side ideas favor all sorts of government policies to provide the necessary capital, labor, technologies, infrastructure, and other inputs necessary to stimulate economic innovation and growth. Neoliberalism is a particularly conservative variant of supply-side thinking that tends to favor less rather than more government intervention in order to facilitate an adequate supply of inputs through the free market. Central to the neoliberal program are things like tax cuts, reductions in welfare spending, and less regulation of business. In order to examine whether some knowledge regimes are more likely to produce certain types of ideas rather than others we examined key reports from the national councils of economic advisors in each country and found that there were important differences along these lines.

The first question takes policymakers' thinking as the dependent variable. The second question takes the ideas to which they are exposed as the dependent variable. The two questions are related sequentially insofar as the national character of a knowledge regime influences the type of ideas that policy research organizations produce and that are then disseminated in order to influence policymakers' thinking.

Our results shed light on three important literatures. The first concerns the specialized research on think tanks. Evidence from our interviews confirms what others have found—although we have done so in a comparative cross-national context—namely that determining which policy research organizations are the most influential is difficult if not impossible.[1] The second literature is about the shifting nature of ideas and policy paradigms like Keynesianism and neoliberalism.[2] Contrary to what several researchers suggest we find in reports from the national councils of economic advisors that policy paradigms are not hegemonic but coexist and compete with one another. And paradigms often evolve gradually rather than shift abruptly from

[1]See, for example, Abelson (2002), Ricci (1993), Weidenbaum (2009), and Weilemann (2000, p. 185).
[2]See, for example, Campbell and Pedersen (2001a), Crouch (2011), Fourcade (2009), Fourcade-Gourinchas and Babb (2002), Hall (1992, 1993), and Mudge (2008).

one to another. The third literature concerns globalization and the diffusion of neoliberalism. We discovered that at least in the national council reports the degree to which neoliberalism diffused across countries and resulted in some sort of neoliberal convergence was limited. This supports what some—but not all—researchers have found. But they explained the absence of convergence in terms of cross-national differences in things like elite and class coalitions, political institutions, and economic circumstances.[3] They neglected the effects of differences in the character of knowledge regimes, which we found to be significant.

It is worth mentioning that the literatures on hegemonic paradigms, globalization, and the diffusion of neoliberalism to which we refer appeared before the 2008 international financial crisis. We now know that the crisis generated much talk in academic and policymaking circles about the return of Keynesian ideas as a challenge to neoliberalism.[4] And aggressive Keynesian-style stimulus packages appeared in several countries too, perhaps most notably the United States during the George W. Bush administration—an administration famous for its passion for lower taxes and less government spending on social programs. So both neoliberal and Keynesian ideas are now more in play in many countries than they were before the crisis. Our results, however, suggest that they were both still very much in play before the crisis hit in all four of our countries.

Before discussing any of this, however, we need to address the methodological difficulties involved in ascertaining influence. Then we turn to the influence of individual policy research organizations and the influence of knowledge regimes as fields.

The Difficulties of Ascertaining Influence

Establishing the extent to which *individual* policy research organizations influence policymakers is a notoriously tricky business. Many things can affect what policymakers do, including but not limited to the analyses, recommendations, and other ideas coming from their favorite policy research organizations. Elections, public opinion, individual and organizational arm twisting, institutional constraints, and general political and economic circumstances matter too.[5] Indeed, as John Kingdon showed, the policymaking process is like

---

[3] See, for example, Babb (2001), Crouch (2011), Dezalay and Garth (2002), Fourcade-Gourinchas and Babb (2002), Harvey (2005), and Prasad (2006).
[4] Krugman 2009; Skidelsky 2009; Stiglitz 2009.
[5] Lindvall (2009) has much to say about this complexity but concludes in the end that ideas still matter.

a garbage can with all sorts of things tossed in that may influence outcomes.[6] Disentangling all this is difficult.[7]

One common way to do so is to develop detailed historical case studies of how policymakers crafted a particular policy at a particular time.[8] Given our interest in four countries and how their knowledge regimes changed over time, this would have required us to construct an unmanageable number of case studies. Furthermore, even if one could occasionally find clear evidence that a particular organization had provided policymakers with a particular idea in a particular case, it would still be difficult to generalize more broadly about which organizations were more influential than others. Alternatively, one might interview policymakers themselves (or their staffs) and ask which policy research organizations they tended to depend on most for analysis, recommendations and other ideas.[9] In our case, this was impossible because we simply did not have the contacts or other resources necessary to survey or conduct interviews with policymakers and staff in all four of our countries.

As a result, we asked people during our interviews how influential they thought their policy research organizations were in terms of affecting the thinking of policymakers.[10] And if they said that their organization was influential, which most of them did, we asked them in effect to prove it. For reasons that will become clear later it was difficult to tell from the interviews how much influence organizations had.

Establishing the extent to which the structure and practices of a knowledge regime as a *field* influences the kinds of ideas policy research organizations tend to produce in the first place is equally dicey. One way to do this would be to analyze the content of reports from several policy research organizations in each of our four knowledge regimes to see if in the aggregate there were associations between different knowledge regimes and the sorts of ideas their organizations typically produced. Another approach would be to analyze a similar set of documents from a knowledge regime at different points in time to see whether changes in the knowledge regime were associated with changes in the types of ideas it tended to produce. However, either approach would require a team of researchers to code and analyze a large

---

[6]Kingdon 1995.

[7]Abelson (2002) provides an extended discussion of the methodological difficulties in establishing whether think tanks are influential. For general discussions of the methodological difficulties in establishing whether ideas affect policymaking, see Berman (1998), Blyth (1997), and the methodological essays in Béland and Cox (2011).

[8]See, for example, Babb (2001), Blyth (2002), Hall (1989b), Rich (2004, chap. 4), Rueschemeyer and Skocpol (1996), and Weidenbaum (2009).

[9]This is what Rich (2004, Appendix A) did in his analysis of U.S. think tanks.

[10]This definition of influence is common in this area of research (e.g., Rich 2004, p. 153).

number of documents and do so in four languages. Again, we did not have the resources to do this.

We did, however, adopt a much scaled down version of this strategy. We analyzed reports from each country's national council of economic advisors— the U.S. Council of Economic Advisors (CEA), the French Council of Economic Analysis (CAE), the German Council of Economic Experts (CEE), and the Danish Economic Council (DØR). We examined reports from 1987, 1997, and 2007 from each council, except the French CAE, which was only established in 1997.[11] The idea was to see whether the content of these reports reflected important features of their knowledge regimes. The methodology involved in analyzing these documents is discussed in the appendix.[12] We did this analysis after concluding our interviews.

We examined reports from these particular organizations for two reasons. First, of all the policy research organizations we visited these were the closest to power insofar as they reported directly to the heads of the executive branch of the government (i.e., president, prime minister, or chancellor) and prepared analytic and advisory reports for them. It stands to reason, then, that if any policy research organizations should have influence on policymakers' thinking, it should be these so their reports are important.[13] Second, of all the policy research organizations we visited these were the most comparable across our four countries. Members of each council were appointed by the head of government and each council prepared analyses and recommendations specifically for them. And in the United States, Germany, and Denmark, their reports also provided overviews of the entire economy and its problems as well as reviews of the policy controversies about how to best manage these problems and how current policies were doing. The French reports focused only on a particular economic problem, such as international competitiveness or unemployment. But they still proved useful for the task at hand.

Keep in mind the limits of the analysis that follows. To reiterate, our analysis of individual organizations relies only on what people told us during our interviews. We did not speak with policymakers or their staffs. Nor did we

---

[11]These included from the United States the CEA's *Economic Report of the President*; from the German CEE the annual *Jahresgutachten des Sachverständingenrat*; and from the Danish DØR the biannual *Dansk Økonomi*. The French CAE does not publish comparable annual reports but rather reports on individual topics from which there are dozens to choose. We picked one from 1997, two from 1998, one from 2007 and one from 2008. We picked reports that we thought were important for issues dealt with by the council reports in other countries. The 1997 report was the first issued by CAE. The 2008 report summarized all of the CAE's reports published between 1997 and 2008. Citations to the reports are as follows: Bureau and Mougeot (1997), Blanchard and Fitoussi (1998), Boyer and Didier (1998), CAE (2007), and CAE (2008). English translations from these documents are Pedersen's.

[12]This involved analyzing approximately 6,500 double-spaced pages of documents.

[13]Abdelal et al. (2010b, p. 234) discusses the benefits of this sort of methodological move.

develop detailed policy case studies to discern which organizations policy-makers were most likely to listen to. Our analysis of knowledge regimes as fields focuses on only a small set of policy analyses and recommendations from the national councils of economic advisors—not from all the organizations we visited. Hence, the conclusions we draw in this chapter are necessarily limited. But we offer them anyway in the hope that they will be intriguing enough to foster more research in the future.

The Influence of Individual Organizations

Virtually all of the people we interviewed thought that their organizations had *directly* influenced policymaking elites by providing information to them through reports, formal testimony, informal meetings, and other means. But they also believed that their organizations had *indirectly* influenced policy-makers by shaping popular discourse and debate in the media, which many presumed affected the issues and policy positions that policymakers consid-ered to be important.[14] The one important difference we found was that the channels of access through which these organizations sought to exert direct influence on policymakers varied according to the institutional arrangement of their policymaking regimes. Nevertheless, it was often difficult to see how much influence these organizations really had—something that some of the people we interviewed actually admitted.

Direct Influence

Most of the policy research organizations we visited tried to exert influence directly by getting face time with politicians, ministers or their staff. This is where it appears that state policy research organizations and in some cases semi-public research organizations doing work for policymakers had a clear advantage over private organizations. For example, the U.S. Congressional Budget Office (CBO) provides Congress with estimates of the effect of pend-ing legislation on the federal budget. The CBO's Robert Murphy explained that this is real influence because

> [w]henever we provide cost analysis—cost estimates—somebody is angry, either the proponents of the bill are upset because we have—they believe we have overestimated the cost of the legislation, [or] the opponents of the bill believe that we've underestimated them. . . . I mean, one interest group or another are upset at what we do be-cause what we do has an impact on the success of legislation.

[14]For further discussion of the importance of elite and popular discourses, see Schmidt (2001, 2002).

He said that the influence of the U.S. Government Accountability Office, where he worked previously, was also evident insofar as its reports occasionally upset politicians.

Other U.S. agencies claimed direct influence over legislation too. CEA, of course, is in direct and regular contact with the White House so their work is placed in front of the president and his staff. According to one CEA official, "We talk to the president—we have input at the highest levels of the government."[15] And the same is true for research organizations in Treasury, the Office of Management and Budget, and the Federal Reserve. But personal relationships matter too. It appeared to a former CEA economist in the George W. Bush administration that people who had been with the president the longest had a bit more influence than others.[16]

Private policy research organizations in America often have a more difficult time getting face time with policymakers than people in state research organizations. This is why lobbying has become such a lucrative business in Washington and why policy research organizations like the Heritage Foundation and others like to be invited to testify before congressional committees. But people in these organizations often preferred more informal contact with policymakers if they could get it.[17] The Urban Institute's Rudolph Penner explained:

> Frankly I would rather have five minutes alone with a congressman than be testifying for an hour, because I'm not one who thinks testimony has all that big an impact. . . . But where the real influence comes, as I said before, is that when you're invited up there to talk to staff, and sometimes staff, if they really like your idea will bring you in to see the senator or the congressman. That is influential.

According to several interviews, one last way in which private policy research organizations in America directly influenced policy was by providing personnel to the government. When a different political party wins office it triggers an exodus of personnel from some of the scholarly and advocacy organizations into the government to replace those who leave. Democratic administrations draw especially from places like the Brookings Institution and the Urban Institute; Republican administrations draw from places like the American Enterprise Institute and Heritage Foundation. According to the Urban

[15]Interview with senior official, CEA.
[16]Interview with Andrew Samwick, former CEA official.
[17]Interviews with Brandon Arnold, Cato Institute; senior official, CBPP. People are often invited to testify before Congress because those who invite them already know more or less what they will say.

Institute's Robert Reischauer, when control of the House, Senate, or White House changes hands, "[t]here's a lot of flow back and forth of these people to places like here, or similar kinds of organizations." William Antholis at Brookings underscored the fact that Washington think tanks provided launching and landing pads for officials coming in and out of government.[18] The Progressive Policy Institute, for instance, told us that they lost several people to the Clinton administration.[19] The same was true for the Center for American Progress when the Democrats regained control of Congress in 2002.[20]

In Paris we also heard often about the importance of gaining direct access to policymakers. Here informal networks were especially important. We were told on several occasions—and it seemed more often than in our other countries—that information and ideas are often disseminated through these networks. We noted in chapter 3 that informal networks are often forged during people's time studying at the Grandes Écoles. These ties serve as keys for opening doors to civil servants and politicians and thus exerting influence. At Enterprise and Progress, for instance, one senior official referred to these ties, stating, "It's amazing that we have such good connections with the political world. So basically, as a lobbying group we are—I will not say powerful because that would be pretentious—but we have some [influence]." He continued by offering the following observation, which was shared by several people we interviewed in Paris: "If you want to have an impact on the legislative process here, you have to have a relationship with the *cabinet*, with these advisors. And so we build up the relationship with them."

We caught a glimpse in our interview with Institute Montaigne's general director of how informal networks facilitate political influence. They had recently published a paper on housing policy. He used his network to leverage an invitation to discuss it with the president's staff:

> I have a good relationship with the woman at L'Elysèe [the president's office]. . . . She had dinner with friends of mine at my place and I know her, and we know people in common. And so after this dinner, we knew each other better so I sent her the paper. And she asked me to come with a researcher and so on and so forth. It's about knowing people, networking, lobbying, informing.

He added that people at Institute Montaigne knew several people on the current president and prime minister's staffs because those people had served previously on one of Montaigne's task forces. He noted that "[i]t's one of the

[18]Email correspondence with William Antholis, Brookings Institution.
[19]Interview with senior official, PPI.
[20]Interview with Sara Rosen Wartell, CAP.

uses" of their task forces. And, as a result, these people "would take us on the telephone; they would react to our proposals if we ask them to; they would facilitate when we invite a minister for a conference or a seminar."

Another venue for making and exercising personal contacts in France is at informal breakfast meetings and discussion groups.[21] Meetings like these are the typical means by which French-style lobbying occurs. But sometimes contacts are made and ideas advanced at the behest of the state, which takes the initiative and invites organizations to come forward with recommendations. The minister of labor, for instance, encouraged Enterprise and Progress to contact its corporate members and come up with ideas for improving labor market policies, such as schemes for reducing unemployment among young people.[22] Another way the government solicits ideas is by asking organizational representatives to serve on the conseils or inviting experts from semi-public research organizations to advise ministers, their staff and their *cabinets*.[23] Less frequently members of research organizations may even gain *cabinet* appointments. The first chair of CAE used to sit in the prime minister's *cabinet* while also chairing CAE.[24]

Personal contacts mattered in Germany too.[25] A senior official at the Foundation Market Economy (SM) explained that utilizing personal contacts was "the most important piece" of his job, which he did with personal handwritten notes to every parliamentarian who received an SM report. But in contrast to France, in Germany channels of access are often more formal. For instance, as discussed in chapter 4, the economic research institutes belong to the German Consortium of Economic Research Institutes (ARGE), which convenes two meetings each year to present data and analysis and discuss policy issues with representatives from the ministries. According to Klaus Zimmermann, ARGE's chair when we interviewed him, these are forums where the research institutes have an opportunity to influence the government's policy thinking.[26] In addition these and other organizations have direct access to ministers and other policymakers at a closed meeting each January where a range of economic issues are discussed.

The Joint Economic Report team and CEE also have formal and direct access to German policymakers on a regular basis. Influence seems to flow

---

[21] Interviews with senior officials, Enterprise and Progress, Foundation Robert Schuman, and CEPII; Paul de Fombelle, Institute Choiseul; François Massardier, Croissance Plus; Michel Rousseau, Foundation Concorde.
[22] Interview with senior official, Enterprise and Progress.
[23] Interview with Dominique David, IFRI.
[24] Interview with Christian de Boissieu, CAE.
[25] Interviews with Dagmar Simon, WZB; with Rolf Langhammer, IfW.
[26] Others were skeptical about the influence stemming from these meetings (interview with Wolfgang Franz, ZEW).

from this. First, regarding the CEE the government is required to deliver an annual economic report in January or February in which it must respond to the CEE's report. So, according to the CEE chairman, "The government is by law forced to say what they think about what we have produced." In other words, the government has to take it seriously.[27] Second, the Joint Economic Reports are influential insofar as the government uses them to guide policy-making in some very specific ways. One is to help fashion its own economic forecasts. Another is to use the Joint Economic Report revenue projections for making decisions about expenditure policies. According to one informed observer, these estimates as well as other parts of the Joint Economic Report forecasts "[v]ery much influence the way that people in the ministries think."[28]

In Denmark we also heard a lot about the influence of formally organized channels of influence. In particular, several people stressed the importance of having members of policy research organizations participate in ad hoc expert commissions or knowledge councils in order to exert direct influence on the policymaking process because they play a large role in creating politically acceptable policy proposals, typically for the prime minister, based on analysis and consensus making.[29] Indeed, being invited to sit on these commissions is a sign "that you have some knowledge somebody will use and can use."[30] And even if an organization does not have one of its members on a commission, it can exert influence by providing analysis to other organizations that do. For instance, the Economic Council of the Labor Movement (AE) provides lots of analysis to the Danish Confederation of Trade Unions (LO), which sits on many commissions and otherwise lobbies the government.[31] Certainly the research units in the LO and other peak associations believe that they have influence due to the fact that the peak organizations they serve are represented on a variety of councils, commissions, and committees; sometimes help the government write legislation; and often help implement legislation once it has been enacted.[32]

Because Denmark is a small country people tend to know each other. So, personal networks are an especially important channel of influence. We learned, for instance, at both LO and the Confederation of Danish Industry

[27] Here again there is ambiguity. Prior to the government's move from Bonn to Berlin some people felt that the public exchange between the government and the CEE as well as the government's January meeting with the research institutes was not a particularly meaningful discussion (Braml 2004, pp. 95–96).
[28] Interview with Rolf Langhammer, IfW.
[29] Interviews with Jan Kæraa Rasmussen, LO; Anders Knutsen, TFV; Jørn Neergaard Larsen, DA.
[30] Interview with Mette Wier, AKF.
[31] Interview with Lars Andersen, AE. In this regard, people we interviewed at AE and SFI also felt that influencing party leaders was important.
[32] Interviews with senior official, DA; Finn Larsen, LO.

(DI) that they had recently been trying to build this sort of informal network. During our interview at DI we were told, "We have strengthened our connections to the government, to the administration . . . as a means to get influence as a result."[33]

In all four countries formal and informal contact with policymakers is important. But policymaking institutions mediate how this happens. First, in the European countries the flow of personnel from private policy research organizations in civil society into the state is not as important as it is in America where private think tanks often provide personnel to new administrations. Why? Because each European state unlike its U.S. counterpart has a permanent senior civil service that does not shift much after the election of a new government.[34] Second, institutions also matter in terms of the targets that policy research organizations try to influence. In the United States organizations were geared variously toward both the executive and legislative branches. In Germany, most of the attention was directed toward the executive branch—the ministries. This makes sense. In Germany there are comparatively fewer public hearings convened by parliament and parliamentary committee work tends to occur out of public view. Moreover, in Germany, thanks to its parliamentary system, legislative business is more centralized within the cabinet and initiatives taken by the chancellor and her or his cabinet are typically backed by their ranks in parliament because as we explained in earlier chapters the political parties are more disciplined than they are in the United States.[35] In this regard Denmark and Germany are similar. The action is directed largely at the ministries in France too thanks to the comparatively weak stature of the legislature in the French presidential system.

Indirect Influence: The Media

In all of our countries we were told many times how important the media had become for indirectly influencing policymakers. For instance, one official at the U.S. Government Accountability Office said, "One of the ways our work has impact is through the press, and we don't engineer that ourselves, but the press uses us hugely. . . . I read the *Washington Post* on the Metro every morning coming to work, and I would say probably two to three, four, even five days a week, there will be an article in there, and I'll say, oh yeah, they picked up our report on X, and the press just loves using us, because it's usually pretty interesting stuff."[36]

[33] Interview with senior official, DI.
[34] Our findings are consistent with Braml (2004, pp. 101–4) and Weilemann (2000).
[35] Braml 2004, chap. 3. As Braml notes, trying to influence members of parliament would be a nearly hopeless strategy in Germany given the strong institutional incentives for party discipline in this parliamentary system.
[36] Interview with senior official, GAO.

Many private policy research organizations in the United States have beefed up their communications staff, spent more time trying to disseminate their analysis and recommendations to the media, and utilized the Internet and other means to influence public debate. One organization president told us that "20 years ago there was very little effort to form relationships with people in the media. Today everybody has a least one person in the organization whose job is to communicate with the media. And some probably even have media training programs."[37] The purpose of all this, of course, is to help shape the policymaking agenda by influencing what is discussed by others in public forums to which policymakers presumably pay attention. Stuart Butler from the Heritage Foundation, which focuses on Congress, captured the general sentiment of many people we interviewed in Washington:

> We think about what influences our primary audience [Congress], and therefore what do we need to do to discuss and provide information, not just to the ultimate audience directly, which we do, but also to those influencing audiences, like the media, like other organizations that are seeking to influence the Hill.

We were told similar things in France. République des Idées, for instance, seeks to bring big policy ideas into the public debate rather than directly to policymakers. Their hope is that policymakers will be sensitive to shifts in public discourse. Foundation Gabriel Peri, the Socialist Party's think tank, is another organization whose mission is to influence public debate rather than policymakers per se. In this regard, reaching the media is the ultimate goal. But for others it is only an intermediate goal—a means for eventually establishing direct contact with policymakers.[38] For instance, we heard at Institute Montaigne that "[o]ur final goal is to influence policy making here, but we know for sure that if we get an article in the press, ministers, *cabinet* members would call and ask for a report they have already received ten times and never read before."

We were surprised to learn that some state policy research organizations in France also seek to influence the public discourse. After all, they already have direct access to their ministers. A senior official at the Directorate for Research, Studies and Statistics (DARES) explained that his department's "main channel" of influence was publishing its studies and then circulating them to

[37]Interview with John Goodman, NCPA.

[38]Communicating with the public and becoming involved in public discourse seemed to be especially important for some business clubs. According to François Massardier from Croissance Plus this was important because in France, "It's not popular to be an entrepreneur," so they try hard to persuade the public to their points of view.

the relevant ministers and civil servants. It turned out that the ministers and their *cabinets* do not necessarily pay attention to the research and policy advice of their research departments. Indeed, he lamented that "[w]e probably are not so much involved in policy advice as the minister that created this department initially would have liked." So in order to garner the attention of ministers it helps, he said, to publish the department's studies first—a lesson he learned working at the Ministry of Finance. Thus, even research departments in some of the most powerful ministries sometimes resort to these indirect influence strategies.

The media have become an important target as well for German policy research organizations who want to influence public debate and thus the political agenda. Whereas researchers have argued that German policy research organizations tended to target an elite audience of policymakers in the 1980s and 1990s, since then many have appealed to a broader public audience.[39] All sorts of policy research organizations have learned that policymakers will often not pay attention to the organization's ideas unless they are reported in the quality media.[40] This is especially important for private organizations that do not have the benefit of institutionalized contacts with the ministries, such as those afforded to the semi-public research institutes involved in the Joint Economic Report.[41]

In Germany, the new private research organizations have been especially keen to develop a media presence. At the Friedrich Ebert Foundation Peter Donaiski told us that organizations like the Bertelsmann Foundation and the Initiative New Social Market Economy (INSM) put lots of effort into running media campaigns—a fact confirmed for us by a senior INSM official. Donaiski added that organizations like INSM have considerable influence over public opinion because they sometimes have special relationships with publishers, magazines, and newspapers so they can "set ideas" very effectively.

The importance of establishing media visibility as a means of influencing the political agenda is evident in the fact that organizations now tend to monitor each other's media presence. For example, Donaiski told us the German party foundations keep an eye on each other's monthly media citation counts—that is, the number of times their reports and staff were mentioned in the media. We also had a conversation with a senior official at the Foundation Market Economy, one of the new private advocacy organizations, about the Berlin Social Science Research Center. He called them an important competitor in part because their president had been pushing her researchers to develop a media profile. He explained that the research organizations whose scientists have high public profiles in the media are influential because "[o]nce

[39] For a discussion of targeting elites, see Braml (2004, p. 163).
[40] Weilemann 2000, pp. 184–85.
[41] Braml 2004, pp. 89–92.

they are well known in Germany, and once they are able to have a thousand or two thousand people listening to them, I mean, they have an impact on policy because politicians are looking [at] who or what people are well known." Thus, as in other countries, gaining media visibility is seen as a back door approach for reaching policymakers.

Danish policy research organizations also felt that an increasingly important way to exert influence was through the media.[42] In this regard, the director of one research organization defined success as "[t]en journalists standing at the press conference" listening to your analysis and recommendations.[43] This is even true of DØR, whose chairman said, "Our real influence rests on our ability to . . . influence the public debate."

We were told that another reason why media attention is so important in Denmark is that politics is driven in large measure by what politicians think of public opinion as reflected in the press.[44] According to a senior official from DI, "I have learned through a lot of years I think that if you are able to demonstrate a problem in the press and also are able to provide a solution in a more direct contact with politicians, the civil service and the citizens, you could all get a lot of things done." The director of AKF agreed, saying that media mattered because "[i]n the end, I think it's because the politicians are very concerned with the media."

The media, then, are a target for policy research organizations. They serve as a conduit through which these organizations try to influence public discourse and the policy agenda. Media are not a producer of analysis and ideas per se but are important nonetheless. Whether this is changing thanks to the proliferation of opinionated cable television programs, blogs, and other media outlets that seek to influence policymaking in their own right is an important question worth exploring in future research.

Claiming Influence

Given all of this effort to exercise influence, do these organizations really have any? Answering this question is far from easy. Most of the people we interviewed claimed that their organizations were influential. But the evidence they presented to substantiate these claims was not always convincing. Their evidence included anecdotes, claims to having influenced the language of political discourse, and various quantitative measures.

Many people we asked about influence provided *anecdotes* as evidence of their organizations' influence. For instance, Sarah Rosen Wartell at the Center for American Progress (CAP) said that she had been told by various

[42]Interviews with Finn Kenneth Hansen, CASA; Mette Wier, AKF.
[43]Interview with Per Schultz Jørgensen, Alternative Welfare Commission.
[44]Interview with Mette Wier, AKF.

presidential candidates that CAP's work had influenced their thinking. Sometimes people claimed that their organization had raised new issues in ways that shifted the political agenda. The president of the National Center for Policy Analysis (NCPA) took credit for the development of health savings accounts, Roth IRAs, and several tax ideas in the Gingrich Contract with America—a conservative economic program—arguing that almost no one else was talking about these things until his organization did. And a senior official at the Hudson Institute insisted that his organization had put the idea of workfare on the public agenda by persuading a governor of Wisconsin to implement it there. The idea, he added, later became part of the Clinton welfare reform in 1996. He also claimed, "Long before anybody else was talking about charter schools we were talking about them. . . . We helped shape both major education and welfare policy reforms in a deep way on the domestic side."

We heard claims about influencing agendas in Denmark too. For instance, the chairman of DØR claimed that they had put retirement policy on the public agenda by publishing "the first report where we made these long-term projections showing that public finances would be unsustainable if we didn't do something—if we didn't react to demographic change—and that was a recurrent theme in many subsequent reports." Furthermore, someone at the Center for Political Studies (CEPOS) said, "We've certainly had some kind of influence on the flat tax debate that wasn't really there before we launched it. So that's not policy but it's an important movement in the direction of policy." Finally, during our interview at *Ugebrevet A4*, the LO's news magazine, we were told that they had influenced public sector reform. How did he know? Common knowledge!

> I think it's a common knowledge among journalists that the reason that the government started this process with Kvalitetsreformen, reform of the public sector . . . was because of articles in *A4* . . . and because of that, it was not all because of us, but it was one of the reasons that the government overnight thought, okay, now we have to have this process.

Beyond agenda setting, however, we also heard anecdotal claims about organizations having swayed policymakers on issues already up for discussion. In France, one political foundation told us that because they had published a "famous" report on French youth that received a lot of media attention, the prime minister's office called and asked for a personal briefing on their findings and a discussion about how to implement some of their policy suggestions.[45] Some claims were even bolder. One came from Croissance Plus,

---

[45] Interviews with senior officials, Foundation for Political Innovation.

where François Massardier said that their policy recommendations for certain amendments to the law governing entrepreneurial activities had been enacted thanks to their lobbying members of Parliament and helping draft new legislative language. Similarly, a senior official at Enterprise and Progress claimed that they were largely responsible for the government reconsidering how to use tax revenues from wealthy individuals. He also said that they pushed for decentralized labor-management bargaining that was written into various laws in the 1990s and early 2000s.

In Germany, many people maintained that their organization's policy recommendations had affected policy reforms too. The Center for European Economic Research (ZEW) took credit for ideas about corporate tax reform and labor market reform that eventually became policy.[46] The chair of CEE claimed credit for CEE successfully promoting certain ideas about pension reform. He also pointed to Chancellor Schröder's Agenda 2010—a 10-point plan designed to revitalize the labor market—that he said was based heavily on a CEE report. Similarly, someone from the Institute for Economic Research in Munich (Ifo) said that their ideas advocating workfare had been adopted by the government as part of an earlier set of labor market reforms recommended by the Hartz Commission, which Schröder established in 2002.[47] Others made similar assertions about their organization's influence.[48]

Sometimes claims of influence were very precise. In Denmark, Anders Knutsen, director of the Think Tank for Future Growth (TFV) insisted that many of his organization's 33 policy recommendations were implemented by the government. The U.S. National Research Council's executive director estimated that 20% of the recommendations from NRC studies were eventually written into law. And the general director of Institute Montaigne in France noted that about 12% of the 600 or so proposals his organization had ever written had become law. But at other times claims of influence were extremely vague. In particular, in France we heard that research departments affiliated with the Treasury and Ministry of Finance were "very, very, very close to power" and thus quite influential.[49] But our respondent did not elaborate.

It is hard to know how much truth there is behind any of these assertions. The most convincing anecdotal claims came from people in one organization speaking positively about another, although these were few and far between. For instance, the Urban Institute's Rudolph Penner argued that in some cases you could see a fairly clear causal link between what a policy research organization did and policy outcomes. One example he gave was a book published by

[46]Interview with Wolfgang Franz, ZEW.
[47]Interview with Paul Kremmel, Ifo.
[48]Interview with Dagmar Simon, WZB.
[49]Interview with senior official, DGTPE.

the American Enterprise Institute, which argued that keeping unsafe drugs off the market was just as important as letting safe ones into it—a book, he said, that influenced the government's decision to pull thalidomide off the market in 1961 after scientists discovered that it caused birth defects. And we heard in several interviews that the Heritage Foundation's policy blueprints had influenced thinking in the Reagan administration. However, even if we believed these claims, it still begs the question of how influential different organizations are in general and whether their influence has changed over time.

Beyond anecdotes, however, some people said that their organization had influence because it changed political *language*. For instance, one person explained that your influence is obvious when you write something and "The next thing you know some member of Congress is using almost the exact same words, and it's being translated into an amendment that gets adopted." But he added that influence like this is hard to discern: "It's just a matter of watching how people change the way they think about an issue over time." He continued, saying, "The advantage of having been here doing this kind of work for over 20 years is I have had the opportunity to see an evolution in thinking, and oftentimes it's things that we were talking about 15 or 10 years ago are now—that at the time were so radical people were just nice enough not to laugh. Now it's common knowledge."[50] Others concurred. Another example of influencing the language of debate came from Sarah Rosen Wartell at CAP who said that she knew that CAP had had influence when politicians and others began using phrases on television and in congressional hearings that had been introduced first by CAP.[51]

In Paris we learned that organizations believed that they had influenced policymakers because specific text from their publications showed up in official statements from top civil servants and politicians.[52] Gilles Finchelstein at Foundation Jean Jaurés claimed that his organization had influenced the presidential elections because one of its pamphlets on low income workers "had been read and used by the two main candidates," Nicolas Sarkozy and Ségolène Royal. We heard a similar assertion at Coe-Rexecode. And at Institute Montaigne we were told that the staffs of both candidates had used paragraphs from Montaigne's documents in their campaign materials. Someone at Montaigne also said that their influence was evident in the fact that they had prepared a document with blueprints for various policies and that it was on Sarkozy's desk the day he came to power, and the desks of the prime minister and everyone in the National Assembly soon thereafter.[53]

[50]Interview with senior fellow, Heritage Foundation.
[51]Her example was the use of the term "strategic deployment," which CAP introduced to refer to reducing U.S. troop levels in Iraq and that had subsequently become ubiquitous.
[52]Interviews with senior officials, Enterprise and Progress and Foundation Robert Schuman; Florent Guénard, République des Idées.
[53]Interview with Philippe Manière, Institute Montaigne.

In Denmark we heard from the director of the Alternative Welfare Commission that his organization's analysis had influenced public discourse regarding welfare reform. He knew this, he said, because he heard on the radio one day a shop steward remark that he believed the Alternative Welfare Commission report more than the government's ad hoc Welfare Commission. He concluded, "I think our scope and our range of influence is much broader than the government's DREAM model based analysis."

A third way in which people tried to convince us that their organizations were influential was by referring to their *citation counts*. Indeed, most private policy research organizations we visited in the United States tracked their citation counts as well as how often they testified before Congress and how often policymakers mentioned their research. Some paid clipping services to gather this information. The Economic Policy Institute's president, for example, was fully aware of his organization's visibility in the media vis-à-vis its competitors. He explained, "When we've done analyses of economics coverage alone in our media hits, and if you scale it by the actual size of the organizations per dollar, we're far better, and we have a good media presence."

French organizations also use citation counts to gauge how well they are affecting public discourse. Many of the private and semi-public research organizations we interviewed counted their press citations and sometimes their citations in the academic literature too.[54] Institute Montaigne, for example, counts media citations as well as the number of their proposals that are discussed in parliament, parliamentary reports, special commissions, and other places.[55]

Organizations in France also pay close attention to the number of times the papers they post on their websites receive hits and are downloaded. For example, Paul de Fombelle at Institute Choiseul proudly announced that his organization was among the top websites listed by Google in some searches for research on topics that their experts covered. Indeed, several organizations told us that they received many website hits, including Enterprise and Progress, which boasted 8,000 to 9,000 recent website visitors. Some organizations use the Internet quite strategically. According to a research fellow at the Foundation for Political Innovation the Internet is very important because "[i]t gives us the opportunity . . . to create a buzz."

When we asked why they collected these sorts of numbers we often heard that they wanted measures of their influence. The general director of Institute Montaigne told us:

[54]Interviews with senior officials at Enterprise and Progress, Foundation Robert Schuman, and CEPII; Paul de Fombelle, Institute Choiseul.
[55]Interview with Philippe Manière, Institute Montaigne.

We have an aim. Our aim is to come up with pragmatic, well intended, benchmarked proposals of public policy and to have them imported within the French law to improve the way France works. And so it would be ridiculous to have this aim and not to measure whether we are getting close or not.

Many German organizations also track their media presence in order to demonstrate their influence on public discourse and the political agenda. A case in point is Ifo, which relies on Media Tenor, a clipping service, to monitor their citations and reported that in 2007, as in years past, Ifo was the German economic research institute most cited in the media.[56] INSM also uses a clipping service and counts how many hits their blog gets—roughly 1,000 per day—which, we were told, is indicative of their ability to influence public debate and thus the political agenda. An INSM senior official said, "We have to measure our success. We don't know if we change the minds of people. But we know if we have an influence on the agenda of politics." Even the Max Planck Institute in Cologne and the Berlin Social Science Research Center (WZB)—two very scholarly research organizations—track media citations. WZB reports these figures to the staff in order to encourage them to elevate their public profiles.[57] Some German organizations report citation counts and website hits in their annual reports.[58]

Danish organizations also track citations. Someone at *Ugebrevet A4* told us that they pay for a professional service to track their own citations as well as competitors', such as *Monday Morning*, which, he said, is cited much less frequently than *A4*.[59] Others do so as well.[60] Some organizations count the number of times people visit their websites too.[61] Still others track the number of times people in the political process refer to their work. For instance, when we asked a senior official at the Danish National Center for Social Research (SFI) if he had a sense of how much impact his organization had on policymaking he said that he did "based on the number of references that are made to the reports that we produced . . . there is a number of reports that is heavily referenced also in the political debates." He said as well that SFI tracked its media citations because "if we want to bridge this gap between the academic and

---

[56]Interview with Paul Kremmel, Ifo.
[57]Interviews with senior official, MPIfG; Dieter Plehwe and Jutta Allmendinger, WZB.
[58]FES Annual Report 2007, p. 17; IW Annual Report 2010 (http://www.iwkoeln.de. Accessed May 2012).
[59]Interview with senior official, *Ugebrevet A4.*
[60]Interviews with Torben Tranæs, Rockwool; Martin Ågerup, CEPOS; Finn Kenneth Hansen, CASA; Mette Wier, AKF.
[61]Interview with senior official, FAOS.

the political world—and we think with the media it's a very important part of bridging that gap—then of course it's important that we are there."

Whether these quantitative measures are valid indicators of influence is an open question. Some people admitted as much and said that they kept track of these things at least as much to impress their funders. In other words, if funders want proof of influence and believe that citations, media appearances, formal testimony before the legislature, and the like constitute such proof, then research organizations will collect data toward that end. Indeed, we heard on at least one occasion that these things impressed donors even if they did not really reflect influence.[62] This was true even at semi-public research organizations like the Center for International Prospective Studies (CEPII) in France that relied heavily on state money. According to a senior official at CEPII, they needed to show the prime minister's office, which funds them, that this was money well spent. We were told the same at policy research organizations in Germany.[63]

It's Voodoo Science

The point is that in the end it is hard to tell how influential a particular organization really is. The fact of the matter is that when we pressed people during our interviews to defend their various claims of organizational influence uncertainty often crept into their responses. Much of what people offered us as proof of their organization's influence could be viewed skeptically. One person we interviewed was especially frank when we asked her how much influence her organization had on policymaking. She said, "This is very difficult to measure. I don't know how to measure that."[64] And then she asked us how *we* thought it could be done! Another person said that, "It's very difficult to measure the success."[65] And a senior official at the Hudson Institute in America exclaimed that, "It's very hard to measure [influence]. I think its voodoo science frankly." We heard this time and again during the interviews.

There are several reasons why ascertaining organizational influence is so difficult. First, even if an organization can demonstrate that its ideas are being picked up by the media and affecting public debate, it is hard to know whether this notoriety actually leads policymakers to take their ideas seriously. The same is true for contacting policymakers directly. Just because a policymaker agrees to read your report, take your call or attend your breakfast meeting does not mean that she will be swayed necessarily by your ideas. To the contrary,

---

[62]Interview with Rudolph Penner, Urban Institute.
[63]Interviews with senior official, INSM; Rolf Kroker, IW. Others confirm that tracking media visibility is especially important for securing funding (Braml 2004, p. 205).
[64]Interview with senior official, CEPII.
[65]Interview with Wolfgang Franz, ZEW.

someone at the Center for Economic Research (OFCE) in France said that when they are called to meet with a minister or her staff or *cabinet*, it is often not because they want OFCE's advice but because "[w]e say something that doesn't please them and they want to convince us that our analysis is wrong!" At Ifo one person told us that although the Ministry of Economics and Technology often studied Ifo's reports and proposals, he could not be sure what impact this had because policy decisions were something that took place behind closed doors.[66] And when we asked someone in the German Ministry of Economics and Technology about whether the closed-door meeting it convened in January with members of various research institutes influenced policymaking he said that it was hard to be sure because this meeting like all others was just one part of a very complex process:

> I mean this meeting is part of the process. I think it should not be overestimated as to its impact. Impact studies are terribly difficult to do because, well, people's minds rarely are changed drastically by any single experience. This is a process and so the impact of such discussions, well, perhaps is to focus minds on certain issues. Yes, but it's difficult to tell that these meetings are crucial in defining the policymaking.[67]

Second, there are often several organizations offering similar ideas and recommendations at the same time so it is hard to determine the etiology of an idea.[68] For instance, the president of the NCPA in America said that in areas like capital gains tax reform many organizations including his were calling for change so it was hard to know how much impact his had. Another person admitted, "To say that a certain law passed because you favored it as opposed to 200 lobbyists and three other people from think tanks favored it is—it's essentially impossible."[69] And someone else explained, "We're always looking . . . for ways to measure impact. I mean, that's always the question: How do you measure it? And there's no easy answer. It's sort of a collage of things that you're trying to put together."[70] The general director of Institute Montaigne in France echoed this view:

> Sometimes we are sure that only [Montaigne] suggested something that has been implemented, so we know it's us. But very often it's

[66]Interview with Paul Kremmel, Ifo.
[67]Interview with senior official, BMWI.
[68]Interview with senior official, CEPII.
[69]Interview with Rudolph Penner, Urban Institute.
[70]Interview with Ted Hand, RFF.

a kind of confluence of different persons, different organizations offering, proposing the same tracks. And if the government decides to follow the track, you never know whether you have been instrumental or not in this decision.

We heard much the same in Denmark where one person said that because ideas emerge in continuing dialogues with people from many organizations, "It is very hard to say where an idea comes from."[71] We were told the same thing in Germany: "So you can't attribute success—even if there is a success—to one institution."[72]

This is compounded by the fact that policy reform often takes a long time. One person in France told us, for instance, that his organization had been pushing for 20 years to reform the state monopoly on employment placement services. But it was only in 2006, he said, that the government finally adopted a new policy, and it was inconceivable that during these two decades his was the only organization weighing in on the issue.[73] So to claim full credit for the reform seemed wildly presumptuous. Others concurred that it often took many years—and a window of opportunity—for an organization's ideas to gain traction, by which time others may have offered similar ideas, or taken credit for ideas initially produced by another organization.[74]

Third, policymakers are not likely to give credit where credit is due. People at Enterprise and Progress in France, for instance, proposed a set of labor market reforms that were intended to reduce unemployment among young workers. They suggested these to various civil servants. Eventually, the Ministry of Labor adopted some of them but took the credit. In the words of one Enterprise and Progress official, "The French government is always like that. You give the idea. They take the idea. And it's their own idea." We heard this elsewhere in France too.[75] Similarly, the chairman of the German CEE lamented, "The politicians do not refer to the Council when enacting a new idea [coming from the Council], a new law because they want to be re-elected and say 'that's my idea.'" In Denmark we were told again, "They [politicians] will not admit it."[76] And one American said, "Most policymakers see themselves as very smart and

[71] Interview with senior official, DI.
[72] Interview with Wolfgang Franz, ZEW. We heard the same thing from Peter Donaiski, FES.
[73] Interview with Bernard Zimmern, IFRAP.
[74] Interviews with William Antholis, Brookings Institution; Karlyn Bowman, AEI. We were told, for example, at RFF in the United States that although they invented it, another organization often took credit for the "cap and trade" idea where businesses would be limited in the amount of air pollution they can generate but could trade credits if they had some to spare with other firms that needed them.
[75] Interviews with senior official, Foundation Robert Schuman; Florent Guénard, République des Idées.
[76] Interview with Per Schultz Jørgensen, Alternative Welfare Commission.

being the source for their own ideas. And see themselves as having ownership of the ideas that they advocate, rather than advocating someone else's ideas."[77]

A final reason, as we mentioned earlier, why determining influence is difficult is that many things affect policymaking. According to one interview, "The truth is . . . there are lots of factors that are going to impact whether a policy decision is made one way or another that are out of our control. I mean we can only do our part."[78] This is entirely in keeping with the general literature on policymaking, which suggests that the policymaking process is often a complex one where the influence of ideas depends on the skill of ideational entrepreneurs, political mobilization, crises and windows of opportunity, long-term agenda setting, access to policymakers and their staffs, and a variety of additional processes and dynamics with different speeds going on at the same time.[79]

So it is often very difficult to determine with confidence which individual policy research organizations are more or less influential. But does this mean that trying to determine influence is a waste of time? Perhaps not if the question is posed at the level knowledge regimes as a field of policy research organizations rather than at the level of individual organizations.

The Influence of Knowledge Regimes as Fields

There were two clear differences across countries in terms of the policy ideas advocated in reports from the national councils of economic advisors. First, councils differed in the *type* of ideas they favored. In particular, some preferred neoliberal or other versions of supply-side ideas more than others. Second, councils differed in the *steadiness* or stability of their convictions over time no matter what type of ideas they embraced. Some either stuck to the same ideas or changed ideas gradually, but others were more erratic and vacillated abruptly between different ideas. All of these differences were consistent with important variations in each country's knowledge regime as reflected in their national councils.

In this regard it is important to recall the essential types of ideas that were in play and that we mentioned earlier. Supply-side ideas favor stimulating economic growth by more effectively supplying necessary inputs to the economy, such as labor or capital, as opposed to boosting growth by pumping up aggregate demand as Keynesians would do. One version of supply-side thinking is neoliberalism, which favors letting the market rather than government supply these inputs. A neoliberal program for improving labor productivity, for example, might involve cutting wages in the private sector to increase the

[77] Interview with senior official, German Marshall Fund.
[78] Interview with senior official, CBPP.
[79] Baumgartner and Jones 1993; Kay 2006; Kingdon 1995.

supply of inexpensive labor. A different supply-side program might advocate spending public money on job training and education to increase the supply of skilled labor.

The United States: Partisanship and Inconsistency

The reports from the U.S. CEA all embraced supply-side ideas. Some also demonstrated a much more pronounced commitment to neoliberalism than their European counterparts and often framed it in partisan ideological language. But this commitment to neoliberalism was also quite erratic as the reports flip-flopped on this issue over time—a clear illustration of the highly partisan atmosphere within which the CEA as well as the rest of the knowledge regime operated.

An important reason for all of this is that unlike the European countries, the CEA is part of the administration—not independent from it. Not surprisingly, then, we found no example of the CEA criticizing the president or the president's administration. Instead, the CEA's reports reflected the highly partisan atmosphere of the American knowledge regime. Their ideological tone was evident in frequent discussions about the appropriate roles of the market and government in economic matters. As a result, there was a mixture of manifesto and analysis in all three reports. Notably, the 1987 report from the Reagan administration spent the first 45 pages describing the economy's performance, but in the rest of this long, 368-page document there was lots of ideologically flavored neoliberal discussion highlighting the need for politicians to address distortions of market mechanisms and disincentives for growth. The embrace of neoliberalism was also evident insofar as the CEA reports were less inclined to worry about serious market failure and discussed it less frequently than the European reports.

Perhaps the most striking feature of the CEA reports in contrast to the European reports was how the CEA's basic understanding of the economy flip-flopped from one period to another while in Europe things were often steadier. This certainly parallels shifting partisan control of the White House and how an escalating crisis of partisanship in the knowledge regime influenced the CEA's reports to the president. It also echoes a lack of unanimity among American economists over theoretical assumptions as well as the appropriate way to manage the economy—something we did not find, for instance, among the brotherhood of economists in the Danish knowledge regime.[80] For instance, the 1987 report from the Reagan era subscribed adamantly to the belief in market efficiency. Hence, the report recommended numerous neoliberal ideas including privatization, fiscal austerity, deregulation, tax cuts, liberalization of

---

[80]Skidelsky (2009) provides an excellent discussion of the deep paradigmatic differences among U.S. economists.

agricultural prices, and more with the intention of "rolling back the state" and not—as in the European cases—of just reforming it and improving its efficiency. This was a supply-side approach whose objective was "to enhance . . . the productive activities of individuals and businesses."[81] In particular, the CEA endorsed Reagan's 1986 Tax Reform Act because it "restores incentives to work, save, and invest, and will substantially boost economic growth and individual well-being," by removing many tax rules that the CEA believed distorted market incentives.[82] Similarly, the Reagan CEA argued that markets were more efficient with less government regulation because regulation distorted competition and restricted choice:[83]

> Government regulation can reduce some risks significantly, but it can also reduce productivity, personal income, and individual choice. . . . In many cases government control of risk is neither efficient nor effective. Markets accommodate individual preferences for avoiding risk and produce information that helps people make informed choices. . . . Because many of the greatest risks are subject to personal control, government regulation can never replace the need for responsible individual action.[84]

But in 1997 the Clinton administration's CEA changed course sharply. In contrast to the Reagan CEA, it did not view markets and the state as antithetical to each other. It argued instead that regulation was often appropriate but that it should be cost-effective and consistent. If the benefits of regulation outweighed the costs, then it should be pursued; if not, then it should be avoided.[85] So while the emphasis was still on regulatory reform it was more nuanced and stressed the need to "refine the role of government in the U.S. market economy," rather than simply reduce it.[86] This combination of enhancing markets through regulatory reform but assuring "cost-effectiveness across regulations" was framed with the concept of *complementarity*. That is, if done properly, government regulation can complement not distort markets and therefore facilitate not hobble competition and growth.[87] This was the Clinton

---

[81]*Economic Report of the President* 1987, p. 50.
[82]*Economic Report of the President* 1987, p. 96.
[83]*Economic Report of the President* 1987, chap. 6.
[84]*Economic Report of the President* 1987, p. 207.
[85]*Economic Report of the President* 1997, pp. 183–96.
[86]*Economic Report of the President* 1997, chap. 6.
[87]*Economic Report of the President* 1997, p. 189. Institutional complementarities, as we discussed earlier in the book, involve the degree to which different policies or institutions fit together in ways that enhance economic performance. The notion of complementarity is especially pronounced in this report where the CEA discusses "using public policy to bring competition to regulated industries" and "markets and public policy as complements" (pp. 196–97).

administration's so-called Third Way approach, which navigated explicitly between two diametrically opposed worldviews: one that worried about government failure and another that worried about market failure.[88] According to the 1997 report, "Over the last four years, this administration has promoted a third vision, one that synthesizes and transcends these two polar worldviews."[89] The CEA provided justification for this approach:

> The conventional emphasis on markets and governments as substitutes, rather than complements, has often led well-meaning, thoughtful people to take extreme positions on the role of the public sector in the economy. Proponents of a strong government role frequently compare real market failures with an idealized vision of a government possessing unlimited information and purely beneficent objectives. Opponents of government often fall prey to the opposite fallacy, contrasting the qualities of an ideal market with the behavior of real governments, which must act upon limited information and often with distorted incentives. Both institutions have limitations; neither measures up to the ideal. A more useful approach is to compare real markets with real policy effects, to understand when and where lines between the public and the private sectors should be drawn.[90]

In 2007 under the George W. Bush administration the CEA changed course again. Although it still believed that "[t]he growth rate of the economy over the long run is determined by its supply-side components," it shifted back toward a neoliberal view with discussions of restraining taxes and government spending, among other things.[91] It did not discuss the complementarities between state and market. Nor did it spend much time worrying about market failure other than to note that "[e]conomists generally attempt to justify government intervention into private market outcomes by suggesting potential market failures that may exist in the absence of any government intervention."[92]

The flip-flopping in CEA philosophy was matched by flip-flopping CEA policy recommendations. The 1987 and 2007 reports emphasized in classic neoliberal language that high taxation was a barrier to economic growth and employment because it undermined market incentives for investment of all kinds, including human capital. In short, if taxes were cut, then the appropriate supply-side investments would follow thanks to unfettered market forces.

---

[88] *Economic Report of the President* 1997, chap. 6.

[89] *Economic Report of the President* 1997, p. 19. The discussion of complementarity was lengthy and involved a number of public policy issues (pp. 190–235).

[90] *Economic Report of the President* 1997, p. 194.

[91] *Economic Report of the President* 2007, p. 39.

[92] *Economic Report of the President* 2007, p. 91.

But the 1997 report, which stressed the complementarity of government and markets, recommended tax reforms mixed with a variety of government supported supply-side labor market policies to improve education, training, and labor market mobility and, in turn, to reduce inequality and poverty—two issues that received considerably more attention in this report as well as the European reports than in either the Reagan or Bush era documents.[93] In contrast, although the Bush CEA report in 2007 also stressed that improved labor productivity was crucial to improving the nation's economic competitiveness it recommended that the way to accomplish this was not through government labor market, education, and job training programs but by letting the market function more effectively by holding down labor costs:

> The United States owes its recent strong per capita growth in large part to strong labor productivity growth. A continuation of this productivity growth is essential to increasing real wages and maintaining the high standard of living in the United States. To remain competitive, U.S. businesses must hold costs down by getting the most out of the inputs they use—that is, they must increase labor productivity.[94]

Indeed, improving productivity by controlling private sector labor costs rather than boosting public sector spending for education and job training was a major difference between the supply-side programs of the left and the right in the United States.

The 2007 report also called for reducing government interference in the market by advocating tax cuts—especially for investors—as the key to improving market efficiency, improving capital investment, cultivating worker skills, attracting foreign investors, encouraging innovation and entrepreneurialism, and facilitating research and development.[95] In the CEA's words, "The goal of pro-growth tax policy is to reduce tax distortions that hamper economic growth. Most economists agree that lower taxes on capital income stimulate greater investment, resulting in greater economic growth, greater international competitiveness, and higher standards of living."[96]

The ideas in the CEA reports exhibited important features of the U.S. knowledge regime as reflected through the CEA itself. First, although all three reports embraced supply-side thinking there was substantial flip-flopping between market-based—that is, neoliberal—and government-based versions of

[93] *Economic Report of the President* 1997, pp. 33, 41, 158ff., and chap. 5.
[94] *Economic Report of the President* 2007, p. 45.
[95] *Economic Report of the President* 2007, pp. 46–47 and chap. 2.
[96] *Economic Report of the President* 2007, chap. 3.

this paradigm. This reflected the highly partisan war of ideas that permeated the knowledge regime and that spilled over into the CEA by virtue of the fact that the composition of the council changed with each administration and, therefore, represented each administration's economic assumptions, ideological predispositions, and policy priorities. Second, as we shall see, the CEA reports tended to be more conservative than many of the European reports. The Reagan and Bush reports were unabashedly neoliberal and expressed little concern over the possibility of market failures. The Clinton CEA was more open to this possibility as well as the utility of government-based supply-side policies and was, therefore, more centrist. The European councils worried more about market failure and favored a stronger role for the government in pursuing supply-side policies than the CEA. The more conservative nature of the CEA's ideas reflected the fact that, as we explained in chapter 2, the ideological range of views found in the U.S. knowledge regime was skewed to the right compared to the range in European countries. Indeed, the labor movement in America did not have institutionalized representation on the CEA like it did on some of the European councils. This, of course, echoed among other things labor's comparatively limited presence in the U.S. knowledge regime in the first place.

France: Fragmentation and Externalization

The French CAE issued reports that displayed neither the partisan flip-flopping nor the propensity for neoliberal thinking of its U.S. counterpart. Instead, they exhibited a more open-minded—that is, eclectic—approach to policy analysis and advising but one that favored a much more significant role for the state in managing the economy than in any of our other countries. This reflected the French externalization strategy for cultivating fresh thinking and new ideas for policymakers.

The CAE's six members, mostly university economists but sometimes drawn from business and government, are appointed by the prime minister and include people from across the political spectrum, not just those sharing views close to his. Its reports mirror the French state's externalization strategy that we discussed in chapter 3 whereby policymakers looked beyond the state's own research units for analysis and advice. As a result, and in contrast to the councils in our other countries, the CAE does not produce reports in-house but rather outsources them to teams of university professors, often including foreigners, and experts from various state and semi-public policy research organizations. Each report focuses on a particular topic rather than a sweeping analysis of the entire economy. By 2008 the CAE had produced 95 of these thematic reports.

CAE reports are almost always published in the name of the authors and not the CAE per se. They generally represent a wide variety of theoretical and methodological perspectives depending on who is commissioned. Contributors range from representatives of the Marxist-inspired French Regulation School on the left to neoliberalism on the right and many others in between. Furthermore, thanks to their reliance on outside academics, these reports are more academic and less ideological and philosophical than reports from the U.S. CEA. They begin usually with a brief set of questions or themes set by the prime minister's office that are then discussed and analyzed by the team of experts appointed by the CAE. A draft is presented at a seminar where written comments are solicited from invited participants. These comments—as well as occasional rejoinders to them from the team—are published in the final report with an executive summary. This is presented at a closing seminar with the prime minister or other ministers, civil servants, university professors, and occasionally people representing the employers and trade unions. The reports themselves generally include a state-of-the-art academic literature review and then a variety of empirical analyses testing competing causal arguments about the topic at hand, such as the determinants of unemployment.[97] They also sometimes compare CAE estimates or forecasts with those from the OECD, IMF, or other organizations in order to get additional information from experts outside the state and to check the accuracy of the report's analysis.[98] The facts that such a wide range of views from outside experts is represented, that a number of additional experts and others are consulted during the report's preparation, and that rejoinders to the central report are included reflect France's quest for fresh thinking through its externalization strategy. And the fact that the reports seldom offer specific policy recommendations as they do in our other countries but instead identify a range of policy options for policymakers to consider is indicative of their open-mindedness.

Despite this open-mindedness, however, the reports we reviewed demonstrated a certain steadiness and consistency in ideas in two important respects. First, they all carried the imprint of French dirigisme insofar as they stressed how the state can strategically create complementarities in ways that boost the private sector's comparative advantage internationally.[99] This view was more pronounced than in the Clinton era report from the U.S. CEA that discussed

---

[97]For an example of the sort of comments that reports receive, see Annexe A to Blanchard and Fitoussi (1998) by INSEE and Direction de la Prévision (p. 64). For an example of the evaluation of the validity of analysis, see the comments by Edmond Malinvaud (pp. 39–43) to Blanchard and Fitoussi (1998). Problems with data, models, and estimating techniques are also presented in Blanchard and Fitoussi (1998, pp. 66, 76ff.).

[98]See, for example, Annexe B to Blanchard and Fitoussi (1998) by Direction de la Prévision (pp. 79–83).

[99]See, for example, CAE (2008, pp. 39, 48), Blanchard and Fitoussi (1998), and Boyer and Didier (1998, pp. 18ff.).

complementarity. Second, and very much following the last point, although the French CAE reports embraced supply-side thinking they were considerably more critical of neoliberalism than the reports from their American counterpart. Their disdain for neoliberalism requires some elaboration.

To begin with, the CAE was openly hostile to neoliberal spending and tax cuts. This was crystal clear in the following denunciation of the idea of neoliberal cuts in unemployment benefits:

> It will be socially unacceptable to reduce substantially the unemployment benefit in the absence of growth and new jobs. . . . When it is nearly impossible to find jobs for certain categories of workers, it is really not useful, probably even cruel, to laud the responsibility of the individual person. For the individual to take on this responsibility it is necessary to ask for help from others in economic and social life.[100]

Nor was the CAE enamored with the idea of supply-side tax cuts for upper income groups as a means of spurring investment. This view, which was a prominent feature of some of the American reports, did not receive much attention at all in the French reports.

Furthermore, discussions about supply-side problems in the economy were often couched in an analysis of institutions and institutional complementarities.[101] For instance, one report considered how institutions governing research and development, finance, education, and training interacted in ways that affected the competitiveness of certain countries and regions.[102] Here as elsewhere the idea of creating complementarities to improve competitiveness was linked to discussions of the need for improving productivity and reducing the so-called output gap—that is, the difference between the actual output of the economy and the estimated output that would be achieved if it were operating at full capacity and maximum efficiency. Many reports implied, therefore, that market failure was a real possibility if institutional complementarities were not achieved—an idea that flies in the face of neoliberals who believe that the most efficient markets are those devoid of much institutional tinkering by the state or anyone else.[103]

---

[100]Blanchard and Fitoussi 1998, pp. 16ff.
[101]See, for example, Boyer and Didier (1998, pp. 44, 51), Bureau and Mougeot (1997, p. 9), and CAE (2008, pp. 48, 51).
[102]Boyer and Didier 1998, p. 48. They refer to publications by Bruno Amable and Robert Boyer among others—all well-known representatives of the French Regulation School of comparative political economy.
[103]The only exception was a chapter from INSEE and Direction de la Prévision in Blanchard and Fitoussi (1998, pp. 63–78).

The CAE reports frequently compared nationally specific types of capitalism in an effort to identify possible sources of national comparative advantage for France. The CAE reports often referred to the concept of comparative advantage, which they took from Michael Porter's work.[104] This theoretical orientation accepts that there is no one "best" form of capitalism and therefore runs very much against the neoliberal grain, which essentially holds that the best form is that which entails the least government interference. All of this was especially clear in the CAE's 2008 report, which summarized over 90 of its previous reports and grounded the analysis in Porter's comparative advantages approach albeit with a strong emphasis on supply-side policies as a way to improve France's economic competitiveness.

The CAE reports also paid close attention to the complexities of the situation at hand and, therefore, the complexities of the solutions required. For example, they called for combining demand-side and supply-side policies, fiscal and monetary policies, and regulation and deregulation as needed.[105] As a result, they advanced concepts like "institutional complexity" and "policy mix" and emphasized the need to create complementarities between productive factors and the public and private sectors.[106] They rejected the view that solutions would arise simply by leaving markets to their own devices.

Finally, and very much in opposition to neoliberalism, these reports stressed that the state should play a key role in facilitating all of this. Hence, the reports included much discussion about how the state should initiate sweeping structural reforms in order to improve French capitalism's international competitive advantage. But for the state to do this effectively it must become more efficient and cost-effective.[107] In other words, in order for the state to help create comparative advantages it must be modernized through cost-benefit analysis: "The excellence of the state is indispensable for the excellence of the companies. . . . And thus, the question of efficiency of the public sector needs more attention."[108] This was especially clear in the 2008 report, which proclaimed that

> [t]he advances in the rationalization of the public finances and
> public services amplify the competitiveness and the opportunity for
> companies, especially the small and medium sized, to be present
> [i.e., competitive] internationally [and that] [t]he public sector
> plays an important role as a mechanism for growth. Its dimensions,

---

[104]Porter 1998. See, for example, CAE (2008, pp. 39, 48), Blanchard and Fitoussi (1998), and Boyer and Didier (1998, pp. 18ff.).
[105]Blanchard and Fitoussi 1998, pp. 10, 33ff., 48.
[106]Bureau and Mougeot 1997.
[107]Bureau and Mougeot 1997.
[108]CAE 2008, p. 64.

however, must correspond to the needs of the users . . . [and] contribute in a positive way to the development of the economy and not to put brakes on it.[109]

Notably, this was a recommendation not for *reducing* but rather for *reforming* the state and making it more efficient.

The CAE reports reflected key aspects of the French knowledge regime. First, their reliance on outside experts was a direct manifestation of the state's externalization strategy for cultivating fresh thinking from outside the state for policymakers. In turn, the CAE's frequent use of outside academics in the preparation of these reports led to considerably less ideological posturing and flip-flopping than we found in the U.S. reports. Indeed, the French reports were more evenly balanced insofar as they typically included a variety of opinions and policy options rather than making firm policy recommendations for one policy or another. Second, the CAE consistently offered a variety of supply-side policy options and favored the state taking a very active role in helping to create institutional complementarities that would bolster the market's performance and without which market failures would more likely occur. The strong emphasis on the state was derivative of France's long-standing dirigiste traditions, which, as we explained in chapter 3, had not been purged from the knowledge regime despite the externalization strategy. Third, the CAE's strong and steadfast aversion to neoliberalism was another reflection of the intellectually diverse composition of its external teams of experts as well as the intentionally diverse political composition of the council itself—both of which resulted from the externalization strategy. Finally, the aversion to neoliberalism was indicative of the fact that the French knowledge regime's ideological spectrum was less skewed toward the right than it was in the United States. The same was true of Germany, which held the social market economy in high regard.

Germany: Coordination and the Social Market Economy

The German CEE embraced supply-side ideas early. There was none of the erratic flip-flopping we found in the U.S. reports. Nor was there as wide a range of opinion as we found in the French reports. And although German supply-side thinking was mixed occasionally with some neoliberalism as well as other perspectives the ideas in the CEE reports were more centrist and moderate than they were in America. These reports were also more analytically sophisticated in how they presented their arguments than were the reports from our other countries. All of this reflected the German knowledge regime's tendencies toward coordination of interorganizational activities, compromise, scientific

[109]CAE 2008, pp. 39, 50.

rigor, and long-standing commitments to principles of both ordoliberalism and the social market economy.

The CEE's tendency for steadiness in its thinking was evident in its early but growing commitment to a moderate type of supply-side economics. According to the CEE's 1997 report it began in response to the stagflation crisis in the early 1970s, which suggested the need for a new economic strategy.[110] The report explained that the CEE's much earlier 1976 report was the turning point insofar as supply-side issues first began to receive attention but that since then the CEE gradually developed a deeper appreciation for and understanding of the supply-side approach. Nevertheless, the report suggested that it was not until 1997 that the CEE finally put supply-side policies ahead of demand-side policies.[111] But it did so with moderation making sure to address opponents of "the last 15 years of supply-side policies in Germany" and identifying "misunderstandings" about the CEE's position on supply-side thinking.[112] On the one hand, it worried about the possibility of the government slipping back into overwhelmingly demand-side policies, which in its opinion had created various "world-wide bad experiences" in the past.[113] On the other hand, it denied the charge that supply-side measures eliminated the need for demand-side policies:

> The criticism of the supply-side oriented economic policy rests to a considerable extent on misunderstandings, for example, when the conception is criticized for being unaware of the importance of demand in an economy. This is wrong; supply-side economic policies must accept the basic ecology of a national economy.[114]

The 1997 turning point was evident in its redefinition of the role that tax policy ought to have in Germany.[115] Here taxation was viewed less from within a demand-side framework where it served in part a redistributive function and more from within a supply-side framework as a means of creating incentives for workers to be more flexible and mobile. The idea was that reorienting tax policy in this way could help more effectively supply labor to the labor market. That said, the CEE stressed in response to its critics that supply-side tax reform could also improve the redistributive efficiency of the tax system.[116]

---

[110]*Jahresgutachten* 1997/98, pp. 148ff. Offe (1981) also explains that German policymakers began to consider supply-side structural policies by the early 1970s. See also Matzner and Streeck (1991).

[111]*Jahresgutachten* 1997/98, p. 172.

[112]*Jahresgutachten* 1997/98, p. 6.

[113]*Jahresgutachten* 1997/98, pp. 174–75.

[114]*Jahresgutachten* 1997/98, p. 6.

[115]*Jahresgutachten* 1997/98, pp. 98ff.

[116]*Jahresgutachten* 1997/98, p. 177.

Evidence that the turn toward supply-side ideas was a slow and steady process was also apparent from a comparison of the three CEE reports we reviewed. The 1987 and 1997 reports offered philosophical and theoretical arguments to justify the supply-side approach. But the 2007 report did not, which suggests that it took a while before the CEE finally felt comfortable enough with the supply-side approach that it no longer felt the need to justify it publicly.

However, the CEE was not immune from the influence of neoliberalism. For example, the reports occasionally invoked concepts like "debureaucratization," "privatization," and "deregulation."[117] All of the CEE reports also encouraged the government to reevaluate the role of the public sector, such as by embarking on structural reforms, decentralizing fiscal authority, and reforming public management practices.[118] But neoliberalism was balanced by other ideas.

In this regard it is worth noting how the CEE's supply-side thinking was stimulated by the emerging crisis of corporatism.[119] As the inflexibility of corporatist wage structures was becoming a problem on the supply-side of the German economy, the CEE's 1987 report called for the social partners to reform wage structures through new wage agreements.[120] This was an issue with which neoliberals would have been happy insofar as wage structure reform meant increasing the amount of dispersion in wages, which would presumably increase competition among workers for better paying jobs and therefore boost productivity and growth. But at the same time the CEE advocated active labor market policies and the coordination of fiscal, labor market, and education policies.[121] It still supported corporatist institutions, such as the continuing representation of employer and worker interests in strong organizations with high membership rates.[122] And it proposed continued cooperation among the government and social partners in order to enhance the productivity of labor and capital and to improve labor market flexibility and labor mobility.[123] The 1997 report echoed many of these sentiments.[124] The balancing and blending of supply-side, neoliberal, and other perspectives in order to advocate for structural changes and institutional reforms in the German economy was typical of the CEE reports we reviewed.[125]

[117] See, for instance, *Jahresgutachten* (1987/88, pp. 188 and 5ff.).
[118] *Jahresgutachten* 1987/88, pp. 10, 14, 24–25, 139ff.; *Jahresgutachten* 1997/98, p. 6, chap. 3; *Jahresgutachten* 2007/8, pp. 6–7.
[119] *Jahresgutachten* 1987/88, pp. 9ff.
[120] *Jahresgutachten* 1987/88, pp. 126ff.
[121] *Jahresgutachten* 1987/88, pp. 19–18, 81.
[122] *Jahresgutachten* 1987/88, p. 184.
[123] *Jahresgutachten* 1987/88, pp. 19, 81–82, 181ff.
[124] *Jahresgutachten* 1997/98, pp. 6, 173ff.
[125] *Jahresgutachten* 1997/98, p. 5.

Several things undoubtedly contributed to the steadiness and moderation of the CEE's reports. First, it prepared them in-house but with considerable input from other interested organizations. In particular, it consulted several ministries, including the Ministry of Economics, the Ministry of Finance, and the Ministry of Labor and Social Policies. It also consulted representatives from the German Bundesbank, the social partners, a number of semi-public scholarly research institutes, and occasionally experts from the European Commission. In other words, the CEE sought input from the actors involved in coordinating wage, fiscal, and monetary policies and the ministries and semi-public policy research organizations responsible for analyzing and monitoring economic developments in Germany. Such widespread consultation and consideration of diverse opinions likely lent stability and moderation to the CEE's ideas over time. One can only wonder whether the U.S. CEA reports might have been more steady and moderate in tone if the CEA had consulted as widely rather than conferring, as it typically did, with only a small handful of organizations close to the administration, notably the Treasury Department and Office of Management and Budget, as well as the Federal Reserve and sometimes a few private forecasters.[126] Of course, far-reaching consultation reflects the German knowledge regime's proclivity for coordinating the activities of policy research organizations and seeking compromise. It is also consistent with corporatism especially insofar as consultation with the social partners is concerned.

The second thing facilitating steadiness and moderation is that the CEE's members are nominated by the minister of economic affairs and appointed by the president, but unlike the U.S. CEA it is not part of the government. Moreover, one of its members is appointed only after receiving the tacit blessing of the labor movement and another is appointed only after receiving similar approval from the business community. None of the members has a political affiliation or an affiliation with the unions, employers, or firms. So, there is little partisan or ideological posturing. Indeed, the composition of the CEE is another reflection of the general tendency throughout the German knowledge regime toward consultation with the social partners and others.

Third, reinforcing the CEE's emphasis on the need for the government, social partners, and others to coordinate their activities was its legislative mandate. The CEE is obliged by law to pay particular attention to three issues when they develop their reports and policy recommendations: (1) price stability, (2) employment, and (3) balance of payments and trade.[127] As a result, its reports made many policy recommendations that covered labor market, fiscal, monetary, education, regulation, welfare, and other policies. Indeed, the German

---

[126]*Economic Report of the President* 1997, p. 286.
[127]*Jahresgutachten* 1997/98, p. 173.

CEE mustered the most comprehensive set of policy recommendations of any of the national economic advisory councils we examined. And it called for the government, social partners, and others to play active roles in devising and implementing them.[128] In doing so it exemplified the penchant for coordination that marked not only the German knowledge regime in particular but the German political economy in general.

Fourth, neoliberalism, which is reminiscent of Germany's ordoliberal tradition, which leans to the right, was softened by the similarly long-standing commitment within the CEE and throughout the knowledge regime to the principles of the social market economy, which leans to the left. The result was reports that tried to blend ideas from both perspectives in pragmatic ways. The moderation and stability that this amalgam fostered was absent both in the French reports, which frequently included several opinions without taking a firm stand one way or the other, and the American reports, which flip-flopped erratically from one administration to the next. In the end, the CEE was inclined less toward state intervention and more toward neoliberalism than the French CAE. But it was more inclined toward state intervention and less toward neoliberalism than the U.S. CEA, at least during the Reagan and Bush eras.

One last word is in order. Stylistically the CEE's reports differed in a notable way from the rest. The CEE included in its reports more equations, models, and quantitative analyses to support its arguments than did its counterparts elsewhere. This is not to say that the other councils lacked such analytic capacities. But the high level of analytical sophistication on display in the CEE reports mirrored the German knowledge regime insofar as mechanisms were in place, such as the Leibniz evaluation process, discussed in chapter 3, that elevated the quality of analysis performed among the semi-public scholarly research institutes and limited political and ideological partisanship from affecting their work. Indeed, the CEE reports were often critical—sometimes harshly—of individual politicians, the government regardless of who was in power, the Bundesbank, and even the European Central Bank once Germany joined the euro zone. Such criticism reflected its political independence and analytic prowess, and may have contributed as well to the moderation of its ideas.

Denmark: Negotiation and Consensus

The reports from DØR were far more averse to supply-side and especially neoliberal ideas than the rest. Indeed, the council's long-standing commitment to demand-side policies was striking. Insofar as it moved to embrace supply-side thinking at all, it was a slow and incremental process. There were no signs of the flip-flopping found in the U.S. reports. This had much to do with the

[128]*Jahresgutachten* 1987/88, p. 139ff.; *Jahresgutachten* 1997/98, p. 6.

composition of the council, its mandate, and the knowledge regime's embrace of the principles of the Danish negotiated economy.

DØR is a semi-public policy research organization funded by the state and consisting of a tripartite council and a chairmanship of four independent economists—the so-called Wise Men—economists who are appointed by the government. The DØR's mandate is to monitor economic developments and analyze short and medium-term economic trends. However, it is also supposed to facilitate consensus among the social partners, the government, and many others and "to contribute to the coordination of different economic interests."[129] The goal of facilitating consensus is why in addition to the Wise Men the council consists of representatives from all the economic interests deemed necessary to coordinate economic policies in Denmark, including various ministries, all the peak associations, the Danish National Bank, organizations representing the local and regional authorities, and others.[130] As such, the composition of the DØR is far more inclusive of a wide swath of organized economic interests than any of the councils in our other countries. However, the Wise Men write the council reports as they see fit.

The DØR takes for granted in all of its reports that markets are imperfect and that state intervention is often necessary to ameliorate market failures. They spend little space defending this view either philosophically or theoretically and accept without question the need to use public expenditures, such as unemployment benefits and other welfare programs, as demand-side automatic stabilizers to help correct economic downturns.[131] Automatic stabilizers are government programs whose spending levels increase automatically and without political discussion when the economy contracts in ways that are supposed to pump up demand and thus stimulate the economy. The DØR endorses automatic stabilizers in all three of the reports we reviewed—a clear indication of its strong commitment to demand-side thinking.[132] The discussion is typically over how much *more* demand-side stimulus is warranted beyond that ensured by the automatic stabilizers.

Conversely, the council's aversion to supply-side thinking was equally apparent. The 1987 report in particular criticizes the supply-side view and sees its value only under rather special circumstances.[133] And although the 1997

---

[129]Danish law no. 574 of June 6, 2007. This language was included in the DØR's enabling legislation and its 2007 revision, which added a fourth member—an environmental economist. We heard the same in an interview with one of the Danish Wise Men.

[130]Interview with Peter Birch Sørensen, Wise Men.

[131]*Dansk Økonomi* 1987 (December), chap. 1, pp. 16, 22; *Dansk Økonomi* 2007 (Spring), p. 110.

[132]See, for example, *Dansk Økonomi* (2007, Spring, p. 110). Automatic stabilizers in Denmark are the product of extensive tripartite agreements over the years and thus another reflection of the consensus-oriented nature of the Danish negotiated economy.

[133]*Dansk Økonomi* 1987 (December), chap. 1, p. 22.

report is less critical it still takes the supply-side approach as being less useful than traditional demand-side thinking. Only the 2007 report acknowledges that supply-side thinking has much value and gives it serious consideration.[134] So even though the DØR gradually came to accept that supply-side solutions may be useful, it was much more reticent and continued to favor demand-side policies more than the other national economic advisory councils.

Not surprisingly, then, the DØR reports rarely discussed neoliberal ideas, such as creating market incentives or deregulating various parts of the economy. One of the few times that any significant attention was paid to neoliberalism was in the 1997 and 2007 reports where the fiscal sustainability of the social contract between the government and citizenry was questioned in view of the demographic fact that the state might not be able to continue meeting its obligations in this regard as the proportion of the population in retirement continued growing relative to the size of the tax-paying labor force. This was elaborated in the 2007 report in the context of concerns over a growing labor shortage, which the council viewed as being perhaps the most serious medium- and long-term problem for the Danish economy.[135] Here the council discussed the need for structural reforms in the labor supply and in doing so introduced microeconomic models based in part on rational expectations theory—one of the theoretical underpinnings of neoliberalism. Nevertheless, and especially in contrast to its U.S. counterpart, the DØR's discussion of the need for supply-side policies in this regard was phrased in pragmatic not ideological terms. There was, for instance, no lofty philosophical language about the inherent virtues of the free market or the necessarily deleterious economic effects of government programs.[136]

The council's aversion to neoliberalism was also obvious in its policy recommendations in all three reports. First, monetarism, which is an important component of neoliberal economic policies, received little attention in the DØR reports. But this was primarily because in 1982 the Danish currency was pegged to the deutsche mark and in 1999 to the euro, leaving Denmark with very little discretion over monetary policy anyway. Second, and more telling in terms of its aversion to neoliberalism, the council reports did not spend time recommending either supply-side tax reform of any kind or cuts in government spending. Instead, it viewed tax reform as a means of income redistribution rather than as a way to create investment incentives through supply-side tax cuts. And it called for dampening the growth of the public sector and making government more efficient rather than downsizing it per se as neoliberals would prefer. Third, the council continued to stress as late

[134]*Dansk Økonomi* 2007 (Spring), chap. 2.
[135]*Dansk Økonomi* 2007 (Spring), p. 27.
[136]*Dansk Økonomi* 2007 (Spring), pp. 93–94.

as 2007 the need for fiscal policies to stimulate demand. So although by 2007 the council recommended a mixture of demand- and supply-side policies it still preferred the demand-side approach and its supply-side ideas were not particularly neoliberal.[137]

The DØR's commitment to demand-side thinking and its aversion to neoliberalism reflect several features of the knowledge regime. First is the general proclivity for negotiation and consensus making, which we found among most of the policy research organizations we visited in Denmark. This is institutionalized in the council itself by virtue of its broadly inclusive membership as well as its mandate to facilitate consensus among the social partners. Indeed, although the Wise Men write their reports on their own, as we explained in chapter 5, they remain somewhat sensitive to the concerns of the social partners and others on the council. Second, throughout the knowledge regime and certainly among the council members there is a taken-for-granted acceptance of the virtues of social democracy and the need for socioeconomic balance, as we also explained in chapter 5. As one person explained off the record, deep down just about everyone in Denmark holds social democratic principles dear—even those in the business community and many of the center-right political parties.[138] Third, support for these sorts of ideas—especially for automatic stabilizers that channel benefits to workers—is surely reinforced by the presence of representatives from the labor unions, which are the strongest and best organized of all of our four countries and whose presence in the knowledge regime is comparatively pronounced.

The steadiness and consistency of the DØR's thinking over time was striking. There was no flip-flopping in DØR reports as there was in the United States. In addition to what we just discussed this was undoubtedly due as well to the fact that the Wise Men were all members of a tight-knit brotherhood of economists that had few serious disagreements. Moreover, their appointments were not contingent on the government that appointed them remaining in power, as were appointments to the U.S. CEA, but were of fixed duration like the case in Germany. Furthermore, their appointments were based on the recommendations of the Wise Men who preceded them. It is unlikely that someone would recommend a replacement whose views differed radically from his or her own. Finally, their reports were also based on consensus making among the Wise Men themselves—another example of the negotiated and consensus-oriented approach that characterizes this knowledge regime.

Given the fact that Denmark's DØR and Germany's CEE both have important corporatist characteristics, confer regularly in one way or another

---

[137] *Dansk Økonomi* 2007 (Spring), pp. 4, 96, 130, 148.

[138] This comment was made in another context to Campbell by a senior official of a leading business peak association.

with the social partners, and are supposed to facilitate in varying degrees interorganizational cooperation, compromise, and coordination, it makes sense that there would be some similarities between them. And there were. For one thing, thanks to their orientations to compromise as well as their independence from the government, neither council's thinking was erratic over time and subject to ideological flip-flopping as it was in the United States. For another thing the ideas of both councils were much closer to each other than they were to those of the U.S. CEA when it came to things like fiscal policy and tax reform. Unlike the Reagan and Bush CEA reports, the DØR and the CEE reports stressed the need for the government and social partners to coordinate their decisions in fiscal, monetary, welfare, and various other policy areas.[139] Furthermore, the U.S. CEA called for supply-side tax reforms to stimulate investment rather than affect income redistribution.[140] But the Danish and German councils acknowledged the need for tax reform to facilitate progressive income redistribute albeit in varying degree. Consider, for example, DØR's view about property taxes:

> Changes in property taxation or in taxation of rental value do have redistributive consequences. An increase in taxation thus will most appropriately have to take place in a situation where prices on land and real estate are rising and where an increase in taxation will limit capital gains rather than cause direct capital losses.[141]

On the other hand, there were some differences in the ideas of the German and Danish councils. First, supply-side thinking was more prevalent in the CEE reports than the DØR reports. Second, although both councils recognized the virtues of progressive tax-based income redistribution, there was an important difference. The CEE was willing to advocate tax reform as long as it did not compromise productivity and investment.[142] But, as the previous quotation suggests, the DØR was less concerned about that. In other words, both councils thought about the investment and redistributive consequences of tax reform, but the Germans put a higher priority on the former while the Danes put a higher priority on the latter. Third, supply-side thinking arrived much later in Denmark than in Germany. Fourth, the DØR was reluctant to soften its position on the importance of demand-side policies and especially automatic stabilizers while the CEE long embraced supply-side thinking and

---

[139] *Dansk Økonomi* 1987 (December), pp. 76ff.
[140] *Economic Report of the President* 1987, pp. 83–96.
[141] *Dansk Økonomi* 1987 (Spring), p. 81.
[142] *Jahresgutachten* 1997/98, p. 177. For a general argument in favor of using incentives to bridge the gap between "growth goals" and "growth reality" (the output gap), see *Jahresgutachten* (1987/88, pp. 10ff.).

monetarism. These differences make sense given the fact that the labor movement in Denmark, which is much stronger to begin with than it is in Germany, has greater representation on the council and in the knowledge regime overall than its counterpart does in Germany. After all, the more influential the views of labor are the more likely it would be that councils would advocate things like automatic stabilizers that benefit labor. The differences in council ideas surely reflect as well the fact that commitments to social democracy run so deep in the Danish knowledge regime whereas in Germany commitment to the social market economy is balanced by the influence of ordoliberalism. Hence, the ideas of the German CEE are somewhat more conservative than those of the Danish DØR.

In sum, ideas in the U.S. CEA reports reflected the partisan and ideological charged character of its knowledge regime. Ideas in reports from the French CAE reflected the externalization of policy analysis and advising in its knowledge regime as well as the French dirigiste tradition. Ideas in the German CEE reports reflected the proclivity for coordination and compromise and balancing ordoliberal and social market principles. And ideas in the Danish DØR reports reflected the inclusive consensus-oriented nature of a knowledge regime steeped in social democratic principles.

Remember that the idea here was to determine through an analysis of reports from the councils of economic advisors whether the nationally specific character of each knowledge regime seemed to influence the sort of ideas coming from it. Based on the limited evidence at hand, it appears that they did. There were clear differences in both the ideas of each council and the degree to which their commitment to these ideas was steady or erratic. And these differences reflected important features of each one's knowledge regime. Nevertheless, we want to urge caution and not overgeneralize. Councils of economic advisors are, as we have said, unique not least because they are particularly close to power and appointed in various ways by the heads of government. So an analysis of reports from other types of policy research organizations is certainly in order. Much work is still required to investigate more thoroughly the relationship between the general character of knowledge regimes and the kinds of ideas they tend to produce.

Conclusions

The essential message of this chapter is that establishing either how individual policy research organizations influence policymakers' thinking or how knowledge regimes overall influence the sorts of ideas to which they may be exposed is a very tricky business. But several implications flow from our analysis.

To begin with, consider the specialized literature on think tanks in light of the evidence we collected in our interviews. Several researchers have tried to determine which policy research organizations in a country have the greatest influence on policymaking. Most conclude that it is extremely hard to do so. For instance, David Ricci wrote that "[p]ower in Washington cannot be measured precisely, yet think tanks surely have a good deal of it." And Murray Weidenbaum, someone who has worked in the world of Washington think tanks for years, confirmed that "[i]t is difficult, and often inaccurate, to present great conclusions about the role and influence of the major think tanks." Both agree that the influence of individual think tanks is idiosyncratic insofar as it varies by organization, issue, and time period.[143] Our results confirm these conclusions especially insofar as the policy research organizations that we visited often admitted that they were not sure how much influence they had. Moreover, where Ricci, Weidenbaum, and others draw such conclusions by examining a single country, we find that this is true across a range of countries, which suggests importantly that the point is more generalizable than previously recognized.

In contrast to what we learned about influence from the interviews we need to be even more circumspect in drawing conclusions from our analysis of reports from national councils of economic advisors. But our reading of these reports offers some tentative insights about important debates in the literature on ideas and policy paradigms. One concerns the nature of economic policy paradigms. A paradigm is a set of theoretical propositions and assumptions about how the economy works that guide policy analysis and the recommendations that flow from it to policymakers. As we have seen, demand-side Keynesianism and supply-side neoliberalism are two well-known economic policy paradigms. Two issues are at stake. The first one is whether single paradigms like these are hegemonic and exclude others or whether they coexist with competing paradigmatic frameworks. The second one, closely related to the first, is how paradigms change. Some argue that paradigm shifts stem from crises that precipitate a sudden rupture with the prevailing paradigm and its displacement by a new one. Others maintain that paradigm shifts evolve slowly and often involve the gradual blending of new paradigmatic elements with old ones such that paradigm shifts do not constitute clear and sharp breaks with the past.[144]

The evidence we have presented from national councils of economic advisors is not consistent with the argument that a single paradigm is hegemonic and not in competition with others. The CAE reports in France, for instance, represent a wide array of paradigmatic views ranging from neoliberalism to

[143]Ricci 1993, p. 2; Weidenbaum 2009, p. 87.
[144]On hegemonic paradigms, see, for example, Peter Hall (1993) who argued that a single coherent paradigm tends to dominate, and Schmidt (2002, pp. 220–25) who suggested that competing paradigms coexist. On paradigmatic ruptures, see Peter Hall (1993). On paradigmatic evolution, see Campbell (2004) and Hay (2001). For an excellent review of both these debates, see Skogstad and Schmidt (2011).

the quasi-Marxist French Regulation School. So in the French case, no single paradigm seems to have been hegemonic. The same was true in Denmark where the DØR simultaneously took insights from the Keynesian demand-side paradigm, notably a continued reverence for automatic stabilizers, and more recently a supply-side paradigm. And the German CEE insisted that it had not entirely abandoned demand-side for supply-side thinking. Moreover, it mixed neoliberal and non-neoliberal versions of supply-side thinking.

Insofar as abrupt or evolutionary paradigm shifts are concerned, our evidence supports the latter view. This is especially evident in the Danish DØR reports, where only recently has the supply-side view started to emerge alongside its demand-side counterpart. The lack of an abrupt paradigm shift is evident as well in the United States. In 1987 neoliberal assumptions about the perils of government failure and the virtues of market efficiency were featured prominently in the Reagan CEA report. But in 1997 the Clinton CEA proposed a "Third Way" strategy recognizing that both market and government failures were possible. And in 2007 the Bush CEA returned to the government failure/market efficiency assumptions. Here, then, we have evidence of an uneven evolutionary process as well as an on-again/off-again blending of elements of both Keynesian market failure assumptions and neoliberal government failure assumptions.[145]

This brings us to the literature on globalization and the diffusion of neoliberalism, a subject closely related to our discussion of convergence in the previous chapter. Many argue that although neoliberal ideas were around for a long time the rise to prominence of neoliberalism took off in the United States and Britain in the wake of the 1970s stagflation crisis and diffused quickly among other countries from there.[146] Yet we have not seen a paradigmatic convergence across our countries in council reports. This is in sharp contrast to those who, for instance, have identified a general convergence among political parties on neoliberal principles.[147] For the most part, none of the European reports displayed nearly as much commitment to neoliberalism as the U.S. reports did. The Danish council, in particular, was averse to neoliberal ideas. And even the degree to which the U.S. reports themselves subscribed to neo-

[145]This suggests as well that paradigms are not monolithic blocks but rather constellations of concepts and ideas from which analysts, advisors, and policymakers can pick and choose as they see fit (e.g., Campbell and Pedersen 2001b).

[146]On the U.S.- and U.K.-based origins of neoliberalism in response to stagflation, see Fourcade-Gourinchas and Babb (2002), Hall (1992, 1993), and Hay (2001). Others have argued that the roots of neoliberalism were more diffuse, not just U.S.- or U.K.-based, and stretch back much earlier than the stagflation crisis. Several scholars trace these roots to the Mont Pèlerin Society, established by Friedrich Hayek and his followers in 1947 (Burgin 2012; Mirowski and Plehwe 2009).

[147]See, in particular, Mudge (2008), who finds that political parties in European countries have converged on neoliberalism. Why political parties but not national councils of economic advisors have shifted like this is worth further investigation.

liberalism was variable, with the Clinton era CEA much less enamored with these ideas than either the Reagan or Bush councils.

To be sure other researchers have shown that neoliberalism diffused unevenly across countries. They argued that this was due to variations in the institutional character of different national political economies, which is why Colin Crouch wrote that we must be cognizant of the "flexibility of the neoliberal paradigm."[148] But the features of political economies to which these researchers refer typically involve only the organization of the policymaking and production regimes—not knowledge regimes. Yves Dezalay and Bryant Garth, for example, explain how the diffusion of neoliberalism to several Latin American countries was mediated by state structures, national politics, and elite coalitions and networks.[149] Rather than paying attention to knowledge regimes they like many others who studied the diffusion of neoliberalism dwell simply on the influence of university economists, notably those from the University of Chicago. They barely mention policy research organizations.[150] Certainly political and economic institutions are important in this regard. However, our analysis suggests that knowledge regimes are also an important yet often neglected part of these diffusion stories. This is an unfortunate oversight particularly because, as we have discussed in previous chapters, they may operate with a degree of independence from the policymaking and production regimes that affect them.

Some researchers who showed that the international diffusion of neoliberalism was uneven have largely discounted the independent causal effects of ideas. Monica Prasad, for instance, maintained that variation in the adoption of neoliberal policies across West European countries was essentially a matter of differences in institutional opportunity structures and the politics they engendered. If ideas were so important, she wondered, why was Britain on the forefront in adopting neoliberal policies when so few British economists actually held neoliberal views? In her view this is a dilemma for those who believe that ideas matter because they "must still explain why ideas that very few people actually believed became so politically powerful."[151] We agree that this is an important question. But we also believe that part of the answer has to do with the organizational and institutional machinery of the knowledge regime that produced and disseminated these ideas in the first place. As we have shown, the degree to which councils of economic advisors advocated neoliberalism varied according to how they were organized and operated and that this reflected some general features of the knowledge regimes of which they

---

[148]Crouch 2011, p. 23.
[149]Dezalay and Garth 2002.
[150]See also Babb (2001), Fourcade-Gourinchas and Babb (2002), Fourcade (2006), and Harvey (2005).
[151]Prasad 2006, p. 20.

were a part. In other words, ideas may have the sort of independent effect she dismisses depending on the knowledge regimes involved.

In sum, let us stress again that we do not mean to overstate our conclusions based on an analysis of reports from only one policy research organization in each country—national councils of economic advisors—even though these organizations are important insofar as they reside close to the centers of power in government. Nevertheless, the evidence at hand suggests that neither supply-side thinking nor neoliberalism was hegemonic within national councils but competed in varying degrees with other views—including demand-side Keynesianism. To the extent that the supply-side and neoliberal paradigms rose and displaced Keynesianism in these organizations they did so in an evolutionary rather than an abrupt way. And the rise of both never precipitated paradigmatic convergence across countries among these organizations. In short, the rise of supply-side and neoliberal thinking as reflected in reports from national councils of economic advisors was incomplete, gradual, and uneven across and within our countries.

Whether one would draw similar conclusions based on analyses of reports from additional organizations in these countries requires much more research. But anecdotal evidence we heard during our interviews would seem to be consistent with these conclusions. As we have explained in previous chapters, there were many policy research organizations inclined to support neoliberalism in each of our countries. But there were also policy research organizations favoring non-neoliberal policy ideas, such as the Economic Policy Institute, the Progressive Policy Institute, the Urban Institute, CBO, and others in the United States; some of the party foundations in France and Germany; some of the German semi-public policy research organizations, notably the Institute for Macroeconomic Forecasting (IMK) and the Economic and Social Research Institute (WSI); and in Denmark many of the expert ad hoc commissions, LO, and some of the university-based research shops like the Employment Relations Research Center (FAOS).

The important point, however, is that although it is hard to know which policy research organizations ultimately influence policymakers' thinking, analyzing reports like we have done may be a useful methodological tool for determining at least how knowledge regimes tend to shape the ideas that are offered to them in the first place. And this is certainly an important form of influence.

Let us not lose sight of the broader institutional context and the fact that the structure of knowledge regimes and their institutional relationships to policymaking and production regimes as we have described them in previous chapters surely operate as selection mechanisms filtering ideas to policymakers. For instance, in the United States the winner-take-all electoral system opens and closes doors for various sorts of ideas from private scholarly and advocacy policy research organizations depending on which party is in power. But whereas this mechanism may filter ideas based on politically partisan criteria, the institutionalized relationships between professional state policy research organizations may filter out partisan ideas in general in favor of more objective analysis and advice. It stands to reason as well that in Germany the Leibniz and Joint Economic Report processes constitute mechanisms that grant certain policy research organizations greater standing in policymaking circles than others and given their emphasis on high-quality scientific analysis filter out ideas that are overly partisan and biased politically. Furthermore, in France, with its long-standing tradition of a powerful centralized state bureaucracy the state and select semi-public policy research organizations have privileged access to policymakers. In contrast, business clubs and other research organizations in the private sector do not and so would appear to rely more heavily on informal networks to make contact with policymakers. All of this surely filtered certain kinds of ideas into and out of serious consideration by policymakers at different times. And in Denmark the expert ad hoc commissions certainly filtered out the more politically partisan ideas while the more general system of institutionalized negotiations did too. The process of negotiation must certainly have filtered out the more politically extreme ideas from both the far left and far right in order to reach consensus. So, in keeping with the general theme of this book, the institutional filters that sift out different ideas are nationally specific.

Finally, in this regard we need to mention again at least briefly the role of the media. As we have shown in this chapter and elsewhere in this book the media have exerted influence on how policy research organizations are organized and operate. The media also serve as a filter through which analysis and other policy ideas percolate to policymakers as well as the public. The rise of partisan media outlets in the United States has certainly contributed to the dissemination of more combative and politically partisan ideas there.[152] Because the media are organized in different ways in different countries, we suspect that their influence on policy research organizations and on filtering their analyses and ideas is also nationally specific and worthy of much more research.

[152]Medvetz 2012.

CONCLUSIONS

8

Summing Up and Normative Implications

In writing this book we have explored territory that has been largely uncharted by comparative political economists, sociologists, and globalization theorists. We have examined the organizational and institutional machinery—knowledge regimes—with which policy analysis, recommendations, and other ideas are produced and disseminated to policymakers. And we have shown how this happened in different ways in the United States, France, Germany, and Denmark as policymakers and others tried to make sense of and cope with their country's political-economic problems after the Golden Age of postwar capitalism as globalization was on the rise. In short, our argument has been about the national origins of policy ideas. But along the way we have made several additional and more specific arguments about comparative political economy, convergence theory, and globalization.

To begin with, much of the scholarship in comparative political economy, including but not restricted to the Varieties of Capitalism School, assumes that understanding national economic policymaking and performance is only a matter of understanding the two-way intersection of politics and economics.[1] We

[1]Several seminal volumes over the years in comparative political economy illustrate the neglect of knowledge regimes and ideas, including, for instance, Katzenstein (1978), Hall and Soskice

have challenged this view and argued that it requires understanding the *three-way* intersection of politics, economics, and ideas—that is, the relationships among policymaking, production, and knowledge regimes. This is something that has not been appreciated in the field of comparative political economy despite efforts to bring the study of ideas and their effects into it. Understanding how knowledge regimes are organized and operate is important because they produce many of the ideas that policymakers are exposed to that may influence them as they grapple with their country's problems. In this sense knowledge regimes constitute a potential source of institutional complementarity that may affect national political-economic performance.

This leads to our next two arguments, which also bear on comparative political economy. First, knowledge regimes have their own unique national character. This is because their organization and operation are influenced by the unique policymaking and production regimes around them. Hence there have long been important and persistent differences among our four knowledge regimes.

Second, beginning in the 1970s each knowledge regime changed as policymakers and others tried to make sense of the challenges to and changes in their country's policymaking and production regimes. These changes were triggered by people's perceptions that their knowledge regimes had become dysfunctional in the sense that they no longer provided ideas to policymakers that were useful for solving their country's problems. In effect, people were reacting to a breakdown of institutional complementarity. Comparative political economists have neglected not only how knowledge regimes are a source of institutional complementarity but also how the breakdown of institutional complementarity is a source of institutional change. However, as we have stressed repeatedly, ours is not a functionalist argument. Even when people try to improve their knowledge regimes and restore institutional complementarity there is no guarantee that they will succeed. There is simply too much trial-and-error experimentation, puzzling, haphazard casting about, muddling through, and struggle for it to be otherwise.

This is not to say, however, that knowledge regimes can simply be reduced to their political-economic environments. That is too deterministic and reminiscent of the old base-superstructure models often associated with some theories of the sociology of knowledge.[2] Our evidence suggests that this view is misleading. Policy research organizations sometimes enjoy considerable autonomy from their surroundings depending, for example, on their sources of

---

(2001b), and Hancké et al. (2007a). The neglect of attention to ideas in comparative political economy was underscored by another important volume by Steinmo and his colleagues (1992), which included an introductory chapter calling in part for more attention to the study of ideas in the field.
[2]Althusser 1968; Domhoff 2010, chap. 4; Gramsci 1971; Marx and Engels 1970.

financial support and the professionalism of their managers and staff. Furthermore, as others have shown, the ideas that these organizations produce, if implemented by policymakers, may feed back in ways that change policymaking and production regimes.[3]

We have also challenged convergence theory as developed by many sociologists, globalization theorists, and others. On the one hand, when knowledge regimes changed in response to the uncertainties associated with the end of the Golden Age they exhibited tendencies toward convergence and did so for reasons that others would have predicted.[4] This was because neither individual policy research organizations nor knowledge regimes per se operated in isolation from one another, and because several mechanisms theorized previously by scholars tended to facilitate a modicum of convergence. These mechanisms included people in policy research organizations learning normatively appropriate ways of operating, more or less blindly copying one another, succumbing to coercion by outsiders who wanted them to adopt particular structures and practices, and competing with each other. But on the other hand, these mechanisms produced only *tendencies* toward convergence—and often weak ones at that. To the extent that there was any movement toward convergence it was very uneven and partial within as well as across countries. As a result, knowledge regimes retained their national character. Why? Because, in contrast to convergence theory, whatever movement there may have been toward convergence was profoundly constrained by the resources and institutions already in place in each knowledge regime and the rest of the political economy. The point is that convergence theory is right about the mechanisms but not about the outcomes. Scholars who maintain that organizational structures and practices diffuse and converge would do well to pay closer attention to those who have argued that change is path-dependent such that new structures and practices develop in ways that are constrained by and therefore still resemble to a considerable degree those that came before.[5]

There is a second lesson in all of this for convergence theory. It is possible to empirically identify the operation of different convergence *mechanisms*. This is important because, as others have pointed out, much previous research on convergence has assumed and theorized but not actually documented these mechanisms at all.[6] In fact, we found that convergence mechanisms tended to occur in nationally specific combinations, which is something that researchers have not recognized previously but that is worth pursuing in future research.

---

[3]See, for example, Abdelal (2009), Abdelal et al. (2010a), Block (1996), Blyth (2002), Campbell (1998), Hall (1992, 1993), Schrad (2010), and Schmidt (2002).
[4]See, for example, Dobbin et al. (2007), Lane (2005), Simmons et al. (2008), and Thatcher (2005).
[5]Campbell 2004, chaps. 3, 5; Pierson 2000a; Streeck and Thelen 2005.
[6]Dobbin et al. 2007; Mizruchi and Fein 1999; Schneiberg and Clemens 2006.

Along these same lines we have shown that the diffusion of neoliberal ideas in reports from national councils of economic advisors across our four knowledge regimes was far from uniform. Thus, our evidence defies those researchers who have argued that globalization precipitated a wholesale neoliberal convergence across countries.[7] Of course, a different group of researchers has suggested that neoliberal convergence has not happened because national political and economic institutions mediated the degree to which policymakers adopted neoliberal ideas or not.[8] We agree with those who point to these mediating effects. However, our evidence indicates that they have missed something important. That is, the national character of *knowledge regimes*—not just production and policymaking regimes—also mediates whatever tendencies there might be toward convergence on neoliberal ideas.

Finally, we offer a novel suggestion for those who have tried to determine how influential ideas are in policymaking. Ascertaining how influential ideas and knowledge regimes are is tough.[9] Often by their own admission *individual* policy research organizations do not know how much if any influence they have on the thinking of policymakers. But our analysis of reports from the national councils of economic advisors suggests albeit tentatively that the national character of knowledge regimes as unique *fields* of policy research organizations influences the types of ideas that policy research organizations produce in the first place and which they later disseminate to policymakers in order to influence their thinking. To our knowledge, no one has taken this promising field-oriented approach to studying ideas and influence.[10]

We hope that others will continue to explore these and related issues. Toward that end we provide a Postscript after this chapter with a few suggestions about how researchers might go about doing this. But before that we address a normative question: Which of our four knowledge regimes is best?

Which Knowledge Regime Is Best?

We have been asked frequently in light of our research which of our four knowledge regimes is the best and what lessons they should take from each other. These are tough normative questions whose answers depend on the criteria by which "best" is defined. In our view, each one has certain advantages

---

[7]Harvey 2005; Mudge 2011.
[8]Campbell and Pedersen 2001b; Prasad 2006; Swank 2002.
[9]A volume by Béland and Cox (2011) includes discussions of the methodological problems in empirically determining the influence of ideas.
[10]Schmidt (2002) comes close insofar as she maps nationally specific types of policy discourse onto different types of political economies. Domhoff (2010, chap. 4) does too for the United States.

and disadvantages relative to the others so it is difficult for us to pick a favorite. Indeed, this is consistent with the general thrust of the Varieties of Capitalism School insofar as it argues that there is no one "best" way to organize capitalism. So, too, there is no one "best" way to organize a knowledge regime.

The U.S. knowledge regime, for example, facilitates great diversity in the types of analysis and policy recommendations it generates. Insofar as heterogeneity of ideas represents a kind of collective brainstorming it may prove useful in generating truly novel ideas that policymakers can use to solve difficult problems. Let a thousand ideational flowers bloom! The downside is that the ideas that come from the private policy research organizations, particularly the advocacy oriented ones, if not some of the state organizations, may be so infused with political ideology as to be of little use for well-reasoned and civil policymaking debate. This, of course, is exacerbated by the big role private funding from wealthy individual and organizational patrons plays in this knowledge regime and the fact that the weight of this funding tends to tilt toward more conservative policy research organizations in line with the rising level of political and ideological partisanship in Washington. Insofar as this has contributed to political gridlock recently where policymakers seem unable or unwilling to agree on much of anything, we are not enthralled with this system.

The French knowledge regime is the least appealing from our point of view. Despite efforts since the late 1990s to seek sources of analysis and policy ideas beyond the state's own policy research units, it appears that they still dominate. This knowledge regime is too insulated to generate much fresh thinking. And we have evidence to support this view. First, some of the newer state research units find it necessary to disseminate their analysis and ideas to the media in the hope of attracting policymakers' attention, which suggests that policymakers are inclined to ignore them otherwise. Second, policymakers have tried to convince some semi-public policy research organizations (e.g., OFCE) that their analysis is wrong rather than taking it to heart when they are in disagreement. Third, subsequent to our interviews we heard from a reliable source off the record about some economists who had originally been called upon to advise the government but were later ignored and ostracized for disagreeing with policymakers and the usual state policy research organizations. Speaking truth to power was not well received. Fourth, there have been until recently serious political obstacles to the formation of private policy research organizations. Thus, although the French externalization strategy was well intentioned it is not clear how well it was implemented.

The German knowledge regime has much to admire. First, its semi-public policy research organizations are impressive in terms of the uniformly high-quality analysis they produce—quality that is ensured thanks to their close affiliations with universities and their participation in the Leibniz evaluation process, which is unique to Germany among our four countries. Second, there are several well-institutionalized channels through which policymakers routinely solicit input from these organizations, such as through the Joint Economic Reports. So unlike in France, external policy research organizations are consulted regularly by policymakers. Third, both business and labor have prominent policy research organizations representing their views. They also have informal representation on the Council of Economic Experts. As a result, German policymakers receive enough analysis and advice from a variety of policy research organizations inside and outside of the state to avoid the sort of insularity and myopia suffered by French policymakers. And the emphasis on high-quality empirical policy research helps avoid the problem of ideologically biased analysis found in some quarters of the U.S. knowledge regime that can contribute to policymaking gridlock.

Finally, Denmark's knowledge regime is also admirable especially insofar as it has turned from ideological to more sophisticated data-based analytical thinking. Denmark's big advantage is that it is the most inclusive of experts from the social partners and many other places. Moreover, the labor and business peak association research units have the institutional capacities to be heard by policymakers insofar as the peak associations participate in the numerous ad hoc expert commissions and are often involved in policy negotiations (and policy implementation) with the government more than anywhere else. We were also impressed by the willingness of many Danish policy research organizations to cooperate with each other in order to produce the best analysis possible and in ways intended to facilitate consensus. A downside to the Danish model, however, is that many of its economic experts are trained at just two universities. While this may contribute to a well-educated brotherhood of economic experts it may also facilitate more myopic or one-sided thinking about economic policy problems than is the case in our other countries.

The point is that there is no one "best" knowledge regime. We admire the heterogeneity of ideas produced in the U.S. knowledge regime—up to a point; the self-critical attitude in France where policymakers spotted and then tried to remedy an excessively insulated and myopic knowledge regime; the comparatively uniform and high level of analytic sophistication of the German knowledge regime; and the nonideological and inclusive nature of the Danish knowledge regime as well as its increased emphasis on analytical sophistication. The more a knowledge regime exhibits *all* of these positive characteristics the better it will be for policymakers and everyone else.

* * * * * * *

We began this book with a story about the birth of an advocacy oriented policy research organization in the United States—the Heritage Foundation. We suggested that this was one of the first signs of change in knowledge regimes after the Golden Age of postwar capitalism. We believe that change will continue as people keep trying to make sense of whatever new problems globalization throws at them. Scrutinizing and understanding these changes is essential if we want to learn more about the national origins of policy ideas.

Postscript

An Agenda for Future Research

Before we wrote this book little research had been done on knowledge regimes. So we view our effort here as only a beginning. And we hope that it will open up new lines of research. With that in mind we offer a series of questions and testable propositions that other researchers might want to consider in the future. These are by no means exhaustive.

Considerations for Comparative Political Economy

To begin with, we have examined only a small handful of countries in arguing that the national character of knowledge regimes is shaped by the policy-making and production regimes with which they are associated. Would the same conclusions obtain if different countries were examined? That is, are our results generalizable? For instance, do other economically advanced democracies with policymaking regimes premised on winner-take-all rather than proportional representation electoral systems have knowledge regimes as riven with competitive wars of ideas as we found in the United States? Britain would be one obvious test case insofar as their "first past the post" system lends itself to single-party rule and dramatic policy shifts rather than compromises when a new party comes to power. Or is the unbridled competition we found in the U.S. knowledge regime simply an idiosyncratic manifestation of American politics? Are knowledge regimes in other countries like Sweden and the Netherlands with proportional representation systems and corporatism prone to interorganizational coordination, compromise, and consensus seeking like they are in Germany and Denmark? Do countries like Japan and South Korea, which are known for their coordinated market economies and developmental states, have statist knowledge regimes like France?[1]

This idea can be extended further. To what extent have developing counties with very different political economies established policy research organizations like those we found in the advanced capitalist democracies? Have the Chinese, for example, built a knowledge regime that in any way resembles those that we have examined? One might suspect that the Chinese political economy is so different from those we have studied that its knowledge regime would lack much resemblance at all to the ones we examined. In particular, we would expect that insofar as any sort of clearly defined knowledge regime existed it would be dominated thoroughly by a very few state policy research organizations. However, semi-public organizations might be present too if during China's economic opening since the 1970s it pursued a French-style externalization strategy to cultivate fresh ideas. Conversely, do countries known for relatively unbridled free markets and crony capitalism, such as Indonesia, have knowledge regimes heavily populated with private policy research organizations similar to the advocacy organizations we found in the United States? Similar questions could be asked of countries in other parts of the world like Eastern Europe, Latin America, and beyond.[2] These questions suggest the following rather basic proposition:

Proposition 1: *The more similar policymaking and production regimes are in another country to those in one of the countries we studied, the more similar its knowledge regime will be as well to the one that we studied.*

We have focused on economic policy. Would the results have been different if we had looked at a different policy area, such as defense, foreign affairs, or the environment? Defense and national security policy, for instance, is often couched in far more secrecy than many policy areas. It is also typically less

[1]For a brief discussion of knowledge regimes in some of these countries, see Campbell and Pedersen (2011).
[2]Research suggests that the form of common institutions in non-Western countries may differ significantly from their form in the West. This is true, for instance, with respect to bankruptcy law in various East Asian countries (Halliday and Carruthers 2010), capitalist property relations in Eastern Europe (Stark 1996), and police, postal, and newspaper systems in Meiji Japan (Westney 1987).

politicized than domestic policies. Perhaps, then, knowledge regimes organized around defense, foreign policy, and national security issues involve fewer policy research organizations overall and in particular fewer private research organizations and more semi-public or state research organizations. In contrast, given the proliferation of environmentally oriented social movements and nongovernmental organizations, environmental policymaking, which is also hotly contested politically, might involve a much wider range of policy research organizations including perhaps entirely new types that we have not found. The possibility for this sort of variation across policy areas follows as well from the fact that within national political economies different sectors are often organized and governed in rather different ways—something that comparative political economists tend to neglect given their propensity for glossing over details like this and generalizing about national political economies.[3] All of this suggests the following:

Proposition 2:   Knowledge regimes focusing on defense and foreign policy will be more insulated, involve fewer policy research organizations, and involve fewer private than state and semi-public policy research organizations than will knowledge regimes focusing on domestic policy.

We have argued that an important reason why knowledge regimes underwent change during the post–Golden Age era was that people perceived in effect that their knowledge regimes no longer complemented the rest of the political economy. In other words, the analysis and other ideas that knowledge regimes produced were no longer deemed useful for helping policymakers make sense of and cope with their country's political-economic problems. Perception was an important part of the story particularly insofar as it helped explain why, for example, the French knowledge regime did not change much for a long time while the Danish and American ones changed much earlier. Insofar as knowledge regimes constitute a source of institutional complementarity for the rest of the political economy, their transformation will not follow automatically just because complementarities break down. Ours is not an argument about functional imperatives. To the contrary, efforts to transform knowledge regimes and restore their complementarities will occur only once people recognize that their knowledge regime has become dysfunctional in this sense. This is consistent with Robert Boyer's notion that institutional complementarities must often be discovered and exploited.[4] Our point is that the reverse is also true:

---

[3]Campbell et al. 1991; Hollingsworth and Boyer 1997; Hollingsworth et al. 1994.
[4]Boyer 2005a, 2005b.

Proposition 3: *The breakdown of the institutional complementarities that knowledge regimes afford the rest of the political economy must be discovered and articulated before anything is done to restore them by transforming knowledge regimes.*

It is worth noting here that national governments have become increasingly interested in studying other national political-economic models in order to identify and better understand their own country's sources of institutional competitiveness and comparative economic advantage. This stems from their concern with making sense of an international economic environment that has become increasingly uncertain and difficult to predict as globalization has unfolded. One way governments have done this, for example, is to pay closer attention to the academic literature and research coming from their knowledge regimes that compares countries and tries to explain cross-national variation in economic performance.[5] We wonder if this curiosity about other countries might translate into efforts to change knowledge regimes, such as by doing more cross-national policy analysis—an emergent trend we have already spotted in our four national cases. In other words, is this another way in which changes in policymaking and production regimes might be affecting the organization and operation of national knowledge regimes? Moreover, is this a deliberate effort to improve the institutional complementarity of national knowledge regimes?

Considerations for Convergence Theory

During our interviews at organizations like the Cato Institute, the Heritage Foundation, and several German political party foundations we were told that they spend considerable effort helping people in other countries around the world set up policy research organizations like their own. Similarly, we were told on a few occasions by neoliberal advocacy organizations that they belonged to something called the Atlas Network, which was an international network of like-minded policy research organizations that met annually to share all sorts of information in order to help each other operate more effectively. And, as discussed in chapter 7, when we visited the U.S. Government Accountability Office, we learned about an international organization, the International Organization of Supreme Audit Institutions (INTOSAI), to which many national accounting offices belonged and that served to benchmark best practices and disseminate information about them to members. Does this matter for diffusion and convergence? Organizational theorists among others

---

[5]Pedersen (2010) documents this trend toward more governmental interest in studying national models in order to improve one's own institutional competitiveness.

have shown in different contexts that when organizations belong to formal networks or associations of this sort they tend to subscribe to the common structures and practices of other members.[6] This suggests the following:

Proposition 4:   *Policy research organizations that belong to national or transnational associations or networks tend to adopt common structures and practices more than organizations that do not belong to such associations or networks.*

Closely related to convergence theory is a literature in organizational sociology concerned with sense making—that is, how organizations make sense of uncertainty in their environments. James March has argued that there are two basic ways in which this happens.[7] One is through "low-intellect learning" where organizations look to the prior successful experiences of their own or other organizations and try to replicate them through mimicry much as convergence theory suggests. The other is through "high-intellect learning" where organizations try to understand the causal structure of the events that have been associated with past successes and then derive actions based on those explanations. In other words, low-intellect learning involves replication of what seems to have worked in the past while high-intellect learning involves analytic reasoning and causal explanations of past successes. March suspects that high-intellect learning is often more successful than low-intellect learning because the world is too complex and past experiences are too limited to achieve success by replication. Furthermore, the lessons of experience are often ambiguous and subject to many interpretations, which can be greatly distorted by one's long-standing, taken-for-granted ideologies and worldviews. We certainly recognize that professional expertise and advice do not always lead to positive outcomes—professionals of various sorts have occasionally led people in disastrous directions. But in this light one might ask whether policymaking regimes that rely more on analysis and advice from scholarly policy research organizations tend to engage more in high-intellect learning and promulgate more successful policies than policymaking regimes that rely more on analysis and advice from advocacy or party policy research organizations. Put differently:

Proposition 5:   *Knowledge regimes that are dominated by policy research organizations favoring scholarly empirical analysis will more likely exhibit high-intellect learning and produce analysis and recommendations that, if adopted by policymakers, lead to successful political-economic outcomes than knowledge*

---

[6]Galaskiewicz 1991; Martin 2006, 2005; Schneiberg 1999. See Strang (2010, pp. 6–7) for a brief review of this literature.
[7]March 2010.

regimes that are dominated by policy research organizations oriented more toward politically partisan advocacy work.

One of the seminal arguments that inspired convergence theory in the first place was made by John Meyer and Brian Rowan who argued that the structures that organizations in a field adopt may be more a matter of formality than substance.[8] That is, organizations often subscribe to certain practices in order to curry favor with important actors in their environment and to establish their own legitimacy. We have assumed for the most part that insofar as individual policy research organizations or knowledge regimes per se have any influence it is by producing ideas that affect the thinking of policymakers as they are trying to make sense of their country's problems. In light of Meyer and Rowan's argument, however, one might wonder instead whether policymakers use the ideas emanating from knowledge regimes simply to legitimize policies that they have already decided to pursue. If this is the case, then people like Mark Blyth are right to argue that ideas are often weapons that policymakers and others use to fight for their interests.[9] The question in this regard is whether knowledge regimes are a source of legitimation or a source of inspiration. To answer this, researchers could explore, for instance, whether policymakers request that policy research organizations appear at congressional or parliamentary hearings or other meetings in order to provide insight for crafting new policies or to provide ammunition to defend against a policymaker's critics and opponents. Does this vary from one country to another? Does it vary from one situation to the next? Is inspiration more likely under crisis conditions? Is legitimation more likely under normal conditions? All of this suggests a reorientation to the propositions about influence that we raised in chapter 7:

Proposition 6:   *The influence of knowledge regimes consists not so much in swaying policymakers but rather in helping policymakers legitimize and justify the policies they want to pursue anyway, particularly in the absence of a crisis when bold new ideas are not deemed necessary.*

Considerations for Globalization and Neoliberal Diffusion

Globalization theorists as well as some comparative political economists argue that a fundamental shift in economic paradigms from Keynesianism to neoliberalism occurred in response to the end of the Golden Age, the outbreak of

[8] Meyer and Rowan 1977.
[9] Blyth 2002, 1997.

stagflation in the 1970s, and then the rise of economic globalization.[10] Some researchers have argued that when a crisis such as this occurs it dramatically upsets the environment and precipitates a sudden shift in policy thinking. These so-called punctuated equilibrium arguments have been challenged by others who have suggested that changes tend to be more incremental and gradual even during crises.[11] We have argued cautiously that this shift toward neoliberalism has been very uneven across our four knowledge regimes—at least in reports from national councils of economic advisors—which is consistent with those who have suggested that the transition from Keynesianism to neoliberalism was a long, haphazard, and incremental process.[12] But what if the stagflation crisis had been more severe? Put in general terms are paradigm shifts more rapid, clear-cut, and consistent within and across countries when crises are more severe? We collected almost all of our data and completed all the interviews in three of our four countries just before the worldwide 2008 financial crisis. We visited Germany only shortly thereafter in the spring of 2009. Many people agree that this was the most serious economic crisis since the Great Depression of the 1930s and substantially worse than the stagflation episode.[13] One could investigate whether this unprecedented crisis had similar or more profound effects in comparison to the crisis of the 1970s in terms of precipitating a paradigm shift across countries. On the one hand, during our German visit we heard rumors that a prominent German economist had proclaimed publicly that the conventional forecasting models no longer worked! And in subsequent email correspondence with a senior official at one of the organizations we visited we were told that the president of DIW, one of Germany's major semi-public economic research institutes, suggested in a public interview that all the institutes stop forecasting for a few years to avoid further embarrassment since none of them anticipated the crash. On the other hand, about two years after we interviewed them for this book we asked several of the people we talked with what effect the 2008 crisis had on their policy research organizations and their knowledge regimes overall. Virtually all of them said that nothing significant had changed yet as a result of the events of 2008, which made sense especially given our argument about the path-dependent, institutionally constrained nature of change in knowledge regimes as well as our argument that not much is likely to change until perceptions of the need for change materialize. Hence, we suggest the following:

[10]Hall 1992, 1993; Harvey 2005.
[11]For punctuated equilibrium arguments, see Baumgartner and Jones (1993) and Krasner (1984). For dissenting views, see Campbell and Pedersen (1996), Hay (2001), and Pierson (1994). For a discussion about how to empirically adjudicate this debate, see Campbell (2004, chap. 2).
[12]Hay 2001.
[13]Krugman 2009; Skidelsky 2009; Stiglitz 2009.

Proposition 7:   *The onset of a political-economic crisis per se—even one as severe as the 2008 financial crisis—will not ensure a rapid, clear-cut, and consistent paradigm shift in ideas emanating from knowledge regimes until people perceive that conventional ideas are outmoded and new ideas are necessary.*

More effort is required to determine whether the overall structure and practices of a knowledge regime influences the type of ideas it tends to produce. Our analysis of this was suggestive but by no means definitive because it was based on documents from only one policy research organization in each of our four knowledge regimes—national councils of economic advisors. More systematic research is in order and would involve analyzing reports from a broader sample of policy research organizations in each knowledge regime. Documents from at least the most prominent organizations in each one should be sampled for different time periods to determine whether changes in the knowledge regime affected the type of ideas they tended to produce and whether systematic differences in the national character of knowledge regimes, such as the degree to which the work of policy research organizations was coordinated or not, were associated with differences in the types of ideas they tended to produce. Based on our comparison of the competitive American case, on the one hand, which was subject to abrupt flip-flopping in policy ideas, and the coordinated and cooperative German and Danish cases, on the other hand, which exhibited more consistency in policy ideas, we suggest the following:

Proposition 8:   *Knowledge regimes with a high level of interorganizational coordination tend to produce more politically moderate and historically stable policy analysis and recommendations than knowledge regimes with a low level of interorganizational coordination.*

Much attention has been paid lately to issues of transnational governance.[14] In this regard, one might wonder whether there are distinctive knowledge regimes at the transnational level, such as the European Union where a number of policy research organizations operate in Brussels in order to influence the European Commission. Notre Europe, for example, is a Paris-based think tank that was founded in 1996 by Jacques Delors, funded primarily by the European Commission and doing research, analyses, seminars and conferences on issues related to European integration.[15] Indeed, some of the organizations we visited during our interviews had offices in Brussels for just this

---

[14]Djelic and Quack 2010; Djelic and Sahlin-Andersson 2006.
[15]http://www.notre-europe.eu/en/about-us/activity-and-statutes/. Accessed May 2012.

purpose. Furthermore, are there transnational knowledge regimes associated with other regional political economies like Mercosur in Latin America and ASEAN in Southeast Asia?[16] What we have in mind here is not the same thing as transnational epistemic communities, which are international networks of individual experts, such as the Mont Pèlerin Society that was integral to the diffusion of neoliberal ideas, but rather fields of policy research organizations operating largely in transnational environments.[17] We have no specific propositions to offer but suggest that this is something worth looking into especially for those interested in issues of transnational governance.

Considerations for the Independence of Expertise

As we noted periodically in earlier chapters, scholars have debated whether experts and the ideas and analyses they produce are independent from surrounding political and economic forces.[18] We have suggested that the answer depends on the particular institutional and organizational circumstances in which they find themselves. Private policy research organizations that are beholden to fickle funders may have less independence than state or semi-public ones whose budgets are more or less ensured. Moreover, as we were told at some of the private organizations, like the Cato Institute and Institute Montaigne, diversifying an organization's resource base among a large number of small donors rather than relying on a small number of large ones is another way to guarantee a modicum of independence. And insofar as independence depends on the availability of financial resources, a more resource rich environment would seem to be more conducive to independence than a resource poor environment. One way to ascertain independence in this regard would be to analyze the contracts and agreements that policy research organizations sign with clients and funders to determine how much freedom they have to plan and execute their research and publish their results without interference from their benefactors. Another would be to explore carefully through interviews of both funders and recipients of such funding the degree to which they expected or were willing to accept strings attached to funding. This suggests two more propositions:

Proposition 9:   *During times of economic expansion and state fiscal surplus when funding is plentiful, policy research organizations*

---

[16]Mercosur stands for Mercado Común del Sur, the Southern Common Market. ASEAN stands for the Association of Southeast Asian Nations.
[17]For discussions of epistemic communities, see, in particular, Haas (1992). Mirowski and Plehwe (2009) provide an excellent collection of essays about the Mont Pèlerin Society.
[18]Domhoff 2010; Gouldner 1979; Gramsci 1971; John Hall 1993; Mannheim 1936; Marx and Engels 1970. For a more general discussion of professional expertise, see Collins and Evans (2007).

are more likely to operate with independence than they are during times of economic contraction and state fiscal deficit when funding is scarce.

Proposition 10: *Private policy research organizations whose funding comes from a large number of small donors are more likely to operate with independence than organizations whose funding comes from a small number of large donors.*

There is, of course, a vast literature on the professions that argues that professionals are likely to resist control by outside sources, such as funders or state regulators. Instead, they seek to operate with autonomy and regulate their own activities as guided by their professional norms, standards and expertise. Some organizations grant less leeway to their professionals than others, particularly if professionals are subordinate to administrative control, are subject to frequent supervision by nonprofessional managers, and work where the boundaries separating managers and professionals are not clearly defined.[19] Professionally trained economists play an important role in our knowledge regimes. We occasionally heard statements from people we interviewed suggesting that when professional economists ran policy research organizations they insisted that their organizations operate independently of external forces. One might expect this especially of policy research organizations affiliated with universities, as in Germany or Denmark, because norms of academic and intellectual freedom are strong among academics. The question is whether a professional orientation is another source of independence for policy research organizations. At least two propositions seem worth pursuing:

Proposition 11: *Policy research organizations managed by professionals with advanced degrees are more likely to operate independently than other organizations.*

Proposition 12: *Policy research organizations with close connections to universities are more likely to operate independently than other organizations.*

We should mention here that we found little evidence that either universities or the media played large roles in our knowledge regimes. Insofar as universities are concerned for the most part they operated on the margins training personnel, competing for staff and resources but only occasionally housing or otherwise sponsoring policy research organizations. We wonder, however, whether this is changing. Are universities gradually coming to play more important roles in knowledge regimes? Does this vary depending on whether a country has many private universities, as in the United States, or largely public

---

[19]Scott and Davis (2007, pp. 147–49) provide an overview of this literature.

universities, as in Europe? And does this sort of activity vary among private and public universities?[20]

Similarly, the media were mentioned in many of our interviews but only as a channel through which policy research organizations tried to influence policymakers by shaping public discourse—not as an important player in knowledge regimes. This surprised us because scholars have argued that the media are an important source of information that can influence public opinion and policymaking. This leads us to wonder whether through the recent advent of smash mouth talk radio and partisan cable television news shows, like those featured on Fox News and MSNBC in the United States, the media now constitute a source of ideas in their own right rather than just a neutral channel for the dissemination of ideas formulated elsewhere.[21] This sort of media has a much greater presence in the United States than Europe, so we are also curious whether the media's effects along these lines vary on either side of the Atlantic. And if the number of such media outlets has increased in countries like Germany and Denmark, have they begun to undermine the coordinated and consensus-oriented nature of these knowledge regimes?

The point is that universities, academics, the media, and public intellectuals fell largely outside the scope of our research. Might they play a more important role going forward or in other countries or other policy areas? And if so, then are universities more inclined toward March's high-intellect approach to sense making while the media are more inclined to the low-intellect approach? These are also questions worth pursuing in the future to better understand the national origins of policy ideas.

---

[20]Domhoff (2010, chap. 4) argues that U.S. universities are an important source of policy ideas from time to time.

[21]In particular, much has been written lately about Fox News as being more of a propaganda machine for conservative ideas than a conventional news source (Brock and Rabin-Havt 2012; Skocpol and Williamson 2012, chap. 4). Others, of course, have accused the U.S. media of having a liberal bias (Dye 1995, chap. 4).

Appendix

Research Design and Methods

In the middle of our research we were sitting on a park bench one morning in Paris waiting for an interview appointment. It was a quiet moment of reflection. Referring to the project one of us remarked, "It isn't rocket science but it sure is fun!" Indeed, it was fun doing this project. But even though it didn't involve rocket science, we did try to be as methodologically careful and systematic as we could. What follows, then, is a discussion of the research design and methods we used for collecting and analyzing data for this book. Specifically we address (1) our sampling of countries and policy research organizations, (2) our interview procedures, (3) the organizational documents we collected, (4) coding of interviews and documents, and (5) a final validity check on our analysis.

The Sample

We selected for study the United States, France, Germany, and Denmark because most researchers agree that they are good examples of the basic types of advanced capitalist political economies: liberal, statist, and corporatist,

343

respectively.[1] We picked Denmark as well because it is more of a hybrid case than many people realize that combines elements of the other three and because it is a small country whereas the others are large.[2] As discussed in chapter 1 we selected within each country four types of research organizations to study based on the important ideal types identified in the literatures on ideas and think tanks: scholarly, advocacy, party, and state policy research organizations. More specifically, we drew an initial "purposive sample" of 4 organizations of each type from each country.[3] This initially gave us 16 organizations per country and 64 organizations overall.

We sampled organizations from each country in the following way. First, we solicited the advice of knowledgeable experts in these countries whom we asked by means of a brief email survey to identify the most important policy research organizations of each type in their country.[4] Second, we consulted a well-known ranking of the most important think tanks around the world, which is based on an international survey of hundreds of think tank directors and scholars familiar with these organizations.[5] Each time an organization was mentioned by an expert it received one point. Each organization listed in the international ranking received an additional point. We tallied the points and ranked the organizations according to how many points they received. At this point we made sure that none of the important organizations mentioned in the secondary literature were omitted. If they were, which was extremely rare, then we added them to the sample. The four organizations in each type (i.e., scholarly, advocacy, party, state) with the most points were selected in each country. When we approached them if they declined to be interviewed or did not respond to our requests after several attempts we moved to the next organization on the list for that type. Insofar as we used country experts and the international ranking to identify organizations we relied on the so-called reputational method of sampling, which uses knowledgeable observers to help identify representative organizations or actors in a field.[6] Finally, once we were in the field we added organizations that people identified during interviews as being especially important but that we had overlooked. Through this

---

[1]See, for example, Crouch and Streeck (1997), Dore et al. (1999), Hall and Soskice (2001b), Katzenstein (1978), Kenworthy (2004), Schmidt (2002), Thelen (2004), and Ziegler (1997).

[2]Campbell and Hall 2006; Campbell and Pedersen 2007a, 2007b; Kenworthy 2006; Pedersen 2006a, 2006b.

[3]Scholars utilizing a purposive sample select subjects—organizations in this case—based on specific questions and purposes of the research in lieu of random sampling and on the basis of information available about these subjects (Tashakkori and Teddlie 1998, p. 76).

[4]We contacted seven experts in the United States, six in France plus the French embassy in Copenhagen, seven in Denmark, and eight in Germany.

[5]*Survey of Think Tanks* 2007.

[6]Hunter 1969.

additional snowball sampling approach we increased our sample size from the initial 64 organizations to 75.[7]

We received positive responses from slightly more than 85% of the organizations that we contacted for interviews, which others have argued is enough to yield negligible sampling bias.[8] In all, 13 organizations declined interviews. Of those that declined 54% were in Germany. The rest were distributed quite evenly across the other three countries. The German refusals included two political party foundations, three private foundations, two prominent economic research institutes, and one ministerial cabinet. It is unclear why German organizations were more reluctant to talk with us than those in other countries—especially since the German embassy in Copenhagen and the Danish embassy in Berlin agreed to help once we ran into trouble. In fact, we inquired about this during the course of our interviews in Germany and nobody could think why these organizations would have been hesitant to speak with us. However, because we still managed to secure interviews with other organizations of the same types we do not believe that our German subsample suffers from significant nonrespondent bias.

There are a few limitations to our sample. First, it is not a random sample. We are not aware of lists of all the relevant organizations in all four countries from which such a sample could be drawn. Rather it is a sample of the most prominent organizations in each country based primarily on their reputations as viewed by experts in these matters. Second, we would have liked to interview more organizations because large samples tend to be more advantageous than small ones for various reasons. But limited resources precluded us from interviewing more organizations in each country especially because our use of in-depth interviews was very time consuming. Nevertheless, by the end of interviewing in each country we were not finding much new information, so saturation was achieved and additional interviews promised to be only marginally helpful.[9] That we achieved saturation by interviewing organizations with very different perspectives on the field lends further credibility to our findings.[10] Third, we sampled organizations based on what the most prominent ones were in 2007. Some of these might not have been the most prominent organizations 30 years ago. Indeed, some of the organizations we selected did not even exist then, such as the Center for American Progress, which was established in 2002, and the French Council of Economic Analysis, which was

[7] A 76th organization agreed to an interview, but we lost it by accidentally double-booking two interviews at the same time in Paris. We were unable to reschedule that interview. Estimates suggest that there are between 200 and 374 nationally focused think tanks in the United States, 162 in France, 187 in Germany, and 30 in Denmark (Rich 2004, chap. 1; *Survey of Think Tanks* 2007).
[8] Gerson 1985, p. 244.
[9] Rubin and Rubin 2005, p. 67.
[10] Rubin and Rubin 2005, p. 68.

established in 1997. But we have no evidence to suggest that organizations in our sample that were at least 30 years old have become more prominent over time. In other words, the older organizations in our sample would most likely have been included in the sample if we had done this research a decade or two ago. On the other hand, there may have been prominent organizations 30 years ago that had become less prominent today, thereby escaping our sample. In fact, we are aware of only one important case like this—the French Planning Commissariat, which was disbanded in 2006 and replaced by the Center for Strategic Analysis, which we did include in the sample.

In order to make the project more manageable we restricted our focus to the general area of national economic policy and the policy research organizations operating in this policy area—one with which we were already familiar. We only sampled organizations with a major focus on national-level policymaking. So, for example, we did not include the Council on Foreign Relations in the United States. While it might seem sensible to restrict the research even more narrowly to organizations focusing on a very specific policy area, such as tax policy or welfare policy, the importance of particular policy areas is not always uniform across countries over the years. For example, health care policy has been high on the political agenda in the United States for the past 30 years, but labor market policy has not. The opposite has been true of France. Hence, we adopted a broad view of economic policy, including, for example, trade, macroeconomic, monetary, and labor market policy, among others. This was not difficult given the fact that economic policy issues were among the most frequently cited areas of interest among private research organizations worldwide in the late 1990s.[11]

Once we had drawn the initial sample our plan was to set up interviews at each organization and collect a variety of organizational documents from them. We decided to focus on the 1980s through 2007 because it was a time when major policy and institutional changes were pursued in many advanced capitalist countries due to the decline of the Golden Age of late-twentieth-century capitalism and the rise of economic globalization and a variety of problems stemming from it.[12] Old policy ideas, notably Keynesianism, fell into disrepute and the environment for knowledge regimes became increasingly uncertain.[13] Hence, research organizations were particularly active and subject to pressures for change during this period.[14]

[11] *Survey of Think Tanks* 2007.
[12] Campbell 2004; Campbell and Pedersen 2001a; Guillén 2001a.
[13] Babb 2007; Blyth 2002; Campbell 1998, 2004; Fourcade 2006; Fourcade-Gourinchas and Babb 2002; Hall 1992, 1993; McNamara 1998.
[14] See, for example, Blyth (2002), Campbell (1998), and *Survey of Think Tanks* (2007).

The Interviews

We began arranging interviews by gathering information from each organization's website to identify leaders who had long histories with the organization in top managerial and/or top research positions. Then we emailed them a letter on university letterhead that introduced ourselves, described the project, outlined the general sorts of questions we wanted to discuss, and identified the types of documents we wanted to collect. It also said approximately when we wanted to do the interview and explained that we would follow up soon by telephone. Virtually everyone who agreed to an interview agreed to be interviewed in person.[15] A small handful of the interviews were conducted by telephone for logistical and scheduling reasons. In many cases we interviewed the president or executive director of the organization, although we interviewed senior researchers in some as well. On a few occasions we spoke with people from the organization's communications or public relations departments. We conducted virtually all the interviews in the respondents' office and at their convenience in order to put them at ease and achieve rapport. In the end, we conducted 101 interviews in 75 policy research organizations across our four countries from spring 2008 through summer 2009.[16] Interviews averaged 90 minutes in length.[17]

Our interview protocol was approved in advance by Dartmouth College's institutional review board. We obtained written consent from everyone we interviewed including whether they would let us reveal their identity when we published our results. Not everyone agreed to have their identity revealed, which is why only some are mentioned by name in the text.

Interviews were especially appropriate in this case for three reasons. First, we were interested not just in the formal organization of knowledge production and dissemination, but also the informal and substantive *processes* involved. In-depth interviews are especially useful for uncovering processes of change.[18] The formal structures of organizations are more easily observed and more likely to change in reaction to environmental pressures than are the informal and substantive processes by which they seek to achieve their goals.[19]

---

[15]In many cases it took several requests before people finally agreed to be interviewed. The people we wanted to interview were extremely busy, so we had to be persistent.

[16]We interviewed 35 people in 19 organizations in the United States (April 2008 and August 2009), 21 people in 19 organizations in Denmark (May and July 2008), 23 people in 19 organizations in France (June 2008), and 22 people in 18 organizations in Germany (April, May, June, and August 2009).

[17]Interviews averaged 67 minutes in the United States, 85 minutes in Denmark, 85 minutes in France, and 87 minutes in Germany.

[18]See, for example, Gerson (1985, p. 241).

[19]Meyer and Rowan 1977.

This seems to be true for knowledge-producing professions, such as economics.[20] While an organization's official documents (e.g., mission statements, organizational bylaws, policy briefs) are often fine for revealing formal changes, they may be less useful insofar as informal and substantive organizational processes are concerned. In-depth interviews, which provide an opportunity to probe respondents with follow-up questions, are better suited for learning about such processes.

Second, we wanted to learn as much as we could about the structure, functioning, and development of the field of policy research organizations in each knowledge regime. Interviews were crucial for helping us understand which organizations were more important than others, which organizations were viewed as competitors, and which organizations tended to collaborate with each other. And, of course, we spent much time during the interviews talking about how these fields had changed over time.

Third, following on this last point, much research has failed to show clearly which mechanisms have caused change in an organizational field when it occurred.[21] This is because a lot of the otherwise excellent research on organizational fields has been quantitative, based on a large number of cases, and geared, therefore, more to determining the degree to which a field has converged on a common set of practices than to identifying the reasons why such convergence may have occurred.[22] Furthermore, little research has actually tested for different mechanisms in a particular set of cases.[23] Interviews are appropriate for identifying these mechanisms. If change is detected, then respondents can be asked to explain what exactly caused it. Similarly, if change is not detected, then they can be asked to explain why it did not.

We used an in-depth, semistructured, open-ended interview protocol in order to ensure comparability across interviews.[24] Open-ended interviews also allowed us to probe and accommodate new theoretical insights as they occurred. The interviews focused on three levels of analysis. First, at the level of the *organization*, we asked about the organization's structure (e.g., how it is financed, how it is staffed, whether staff are professionals or not, how authority is structured) and goals (e.g., whether it seeks primarily to generate knowledge, influence politicians, or influence the media/public debate, and how successful it is in accomplishing its goals). We also asked about the organization's practices (e.g., how research is conducted, how much autonomy researchers have, how research results are disseminated, whether its strategy for

[20]Fourcade 2009.
[21]Mizruchi and Fein 1999; Schneiberg and Clemens 2006.
[22]See, for example, Meyer et al. (1997a, 1997b).
[23]Dobbin et al. 2007; Mizruchi and Fein 1999. There are exceptions, such as Bartley (2007), Simmons et al. (2008), and Halliday and Carruthers (2007).
[24]Briggs 1986; Gerson 1985, p. 245; Gubrium and Holstein 2001; Hammersly and Atkinson 1995.

influencing policy focuses on politicians, bureaucrats, staffers, media, and so on). Finally, we asked about the degree to which change has occurred over the past 30 years in any of this, and what the causes were (e.g., whether normative, mimetic, coercive, or competitive mechanisms were operating).

Second, at the level of the *national field* of research organizations, we asked about the organization's relationships with other research organizations within their country (e.g., the degree to which they monitor other research organizations, who they monitor and why, the degree to which they cooperate/compete with other organizations, what organizations they cooperate/compete with, what form that cooperation/competition takes). We also asked how this has changed over the past 30 years and what the causes were (e.g., whether normative, mimetic, coercive or competitive mechanisms were operating). We asked similar questions about the general structure and functioning of the national field overall (e.g., how much research organizations in general monitor/cooperate/compete, what form it takes typically, how it has changed, and why). In particular, we asked about the degree to which convergence has occurred over the past 30 years among organizations within the field on a common set of structures, goals, and practices (as defined in the organizational-level questions, outlined above), and why it had or had not happened.

Third, at the level of the *international field* of research organizations, we asked about the organization's relationships with research organizations in other countries (e.g., the degree to which they monitor other research organizations, the degree to which they cooperate with other organizations, what organizations they monitor and cooperate with, what form that cooperation takes). We also inquired about how all of this had changed over the past 30 years and what the causes were (e.g., whether normative, mimetic, coercive, or competitive mechanisms were operating). In particular, we asked about the degree to which convergence has occurred over the past 30 years between research organizations in the respondent's country and those in other countries on a common set of structures, goals, and practices (as defined in the organizational-level questions outlined above), and why it had or had not happened.

We piloted a preliminary draft of the interview protocol in order to ensure clarity and made the appropriate modifications. We shared the basic questions with respondents prior to the interview. Many of them arrived for the interviews with those questions in hand prepared to run through them. Some even had notes in the margins indicating that they had given them some thought prior to the interview. We conducted all but two of the interviews in English. Pedersen conducted two in French. English was generally not a problem in the European cases because virtually all of the Europeans we interviewed were fluent in the language. When they stumbled in English, Pedersen was able to help with translation on the spot because he is fluent in English, Danish, French, and German. We initially requested one hour for the interviews, but most ran longer than that. In some cases people delayed their next appointments on the spot in order to continue the interview. They said this was because they found the interviews to be interesting and as a result were willing to extend the time originally allotted. Indeed, many told us that they had never thought about some of the issues we raised—especially those regarding their organization and change in the knowledge regime as a whole. Several people asked to see our results when they became available. Some even asked us to return to present the results at seminars for their colleagues and in some cases also for people from other organizations in the field.

We conducted almost all of the interviews together as a team.[25] We recorded them all on digital voice recorders and had them transcribed professionally and verbatim as computerized word processing documents. When the transcriber was unclear about what was being said on the recording, such as when there was overlapping dialogue, she marked the ambiguous section in the transcript. We then "cleaned" these transcripts by comparing the ambiguous sections against the recordings and making the necessary corrections if possible on the computerized transcript. This was a lengthy process.

There are, of course, potential problems with interviewing. First, trying to ascertain change over 30 years through interviews was sometimes difficult insofar as some respondents could speak about only recent activities in their organization and knowledge regime. However, we made every effort to find people who had been with their organizations long enough to provide narratives that reflected changes during this period. And although retrospective answers may be problematic in the abstract, it appeared to be less so in the moment because people were quick to tell us whenever they could not answer a question about the past. Moreover, we also gauged change whenever possible by comparing what we learned in one interview with what we learned in other interviews. We were also able to check some of the information gleaned in interviews about a particular organization and knowledge regime with what annual reports or the secondary literature said. This technique has been used successfully by other researchers who have compared their own research on an organization or organizational field with that done previously by others on the same organization or field.[26]

Second, a common problem with this type of interviewing is respondent bias—that is, respondents may offer official accounts reflecting what they

---

[25]In hindsight this afforded us some benefits. First, interviewing is intensive and tiring, especially when more than two long interviews are conducted per day. Having two interviewers helped keep interviews on track. Second, sometimes one of us would think of helpful follow-up questions that the other might have missed. Third, because we were trained in different intellectual traditions and have different levels of familiarity with our four countries, we often challenged each other's assumptions and interpretations about the cases when we discussed the interviews later. In short, by virtue of our different backgrounds we did not let each other take much for granted.
[26]Burawoy 1979.

believe should happen or what is deemed desirable rather than what actually does happen.[27] We tried to be sensitive to the possibility that our interviewees were "spinning" us like this by keeping a skeptical eye and discovered in some cases that they were. In order to rectify this problem on the spot we carefully probed the initial responses during the interviews, such as by asking for specific examples. We also remained attentive to information in other interviews, documents, and the secondary literature that contradicted what they told us. Third, we always tried to remain sensitive to the possibility that people bring their own subjective perceptions of things to an interview. And we used documents and the secondary literature wherever possible to check if there seemed to be a problem in this regard.

Despite potential problems like these, our confidence in the validity of much of the information we gathered during interviews was bolstered in another important way. As noted above, by the time we had finished interviewing in each country we had reached a saturation point where people were telling us things that we had heard before from others. Much of what each one told us was consistent with what others had said—that is, there was considerable consistency across interviews. This was comforting methodologically because the backbone of our analysis was going to be based on the interview data.

In the course of interviewing we kept careful field notes on a daily basis. Usually in cafes or hotel lobbies with a laptop computer we "debriefed" ourselves on the day's interviews. We tracked important themes, stories, trends, and other things that had come to light that day. By doing this every day we managed to begin a very rudimentary kind of analysis while we were in the field and things were fresh in our minds. As it turned out, these field notes, which ran from 20 to 25 single-spaced pages per country, were extremely helpful in sketching out some of the major story lines in our country cases as well as some of the important themes and insights of the analysis. We used them soon after we had concluded interviewing to begin fleshing out an outline of this book.

Finally, we discovered an extremely useful methodological technique during the interviews. Early in the third set of interviews—those we conducted in France—we drew a map of the knowledge regime as best we understood it up to that point. The next day we shared it with our interviewees and asked them whether it looked right to them and where their organizations fit in among the rest. Based on their responses we modified the sketch and used it again the next day in an iterative fashion such that the map evolved as the interviews proceeded. This technique not only helped us better understand the knowledge regime but also appealed to our respondents because they could

[27]Gerson 1985, pp. 246–47.

literally see what we were trying to figure out. It is unfortunate that we did not use this technique in all four countries.

Organizational Documents

As noted above, to compensate somewhat for the potential problems associated with interview data, we also collected during the interviews two types of documents from each organization in order to obtain additional information. These included (1) annual reports and (2) policy documents that our respondents felt were representative of their organization's work. We asked for annual reports and documents from 1987, 1997, and 2007 or as close to those years as possible. Our intent in collecting annual reports was to gather information about basic organizational facts, such as budget and staffing size, organizational structure, and the like. The policy documents included, for instance, policy briefs, scholarly publications, and reports commissioned by government agencies, which we planned to use as further background information on each organization's activities and to determine what sort of policy recommendations they made over time. We were especially interested in seeing whether neoliberalism became a more prominent perspective in the four knowledge regimes. We also gathered information from each organization's website. The annual reports proved to be especially helpful insofar as they balanced the interviews and compensated for faulty recall among interviewees. Most of the U.S., German, and Danish organizations provided everything we asked for. The French organizations proved to be more difficult especially where annual reports were concerned because many of these organizations did not issue such reports until sometime after 1997, if ever.

Coding and Analysis

Our data enabled us to examine how each knowledge regime was organized, how it operated, how different types of organizations produced knowledge, how they interacted with each other at home and abroad, how they tried to influence the policymaking process, how this changed over time, and how all of this varied across countries. The comparisons of interest were as follows: (1) comparisons of research organizations within national knowledge regimes, (2) comparisons of knowledge regimes across countries, and (3) comparisons of knowledge regimes over time.

Interviews

We analyzed the interview data with ATLAS.ti (version 6) qualitative data analysis software. To do this we developed a coding scheme from our working hypotheses, field notes, and expectations about how fields of organizations might change or not in response to uncertainty in their surrounding environments. This was an iterative process that took several months during which we worked with a team of students to refine and clarify the coding scheme and establish its intercoder reliability. The goal here was to devise a coding scheme with categories that were simple and unambiguous.[28] Hence, we adopted basic procedures used in much archival research to standardize data collection and ensure reliability.[29] Eventually, we established intercoder reliability of about 96% for the coding scheme by the "negotiated agreement method."[30]

Once this coding scheme was set and an acceptable level of reliability had been achieved, Campbell and a research assistant then proceeded to code all the interviews in ATLAS.ti. As this process unfolded he also generated a second set of codes regarding themes that were not covered by the first set of codes but that seemed important enough to track as they came to light. As such, each interview was coded with one set of codes that was created ahead of time through a combination of deduction and induction and that remained unchanged throughout the process, and another set of codes that was created inductively and that evolved as coding proceeded. Thus, we were able to code in ways that would help us test our initial working hypotheses but that would also let us identify new theoretical insights that we had not anticipated as is characteristic of the grounded theory approach to research.[31] The coding process in ATLAS.ti was done primarily to facilitate easy and accurate data retrieval from the interview transcripts. During the coding process Campbell also wrote detailed summaries in ATLAS.ti of what was said in each interview for later reference. Overall, he and his assistant each coded 5,504 double-spaced printed pages of interview transcripts.[32]

Policy Reports

Among the policy documents we collected we gathered information from policy reports from each country's council of economic advisors. The idea was to determine the degree to which each council report represented policy recommendations that were consistent or not with neoliberalism. This was a two-step process. First, following the common understanding of neoliberalism we coded the council reports from all four countries to determine

---

[28]See, for example, Krippendorf (1980), Roberts (1997), and Weber (1990).
[29]See, for example, Armstrong et al. (1997) and Mauthner et al. (1998).
[30]Garrison et al. 2006; Morrissey 1974, pp. 214–15. For detailed discussion of the interview coding methodology that we developed, see Campbell et al. (2013).
[31]See, for example, Glaser and Strauss (1967) and Rubin and Rubin (2005).
[32]More specifically, we had about 1,314 pages of transcripts from the Danish interviews, 1,326 pages from the French interviews, 1,318 pages from the German interviews, and 1,546 pages from the U.S. interviews.

how many neoliberal themes were favored in each one.[33] The themes included limited/reduced government spending, limited/reduced taxes, limited/reduced regulations, maximizing labor force participation (vs. full employment), equal opportunity (vs. equal outcomes), free trade, decentralized political authority, privatization, use of incentives to achieve goals (vs. mandating goals by law), price stability, monetary policy, and securing private economic benefits from public intervention. Because we were interested only in gathering straightforward data based on explicit statements in the reports that required little interpretation we did not worry about intercoder reliability. Pedersen then coded these reports using an Excel spread sheet. This scheme was fairly simple in the sense that it determined only the degree to which a policy document favored neoliberal policies or not. It was not sensitive enough to help differentiate among different types of neoliberal or non-neoliberal policy positions.

At the same time, and in an effort to compensate for these problems, Pedersen used ATLAS.ti to tag statements in the documents that corroborated his coding decisions. In this way he coded about 6,500 double-spaced pages of policy reports. He also took careful notes on each report in order to track their more subtle aspects. In particular, he tracked the process by which a council went about writing its report; the specific policy areas it discussed; the sorts of analysis, forecasting, and recommendations it included; its writing style; and the methodologies involved. Thus, he deployed both a deductive and inductive approach to gathering data from the documents much as Campbell did for gathering data from the interview transcripts. His inductive approach represents a rudimentary form of discourse analysis.

Annual Reports

Finally, we also worked with another team of students to gather data from the annual reports. Students in the United States worked on the U.S. reports and a Danish student, who was fluent in Danish, German, and French, worked on the reports from the other countries. We were interested in collecting rather basic and explicit information from these reports on things like organizational budgets, staffing, structure, and so on for which we developed a coding scheme. These data were entered into Excel spreadsheets.

We standardized the budget data from the annual reports in terms of 2009 U.S. dollars. First, using various online calculators we converted all budget data for France, Germany, and Denmark into U.S. dollars for the corresponding

---

[33]For common understandings of neoliberalism, see, for example, Crouch (2011), Mirowski and Plehwe (2009), and Skidelsky (2009). We drew particular inspiration for this from Mudge's (2011) coding of neoliberalism in European and North American political party platforms.

years. For instance, data that were given as 1987 French francs were converted into 1987 dollars. And German or Danish data that were given as 2002 euros or kroner, respectively, were converted into 2002 dollars. Next, we converted all the dollar amounts for all countries and years into 2009 U.S. dollars using another online calculator that accounted for the effects of inflation on the dollar. Thus, all budget data for all countries were finally expressed in terms of inflation adjusted 2009 U.S. dollars. This allowed the possibility for us to make meaningful budgetary comparisons among organizations, over time, and across countries without worrying about whether the differences were due to variation in inflation.[34] Unless noted otherwise all budget data in this book are drawn from these reports and given as 2009 U.S. dollars.

The interview data were the most useful and constitute the heart of our analysis. This is because these data were the most systematic and comparable across organizations and countries. After all, we asked the same basic questions of everyone we interviewed. In contrast, the annual report data were problematic. First, not all organizations published annual reports so some data that we wanted to collect did not exist. The U.S. and German organizations were most likely to do so for the three time periods in question, 1987, 1997, and 2007, but even then not all of them did. Government organizations, for instance, were much less likely to publish annual reports than organizations in civil society. And until 2007 virtually none of the French organizations had such reports to give us. This was not because they refused to share reports but rather because they did not exist in the first place. Second, even when we had reports they did not always contain the data that we hoped to gather, including, for example, basic data on revenues and expenditures. Hence, there were significant missing data problems in terms of the annual reports. In short, requirements and standards for reporting organizational information through annual reports varied dramatically across organizations and countries and over time. Things were best in the United States but not as good in the other countries, especially France.

None of this should be too surprising. Cross-national research is notoriously difficult in terms of finding comparable data in several countries. The problem is compounded when a historical dimension is added and longitudinal data are desired. These difficulties are especially pronounced when a new field of research is being addressed, which is what we were doing. We recognize the limitations of our data. We also believe, however, that it is worth using them as best we can to break new empirical and theoretical ground.

---

[34]Details including information about the online conversion tools are available from the authors.

Validity and Case Study Integrity

Qualitative analysis, such as the case study approach we have used here, is susceptible potentially to validity problems because the analyst combs through and interprets vast amounts of qualitative data, such as the interviews and documents used in this study, in order to write the case study. Skeptics might question the validity of those interpretations. And researchers themselves might worry about this problem as well they should.

In this study, two issues concerned us about the validity of our case studies or what others have called case study integrity. First, we knew the U.S. and Danish political economies very well having done research on them for much of our careers. At issue then was the possibility that whatever taken-for-granted assumptions we had about these two cases might have clouded or biased our interpretation of them. Second, we were less familiar with the French and German political economies and therefore worried that this might lead us to misinterpret the data or overlook things and thus draw erroneous conclusions about these cases.

In order to check the integrity of our case studies, once we had written polished drafts of each country case study (i.e., chapters 2–5) we sent them by email to many of the people we had interviewed in the first place for that chapter. The French received the chapter on France, the Germans received the chapter on Germany, and so on. We asked them to read it and provide us with whatever comments they wanted, including especially comments on things that we may have gotten wrong. We also asked them to comment on anything important that may have changed in their organization or knowledge regime since we had interviewed them. We were unable to reach everyone we interviewed. Some had moved on to other organizations or retired, and some did not respond to our request. But each of those who did respond graciously offered comments and suggestions that were helpful. These comments were of three varieties. First, respondents commented on extremely minor factual or interpretive details that they felt should be corrected in the final draft. Second, virtually everyone said that they agreed with the overall thrust of our interpretations. Nobody raised significant issues or disagreed with the story lines we had developed in the chapters. And many of them said that they had learned things from our analyses and were grateful that we had returned to them with these drafts. Third, most people said that not much had changed since we had interviewed them. We took all of their comments into consideration when we prepared the final manuscript. As a result, we are confident in the validity of our case studies.

References

Abbott, Andrew. 1993. "The Sociology of Work and Occupations." *Annual Review of Sociology* 19:187–209.

———. 1988. *The System of Professions*. Chicago: University of Chicago Press.

Abdelal, Rawi. 2009. "Constructivism as an Approach to International Political Economy." Pp. 62–77 in *Routledge Handbook of International Political Economy*, edited by Mark Blyth. London: Routledge.

Abdelal, Rawi, Mark Blyth, and Craig Parsons, editors. 2010a. *Constructing the International Economy*. Ithaca: Cornell University Press.

———. 2010b. "Reconstructing IPE: Some Conclusions Drawn from a Crisis." Pp. 227–40 in *Constructing the International Economy*, edited by Rawi Abdelal, Mark Blyth, and Craig Parsons. Ithaca: Cornell University Press.

Abelson, Donald E. 2004. "The Business of Ideas: The Think Tank Industry in the United States." Pp. 215–31 in *Think Tank Traditions*, edited by Diane Stone and Andrew Denham. Manchester: Manchester University Press.

———. 2002. *Do Think Tanks Matter?* Montreal: McGill-Queen's University Press.

———. 2000. "Do Think Tanks Matter? Opportunities, Constraints and Incentives for Think Tanks in Canada and the United States." *Global Society* 14(2)13–36.

———. 1998. "Think Tanks in the United States." Pp. 107–27 in *Think Tanks across Nations: A Comparative Perspective*, edited by Diane Stone, Andrew Denham, and Mark Garnett. Manchester: Manchester University Press.

———. 1992. "A New Channel of Influence: American Think Tanks and the News Media." *Queen's Quarterly* 99(4)849–72.

Albert, Michel. 1993. *Capitalism vs. Capitalism*. New York: Four Walls Eight Windows.

Althusser, Louis. 1968. *For Marx*. London: Verso.

Amable, Bruno. 2003. *The Diversity of Modern Capitalism*. New York: Oxford University Press.

Anthony, Denise, Ajit Appari, and Eric Johnson. 2012. "Institutionalizing Compliance: Institutional Forces in Hospital Compliance with HIPPA." Unpublished manuscript, Department of Sociology, Dartmouth College.

Armstrong, David, Ann Gosling, John Weinman, and Theresa Marteau. 1997. "The Place of Inter-Rater Reliability in Qualitative Research: An Empirical Study." *Sociology* 31(3)597–606.

Babb, Sarah. 2007. "Embeddedness, Inflation, and International Regimes: The IMF in the Early Postwar Period." *American Journal of Sociology* 113:128–64.

———. 2001. *Managing Mexico*. Princeton: Princeton University Press.

Bai, Matt. 2007. *The Argument: Billionaires, Bloggers, and the Battle to Remake Democratic Politics*. New York: Penguin.

Bartley, Tim. 2007. "Institutional Emergence in an Era of Globalization: The Rise of Transnational Private Regulation of Labor and Environmental Conditions." *American Journal of Sociology* 113:297–351.

Baumgartner, Frank, and Bryan Jones. 1993. *Agendas and Instability in American Politics*. Chicago: University of Chicago Press.

Béland, Daniel, and Robert Cox, editors. 2011. *Ideas and Politics in Social Science Research*. New York: Oxford University Press.

Berman, Sheri. 2006. *The Primacy of Politics: Social Democracy and the Making of Europe's Twentieth Century*. New York: Cambridge University Press.

——. 1998. *The Social Democratic Moment: Ideas and Politics in the Making of Interwar Europe*. Cambridge, MA: Harvard University Press.

Bernard, H. Russell. 2000. *Social Research Methods: Qualitative and Quantitative Approaches*. Thousand Oaks, CA: Sage.

Bimber, Bruce. 1996. *The Politics of Expertise in Congress: The Rise and Fall of the Office of Technology Assessment*. Albany: State University of New York Press.

Blair, Peter. 2011. "Scientific Advice for Policy in the United States: Lessons from the National Academies and the Former Congressional Office of Technology Assessment." Pp. 297–333 in *The Politics of Scientific Advice*, edited by Justus Lentsch and Peter Weingart. New York: Cambridge University Press.

Blanchard, Olivier, and Jean-Paul Fitoussi. 1998. *Croissance et chomage*. Paris: La Documentation Française.

Block, Fred. 2008. "Swimming Against the Current: The Rise of a Hidden Developmental State in the United States." *Politics and Society* 36:169–206.

——. 1996. *The Vampire State*. New York: New Press.

Blyth, Mark M. 2013. *Austerity: The History of a Dangerous Idea*. New York: Oxford University Press.

——. 2011. "Ideas, Uncertainty and Evolution." Pp. 83–103 in *Ideas and Politics in Social Science Research*, edited by Daniel Béland and Robert Cox. New York: Oxford University Press.

——. 2002. *Great Transformations: The Rise and Decline of Embedded Liberalism*. New York: Cambridge University Press.

——. 1997. "Any More Bright Ideas? The Ideational Turn of Comparative Political Economy." *Comparative Politics* 29(2)229–50.

Boli, John, and George Thomas, editors. 1999. *Constructing World Culture*. Stanford: Stanford University Press.

Bourdieu, Pierre. 2001. *Firing Back*. New York: New Press.

Bourgeault, Ivy Lynn, Cecilia Benoit, and Kristine Hirschkorn. 2009. "Introduction: Comparative Perspectives on Professional Groups—Current Issues and Critical Debates." *Current Sociology* 57(4)475–85.

Boyer, Robert. 2005a. "Coherence, Diversity and Evolution of Capitalisms: The Institutional Complementarity Hypothesis." Unpublished manuscript, Centre National de la Recherche Scientifique, Paris.

——. 2005b. "Complementarity in Regulation Theory." *Socio-Economic Review* 3(2)366–71.

——. 1997. "French Statism at the Crossroads." Pp. 71–101 in *Political Economy of Modern Capitalism*, edited by Colin Crouch and Wolfgang Streeck. Thousand Oaks, CA: Sage.

Boyer, Robert, and Michel Didier. 1998. *Innovation et croissance*. Paris: La Documentation Française.

Boyer, Robert, and Daniel Drache, editors. 1996. *States Against Markets: The Limits of Globalization*. New York: Routledge.

Braml, Josef. 2004. *Think Tanks versus "Denkfabriken"? U.S. and German Policy Research Institutes Coping with and Influencing Their Environments*. Baden-Baden: Nomos Verlagsgesellschaft.

Briggs, Charles. 1986. *Learning How to Ask*. New York: Cambridge University Press.

Brint, Steven. 1994. *In an Age of Experts: The Changing Role of Professionals in Politics and Public Life*. Princeton: Princeton University Press.

Brock, David, and Ari Rabin-Havt. 2012. *The Fox Effect*. New York: Anchor Books.

Burawoy, Michael. 1979. *Manufacturing Consent*. Chicago: University of Chicago Press.

Bureau, Dominique, and Michel Mougeot. 1997. *Performance, incitations et gestion publique*. Paris: Les Documentation Française.

Burgin, Angus. 2012. *The Great Persuasion: Reinventing Free Markets since the Depression*. Cambridge, MA: Harvard University Press.

Burla, Laila, Birte Knierim, Jürgen Barth, Katharina Liewald, Margreet Duetz, and Thomas Abel. 2008. "From Text to Codings: Inter-coder Reliability Assessment in Qualitative Content Analysis." *Nursing Research* 57(2)113–17.

Buttel, Fred. 2000. "World Society, the Nation-State, and Environmental Protection: Comment on Frank, Hironaka, and Schofer." *American Sociological Review* 65:117–22.

Camic, Charles, Neil Gross, and Michèle Lamont, editors. 2011a. *Social Knowledge in the Making.* Chicago: University of Chicago Press.

Camic, Charles, Neil Gross, and Michèle Lamont. 2011b. "The Study of Social Knowledge Making." Pp. 1–40 in *Social Knowledge in the Making*, edited by Charles Camic, Neil Gross, and Michèle Lamont. Chicago: University of Chicago Press.

Campbell, John L. 2011. "The U.S. Financial Crisis: Lessons for Theories of Institutional Complementarity." *Socio-Economic Review* 9:211–34.

———. 2010. "Institutional Reproduction and Change." Pp. 87–117 in *The Oxford Handbook of Comparative Institutional Analysis*, edited by Glenn Morgan, John L. Campbell, Colin Crouch, Ove K. Pedersen, and Richard Whitley. New York: Oxford University Press.

———. 2004. *Institutional Change and Globalization.* Princeton: Princeton University Press.

———. 2002. "Ideas, Politics, and Public Policy." *Annual Review of Sociology* 38:21–38.

———. 1998. "Institutional Analysis and the Role of Ideas in Political Economy." *Theory and Society* 27:377–409.

Campbell, John L., and John A. Hall. 2009. "National Identity and the Political Economy of Small States." *Review of International Political Economy* 16(4)1–26.

———. 2006. "The State of Denmark." Pp. 3–49 in *National Identity and the Varieties of Capitalism: The Danish Experience*, edited by John L. Campbell, John A. Hall, and Ove K. Pedersen. Montreal: McGill-Queen's University Press.

Campbell, John L., John A. Hall, and Ove K. Pedersen, editors. 2006. *National Identity and the Varieties of Capitalism: The Danish Experience.* Montreal: McGill-Queen's University Press.

Campbell, John L., J. Rogers Hollingsworth, and Leon N. Lindberg, editors. 1991. *Governance of the American Economy.* New York: Cambridge University Press.

Campbell, John L., and Leon N. Lindberg. 1990. "Property Rights and the Organization of Economic Activity by the State." *American Sociological Review* 55:634–47.

Campbell, John L., and Ove K. Pedersen. 2011. "Knowledge Regimes and Comparative Political Economy." Pp. 167–90 in *Ideas and Politics in Social Science Research*, edited by Daniel Béland and Robert Cox. New York: Oxford University Press.

———. 2007a. "Institutional Competitiveness in the Global Economy: Denmark, the United States and the Varieties of Capitalism." *Regulation and Governance* 1(3)230–46.

———. 2007b. "The Varieties of Capitalism and Hybrid Success: Denmark in the Global Economy." *Comparative Political Studies* 40(3)307–32.

———, editors. 2001a. *The Rise of Neoliberalism and Institutional Analysis.* Princeton: Princeton University Press.

———. 2001b. "The Second Movement in Institutional Analysis." Pp. 249–82 in *The Rise of Neoliberalism and Institutional Analysis*, edited by John L. Campbell and Ove K. Pedersen. Princeton: Princeton University Press.

———. 1996. "The Evolutionary Nature of Revolutionary Change in Postcommunist Europe." Pp. 207–49 in *Legacies of Change: Transformations of Postcommunist European Economies*, edited by John L. Campbell and Ove K. Pedersen. New York: Aldine de Gruyter.

Campbell, John L., Charles Quincy, Jordan Osserman, and Ove K. Pedersen. 2013. "Coding In-Depth Semi-structured Interviews: Problems of Unitization and Inter-coder Reliability and Agreement." *Sociological Methods and Research* 42(3)294–320.

Castles, Francis G. 2000. "Federalism, Fiscal Decentralization and Economic Performance." Pp. 171–90 in *Federalism and Political Performance*, edited by Ute Wachendorfer-Schmidt. London: Routledge.

Center for Responsive Politics. 2010. http://www.opensecrets.org/. Accessed December 13, 2010.

Chandler, Alfred D. 1977. *The Visible Hand.* Cambridge, MA: Harvard University Press.

Christiansen, Peter Munk, and Asbjørn Sonne Nørgaard. 2003. *Faste Forhold—Flygtige Forbind-elser*. Aarhus: Aarhus Universitetsforlag.

Clawson, Dan, Alan Neustadtl, and Mark Weller. 1998. *Dollars and Votes*. Philadelphia: Temple University Press.

Cohen, Stephen. 1977. *Modern Capitalist Planning: The French Model*, 2nd edition. Berkeley: University of California Press.

Coleman, David A. 1991. "Policy Research—Who Needs It?" *Governance: An International Journal of Policy and Administration* 4(4)420–55.

Collins, Harry, and Robert Evans. 2007. *Rethinking Expertise*. Chicago: University of Chicago Press.

Conseil d'Analyse Économique. 2007. *La France dans 15 ans. Perspective èconomiques*. Paris: La Documentation Française.

Conseil d'Analyse Économique. 2008. *La France dans 15 ans. Perspective èconomiques*. Paris: La Documentation Française.

Crafts, Nicholas. 2000. "Globalization and Growth in the Twentieth Century." Pp. 1–51 in *World Economic Outlook: Supporting Studies*. Washington, DC: International Monetary Fund.

Crouch, Colin. 2011. *The Strange Non-death of Neoliberalism*. London: Polity.

———. 2005. *Capitalist Diversity and Change*. New York: Oxford University Press.

Crouch, Colin, and Wolfgang Streeck, editors. 1997. *Political Economy of Modern Capitalism*. Thousand Oaks, CA: Sage.

Culpepper, Pepper. 2010. *Quiet Politics and Business Power: Corporate Control in Europe and Japan*. New York: Cambridge University Press.

———. 2006. "Capitalism, Coordination, and Economic Change: The French Political Economy since 1985." Pp. 29–49 in *Changing France: The Politics That Markets Make*, edited by Pepper Culpepper, Peter A. Hall, and Bruno Palier. New York: Palgrave.

———. 2001. "Employers, Public Policy, and the Politics of Decentralized Cooperation in Germany and France." Pp. 275–306 in *Varieties of Capitalism*, edited by Peter A. Hall and David Soskice. New York: Oxford University Press.

Cyert, Richard, and James March. 1963. *A Behavioral Theory of the Firm*. Englewood Cliffs, NJ: Prentice Hall.

Czarniawska, Barbara, and Guje Sevon, editors. 1996. *Translating Organizational Change*. New York: Aldine de Gruyter.

Davis, Gerald, Kristina Diekmann, and Catherine Tinsley. 1994. "The Decline and Fall of the Conglomerate Firm in the 1990s: The Deinstitutionalization of an Organizational Form." *American Sociological Review* 59:547–70.

Davis, Gerald, Doug McAdam, W. Richard Scott, and Mayer Zald, editors. 2005. *Social Movements and Organization Theory*. New York: Cambridge University Press.

Day, Alan J. 2000. "Think Tanks in Western Europe." Pp. 103–38 in *Think Tanks and Civil Societies*, edited by James G. McGann and R. Kent Weaver. New York: Transaction.

Deeg, Richard. 2010. "Institutional Change in Financial Systems." Pp. 309–34 in *The Oxford Handbook of Comparative Institutional Analysis*, edited by Glenn Morgan, John L. Campbell, Colin Crouch, Ove K. Pedersen, and Richard Whitley. New York: Oxford University Press.

Dehejia, Vivek H., and Philipp Genschel. 1999. "Tax Competition in Europe." *Politics and Society* 27(3)403–30.

De Lamothe, A. Dutheillet. 1965. "Ministerial Cabinets in France." *Public Administration* 43:365–79.

Desai, Radhika. 1994. "Second-Hand Dealers in Ideas: Think Tanks and Thatcherite Hegemony." *New Left Review* 203:27–64.

Desmoulins, Lucile. 2000. "French Public Policy Research Institutes and Their Political Impact as Another Illustration of French Exceptionalism." Pp. 139–68 in *Think Tanks and Civil Societies*, edited by James G. McGann and R. Kent Weaver. New York: Transaction.

DeVries, Raymond, Robert Dingwall, and Kristina Orfali. 2009. "The Moral Organization of the Professions: Bioethics in the United States and France." *Current Sociology* 57(4)555–79.

Dezalay, Yves, and Bryant Garth. 2002. *The Internationalization of Palace Wars*. Chicago: University of Chicago Press.

Dickinson, Matthew J. 2005. "The Executive Office of the President: The Paradox of Politicization." Pp. 135–73 in *The Executive Branch*, edited by Joel Aberbach and Mark Peterson. New York: Oxford University Press.

DiMaggio, Paul, editor. 2001. *The Twenty-First-Century Firm*. Princeton: Princeton University Press.

DiMaggio, Paul, and Walter Powell. 1983. "The Iron Cage Revisited: Institutional Isomorphism and Collective Rationality in Organizational Fields." *American Sociological Review* 48:147–60.

Djelic, Marie-Laure. 1998. *Exporting the American Model: The Postwar Transformation of European Business*. New York: Oxford University Press.

Djelic, Marie-Laure, and Sigrid Quack, editors. 2010. *Transnational Communities: Shaping Global Economic Governance*. New York: Cambridge University Press.

Djelic, Marie-Laure, and Kristin Sahlin-Andersson, editors. 2006. *Transnational Governance: Institutional Dynamics of Regulation*. New York: Cambridge University Press.

Dobbin, Frank. 2005. "Comparative and Historical Approaches to Economic Sociology." Pp. 26–48 in *The Handbook of Economic Sociology*, 2nd edition, edited by Neil Smelser and Richard Swedberg. Princeton: Princeton University Press.

———. 2004. "The Sociological View of the Economy." Pp. 1–48 in *The New Economic Sociology*, edited by Frank Dobbin. Princeton: Princeton University Press.

———. 1994. *Forging Industrial Policy*. New York: Cambridge University Press.

———. 1992. "The Origins of Private Social Insurance: Public Policy and Fringe Benefits in America." *American Journal of Sociology* 97:1416–50.

Dobbin, Frank, Beth Simmons, and Geoffrey Garrett. 2007. "The Global Diffusion of Public Policies: Social Construction, Coercion, Competition, or Learning?" *Annual Review of Sociology* 33:449–72.

Domhoff, G. William. 2010. *Who Rules America?* New York: McGraw-Hill.

Dore, Ronald, William Lazonick, and Mary O'Sullivan. 1999. "Varieties of Capitalism in the Twentieth Century." *Oxford Review of Economic Policy* 15(4)102–20.

Doremus, Paul, William Keller, Louis Pauly, and Simon Reich. 1998. *The Myth of the Global Corporation*. Princeton: Princeton University Press.

Due, Jesper, Jørgen Steen Madsen, and Mie Dalskov Phil. 2010. *Udviklingen i den Faglige Organisering: Årsager og Konsekvenser for den Danske Model*. LO-Dokumentation, no. 1, Copenhagen, Denmark.

Duina, Francesco. 2003. "National Legislatures in Common Markets: Autonomy in the European Union and Mercosur." Pp. 183–212 in *The Nation-State in Question*, edited by T. V. Paul, G. John Ikenberry, and John A. Hall. Princeton: Princeton University Press.

———. 1999. *Harmonizing Europe: Nation-States within the Common Market*. Albany: State University of New York Press.

Dunn, Graham. 1989. *Design and Analysis of Reliability Studies: The Statistical Evaluation of Measurement Errors*. New York: Oxford University Press.

Dye, Thomas. 1995. *Who's Running America?* Englewood Cliffs, NJ: Prentice Hall.

Dyson, Kenneth. 1982. "West Germany: The Search for a Rationalist Consensus." Pp. 17–46 in *Policy Styles in Western Europe*, edited by Jeremy Richardson. London: George Allen and Unwin.

Edelman, Lauren. 1992. "Legal Ambiguity and Symbolic Structures: Organizational Mediation of Civil Rights Law." *American Journal of Sociology* 97:1531–76.

Edin, Kathryn, and Maria Kefalas. 2005. *Promises I Can Keep: Why Poor Women Put Motherhood before Marriage*. Berkeley: University of California Press.

Edin, Kathryn, and Laura Lein. 1997. *Making Ends Meet: How Single Mothers Survive Welfare and Low-Wage Work*. New York: Russell Sage Foundation.

Edsall, Thomas Byrne. 2012. *The Age of Austerity*. New York: Doubleday.

Eichengreen, Barry. 2008. *The European Economy since 1945: Coordinated Capitalism and Beyond*. Princeton: Princeton University Press.

Elster, Jon. 1989. *Nuts and Bolts for the Social Sciences*. New York: Cambridge University Press.

Engel, Mimi. 2007. "Mixing Methods: Reliability and Validity across Quantitative and Qualitative Measures of Relationship Quality." Pp. 255–76 in *Unmarried Couples with Children*, edited by Paula England and Kathryn Edin. New York: Russell Sage Foundation.

England, Paula, and Kathryn Edin. 2007. "Unmarried Couples with Children: Hoping for Love and the White Picket Fence." Pp. 3–21 in *Unmarried Couples with Children*, edited by Paula England and Kathryn Edin. New York: Russell Sage Foundation.

Esping-Andersen, Gøsta. 1985. *Politics Against Markets: The Social Democratic Road to Power*. Princeton: Princeton University Press.

Evans, Peter, Dietrich Rueschemeyer, and Theda Skocpol, editors. 1985. *Bringing the State Back In*. New York: Cambridge University Press.

Evetts, Julia. 2006. "Short Note: The Sociology of Professional Groups—New Directions." *Current Sociology* 54(1)133–43.

Fahy, Patrick. 2001. "Addressing Some Common Problems in Transcript Analysis." *International Review of Research in Open and Distance Learning* 1(2). http://www.irrodl.org/index.php/irrodl/article/view/321.

Fantasia, Rick, and Kim Voss. 2004. *Hard Work: Remaking the American Labor Movement*. Berkeley: University of California Press.

Feulner, Edwin. 2000. "The Heritage Foundation." Pp. 67–85 in *Think Tanks and Civil Societies*, edited by James G. McGann and R. Kent Weaver. New York: Transaction.

Fieschi, Catherine, and John Gaffney. 2004. "French Think Tanks in Comparative Perspective." Pp. 105–20 in *Think Tank Traditions*, edited by Diane Stone and Andrew Denham. Manchester: Manchester University Press.

———. 1998. "French Think Tanks in Comparative Perspective." Pp. 42–58 in *Think Tanks across Nations: A Comparative Perspective*, edited by Diane Stone, Andrew Denham, and Mark Garnett. Manchester: Manchester University Press.

Fischer, Frank. 1991. "American Think Tanks: Policy Elites and the Politicization of Expertise." *Governance: An International Journal of Policy and Administration* 4(3)332–53.

Fligstein, Neil. 1990. *The Transformation of Corporate Control*. Cambridge, MA: Harvard University Press.

Fligstein, Neil, and Doug McAdam. 2012. *A Theory of Fields*. New York: Oxford University Press.

Fourcade, Marion. 2009. *Economists and Societies*. Princeton: Princeton University Press.

———. 2006. "The Construction of a Global Profession: The Transnationalization of Economics." *American Journal of Sociology* 112:145–94.

Fourcade-Gourinchas, Marion, and Sarah Babb. 2002. "The Rebirth of the Liberal Creed: Paths to Neoliberalism in Four Countries." *American Journal of Sociology* 108:533–79.

Frank, David, Ann Hironaka, and Evan Schofer. 2000. "The Nation-State and the Natural Environment of the Twentieth Century." *American Sociological Review* 65:96–116.

Freeman, Richard B. 2007. *America Works: Critical Thoughts on the Exceptional U.S. Labor Market*. New York: Russell Sage.

Freidson, Eliot. 1994. *Professionalism Reborn*. Chicago: University of Chicago Press.

———. 1984. "The Changing Nature of Professional Control." *Annual Review of Sociology* 10:1–20.

Furner, Mary O., and Barry Supple, editors. 1990. *The State of Economic Knowledge*. New York: Cambridge University Press.

Gaffney, John. 1991. "The Political Think-Tanks in the UK and the Ministerial Cabinets in France." *West European Politics* 14(11)1–17.

Galaskiewicz, Joseph. 1991. "Making Corporate Actors Accountable: Institution-Building in Minneapolis-St. Paul." Pp. 293–310 in *The New Institutionalism in Organizational Analysis*, edited by Walter W. Powell and Paul J. DiMaggio. Chicago: University of Chicago Press.

Garrett, Geoffrey. 1998. *Partisan Politics in the Global Economy*. New York: Cambridge University Press.

Garrett, Geoffrey, Frank Dobbin, and Beth Simmons. 2008. "Conclusion." Pp. 344–60 in *The Global Diffusion of Markets and Democracy*, edited by Beth Simmons, Frank Dobbin, and Geoffrey Garrett. New York: Cambridge University Press.

Garrison, D. R., M. Cleveland-Innes, Marguerite Koole, and James Kappelman. 2006. "Revisiting Methodological Issues in Transcript Analysis: Negotiated Coding and Reliability." *Internet and Higher Education* 9:1–8.

Gellner, Winand. 1998. "Think Tanks in Germany." Pp. 82–106 in *Think Tanks across Nations: A Comparative Perspective,* edited by Diane Stone, Andrew Denham, and Mark Garnett. Manchester: Manchester University Press.

———. 1995. "The Politics of Policy 'Political Think Tanks' and Their Markets in the U.S. Institutional Environment." *Presidential Studies Quarterly* 25(3)497–510.

Gereffi, Gary. 2005. "The Global Economy: Organization, Governance, and Development." Pp. 160–82 in *The Handbook of Economic Sociology,* 2nd edition, edited by Neil Smelser and Richard Swedberg. Princeton: Princeton University Press.

Gerson, Kathleen. 1985. *Hard Choices.* Berkeley: University of California Press.

Glaser, Barney, and Anselm Strauss. 1967. *The Discovery of Grounded Theory.* New York: Aldine de Gruyter.

Goldstein, Judith, and Robert O. Keohane, editors. 1993. "Ideas and Foreign Policy: An Analytic Framework." Pp. 3–30 in *Ideas and Foreign Policy,* edited by Judith Goldstein and Robert Keohane. Ithaca: Cornell University Press.

Gouldner, Alvin. 1979. *The Future of Intellectuals and the Rise of the New Class.* New York: Oxford University Press.

Goyer, Michel. 2006. "Varieties of Institutional Investors and National Models of Capitalism: The Transformation of Corporate Governance in France and Germany." *Politics and Society* 34:399–430.

Gramsci, Antonio. 1971. *Selections from the Prison Notebooks.* New York: International.

Grayson, Kent, and Roland Rust. 2001. "Interrater Reliability Assessment in Content Analysis." *Journal of Consumer Psychology* 10(1–2)71–73.

Grønnegaard Christensen, Jørgen, Poul Erik Mouritzen, and Asbjørn Sonne. 2009. *De Store Kommissioner.* Odense: Syddansk Universitetsforlag.

Grunberg, Gérard. 2006. "The French Party System and the Crisis of Representation." Pp. 223–43 in *Changing France: The Politics That Markets Make,* edited by Pepper Culpepper, Peter A. Hall, and Bruno Palier. New York: Palgrave.

Gubrium, Jaber, and James Holstein. 2001. *Handbook of Interview Research: Context and Method.* Thousand Oaks, CA: Sage.

Guillén, Mauro. 2001a. "Is Globalization Civilizing, Destructive, or Feeble? A Critique of Five Key Debates in the Social Science Literature." *Annual Review of Sociology* 27:235–60.

———. 2001b. *The Limits of Convergence: Globalization and Organizational Change in Argentina, South Korea and Spain.* Princeton: Princeton University Press.

———. 1994. *Models of Management: Work, Authority and Organization in a Comparative Perspective.* Chicago: University of Chicago Press.

Gulati, Ranjay. 2007. *Managing Network Resources: Alliances, Affiliations, and Other Relational Assets.* New York: Oxford University Press.

Guyomarch, Alain. 1999. "'Public Service,' 'Public Management' and the 'Modernization' of French Public Administration." *Public Administration* 77(1)171–93.

Haas, Peter M. 1992. "Introduction: Epistemic Communities and International Policy Coordination." *International Organization* 46(1)1–36.

Hacker, Jacob S., and Paul Pierson. 2010. *Winner-Take-All Politics.* New York: Simon & Schuster.

Hage, Jerald, and Jonathon Mote. 2008. "Transformational Organizations and Institutional Change: The Case of the Institut Pasteur and French Science." *Socio-Economic Review* 6:313–36.

Hall, John A. 1993. "Ideas and Social Sciences." Pp. 31–56 in *Ideas and Foreign Policy,* edited by Judith Goldstein and Robert Keohane. Ithaca: Cornell University Press.

Hall, Peter A. 2010. "Historical Institutionalism in a Rationalist and Sociological Perspective." Pp. 204–24 in *Explaining Institutional Change,* edited by James Mahoney and Kathleen Thelen. New York: Cambridge University Press.

———. 2007. "The Evolution of Varieties of Capitalism." Pp. 39–88 in *Beyond Varieties of Capitalism*, edited by Bob Hancké, Martin Rhodes, and Mark Thatcher. New York: Oxford University Press.

———. 2006a. "Danish Capitalism in Comparative Perspective." Pp. 441–52 in *National Identity and the Varieties of Capitalism: The Danish Experience*, edited by John L. Campbell, John A. Hall, and Ove K. Pedersen. Montreal: McGill-Queen's University Press.

———. 2006b. "Introduction: The Politics of Social Change in France." Pp. 1–26 in *Changing France: The Politics That Markets Make*, edited by Pepper Culpepper, Peter A. Hall, and Bruno Palier. New York: Palgrave.

———. 2005. "Institutional Complementarity: Causes and Effects." *Socio-Economic Review* 3(2)373–77.

———. 1993. "Policy Paradigms, Social Learning, and the State: The Case of Economic Policy-making in Britain." *Comparative Politics* 25(3)275–96.

———. 1992. "The Movement from Keynesianism to Monetarism: Institutional Analysis and British Economic Policy in the 1970s." Pp. 90–113 in *Structuring Politics: Historical Institutionalism in Comparative Perspective*, edited by Sven Steinmo, Kathleen Thelen, and Frank Longstreth. New York: Cambridge University Press.

———. 1989a. "Conclusion: The Politics of Keynesian Ideas." Pp. 361–93 in *The Political Power of Economic Ideas*, edited by Peter A. Hall. Princeton: Princeton University Press.

———, editor. 1989b. *The Political Power of Economic Ideas*. Princeton: Princeton University Press.

———. 1986. *Governing the Economy: The Politics of State Intervention in Britain and France*. New York: Oxford University Press.

Hall, Peter A., and David Soskice. 2001a. "An Introduction to Varieties of Capitalism." Pp. 1–70 in *Varieties of Capitalism*, edited by Peter A. Hall and David Soskice. New York: Oxford University Press.

———, editors. 2001b. *Varieties of Capitalism*. New York: Oxford University Press.

Hallerberg, Mark. 1996. "Tax Competition in Wilhelmine Germany and Its Implications for the European Union." *World Politics* 48(3)324–57.

Halliday, Terence, and Bruce Carruthers. 2010. *Bankrupt: Global Lawmaking and Systemic Financial Crisis*. Stanford: Stanford University Press.

———. 2007. "The Recursivity of Law: Global Norm Making and National Lawmaking in the Globalization of Corporate Insolvency Regimes." *American Journal of Sociology* 112:1135–1202.

Hammersly, Martyn, and Paul Atkinson. 1995. "Insider Accounts: Listening and Asking Questions." Pp. 124–56 in *Ethnography: Principles in Practice*, 2nd edition, edited by Martyn Hammersly and Paul Atkinson. London: Routledge.

Hancké, Bob, Martin Rhodes, and Mark Thatcher, editors. 2007a. *Beyond Varieties of Capitalism*. New York: Oxford University Press.

———. 2007b. "Introduction: Beyond Varieties of Capitalism." Pp. 3–38 in *Beyond Varieties of Capitalism*, edited by Bob Hancké, Martin Rhodes, and Mark Thatcher. New York: Oxford University Press.

Hannan, Michael, and John Freeman. 1977. "The Population Ecology of Organizations." *American Journal of Sociology* 82:929–64.

Harvey, David. 2005. *A Brief History of Neoliberalism*. New York: Oxford University Press.

Hattam, Victoria. 1993. *Labor Visions and State Power*. Princeton: Princeton University Press.

Hay, Colin. 2001. "The 'Crisis' of Keynesianism and the Rise of Neoliberalism in Britain: An Ideational Institutionalist Approach." Pp. 193–218 in *The Rise of Neoliberalism and Institutional Analysis*, edited by John L. Campbell and Ove K. Pedersen. Princeton: Princeton University Press.

Heclo, Hugh. 1974. *Modern Social Politics in Britain and Sweden*. New Haven: Yale University Press.

Hedström, Peter, and Richard Swedberg. 1998. *Social Mechanisms: An Analytical Approach to Social Theory*. New York: Cambridge University Press.

Held, David, Anthony McGrew, David Goldblatt, and Jonathan Perraton. 1999. *Global Transfor-mations*. Stanford: Stanford University Press.

Heugens, Pursey, and Michel W. Lander. 2009. "Structure! Agency! And Other Quarrels: A Meta-Analysis of Institutional Theories of Organizations." *Academy of Management Journal* 52(1)61–85.

Hicks, Alexander, and Lane Kenworthy. 1998. "Cooperation and Political Economic Performance in Affluent Democratic Capitalism." *American Journal of Sociology* 103:1631–72.

Hirsch, Paul M. 1997. "Sociology without Social Structure: Neoinstitutional Theory Meets Brave New World." *American Journal of Sociology* 102:1702–23.

Hirsch, Paul M., and Michael Lounsbury. 1997. "Ending the Family Quarrel: Toward a Reconcili-ation of 'Old' and 'New' Institutionalisms." *American Behavioral Scientist* 40(4)406–18.

Hodson, Randy. 1999. *Analyzing Documentary Accounts*. Thousand Oaks, CA: Sage.

Hollingsworth, J. Rogers. 1997. "The Institutional Embeddedness of American Capitalism." Pp. 133–47 in *Political Economy of Modern Capitalism*, edited by Colin Crouch and Wolf-gang Streeck. Thousand Oaks, CA: Sage.

Hollingsworth, J. Rogers, and Robert Boyer, editors. 1997. *Contemporary Capitalism: The Em-beddedness of Institutions*. New York: Cambridge University.

Hollingsworth, J. Rogers, Philippe Schmitter, and Wolfgang Streeck, editors. 1994. *Governing Capitalist Economies*. New York: Oxford University Press.

Höpner, Martin. 2005. "What Connects Industrial Relations and Corporate Governance? Ex-plaining Institutional Complementarity." *Socio-Economic Review* 3(2)331–58.

Howell, Chris. 2009. "The Transformation of French Industrial Relations: Labor Representation and the State in a Post-*Dirigiste* Era." *Politics and Society* 37:229–56.

Hruschka, Daniel, Deborah Schwartz, Daphne Cobb St. John, Erin Picone-Decaro, Richard Jenkins, and James Carey. 2004. "Reliability in Coding Open-Ended Data: Lessons Learned from HIV Behavioral Research." *Field Methods* 16(3)307–31.

Hunter, Floyd. 1969. *Community Power Structure: Power of Decision Makers*. Chapel Hill: Uni-versity of North Carolina Press.

International Bank for Reconstruction and Development/World Bank. 2004. *Doing Business in 2004: Understanding Regulation*. Washington, DC: World Bank/Oxford University Press. http://www.doingbusiness.org/~/media/FPDKM/Doing%20Business/Documents/Annual -Reports/English/DB04-FullReport.pdf. Accessed February 2012.

Iversen, Torben. 1999. *Contested Economic Institutions*. New York: Cambridge University Press.

Jacoby, Sanford. 2005. *The Embedded Corporation: Corporate Governance and Employment Rela-tions in Japan and the United States*. Princeton: Princeton University Press.

James, Simon. 1993. "The Idea Brokers: The Impact of Think Tanks on British Government." *Public Administration* 71(Winter)491–506.

Joyce, Philip G. 2011. *The Congressional Budget Office: Honest Numbers, Power and Policymak-ing*. Washington, DC: Georgetown University Press.

Judt, Tony. 2006. *Postwar: A History of Europe since 1945*. New York: Penguin.

Kalev, Alexandra, Frank Dobbin, and Erin Kelly. 2006. "Best Practices or Best Guesses? Di-versity Management and the Remediation of Inequality." *American Sociological Review* 71:589–617.

Kapstein, Ethan. 1994. *Governing the Global Economy: International Finance and the State*. Cambridge, MA: Harvard University Press.

Katzenstein, Peter J. 2003. "Small States and Small States Revisited." *New Political Economy* 8(1)9–30.

———, editor. 1996. *The Culture of National Security*. New York: Columbia University Press.

———. 1987. *Policy and Politics in West Germany*. Philadelphia: Temple University Press.

———. 1985. *Small States in World Markets: Industrial Policy in Europe*. Ithaca: Cornell Univer-sity Press.

———. 1984. *Corporatism and Change: Austria, Switzerland, and the Politics of Industry*. Ithaca: Cornell University Press.

———, editor. 1978. *Between Power and Plenty*. Madison: University of Wisconsin Press.

Kay, Adrian. 2006. *The Dynamics of Public Policy*. Cheltenham: Edward Elgar.

Kenworthy, Lane. 2011. *Progress for the Poor*. New York: Oxford University Press.

———. 2006. "Institutional Coherence and Macroeconomic Performance." *Socio-Economic Review* 4:69–91.

———. 2004. *Egalitarian Capitalism*. New York: Russell Sage Foundation.

———. 1997. "Globalization and Economic Convergence." *Competition and Change* 2:1–64.

Kingdon, John. 1995. *Agendas, Alternatives, and Public Policies*, 2nd edition. New York: HarperCollins.

Kitschelt, Herbert, Peter Lange, Gary Marks, and John Stephens, editors. 1999. *Continuity and Change in Contemporary Capitalism*. New York: Cambridge University Press.

Kjær, Peter, and Ove K. Pedersen. 2001. "Translating Liberalization: Neoliberalism in the Danish Negotiated Economy." Pp. 219–48 in *The Rise of Neoliberalism and Institutional Analysis*, edited by John L. Campbell and Ove K. Pedersen. Princeton: Princeton University Press.

Knorr Cetina, Karin. 1999. *Epistemic Communities*. Cambridge, MA: Harvard University Press.

Krasner, Stephen. 1984. "Approaches to the State: Alternative Conceptions and Historical Dynamics." *Comparative Politics* 16(2)223–46.

Krippendorf, Klaus. 1980. *Content Analysis: An Introduction to Its Methodology*. Beverley Hills, CA: Sage.

Kristensen, Peer Hull, and Jonathan Zeitlin. 2005. *Local Players in Global Games*. New York: Oxford University Press.

Krugman, Paul. 2009. *The Return of Depression Economics and the Crisis of 2008*. New York: Norton.

Kuhlmann, Ellen, Judith Allsop, and Mike Saks. 2009. "Professional Governance and Public Control: A Comparison of Healthcare in the United Kingdom and Germany." *Current Sociology* 57(4)511–28.

Kurasaki, Karen S. 2000. "Intercoder Reliability from Validating Conclusions Drawn from Open-Ended Interview Data." *Field Methods* 12(3)179–94.

Lallement, Michel. 2006. "New Patterns of Industrial Relations and Political Action since the 1980s." Pp. 50–79 in *Changing France: The Politics That Markets Make*, edited by Pepper Culpepper, Peter A. Hall, and Bruno Palier. New York: Palgrave.

Lane, Christel. 2005. "Institutional Transformation and System Change: Changes in the Corporate Governance of German Corporations." Pp. 78–109 in *Changing Capitalisms? Internationalization, Institutional Change, and Systems of Economic Organization*, edited by Glenn Morgan, Richard Whitley, and Eli Moen. New York: Oxford University Press.

Lash, Scott, and John Urry. 1987. *The End of Organized Capitalism*. Madison: University of Wisconsin Press.

Lees-Marshment, Jennifer. 2009. *Political Marketing: Principles and Applications*. London: Routledge.

Le Galès, Patrick. 2006. "The Ongoing March of Decentralization within the Post-Jacobin State." Pp. 198–219 in *Changing France: The Politics That Markets Make*, edited by Pepper Culpepper, Peter A. Hall, and Bruno Palier. New York: Palgrave.

Lehmbruch, Gerhard. 1979. "Consociational Democracy, Class Conflict and the New Corporatism." Pp. 53–61 in *Trends toward Corporatist Intermediation*, edited by Philippe C. Schmitter and Gerhard Lehmbruch. London: Sage.

Leicht, Kevin, and Mary Fennell. 1997. "The Changing Organizational Context of Professional Work." *Annual Review of Sociology* 23:215–31.

Leicht, Kevin, Tony Walter, Ivan Sainsaulieu, and Scott Davies. 2009. "New Public Management and New Professionalism across Nations and Contexts." *Current Sociology* 57(4)581–605.

Levy, Jonah. 1999. *Tocqueville's Revenge: State, Society, and Economy in Contemporary France*. Cambridge, MA: Harvard University Press.

Lindblom, Charles. 1959. "The Science of Muddling Through." *Public Administration Review* 19:79–88.

Lindvall, Johannes. 2009. "The Real but Limited Influence of Expert Ideas." *World Politics* 61(4)703–30.

MacDonald, Keith M. 1995. *The Sociology of the Professions*. Thousand Oaks, CA: Sage.

Madsen, Per Kongshøj. 2006. "How Can It Fly? The Paradox of a Dynamic Labor Market in a Scandinavian Welfare State." Pp. 321–55 in *National Identity and the Varieties of Capitalism: The Danish Experience*, edited by John L. Campbell, John A. Hall, and Ove K. Pedersen. Montreal: McGill-Queen's University Press.

Mahoney, James, and Kathleen Thelen, editors. 2010a. *Explaining Institutional Change*. New York: Cambridge University Press.

———. 2010b. "A Theory of Gradual Institutional Change." Pp. 1–37 in *Explaining Institutional Change*, edited by James Mahoney and Kathleen Thelen. New York: Cambridge University Press.

Mannheim, Karl. 1936. *Ideology and Utopia*. New York: Harcourt, Brace and World.

Mansbridge, Jane. 1992. "A Deliberative Perspective on Neocorporatism." *Politics and Society* 20(4)493–504.

March, James. 2010. *The Ambiguities of Experience*. Ithaca: Cornell University Press.

Marcussen, Martin. 2000. *Ideas and Elites: The Social Construction of Economic and Monetary Union*. Aalborg, Denmark: Aalborg University Press.

Marglin, Stephen, and Juliet Schor, editors. 1990. *The Golden Age of Capitalism*. New York: Oxford University Press.

Marier, Patrik. 2002. "Where Did All the Bureaucrats Go? Role and Influence of the Public Bureaucracy in the Swedish and French Pension Reform Debate." Paper presented at the European Consortium for Political Research, Turin, Italy, March 22–27.

Martin, Cathie Jo. 2006. "Corporatism in the Postindustrial Age: Employers and Social Policy in the Little Land of Denmark." Pp. 271–94 in *National Identity and the Varieties of Capitalism: The Danish Experience*, edited by John L. Campbell, John A. Hall, and Ove K. Pedersen. Montreal: McGill-Queen's University Press.

———. 2005. "Corporatism from the Firm Perspective." *British Journal of Political Science* 35(1)127–48.

Marx, Karl, and Frederick Engels. 1970. *The German Ideology*. New York: International.

Mason, Jennifer. 2002. *Qualitative Researching*, 2nd edition. Thousand Oaks, CA: Sage.

Matzner, Egon, and Wolfgang Streeck, editors. 1991. *Beyond Keynesianism*. Aldershot: Edward Elgar.

Mauthner, Natasha, Odette Parry, and Kathryn Backett-Milburn. 1998. "The Data Are Out There, or Are They? Implications for Archiving and Revisiting Qualitative Data." *Sociology* 32(4)733–45.

McGann, James G., and R. Kent Weaver, editors. 2000. *Think Tanks and Civil Societies*. New York: Transaction.

McKenzie, Richard B., and Dwight R. Lee. 1991. *Quicksilver Capital*. New York: Free Press.

McNamara, Kathleen. 1998. *The Currency of Ideas: Monetary Politics in the European Union*. Ithaca: Cornell University Press.

Medvetz, Thomas. 2012. *Think Tanks in America*. Chicago: Chicago University Press.

Meyer, John W., John Boli, George M. Thomas, and Francisco O. Ramirez. 1997a. "World Society and the Nation State." *American Journal of Sociology* 103(1)144–81.

Meyer, John W., David Frank, Ann Hironaka, Evan Schofer, and Nancy B. Tuma. 1997b. "The Structuring of a World Environmental Regime, 1870–1990." *International Organization* 51:623–51.

Meyer, John W., and Brian Rowan. 1977. "Institutionalized Organizations: Formal Structure as Myth and Ceremony." *American Journal of Sociology* 83:340–63.

Miles, Matthew B., and A. Michael Huberman. 1984. *Qualitative Data Analysis: A Sourcebook of New Methods*. Beverly Hills, CA: Sage.

Mirowski, Philip, and Dieter Plehwe, editors. 2009. *The Road from Mont Pelerin: The Making of the Neoliberal Thought Collective*. Cambridge, MA: Harvard University Press.

Mizruchi, Mark S., and Lisa C. Fein. 1999. "The Social Construction of Organizational Knowledge: A Study of the Uses of Coercive, Mimetic, and Normative Isomorphism." *Administrative Science Quarterly* 44:653–83.

Morgan, Glenn, John L. Campbell, Colin Crouch, Ove K. Pedersen, and Richard Whitley, editors. 2010. *The Oxford Handbook of Comparative Institutional Analysis.* New York: Oxford University Press.

Morrissey, Elizabeth R. 1974. "Sources of Error in the Coding of Questionnaire Data." *Sociological Methods and Research* 3(2)209–32.

Mudge, Stephany. 2011. "What's Left of Leftism? Neoliberal Politics in Western Party Systems, 1945–2008." *Social Science History* 35:337–80.

———. 2008. "What Is Neoliberalism?" *Socio-Economic Review* 4:703–31.

Mueller-Jentsch, Walther. 1995. "Germany: From Collective Voice to Co-Management." Pp. 53–78 in *Works Councils*, edited by Joel Rogers and Wolfgang Streeck. Chicago: University of Chicago Press.

Obach, Brian. 2010. "Political Opportunity and Social Movement Coalitions: The Role of Policy Segmentation and Nonprofit Tax Law." Pp. 197–218 in *Strategic Alliances: Coalition Building and Social Movements*, edited by Nella Van Dyke and Holly McCammon. Minneapolis: University of Minnesota Press.

Offe, Claus. 1981. "The Attribution of Public Status to Interest Groups: Observations on the West German Case." Pp. 123–58 in *Organizing Interests in Western Europe*, edited by Suzanne Berger. New York: Cambridge University Press.

Organization for Economic Cooperation and Development. 2004. *Employment Outlook, 2004.* Paris: OECD.

Orren, Karen, and Stephen Skowronek. 1994. "Beyond the Iconography of Order: Notes for a 'New Institutionalism.'" Pp. 311–30 in *The Dynamics of American Politics*, edited by Lawrence D. Dodd and Calvin Jillson. Boulder: Westview.

Øhrgaard, Per. 2012. "Fichte and Grundtvig as Educators of the People." Unpublished manuscript, Department of Business and Politics, Copenhagen Business School.

Østergård, Uffe. 2006. "Denmark: A Big Small State—The Peasant Roots of Danish Modernity." Pp. 51–98 in *National Identity and the Varieties of Capitalism: The Danish Experience*, edited by John L. Campbell, John A. Hall, and Ove K. Pedersen. Montreal: McGill-Queen's University Press.

Palier, Bruno. 2006. "The Long Good Bye to Bismarck? Changes in the French Welfare State." Pp. 107–28 in *Changing France: The Politics That Markets Make*, edited by Pepper Culpepper, Peter A. Hall, and Bruno Palier. New York: Palgrave.

Palier, Bruno, and Kathleen Thelen. 2012. "Dualization and Institutional Competitiveness: Industrial Relations, Labor Market and Welfare State Changes in France and Germany." Pp. 201–25 in *The Age of Dualization: Structures, Policies, Politics and Divided Outcomes*, edited by Patrick Emmenegger, Silja Häusermann, Bruno Palier, and Martin Seeleib-Kaiser. New York: Oxford University Press.

———. 2010. "Institutionalizing Dualism: Complementarities and Change in France and Germany." *Politics and Society* 38:119–48.

Palmquist, Michael E., Kathleen M. Carley, and Thomas A. Dale. 1997. "Applications of Computer-Aided Text Analysis: Analyzing Literary and Nonliterary Texts." Pp. 171–89 in *Text Analysis for the Social Sciences*, edited by Carl W. Roberts. Mahwah, NJ: Lawrence Erlbaum.

Parsons, Craig. 2007. *How to Map Arguments in Political Science.* New York: Oxford University Press.

Pauly, Louis. 1998. *Who Elected the Bankers? Surveillance and Control in the World Economy.* Ithaca: Cornell University Press.

Pedersen, Ove K. 2011. *Konkurrencestaten.* Copenhagen: Hans Reitzels Forlag.

———. 2010. "Institutional Competitiveness: How Nations Came to Compete." Pp. 625–58 in *The Oxford Handbook of Comparative Institutional Analysis*, edited by Glenn Morgan, John L. Campbell, Colin Crouch, Ove K. Pedersen, and Richard Whitley. New York: Oxford University Press.

———. 2006a. "Denmark: An Ongoing Experiment." Pp. 453–70 in *National Identity and the Varieties of Capitalism: The Danish Experience*, edited by John L. Campbell, John A. Hall, and Ove K. Pedersen. Montreal: McGill-Queen's University Press.

———. 2006b. "Negotiated Economy: Corporatism and Beyond." Pp. 245–70 in *National Identity and the Varieties of Capitalism*, edited by John L. Campbell, John A. Hall, and Ove K. Pedersen. Montreal: McGill-Queen's University Press.

———. 1991. "Nine Questions to a Neoinstitutional Theory in Political Science." *Scandinavian Political Studies* 14(2)125–48.

Pierson, Paul. 2000a. "Increasing Returns, Path Dependence, and the Study of Politics." *American Political Science Review* 94(2)251–67.

———. 2000b. "Not Just What, but When: Timing and Sequence in Political Processes." *Studies in American Political Development* 14(Spring)72–92.

———. 1994. *Dismantling the Welfare State? Reagan, Thatcher and the Politics of Retrenchment.* New York: Cambridge University Press.

Piore, Michael J. 1995. *Beyond Individualism: How Social Demands of the New Identity Groups Challenge American Political and Economic Life.* Cambridge, MA: Harvard University Press.

Piore, Michael J., and Charles F. Sabel. 1984. *The Second Industrial Divide.* New York: Basic Books.

Porter, Michael. 1998. *The Competitive Advantage of Nations.* New York: Free Press.

Prasad, Monica. 2012. *The Land of Too Much: American Abundance and the Paradox of Poverty.* Cambridge, MA: Harvard University Press.

———. 2006. *The Politics of Free Markets: The Rise of Neoliberal Economic Policies in Britain, France, Germany and the United States.* Chicago: Chicago University Press.

———. 2005. "Why Is France so French? Culture, Institutions and Neoliberalism, 1974–1981." *American Journal of Sociology* 111:357–407.

Ptak, Ralf. 2009. "Neoliberalism in Germany: Revisiting the Ordoliberal Foundations of the Social Market Economy." Pp. 98–138 in *The Road from Mont Pelerin: The Making of the Neoliberal Thought Collective*, edited by Philip Mirowski and Dieter Plehwe. Cambridge, MA: Harvard University Press.

Ricci, David. 1993. *The Transformation of American Politics.* New Haven: Yale University Press.

Rich, Andrew. 2004. *Think Tanks, Public Policy, and the Politics of Expertise.* New York: Cambridge University Press.

Richardson, Jeremy, editor. 1982. *Policy Styles in Western Europe.* London: George Allen and Unwin.

Roberts, Carl W. 1997. "Semantic Text Analysis: On the Structure of Linguistic Ambiguity in Ordinary Discourse." Pp. 55–78 in *Text Analysis for the Social Sciences*, edited by Carl W. Roberts. Mahwah, NJ: Lawrence Erlbaum.

Roe, Mark J. 2003. *Political Determinants of Corporate Governance: Political Context, Corporate Impact.* New York: Oxford University Press.

Rose, Richard. 2005. "Giving Direction to Government in Comparative Perspective." Pp. 72–99 in *The Executive Branch*, edited by Joel Aberbach and Mark Peterson. New York: Oxford University Press.

Rosenthal, Robert. 1987. *Judgment Studies: Design, Analysis, and Meta-Analysis.* New York: Cambridge University Press.

Rubin, Herbert, and Irene Rubin. 2005. *Qualitative Interviewing.* Thousand Oaks, CA: Sage.

Rueschemeyer, Dietrich and Theda Skocpol, editors. 1996. *States, Social Knowledge, and the Origins of Modern Social Policies.* Princeton: Princeton University Press.

Ruggie, John Gerald. 1982. "International Regimes, Transactions, and Change: Embedded Liberalism in the Postwar Economic Order." *International Organization* 36(2)379–99.

Sabel, Charles. 1993. "Studied Trust: Building New Forms of Cooperation in a Volatile Economy." Pp. 104–44 in *Explorations in Economic Sociology*, edited by Richard Swedberg. New York: Russell Sage Foundation.

Sabel, Charles, Archon Fung, and Bradley Karkkainen. 2000. *Beyond Backyard Environmentalism.* Boston: Beacon.

Salisbury, Robert. 1979. "Why No Corporatism in America?" Pp. 213–30 in *Trends toward Corporatist Intermediation*, edited by Philippe C. Schmitter and Gerhard Lehmbruch. London: Sage.

Schmidt, Vivien A. 2002. *The Futures of European Capitalism*. New York: Oxford University Press.

———. 2001. "Discourse and the Legitimation of Economic and Social Policy Change in Europe." Pp. 229–72 in *Globalization and the European Political Economy*, edited by Steven Weber. New York: Columbia University Press.

———. 2000. "Democracy and Discourse in an Integrating Europe and a Globalizing World." *European Law Journal* 6:277–300.

Schmidt, Vivien A., and Mark Thatcher, editors. 2013. *Resilient Liberalism in Europe's Political Economy*. New York: Cambridge University Press.

Schmitter, Philippe. 1979. "Still the Century of Corporatism?" Pp. 7–52 in *Trends toward Corporatist Intermediation*, edited by Philippe C. Schmitter and Gerhard Lehmbruch. London: Sage.

Schneiberg, Marc. 2007. "What's on the Path? Path Dependence, Organizational Diversity and the Problem of Institutional Change in the U.S. Economy, 1900–1950." *Socio-Economic Review* 5(1)47–80.

———. 2002. "Organizational Heterogeneity and the Production of New Forms: Politics, Social Movements and Mutual Companies in American Fire Insurance, 1900–1930." *Research in the Sociology of Organizations* 19:39–89.

———. 1999. "Political and Institutional Conditions for Governance by Association: Private Order and Price Controls in American Fire Insurance." *Politics and Society* 27(1)67–103.

Schneiberg, Marc, and Tim Bartley. 2001. "Regulating American Industries: Markets, Politics, and the Institutional Determinants of Fire Insurance Regulation." *American Journal of Sociology* 107:101–46.

Schneiberg, Marc, and Elisabeth Clemens. 2006. "The Typical Tools for the Job: Research Strategies in Institutional Analysis." *Sociological Theory* 24:195–227.

Schrad, Mark Lawrence. 2010. *The Political Power of Bad Ideas*. New York: Oxford University Press.

Schwartz, Herman. 2001. "The Danish 'Miracle'? Luck, Pluck, or Stuck?" *Comparative Political Studies* 3(2)131–55.

———. 1994. "Small States in Big Trouble: State Reorganization in Australia, Denmark, New Zealand, and Sweden in the 1980s." *World Politics* 46:527–55.

Sciulli, David. 2005. "Continental Sociology of Professions Today: Conceptual Contributions." *Current Sociology* 53(6)915–42.

Scott, W. Richard. 2008. *Institutions and Organizations*. Thousand Oaks, CA: Sage.

Scott, W. Richard, and Gerald F. Davis. 2007. *Organizations and Organizing: Rational, Natural and Open System Perspectives*. Upper Saddle River, NJ: Pearson Prentice Hall.

Searls, Ella. 1978. "The Fragmented French Executive: Ministerial Cabinets in the Fifth Republic." *West European Politics* 1(2)161–76.

Senghass, Dieter. 1985. *The European Experience: A Historical Critique of Development Theory*. Leamington Spa, UK: Berg.

Shonfield, Andrew. 1965. *Modern Capitalism*. London: Oxford University Press.

Simmons, Beth, Frank Dobbin, and Geoffrey Garrett, editors. 2008. *The Global Diffusion of Markets and Democracy*. New York: Cambridge University Press.

Skidelsky, Robert. 2009. *Keynes: The Return of the Master*. New York: Public Affairs.

Skocpol, Theda, and Vanessa Williamson. 2012. *The Tea Party and the Remaking of Republican Conservatism*. New York: Oxford University Press.

Skogstad, Grace. 2011. "Conclusion." Pp. 235–53 in *Policy Paradigms, Transnationalism and Domestic Politics*, edited by Grace Skogstad. Toronto: University of Toronto Press.

Skogstad, Grace, and Vivien Schmidt. 2011. "Introduction: Policy Paradigms, Transnationalism, and Domestic Politics." Pp. 3–35 in *Policy Paradigms, Transnationalism and Domestic Politics*, edited by Grace Skogstad. Toronto: University of Toronto Press.

Skowronek, Stephen. 1982. *Building a New American State*. New York: Cambridge University Press.

Smith, Andy. 2006. "The Government of the European Union and a Changing France." Pp. 179–97 in *Changing France: The Politics That Markets Make*, edited by Pepper Culpepper, Peter A. Hall, and Bruno Palier. New York: Palgrave.

Smith, James. 1991. *The Idea Brokers: Think Tanks and the Rise of the New Policy Elite*. New York: Free Press.

———. 1989. "Think Tanks and the Politics of Ideas." Pp. 175–94 in *The Spread of Economic Ideas*, edited by David Colander and A. W. Coats. New York: Cambridge University Press.

Soskice, David. 2007. "Macroeconomics and Varieties of Capitalism." Pp. 89–121 in *Beyond Varieties of Capitalism*, edited by Bob Hancké, Martin Rhodes, and Mark Thatcher. New York: Oxford University Press.

———. 1999. "Divergent Production Regimes: Coordinated and Uncoordinated Market Economies in the 1980s and 1990s." Pp. 101–35 in *Continuity and Change in Contemporary Capitalism*, edited by Herbert Kitschelt, Peter Lange, Gary Marks, and John Stephens. New York: Cambridge University Press.

Spence, Michael. 1981. "The Learning Curve and Competition." *Bell Journal of Economics* 12(1)49–70.

Stark, David. 1996. "Recombinant Property in East European Capitalism." *American Journal of Sociology* 101(4)993–1027.

Stedman Jones, Daniel. 2012. *Masters of the Universe: Hayek, Friedman, and the Birth of Neoliberal Politics*. Princeton: Princeton University Press.

Steinmo, Sven. 2010. *The Evolution of Modern States*. New York: Cambridge University Press.

———. 1993. *Taxation and Democracy*. New Haven: Yale University Press.

Steinmo, Sven, Kathleen Thelen, and Frank Longstreth, editors. 1992. *Structuring Politics: Historical Institutionalism in Comparative Perspective*. New York: Cambridge University Press.

Stiglitz, Joseph. 2009. *Freefall: America, Free Markets, and the Sinking of the World Economy*. New York: Norton.

Stinchcombe, Arthur. 1990. *Information and Organizations*. Berkeley: University of California Press.

Stone, Diane. 2004. "Introduction: Think Tanks, Policy Advice and Governance." Pp. 1–18 in *Think Tank Traditions*, edited by Diane Stone and Andrew Denham. Manchester: Manchester University Press.

Stone, Diane, and Andrew Denham, editors. 2004. *Think Tank Traditions*. Manchester: Manchester University Press.

Stone, Diane, Andrew Denham, and Mark Garnett, editors. 1998. *Think Tanks across Nations: A Comparative Perspective*. Manchester: Manchester University Press.

Strang, David. 2010. *Learning by Example: Imitation and Innovation at a Global Bank*. Princeton: Princeton University Press.

Strang, David, and Ellen Bradburn. 2001. "Theorizing Legitimacy or Legitimating Theory? Neoliberal Discourse and HMO Policy, 1970–1989." Pp. 129–58 in *The Rise of Neoliberalism and Institutional Analysis*, edited by John L. Campbell and Ove K. Pedersen. Princeton: Princeton University Press.

Streeck, Wolfgang. 2009. *Reforming Capitalism: Institutional Change in the German Political Economy*. New York: Oxford University Press.

———. 2005. "Requirements for a Useful Concept of Complementarity." *Socio-Economic Review* 3(2)363–66.

———. 1997a. "Beneficial Constraints: On the Economic Limits of Rational Voluntarism." Pp. 197–219 in *Contemporary Capitalism: The Embeddedness of Institutions*, edited by J. Rogers Hollingsworth and Robert Boyer. New York: Cambridge University Press.

———. 1997b. "German Capitalism: Does It Exist? Can It Survive?" Pp. 33–54 in *Political Economy of Modern Capitalism*, edited by Colin Crouch and Wolfgang Streeck. Thousand Oaks, CA: Sage.

Streeck, Wolfgang, and Philippe C. Schmitter. 1985. "Community, Market, State—and Associations? The Prospective Contribution of Interest Governance to Social Order." Pp. 1–29 in *Private Interest Government*, edited by Wolfgang Streeck and Philippe C. Schmitter. Beverly Hills, CA: Sage.

Streeck, Wolfgang, and Kathleen Thelen, editors. 2005. *Beyond Continuity*. New York: Oxford University Press.

Stucke, Andreas. 2011. "Quality Assurance through Procedures—Policy Advice by the German Science Council." Pp. 157–74 in *The Politics of Scientific Advice*, edited by Justus Lentsch and Peter Weingart. New York: Cambridge University Press.

Suleiman, Ezra. 1987. *Private Power and Centralization in France*. Princeton: Princeton University Press.

Survey of Think Tanks. 2007. Philadelphia: Foreign Policy Research Institute, Think Tanks and Civil Societies Program, University of Pennsylvania.

Swank, Duane. 2002. *Global Capital, Political Institutions and Policy Change in Developed Welfare States*. New York: Cambridge University Press.

Tashakkori, Abbas, and Charles Teddlie. 1998. *Mixed Methodology: Combining Qualitative and Quantitative Approaches*. Thousand Oaks, CA: Sage.

Thatcher, Mark. 2007. "Reforming National Regulatory Institutions: The EU and Cross-National Variety in European Network Industries." Pp. 147–72 in *Beyond Varieties of Capitalism*, edited by Bob Hancké, Martin Rhodes, and Mark Thatcher. New York: Oxford University Press.

———. 2005. "The Third Force? Independent Regulatory Agencies and Elected Politicians in Europe." *Governance: An International Journal of Policy, Administration and Institutions* 18(3)347–74.

Thelen, Kathleen. 2004. *How Institutions Evolve*. New York: Cambridge University Press.

———. 2003. "How Institutions Evolve: Insights from Comparative Historical Analysis." Pp. 208–40 in *Comparative Historical Analysis in the Social Sciences*, edited by James Mahoney and Dietrich Rueschemeyer. New York: Cambridge University Press.

———. 2000. "Why German Employers Cannot Bring Themselves to Dismantle the German Model." Pp. 138–69 in *Unions, Employers and Central Banks*, edited by Torben Iversen, Jonas Pontousson, and David Soskice. New York: Cambridge University Press.

———. 1999. "Historical Institutionalism in Comparative Politics." *Annual Review of Political Science* 2:369–404.

Thelen, Kathleen, and Ikuo Kume. 1999. "The Effects of 'Globalization' on Labor Revisited: Lessons from Germany and Japan." *Politics and Society* 27:476–504.

Thelen, Kathleen and Sven Steinmo. 1992. "Historical Institutionalism in Comparative Politics." Pp. 1–32 in *Structuring Politics: Historical Institutionalism in Comparative Analysis*, edited by Sven Steinmo, Kathleen Thelen, and Frank Longstreth. New York: Cambridge University Press.

Thomas, George, John Meyer, Francisco Ramirez, and John Boli, editors. 1987. *Institutional Structure: Constituting State, Society and the Individual*. Thousand Oaks, CA: Sage.

Thunert, Martin. 2004. "Think Tanks in Germany." Pp. 71–88 in *Think Tank Traditions*, edited by Diane Stone and Andrew Denham. Manchester: Manchester University Press.

———. 2000. "Players Beyond Borders? German Think Tanks as Catalysts of Internationalization." *Global Society* 24(2): 191–211.

Tiefken, Sven T. 2007. *Expertkommissionen im Politischen Prozess*. Berlin: Springer.

Tolbert, Pamela, and Lynne Zucker. 1983. "Institutional Sources of Change in the Formal Structure of Organizations: The Diffusion of Civil Service Reform." *Administrative Science Quarterly* 28:22–39.

United Nations. 2006. *Republic of France Public Administration Country Profile*. New York: United Nations, Division for Public Administration and Development Management, Department of Economic and Social Affairs.

U.S. Central Intelligence Agency. 2011. *CIA World Factbook*. Washington, DC: CIA. https://www.cia.gov/library/publications/the-world-factbook.

Visser, Jelle. 2009. "ICTWSS Data Base (Institutional Characteristics of Trade Unions, Wage Setting, State Intervention, and Social Pacts in 34 countries between 1960 and 2007." Amsterdam: University of Amsterdam, Amsterdam Institute for Advanced Labor Studies.

———. 2006. "Union Membership Statistics in 24 Countries." *Monthly Labor Review* 129(1)38–49.

Vogel, David. 1986. *National Styles of Regulation*. Ithaca: Cornell University Press.

Wagner, Gert. 2011. "Quality Control for the Leading Institutes of Economic Research in Germany: Promoting Quality within and Competition between the Institutes." Pp. 215–28 in *The Politics of Scientific Advice*, edited by Justus Lentsch and Peter Weingart. New York: Cambridge University Press.

Weaver, R. Kent, and James McGann. 2000. "Think Tanks and Civil Societies in a Time of Change." Pp. 1–37 in *Think Tanks and Civil Societies*, edited by James McGann and R. Kent Weaver. New Brunswick: Transaction.

Weber, Max. 1958. *The Protestant Ethic and the Spirit of Capitalism*. New York: Scribner.

———. 1946. "The Social Psychology of the World Religions." Pp. 267–301 in *From Max Weber*, edited by Hans Gerth and C. Wright Mills. New York: Oxford University Press.

Weber, Robert P. 1990. *Basic Content Analysis*, 2nd edition. Newbury Park, CA: Sage.

Weick, Karl. 1995. *Sensemaking in Organizations*. Thousand Oaks, CA: Sage.

Weidenbaum, Murray. 2009. *The Competition of Ideas: The World of the Washington Think Tanks*. New Brunswick: Transaction.

Weilemann, Peter R. 2000. "Experiences of a Multidimensional Think Tank: The Konrad-Adenauer-Stiftung." Pp. 169–86 in *Think Tanks and Civil Societies*, edited by James G. McGann and R. Kent Weaver. New York: Transaction.

Weir, Margaret, and Theda Skocpol. 1985. "State Structures and the Possibilities for 'Keynesian' Responses to the Great Depression in Sweden, Britain and the United States." Pp. 107–67 in *Bringing the State Back In*, edited by Peter Evans, Dietrich Rueschemeyer, and Theda Skocpol. New York: Cambridge University Press.

Weiss, Linda, editor. 2003. *States in the Global Economy*. New York: Cambridge University Press.

———. 1998. *The Myth of the Powerless State*. Ithaca: Cornell University Press.

Westney, D. Eleanor. 1987. *Imitation and Innovation: The Transfer of Western Organizational Patterns in Meiji Japan*. Cambridge, MA: Harvard University Press.

Westphal, James, Ranjay Gulati, and Steven Shortell. 1997. "Customization or Conformity: An Institutional and Network Perspective on the Content and Consequences of TQM Adoption." *Administrative Science Quarterly* 42:366–94.

Wilsford, David. 2001. "Running the Bureaucratic State: Administration in France." Pp. 963–77 in *Handbook of Comparative and Development Public Administration*, edited by Ali Farazmand. New York: Marcel Dekker.

Wilthagen, Ton, and Frank Tros. 2004. "The Concept of 'Flexicurity': A New Approach to Regulating Employment and Labor Markets." *Transfer* 10(2)166–86.

Zak, Paul J., and Stephen Knack. 2001. "Trust and Growth." *Economic Journal* 111(April) 295–321.

Zeitlin, Jonathan. 2003. "Introduction." Pp. 1–32 in *Governing Work and Welfare in a New Economy: European and American Experiments*, edited by Jonathan Zeitlin and David Trubek. New York: Oxford University Press.

Ziegler, J. Nicholas. 1997. *Governing Ideas: Strategies for Innovation in France and Germany*. Ithaca: Cornell University Press.

Zysman, John. 1983. *Governments, Markets, and Growth*. Ithaca: Cornell University Press.

Index

coercion: convergence and, 236–37, 239, 249–56, 259–62, 272; Denmark and, 14, 259–62, 272; France and, 14, 253–56; normative implications and, 327; partisanship and, 14, 249–53; United States and, 14, 249–53

collective bargaining, 41, 85n4, 131, 174

Cologne Institute for Economic Research (IW): convergence and, 243, 258; coordination/compromise policy and, 136–39, 142n68, 144, 148, 151n102, 156, 158n132, 166–67; influence and, 294n58, 295n63

Committee for Economic Development, 77

Committee for Responsible Federal Budget, 77

Communists: Denmark and, 176; France and, 86–87, 98, 118; Germany and, 131, 171

comparative political economy, 215, 232; advocacy organizations and, 220–22; capitalism and, 219–22; competition and, 221, 223; consensus and, 221; considerations for, 332–35; convergence and, 233, 236, 272, 274–75; cooperation and, 220–21, 223; crisis of ideas and, 221; crisis of ideology and, 222; economic forecasts and, 222; economic institutions and, 219; Foundation Market Economy (SM) and, 222; future research and, 332–35; Germany and, 129, 147, 168; globalization and, 219, 222; Golden Age and, 219, 222; Heritage Foundation and, 223, 225, 228–29; influence and, 305n102; Initiative New Social Market Economy (INSM) and, 222; institutional complementarity and, 219–23; intention and, 219; knowledge regimes and, 2, 4, 6–17, 22–25, 27, 29, 33–34; Marxism and, 223; negotiation and, 223; normative implications and, 325–26; orientation of, 2; perception and, 221–22; policy analysis and, 220, 223; policymakers and, 219–20; policy research organizations and, 220, 223; production regimes and, 219, 222; reform and, 219–21; research organizations and, 220–23; taxes and, 220; think tanks and, 221; United States and, 40

competition: absence of in civil society, 114–19; comparative political economy and, 221, 223; convergence and, 235–39, 249–53, 253, 257n71, 262, 272–75; crisis of corporatism and, 161–68; Denmark and, 173, 176, 185–86, 195, 201, 203, 206–10, 213; France and, 84, 94, 96, 106–7, 114–25, 253, 280; future research and, 332–33, 335, 339; Germany and, 26, 129–34, 157, 160n144, 161–69, 218, 221, 223, 257n71; globalization and, 185 (see also globalization); influence and,

280, 288, 293–94, 300, 302, 305–6, 309, 317; Internet and, 67; knowledge regimes and, 3, 5, 11, 13–14, 21–27, 31, 35; media and, 59, 62–64, 67; partisanship and, 39–43, 57, 59–67, 74, 78, 80–82, 216, 217, 249–53; policy research organizations and, 60–64; private organizations and, 60–64; race to the bottom and, 13; research design and, 348–49; research talent and, 62; state research organizations and, 64–67; taxes and, 13; United States and, 14, 26, 39–43, 57, 59–67, 74, 78, 80–82, 216, 217, 249–53

compromise: Denmark and, 1, 43, 172, 174n6, 175, 191–93, 199, 204, 208, 213; future research and, 332–33; Germany and, 32, 129–30, 132, 134, 149–63, 166n165, 167–70; independent policy analysis and, 225; influence and, 307, 310, 315–16; knowledge regimes and, 3, 7, 24, 32; United States and, 43, 75–76

Concord Coalition, 76–77

Confederation of Danish Employers (DA): convergence and, 247, 261, 263; European Union (EU) and, 201; negotiation and, 174–75, 177–78, 183–87, 190, 194–95, 198, 201–4, 209–10, 212

Confederation of Danish Industry (DI): convergence and, 286, 289; influence and, 285–86; negotiation and, 175, 185–87, 193, 195, 209, 212n146

Confederation of Professionals (FTF), 174

Congressional Budget Office (CBO): convergence and, 241, 246, 251–53, 267, 269; independent policy analysis and, 224–25; influence and, 281, 320; partisanship and, 53–57, 62, 65–66, 71, 81, 83

Congressional Research Service (CRS): convergence and, 266, 267n96; independent policy analysis and, 224; partisanship and, 53–57, 65–66, 71, 83

consensus: brotherhood of economists and, 197–99; comparative political economy and, 221; convergence and, 239, 244, 259–62; Denmark and, 1, 14, 25, 26, 172–73, 175–76, 178, 182, 185, 187–88, 191–99, 204, 208–11, 213, 218, 221, 239, 244, 259–62, 285, 311–16, 321, 330, 333; France and, 93, 109, 122; future research and, 342; Germany and, 133, 150, 153–55, 157, 333, 342; Golden Age and, 5; influence and, 285, 311–16, 321; knowledge regimes and, 5, 9, 14, 25, 26; negotiation and, 172–73, 175–76, 178, 182, 185, 187–88, 191–99, 204, 208–11, 213, 311–16; normative implications and,

consensus (*continued*)
330, 333; United States and, 56, 77; Washington Consensus and, 9

conservative parties, 131, 175, 200n105

Contract with America, 48, 290

convergence, 232; advocacy organizations and, 234, 240n25, 244–50, 255, 258, 263, 267–68, 270–71, 274–75; American Enterprise Institute (AEI) and, 244, 246, 248, 250, 267n98; banks and, 239, 241, 274n113; Berlin Social Science research Center (WZB) and, 247; Brookings Institution and, 240, 244, 246, 248–50, 254–55; causality and, 233, 237; Center for Alternative Social Analysis (CASA) and, 261, 270; Center for American Progress (CAP) and, 244, 247–48, 250–51, 253, 265; Center for Economic Research (OFCE) and, 254–55, 260n83, 263–64; Center for European Economic Research (ZEW) and, 243; Center for International Perspective Studies (CEPII) and, 242, 246, 248, 263, 264; Center for Labor Market Research (CARMA) and, 259, 270; Center for Political Studies (CEPOS) and, 241, 244, 247, 271; Center on Budget and Policy Priorities (CBPP) and, 263; coercion and, 236–37, 239, 249–56, 259–62, 272; Cologne Institute for Economic Research (IW) and, 243, 258; competition and, 235–39, 249–53, 257n71, 262, 272–75; Confederation of Danish Employers (DA) and, 247, 261, 263; Confederation of Danish Industry (DI) and, 286, 289; Congressional Budget Office (CBO) and, 241, 246, 251–53, 267, 269; Congressional Research Service (CRS) and, 267n96; consensus and, 239, 244, 259–62; constraints and, 233–39, 263–75; cooperation and, 251n57, 253, 259, 262, 270, 273; corporatist regimes and, 27, 256, 266, 269–71; Council of Economic Advisors (CEA) and, 244, 267; Council of Economic Analysis (CAE) and, 255, 267–68; Council of Economic Experts (CEE) and, 255–58, 267–68; crisis of ideas and, 253, 271; crisis of ideology and, 260–62; cross-national effects and, 233, 238–43, 253, 263, 266–68; Danish Confederation of Trade Unions (LO) and, 243, 247, 261n86, 263, 269; Danish Economic Council (DØR) and, 240, 260n83, 261; Danish National Center for Social Research (SFI) and, 260–61; Danish Rational Economic Agent Model (DREAM) and, 243, 259, 261; Denmark and, 197, 239, 243–44, 247–48, 259–63,
270–71, 274; dissemination and, 245–49; Economic and Social Research Institute (WSI) and, 243n33, 269; Economic Council of the Labor Movement (AE) and, 243, 259; economic forecasts and, 234, 241–42, 248, 251–52, 256, 260, 267, 269; economic institutions and, 237, 269–72; economic policy analysis and, 241–45; Economic Policy Institute (EPI) and, 246, 249–50, 253, 269–70; Employment Relations Research Center (FAOS) and, 260, 270; European Union (EU) and, 239, 260; executive branch and, 251–52; expertise and, 261; Foundation Market Economy (SM) and, 244, 271; France and, 239, 242, 244, 246–48, 253–56, 262–64, 267–68, 271, 274; French Institute for Research on Public Administration (IFRAP) and, 240, 246, 255, 267, 271; French Institute of International Relations (IFRI) and, 246, 248, 254; funding and, 245, 251, 253, 255, 264–66, 269–70, 272–75; future research and, 335–37; General Directorate of the Treasury and Economic Policy (DGTPE) and, 242, 254; German Institute for Economic Research (DIW) and, 257n71, 260n83; Germany and, 157, 159–60, 239–40, 243–44, 247–48, 254–58, 261n84, 262, 264n90, 267–72; globalization and, 236, 239, 270; Golden Age and, 234, 236, 253, 260, 270–71; governance and, 238; Government Accountability Office (GAO) and, 268–69; Heritage Foundation and, 240–41, 244–45, 249–51, 255, 267n98; influence and, 278, 318, 320; Initiative New Social Market Economy (INSM) and, 241, 244, 247–48, 271; Institute for Economic Research at the University of Munich (Ifo) and, 257–58, 260n83; Institute for Employment Research (IAB) and, 243, 269; Institute for Macroeconomic Forecasting (IMK) and, 243n33, 269; International Monetary Fund (IMF) and, 13, 241, 260n83, 274n113; Keynesianism and, 243; Kiel Institute for the World Economy (IfW) and, 260n83; knowledge regimes and, 4, 6, 12–14, 19, 27–29, 33–34, 234; labor and, 243–44, 255, 261n86, 263, 269–71; Leibniz Association and, 257–58, 261n84, 264n90, 272; limits of, 233–75; lobbyists and, 249, 267, 271; media and, 27, 245–51, 258, 266–67, 273; mimetic mechanisms and, 235–39, 249, 253–58, 262, 269, 273–75; mimicry and, 13–14, 239, 249–53, 258, 262, 273, 336; National Center for Policy Analysis (NCPA) and, 240, 263;

coordination/compromise policy (*continued*) 284–85, 288, 321, 330; Kiel Institute for the World Economy (IfW) and, 135, 136n24, 138, 144, 146n87, 149n98, 151n102, 158–59, 163, 166n165; Konrad Adenauer Foundation (KAS) and, 142–43, 166; Leibniz Association and, 138n42, 149n98, 158–61, 166–69, 171, 192, 197, 222–23, 257–58, 261n84, 264n90, 272, 311, 321, 329–30; Ludwig Maximilian University in Munich (LMU) and, 146; Max Planck Institute for the Study of Societies (MPIfG) and, 147–48, 162n150; ministerial research units and, 140–41; party foundations and, 141–43; policy analysis and, 130, 134, 135n22, 138, 140n57, 143, 148–64, 168; political–economic environment and, 130–35; political economy and, 233–39, 249, 252–53, 256, 258–59, 262, 271–75; Rhine-Westphalia Institute for Economic Research (RWI) and, 135, 136n24, 139, 163; semi-public scholarly research organizations and, 135–49, 153–54, 158–60, 167–71, 218; Social Democratic Party (SPD) and, 131–32, 140; social market economy and, 307–11; think tanks and, 134, 135n22, 137–38, 142–44, 148, 165, 167–68

Coors, Joseph, 1

Copenhagen Business School, 207

Copenhagen Institute, 188

corporatist regimes: bargaining and, 7; competition and, 161–68; convergence and, 27, 256, 266, 269–71; Denmark and, 25, 31–32, 59, 172–74, 177–78, 180, 182, 191, 200–201, 203, 209–11, 218, 227, 269–70, 314–15; France and, 86, 89, 94, 105–6, 124; Germany and, 24, 31–32, 59, 129–33, 139, 148–49, 161, 163–64, 167–71, 227, 256, 270–71, 309, 314–15; independent policy analysis and, 227; influence and, 309, 314–15; research design and, 343–44; United States and, 51, 59, 269, 270; Varieties of Capitalism School and, 33

Council of Economic Advisors (CEA): convergence and, 244, 267; France and, 91; influence and, 280, 282, 299–305, 310–11, 314–16, 318–19; partisanship and, 53–57, 66

Council of Economic Analysis (CAE): convergence and, 255, 267–68; dirigisme and, 91–94, 104n95, 109, 122–23, 127; influence and, 280, 284, 303–7, 311, 316–17; research design and, 345–46

Council of Economic Experts (CEE): convergence and, 255–58, 267–68; coordination/compromise policy and, 139–41, 148,

152–55, 157, 160, 167–68; influence and, 280, 284–85, 291, 297, 307–11, 314–16, 318

crisis of corporatism: competition and, 161–68; Germany and, 24, 26, 130, 134, 161–68, 178, 216, 218, 222, 270, 309; Golden Age and, 24, 26, 130, 134, 161–68, 178, 216, 218, 222, 270, 309

crisis of ideas: comparative political economy and, 221; convergence and, 253, 271; externalization and, 106–14; France and, 23, 84–85, 106–14, 124, 126, 221, 253; Golden Age and, 23, 84–85, 106–14, 124, 126, 217, 221, 271

crisis of ideology: comparative political economy and, 222; convergence and, 260–62; Denmark and, 24–25, 173, 199–211, 218, 222, 260–62; Golden Age and, 24–25, 173, 199–211

crisis of partisanship, 22–23, 26, 69–75, 80–81, 178, 216, 299

Croissance Plus, 97n67, 99–100, 111, 115, 287n38, 290

Daily Show, The (TV show), 63

Danish Center for Governmental Research (AKF), 180–81, 289

Danish Chamber of Commerce, 175

Danish Confederation of Professional Associations (AC), 174

Danish Confederation of Trade Unions (LO): convergence and, 243, 247, 261n86, 263, 269; independent policy analysis and, 224; influence and, 285, 320; negotiation and, 174, 177, 185–86, 191, 194–96, 201, 203n115, 204–5, 208–11, 214

Danish Economic Council (DØR): convergence and, 240, 260n83, 261; independent policy analysis and, 225; influence and, 280, 289–90, 311–18; negotiation and, 179, 181–82, 185, 192–98, 203n117, 205–7, 212–14

Danish Elderly Association, 206

Danish Federation of Small and Medium Sized Enterprises, 175

Danish National Bank, 312

Danish National Center for Social Research (SFI): convergence and, 260–61; influence and, 285n31, 294; negotiation and, 180–81, 206–7

Danish People's Party, 176

Danish Rational Economic Agent Model (DREAM): convergence and, 243, 259, 261; influence and, 293; negotiation and, 179, 181–82, 198, 202–3, 208

Danish Regions (DR), 174, 177

and, 98–99, 101n86, 115, 119n156, 126n176, 246, 292; Foundation Robert Schuman and, 98, 115, 115–19; fragmentation and, 303–7; French Institute for Research on Public Administration (IFRAP) and, 96–97, 101, 103n94, 105, 111–12, 114–17, 126, 224, 240, 246, 255, 267, 271; French Institute of International Relations (IFRI) and, 94–95, 105n99, 115n138, 116–19, 246, 248, 254; funding and, 94–95, 99–100, 109n112, 116, 119, 126; future research and, 325, 330, 333; Gaullists and, 86–88, 98, 111–12; General Directorate of the Treasury and Economic Policy (DGTPE) and, 91, 109, 111, 114, 116, 120, 122–23, 242, 254; globalization and, 85, 89, 99, 106–8, 111, 113–14, 124; Golden Age and, 20, 23–24, 85, 87, 89, 106–7, 110, 113–14, 123; Grandes Écoles system and, 87, 91, 101, 103–4, 109, 127, 216, 226–28, 283; inflation and, 106; influence and, 284, 286–88, 290–91, 293–97, 303–7, 317, 320–21; informal personal networks and, 103–6; Institute Choiseul and, 100, 102–3, 105n99, 115, 117–19, 247, 293; Institute for Economic and Social Research (IRES) and, 94–95, 106, 108; Institute for Enterprise (IDEP) and, 99, 111, 115, 117n148; Institute Montaigne and, 96–97, 98n73, 105n99, 105n100, 111–12, 114–19, 126, 221, 244, 246, 248, 255, 263, 271, 283, 287, 291–93, 296, 340; institutional complementarity and, 85, 106, 123, 125–26; intellectuals and, 101–2; intention and, 120; Keynesianism and, 92, 95, 107, 111, 117; labor and, 85–86, 88–89, 91–96, 105–6, 108–9, 115, 117, 119–21, 123, 284, 291, 297; lobbyists and, 97–101; Marxism and, 92; media and, 96, 102, 103n94; methodology on analysis of, 31–35; mimetic mechanisms and, 14, 253–56; Ministry for Work, Solidarity and Civil Service and, 120; Ministry of Finance and, 86, 88, 89n29, 91, 114n133, 119–20, 288, 291; Ministry of Labor and, 297; Mitterrand and, 87–88, 107; Movement of French Enterprises (MEDEF) and, 88, 94–95; National Assembly and, 86, 104, 292; National Center for Scientific Research (CNRS) and, 97n66, 108n111; National Council for Statistical Information (CNIS) and, 90, 120–22; National Council of French Employers (CNPF) and, 85, 88; National Front (FN) and, 87; National Institute for Statistics and Economic Studies (INSEE) and, 90–91, 94–96, 101, 104, 108, 114, 120–24, 127, 168, 179, 240, 260n83, 304n97,

305n103; National School of Administration (ENA) and, 87, 101n89, 105, 109, 116; National School of Statistics and Economic Administration (ENSAE) and, 101, 104, 109; negotiation and, 127; neoliberalism and, 86n11, 87–88, 91, 96, 107, 111, 118; normative implications and, 14, 253–56, 325, 330; parliament and, 86n11, 96, 98–99, 103, 127, 291, 293; perception and, 116n140, 125–26; philanthropy and, 104–5, 124–25; Planning Commissariat and, 86, 88, 90, 92, 94, 108, 121, 122n165, 272, 346; policymakers and, 84, 90, 92, 94, 100–113, 123–26; policymaking regimes and, 86–87, 93n47, 98, 104–5, 112–13, 123–24; policy recommendations and, 92–93, 96; policy research organizations and, 84, 89–98, 101, 103–28; political economy and, 85–90, 106, 114, 123–25, 130–35; political foundations and, 98–99; political institutions and, 105; populism and, 86n11; postwar era and, 85–88, 94, 123–24; presidential system of, 86–87; price setting and, 86; private money and, 18–19, 105, 112, 115, 126; production regimes and, 85, 88–89, 104–7, 112–13, 123; productivity and, 106; Rally for the Republic (RPR) and, 86–87, 98; reform and, 88, 107, 114, 121–22, 124, 297, 306–7; République des Idées and, 102, 113, 115, 117, 118n151, 247, 287; research design and, 343–46, 347n16, 347n17, 351, 354–56; research organizations and, 84, 89–96, 100–128; Retirement Advisory Council (COR) and, 93, 105, 109–10, 120, 122–23; Saint Simon Society and, 102; Sarkozy and, 110, 116, 121n164, 292; scholarly research organizations and, 90, 93–95, 99–100, 101n86, 108, 112, 121, 123, 125–26, 221; Socialists and, 86–88, 98, 109–10, 116n140, 287; stagflation and, 84, 88, 107, 124; state research organizations and, 84, 89–94, 104, 122–23, 216; statist regimes and, 14, 86, 89, 125, 216, 217, 227, 253, 271, 352; taxes and, 58–59, 95n58, 105, 112–13, 124; Terra Nova and, 115; think tanks and, 96, 98, 105, 108–19, 123–24; Timbeau and, 101n86, 107–10, 116, 118, 127; Tocqueville's revenge and, 107; Union for a Popular Movement (UMP) and, 87, 98, 110; Union for French Democracy (UDF) and, 86–87, 98; universities and, 58–59, 91–93, 101–4, 109, 116n139, 226, 303–4

Franz, Wolfgang, 146, 147, 153, 159, 243, 256–57

Free Democratic Party (FDP), 131, 141

French Institute for Research on Public Administration (IFRAP): convergence and, 240, 246, 255, 267, 271; dirigisme and, 96–97, 101, 103n94, 105, 111–12, 114–17, 126; independent policy analysis and, 224

French Institute of International Relations (IFRI): convergence and, 246, 248, 254; dirigisme and, 94–95, 105n99, 115n138, 116–19

French Regulation School, 304

Friedrich Ebert Foundation (FES), 98n71, 141–42, 247, 294n58, 297n72

Friedrich Naumann Foundation, 141, 142n64

functionalism, 11, 15–16, 221, 326

funding: convergence and, 245, 251, 253, 255, 264–66, 269–70, 272–75; Denmark and, 185, 187, 189, 195, 206–7, 210, 212; France and, 94–95, 99–100, 109n112, 116, 119, 126; future research and, 340–41; Germany and, 134–36, 138, 142–43, 145, 147–48, 158–59, 162, 165–66, 168, 170; government, 135, 166n166, 170, 185, 207; influence and, 295n63; normative implications and, 329; philanthropy and, 42, 44, 104–5, 124–25, 223; private, 22, 27, 58–59, 138, 145, 253, 264–66, 274, 329; public, 126, 138; state, 27; tax deductions and, 22; United States and, 44, 46, 50, 52, 58–62, 64–65, 67–68, 71, 80, 82

Future of Children, The (Brookings Institution), 57

future research: advocacy organizations and, 335–37; capitalism and, 333; causality and, 336; comparative political economy and, 332–35; competition and, 332–33, 335, 339; compromise and, 332–33; consensus and, 342; convergence and, 335–37; cooperation and, 339; democracy and, 332–33; Denmark and, 325, 330, 333, 341–42; economic forecasts and, 338; European Union (EU) and, 339; expertise and, 336, 340–42; expertise independence and, 340–42; France and, 325, 330, 333; funding and, 340–41; German Institute for Economic Research (DIW) and, 338; Germany and, 333, 335, 338–39, 341–42; globalization and, 335, 337–40; Golden Age and, 334, 337; governance and, 339–40; Heritage Foundation and, 335; institutional complementarity and, 334–35; Keynesianism and, 337–38; media and, 341–42; neoliberalism and, 335, 337–40; parliament and, 337; perception and, 334, 338; policy analysis and, 335, 339; policymakers and, 332–37, 342; policy research organizations and, 333–42;

production regimes and, 332–33, 335; research organizations and, 333–42; scholarly research organizations and, 336; stagflation and, 338; state research organizations and, 334; statist regimes and, 333; think tanks and, 339; United States and, 332–33, 341–42; universities and, 341–42

Garth, Bryant, 319

Gaullists, 86–88, 98, 111–12

General Directorate of the Treasury and Economic Policy (DGTPE): convergence and, 242, 254; dirigisme and, 91, 109, 111, 114, 116, 120, 122–23

German Consortium of Economic Research Institutes (ARGE), 153–55, 284

German Council of Science and Humanities (Wissenschaftsrat), 141, 158, 160, 257–58

German Institute for Economic Research (DIW): convergence and, 257n71, 260n83; coordination/compromise policy and, 94n56, 135–39, 146–47, 150, 158n132, 160, 166; future research and, 338

German National Science Council (DFG), 136

Germany: advocacy organizations and, 130, 134, 138, 143–49, 158n132, 163–69, 221–22, 224; Agenda 2010 and, 291; banks and, 130n6, 134, 137, 138n42, 140, 154, 166, 310–11; Berlin Social Science Research Center (WZB) and, 138n42, 142n68, 147–48, 152n111, 164n156, 166n165, 167, 247, 294; Bertelsmann Foundation and, 144, 247, 271, 288; Brookings Institution and, 137, 138n41, 146; Bundestag and, 132, 134, 143, 148, 155, 175; Bundeswehr Institute of Social Sciences (SOWI) and, 146n89, 160n43; cabinet members and, 132, 140, 141n58, 286, 345; capitalism and, 130, 134, 165; Center for European Economic Research (ZEW) and, 135–39, 146–47, 159, 166n165, 243, 284n26, 291; Christian Democratic Union (CDU) and, xvii, 131–32, 140, 143; Christian Social Union (CSU) and, 131–32, 140–41; coercion and, 14; Cologne Institute for Economic Research (IW) and, 136–39, 142n68, 144, 148, 151n102, 156, 158n132, 166–67, 243, 258, 294n58, 295n63; Communists and, 131, 171; competition and, 26, 129–34, 157, 160n144, 161–69, 218, 221, 223, 257n71; compromise and, 32, 129–30, 132, 134, 149–63, 166n165, 167–70; Confederation of Danish Employers (DA) and, 247; consensus and, 133, 150, 153–55, 157, 333, 342; convergence and, 157, 159–60,

239–40, 243–44, 247–48, 254–58, 261n84, 262, 264n90, 267–72; cooperation and, 131, 146; coordination and, 307–11; corporatist regimes and, 24, 31–32, 59, 129–33, 139, 148–49, 161, 163–64, 167–71, 227, 256, 270–71, 309, 314–15; Council of Economic Experts (CEE) and, 139–41, 148, 152–55, 157, 160, 167–68, 255–58, 267–68, 280, 284–85, 291, 297, 307–11, 314–16, 318; crisis of corporatism and, 24, 26, 130, 134, 161–68, 178, 216, 218, 222, 270, 309; current knowledge regime of, 135–71; demands for scientific policy advice and, 156–58; democracy and, 142, 144; Diet of German Industry and Commerce and, 130; Economic and Social Research Institute (WSI) and, 135–38, 140n57, 146, 148, 158n132, 167, 243n33, 269, 320; economic forecasts and, 135, 137–39, 141–42, 149–55, 159–60, 162, 167, 171; economic science and, 156–61; Essen Institute and, 138, 166; European Union (EU) and, 162n150; executive branch and, 132, 139, 218, 286; expertise and, 132–33, 140, 146, 152, 156, 163; Federal Employment Agency and, 136, 138, 243; federalist structure of, 24, 132–34, 144, 148, 158; Federal Ministry of Economics and Technology (BMWI) and, 141, 149, 149n98, 151–54, 256, 296; Federation of German Employer Associations (BDA) and, 130, 155n122; Federation of German Industry (BDI) and, 130–31, 134, 155n122, 164; Federation of German Trade Unions (DGB) and, 131, 134, 136; Foundation Market Economy (SM) and, 145, 163–64, 167, 222, 244, 271, 284; Free Democratic Party (FDP) and, 131, 141; Friedrich Ebert Foundation (FES) and, 98n71, 141–43, 145n82, 166n166, 170n171, 247, 294n58, 297n72; Friedrich Naumann Foundation and, 141, 142n64; funding and, 134–36, 138, 142–43, 145, 147–48, 158–59, 162, 165–66, 168, 170; future research and, 333, 335, 338–39, 341–42; German Consortium of Economic Research Institutes (ARGE) and, 153–55, 284; German Institute for Economic Research (DIW) and, 94n56, 135–39, 146–47, 150, 158n132, 160, 166, 257n71, 260n83, 338; German National Science Council (DFG) and, 136; globalization and, 130, 133–34, 144, 149, 156–57, 160–63, 167–68; Golden Age and, 20, 24, 130, 133, 149, 156–57, 161–68; Halle Institute for Economic Research (IWH) and, 135, 136n24,

163; Hamburg Institute for International Economics Archive (HWWA) and, 159; Hanns Seidel Foundation and, 141, 142n64, 142n66; Hans Böckler Foundation and, 136, 138, 269; Heinrich Böll Foundation and, 141–43, 166; inflation and, 140, 162; influence and, 280, 284, 286, 288–89, 291, 294–98, 307–11, 314–16, 318, 320–21; Initiative New Social Market Economy (INSM) and, 142n68, 144–45, 158n132, 163, 166–67, 222, 224, 241, 244, 247–48, 271, 288, 294; Institute for Economic Research at the University of Munich (Ifo) and, 94n56, 135–38, 146–47, 149n98, 150, 157, 159, 163, 166, 257–58, 260n83, 291, 294, 296; Institute for Employment Research (IAB) and, 136–39, 146n87, 156, 159–60, 243, 269; Institute for Macroeconomic Forecasting (IMK) and, 135–38, 146, 148, 150–51, 163, 166–67, 243n33, 269, 320; institutional complementarity and, 130, 161, 169; International Monetary Fund (IMF) and, 137, 138n42, 157; January meeting and, 153–55; Joint Economic Report and, 141, 148–55, 160, 162, 165, 168–71, 192, 221, 223, 256, 258, 284–85, 288, 321, 330; Keynesianism and, 131, 138–40, 150n99, 151, 155, 158n132; Kiel Institute for the World Economy (IfW) and, 135, 136n24, 138, 144, 146n87, 149n98, 151n102, 163, 166n165, 260n83; Konrad Adenauer Foundation (KAS) and, 141–43, 166; labor and, 129–34, 136, 137n33, 139–40, 145, 148, 150–56, 158n132, 161, 164, 167, 169, 227, 243, 269, 271, 291, 308–9, 316, 330; Left Party and, 131, 141–42; Leibniz Association and, 138n42, 149n98, 158–61, 166–69, 171, 192, 197, 222–23, 257–58, 261n84, 264n90, 272, 311, 321, 329–30; lobbyists and, 142, 145–46, 163–67; Ludwig Maximilian University in Munich (LMU) and, 146; Max Planck Institute for the Study of Societies (MPIfG) and, 147–48, 162n150; media and, 144, 148, 166n166; methodology on analysis of, 31–35; mimetic mechanisms and, 14, 256–58; ministerial research units and, 140–41; Ministry of Economics and, 310; Ministry of Finance and, 310; Ministry of Labor and Social Policies and, 310; negotiation and, 131–32, 143, 150, 170n171; neoliberalism and, 134, 138n45, 140n57, 144, 155, 163, 311; normative implications and, 14, 256–59, 325, 329–30; Organization for Economic Cooperation and Development

Germany (*continued*)

(OECD) and, 137, 138n42, 157; parliament and, 131–32, 142n69, 145, 155, 168, 170, 284, 286; partisanship and, 132, 138, 140, 143; party foundations and, 141–43; perception and, 130, 134, 149, 169; policy analysis and, 130, 134, 135n22, 138, 140n57, 143, 148–64, 168; policymakers and, 129, 131–37, 142, 144–45, 148, 154, 156, 160, 162, 165–71; policy recommendations and, 149–51, 154, 164, 169; policy research organizations and, 129–30, 134–35, 139–49, 153–56, 160–71; political economy and, 106, 129–34, 147–49, 156, 161–62, 167–71; postwar era and, 130, 133, 154; production regimes and, 130–31, 134, 148, 155, 164, 167–68, 171; productivity and, 161–62, 309; Quandt Foundation and, 144; reform and, 131, 134, 145, 155, 291, 308–9, 315; research design and, 343–45, 347n16, 347n17, 349, 352–56; research organizations and, 129–30, 134–49, 153–71; Rhine-Westphalia Institute for Economic Research (RWI) and, 135, 136n24, 139, 163, 260n83; Rosa Luxemburg Foundation and, 141–42; scholarly research organizations and, 135–49, 153–54, 158–60, 165–71, 218; Schröder and, 155, 162, 291; semi-public scholarly research organizations and, 135–49, 153–54, 158–60, 167–71, 218; Social Democratic Party (SPD) and, 131–32, 140; social market economy and, 307–11; state research organizations and, 140–41, 169, 218; statist regimes and, 129, 168–69; taxes and, 136, 145, 165, 167; think tanks and, 134, 135n22, 137–38, 142–44, 148, 165, 167–68; tripartite system of, 130, 136n28, 139, 148, 155n122, 167; unification of, 24, 156, 158–60, 164–65, 167–69, 218, 222; universities and, 19, 58–59, 135, 139–41, 146–49, 151n102, 154, 158, 160, 166, 218, 227, 243, 329–30, 341; Vodafone Foundation and, 144; wage negotiations and, 131; welfare state and, 133, 151

Gesamtmetall, 144

Gingrich, Newt, 48, 55, 73, 246, 252, 290

globalization, 215, 218, 231–32; comparative political economy and, 219, 222; convergence and, 236, 239, 270; Denmark and, 173, 176–77, 184–86, 199, 203, 211; Dobbin and, 6; France and, 85, 89, 99, 106–8, 111, 113–14, 124; future research and, 335, 337–40; Germany and, 130, 133–34, 144, 149, 156–57, 160–63, 167–68; influence and, 278, 318; neoliberal diffusion and, 337–40;

normative implications and, 325, 327–28, 331; research design and, 346; United States and, 40, 59, 67, 80, 82

Globalization Council, 184–85

Global Transformations (Held), 5

Golden Age, 231; basis of, 20; Bretton Woods and, 5, 20–21, 22n64, 170; comparative political economy and, 219, 222; consensus and, 5; convergence and, 234, 236, 253, 260, 270–71; crisis of corporatism and, 24, 26, 130, 134, 161–68, 178, 216, 218, 222, 270, 309; crisis of ideas and, 23, 84–85, 106–14, 124, 126, 217, 221, 271; crisis of ideology and, 24–25, 173, 199–211; crisis of partisanship and, 22–23; Denmark and, 20, 24–25, 173, 176–78, 199–204, 207, 211; end of, 4–6, 11–13, 20–29, 40, 59, 67, 82, 85, 89, 106–7, 113–14, 123, 133, 149, 157, 161, 163, 165, 167–68, 176, 199, 202–3, 207, 211, 215, 219, 222, 232, 236, 327, 337 (*see also* Globalization); foreign direct investment and, 20; France and, 20, 23–24, 85, 87, 89, 106–7, 110, 113–14, 123; future research and, 334, 337; Germany and, 20, 24, 130, 133, 149, 156–57, 161–68; Keynesianism and, 20; knowledge regimes and, 4–6, 11–13, 20–29, 34–35; normative implications and, 325, 327, 331; OPEC and, 21; productivity and, 20–21; research design and, 346; United States and, 20, 24–25, 40, 59, 67, 80, 82

Goodman, John, 48, 77

governance: convergence and, 238; future research and, 339–40; knowledge regimes and, 7, 30 (*see also* knowledge regimes)

Government Accountability Office (GAO): convergence and, 267–69; future research and, 335; independent policy analysis and, 224; influence and, 282, 286; partisanship and, 53–57, 65–66, 71–72, 77, 81, 83

Gramsci, Antonio, 17, 223

Grandes Écoles system, 87, 91, 101, 103–4, 109, 127, 216, 226–28, 283

Great Depression, 338

Green Party, 87, 131, 141

Growth Forum, 184

Guenard, Florent, 102

Hall, Peter, 2, 7–9, 219n3, 317n144

Halle Institute for Economic Research (IWH), 135, 136n24, 163

Halliday, Terrence, 13, 239

Hamburg Institute for International Economics Archive (HWWA), 159

Hamilton, Douglas, 241

Hanns Seidel Foundation, 141, 142n64, 142n66
Hans Böckler Foundation, 136, 138, 269
Hassett, Kevin, 44–45, 71
Heinrich Böll Foundation, 141–43, 166
Held, David, 5
Heritage Foundation: comparative political
    economy and, 223, 225, 228–29; conver-
    gence and, 240–41, 244–45, 249–51, 255,
    267n98; Denmark and, 188; dirigisme and,
    95, 97, 105; future research and, 335; inde-
    pendent policy analysis and, 220; influence
    and, 282, 287, 292; *Mandate for Leadership*
    and, 1; normative implications and, 330;
    soaring reputation of, 1–2; United States
    and, 45–52, 61n89, 62–63, 68, 70, 72–79, 95
Hicks, Christy, 61n90, 62–63, 245, 249–50,
    265
Hudson Institute, 45, 47, 48n38, 51, 57,
    78n152, 290, 295

idealists: independent policy analysis and,
    223–24, 227–28; knowledge regimes and, 18
independent policy analysis: advocacy orga-
    nizations and, 224–25, 228–29; Brookings
    Institution and, 228; Center for Economic
    Research (OFCE) and, 224; compromise
    and, 225; Congressional Budget Office
    (CBO) and, 224–25; corporatist regimes
    and, 227; Danish Confederation of Trade
    Unions (LO) and, 224; Danish Economic
    Council (DØR) and, 225; French Institute
    for Research on Public Administration
    (IFRAP) and, 224; Heritage Foundation
    and, 220; idealists and, 223–24, 227–28;
    Initiative New Social Market Economy
    (INSM) and, 224; labor and, 223; lobbyists
    and, 225, 229; materialists and, 223–24,
    227; neoliberalism and, 224; normative
    implications and, 226; policy research or-
    ganizations and, 223–28; political economy
    and, 228; political institutions and, 225n9;
    private money and, 225; scholarly research
    organizations and, 227; statist regimes and,
    227; taxes and, 225; think tanks and, 225,
    228–29; universities and, 226, 227–29
inequality, 127, 302
inflation, 1, 20; Denmark and, 200, 208;
    France and, 106; Germany and, 140, 162;
    OPEC and, 21; research design and, 355;
    stagflation and, 4, 9, 11, 21–22, 28; United
    States and, 67
influence, 15; advocacy organizations and,
    282, 288, 321; American Enterprise Institute
    (AEI) and, 282, 292; anecdotal evidence

of, 289–92, 320; banks and, 310–12; Berlin
Social Science Research Center (WZB) and,
294; Brookings Institution and, 282–83,
297n74; cabinet members and, 283–88, 296;
capitalism and, 306; causality and, 291, 304,
319; Center for American Progress (CAP)
and, 289–90, 292; Center for Economic Observation and Research for the Expansion
of Economy and Enterprise Development
(Coe-Rexecode) and, 292; Center for Economic Research (OFCE) and, 296; Center
for European Economic Research (ZEW)
and, 284n26, 291; Center for International
Perspective Studies (CEPII) and, 295; Center for Political Studies (CEPOS) and, 290;
citation counts and, 288, 293–94; claiming,
289–95; Cologne Institute for Economic
Research (IW) and, 294n58, 295n63; competition and, 280, 288, 293–94, 300, 302,
305–6, 309, 317; compromise and, 307, 310,
315–16; Confederation of Danish Industry
(DI) and, 286, 289; Congressional Budget
Office (CBO) and, 281, 320; consensus and,
285, 311–16, 321; convergence and, 278,
318, 320; cooperation and, 309, 315; coordination and, 307–11; corporatist regimes
and, 309, 314–15; Council of Economic Advisors (CEA) and, 280, 282, 299–305, 310–
11, 314–16, 318–19; Council of Economic
Analysis (CAE) and, 280, 284, 303–7, 311,
316–17; Council of Economic Experts
(CEE) and, 280, 284–85, 291, 297, 307–11,
314–16, 318; cross-national effects and,
277–78; Danish Center for Governmental
Research (AKF) and, 289; Danish Confederation of Trade Unions (LO) and, 285, 320;
Danish Economic Council (DØR) and, 280,
289–90, 311–18; Danish National Center
for Social Research (SFI) and, 285n31, 294;
Danish Rational Economic Agent Model
(DREAM) and, 293; democracy and, 314,
316; Denmark and, 280, 285–86, 289–91,
293, 297, 311–16, 318, 320–21; deregulation
and, 299, 306, 309, 313; difficulties of ascertaining, 278–81; direct, 281–86; Directorate
for the Coordination of Research, Studies
and Statistics (DARES) and, 287; Economic
and Social Research Institute (WSI) and,
320; Economic Council of the Labor Movement (AE) and, 285; economic forecasts
and, 285, 304, 310, 320; economic institutions and, 319; Economic Policy Institute
(EPI) and, 320; elections and, 278, 286, 292;
Employment Relations Research Center

influence (*continued*)

(FAOS) and, 320; European Union (EU) and, 13, 89n29; executive branch and, 280, 286; externalization and, 303–7; fields of organizations and, 277–79, 281, 298–316; Foundation Market Economy (SM) and, 284; fragmentation and, 303–7; France and, 284, 286–88, 290–91, 293–97, 303–7, 317, 320–21; Friedrich Ebert Foundation (FES) and, 294n58, 297n72; funding and, 295n63; German Consortium of Economic Research Institutes (ARGE) and, 284; Germany and, 280, 284, 286, 288–89, 291, 294–98, 307–11, 314–16, 318, 320–21; globalization and, 278, 318; Heritage Foundation and, 282, 287, 292; inconsistency and, 299–303; indirect, 286–89; individual organizations and, 281–98; Initiative New Social Market Economy (INSM) and, 288, 294; Institute for Economic Research at the University of Munich (Ifo) and, 291, 294, 296; Institute for Macroeconomic Forecasting (IMK) and, 320; intention and, 300, 307; International Monetary Fund (IMF) and, 304; investment and, 301–2, 305, 313, 315; Keynesianism and, 277–78, 298, 317–18, 320; labor and, 277, 284, 291, 297–99, 302, 304, 308–10, 313–14, 316; Leibniz Association and, 311, 321, 329–30; lobbyists and, 282–84, 291, 296; Marxism and, 304, 318; media and, 27–28, 281, 286–90, 293–95, 321; National Center for Policy Analysis (NCPA) and, 290, 296; National Institute for Statistics and Economic Studies (INSEE) and, 304n97, 305n103; National Research Council (NRC) and, 291; negotiation and, 311–16, 321; neoliberalism and, 277–78, 298–99, 301–14, 317–20; Office of Management and Budget (OMB) and, 310; Organization for Economic Cooperation and Development (OECD) and, 304; parliament and, 284, 286, 291, 293; partisanship and, 299–303; policy analysis and, 290, 303, 316–17; policymakers and, 276–98, 303–4, 307–8, 316–17, 318n145, 320–21; policy recommendations and, 291, 301, 304, 307, 310–13; policy research organizations and, 276–98, 303, 310, 312, 314, 316–17, 319–21; political economy and, 305n102, 311; political institutions and, 278; privatization and, 299, 309; production regimes and, 319–20, 326–27; productivity and, 298–302, 305, 309, 315; Progressive Policy Institute (PPI) and, 283, 320; reform and, 290–91,

293, 296, 297, 300–302, 306–9, 313, 315; research organizations and, 276–95, 298, 303, 310, 312, 314, 316–21; Resources for the Future (RFF) and, 297n74; scholarly research organizations and, 282, 294, 310–11, 320–21; social market economy and, 307–11; stability and, 298, 310–18; stagflation and, 308, 318; state research organizations and, 282; taxes and, 277–78, 290–91, 296, 299–302, 305, 308, 313, 315; Think Tank for Future Growth (TFV) and, 291; think tanks and, 277, 279n7, 279n9, 283, 286–87, 291, 296, 316–17; United States and, 278, 280, 286–87, 293, 297n74, 299–303, 307, 314–15, 318, 320–21; universities and, 303–4, 319–20; voodoo science and, 295–98

Initiative New Social Market Economy (INSM): comparative political economy and, 222; convergence and, 241, 244, 247–48, 271; coordination/compromise policy and, 142n68, 144–45, 158n132, 163, 166–67; independent policy analysis and, 224; influence and, 288, 294

Institute Choiseul, 100, 102–3, 105n99, 115, 117–19, 247, 293

Institute for Economic and Social Research (IRES), 94–95, 106, 108

Institute for Economic Research at the University of Munich (Ifo): convergence and, 257–58, 260n83; coordination/compromise policy and, 94n56, 135–38, 146–47, 149n98, 150, 157, 159, 163, 166; influence and, 291, 294, 296

Institute for Employment Research (IAB): convergence and, 243, 269; coordination/compromise policy and, 136–39, 146n87, 156, 159–60

Institute for Enterprise (IDEP), 99, 111, 115, 117n148

Institute for Macroeconomic Forecasting (IMK): convergence and, 243n33, 269; coordination/compromise policy and, 135–38, 146, 148, 150–51, 163, 166–67; influence and, 320

Institute Montaigne: convergence and, 244, 246, 248, 255, 263, 271; comparative political economy and, 221; dirigisme and, 96–97, 98n73, 105n99, 105n100, 111–12, 114–19, 126; future research and, 340; influence and, 283, 287, 291–93, 296

institutional complementarity: comparative political economy and, 219–23; coordination/compromise policy and, 130, 161, 169; Denmark and, 178, 210, 213; dirigisme and,

knowledge regimes (*continued*)
30–31; universities and, 10, 19, 30; welfare
states and, 4–7, 20. *See also specific country*
Knutsen, Anders, 185, 291
Koch, Charles, 48, 82
Koch, David, 48, 82
Konrad Adenauer Foundation (KAS), 141–43,
166
KPMG, 112
Kroker, Rolf, 156–57, 243

labor: collective bargaining and, 41, 85n4,
131, 174; convergence and, 243–44, 255,
261n86, 263, 269–71; Denmark and, 172,
174–75, 177–79, 183, 185–86, 189, 191–92,
194–96, 198, 201, 204, 206, 211–14, 218,
227, 255, 261n86, 263, 269–70, 313–14,
316, 330; France and, 85–86, 88–89, 91–96,
105–6, 108–9, 115, 117, 119–21, 123, 284,
291, 297; Germany and, 129–31, 133–34,
136, 137n33, 139–40, 145, 148, 150–56,
158n132, 161, 164, 167, 169, 227, 243, 269,
271, 291, 308–9, 316, 330; independent
policy analysis and, 223; influence and, 277,
284, 291, 297–99, 302, 304, 308–10, 313–14,
316; knowledge regimes and, 7–8, 20; normative implications and, 330; research design and, 346, 354; skilled, 299; unions and,
7, 41 (*see also* unions); United States and,
41, 43, 46, 51, 59, 65, 67, 81, 269–70, 302,
310; wage negotiations and, 131
Labor Market Commission, 183–84
Labor Market Report (Confederation of Danish Employers), 186
laissez-faire, 133, 266
Langhammer, Rolf, 144, 171
Larsen, Finn, 195n86, 195n87, 261, 263
Larsen, Jørn Neergard, 183–84, 212
Law Model, 179n24, 202–3
Left Party, 131, 141–42
Leibniz Association: convergence and,
257–58, 261n84, 264n90, 272; Germany
and, 138n42, 149n98, 158–61, 166–69, 171,
192, 197, 222–23, 257–58, 261n84, 264n90,
272, 311, 321, 329–30; influence and, 311,
321, 329–30
Levy, Jonah, 107
Liberal Alliance, 176
liberal parties, 131, 175, 200n105
LMU-Ifo Economics and Business Data
Center, 146
lobbyists: advocacy organizations and, 50,
51n46; American Enterprise Institute (AEI)
and, 267n98; convergence and, 249, 267,

271; Denmark and, 188, 195, 201, 206,
209–10, 212; France and, 97–101; Germany
and, 142, 145–46, 163–67; independent
policy analysis and, 225, 229; influence and,
282–84, 291, 296; knowledge regimes and,
24, 30–31; negotiation and, 206–10; United
States and, 41, 49–51
Local Government Denmark (LGDK), 174, 177
Lorot, Pascal, 103
Ludwig Maximilian University in Munich
(LMU), 146

Mandate for Leadership (Heritage Foundation), 1
Manière, Philippe, 96–97, 98n73, 105n99,
105n100, 111–12, 117, 126, 263–64
Mannheim, Karl, 18, 223
Marxism: comparative political economy and,
223; France and, 92; influence and, 304,
318; knowledge regimes and, 4n9, 17; nor-
mative implications and, 326, 340n18
Massachusetts Institute of Technology
(MIT), 54
Massardier, François, 287n38, 291
materialists: Center for American Progress
(CAP) and, 223–24; independent policy
analysis and, 223–24, 227; knowledge regimes and, 17–18
Max Planck Institute for the Study of Societies
(MPIfG), 147–48, 162n150
Mazo, Michael, 102
McAdam, Doug, 236
McKinsey & Company, 112
media: competition and, 59, 62–64, 67; convergence and, 27, 245–51, 258, 266–67, 273;
Denmark and, 202, 209–10; France and, 96,
102, 103n94; future research and, 341–42;
Germany and, 144, 148, 166n166; influence
and, 27–28, 281, 286–90, 293–95, 321;
knowledge regimes and, 27–28, 30; new,
27, 67, 73–74, 81, 247, 251, 273; normative
implications and, 329; partisanship and, 49,
59, 62–64, 67, 73–74, 76–77, 79, 81; press
releases and, 49, 180, 248; research design
and, 348–49; United States and, 49, 59,
62–64, 67, 73–74, 76–77, 79, 81
Media Tenor, 294
Medicare, 75
Medvetz, Thomas, 43, 71n132
Meese, Edwin, 1
Meyer, John, 12, 337
Micro-Data Labor Supply Model of the Economic Council (MILASMEC), 181n37
Microsoft, 112

negotiation (*continued*)
organizations and, 180–85; Simulation Model of the Economic Council (SMEC) and, 179n24, 181, 185, 198; state research organizations and, 178–80; Think Tank for Future Growth (TFV) and, 185; think tanks and, 185–89, 208

neoliberalism, 232; France and, 86n11, 87–88, 91, 96, 107, 111, 118; future research and, 335, 337–40; Germany and, 134, 138n45, 140n57, 144, 155, 163, 311; independent policy analysis and, 224; influence and, 277–78, 298–99, 301–14, 317–20; knowledge regimes and, 2, 4–6, 9–10, 13, 15–16, 28–29, 34; normative implications and, 328; productivity and, 298–99; research design and, 352–54; rise of, 2, 4–6, 9, 34

New Democrats, 52

Nixon, Richard, 67

nongovernmental organizations (NGOs), 13, 334

normative implications: advocacy organizations and, 329–30; capitalism and, 325, 329, 331; Center for Economic Research (OFCE) and, 329; coercion and, 327; consensus and, 330, 333; convergence and, 13–14, 226, 235–39, 249, 253–62, 269, 273–75, 325–28; cooperation and, 330; cross-national effects and, 335; Denmark and, 176, 259–62, 325, 330; economic institutions and, 328; France and, 14, 253–56, 325, 330; funding and, 329; Germany and, 14, 256–59, 325, 329–30; globalization and, 325, 327–28, 331; Golden Age and, 325, 327, 331; Heritage Foundation and, 330; independent policy analysis and, 226; institutional complementarity and, 326; intention and, 329; knowledge regimes and, 9, 13–14, 27–28, 29n67; labor and, 330; Marxism and, 326, 340n18; media and, 329; negotiation and, 176n16, 330; neoliberalism and, 328; perception and, 326; policy analysis and, 325; policymakers and, 325–31, 328; policy recommendations and, 329; policy research organizations and, 326–30; political economy and, 325–27; research design and, 349; summing up and, 325–31; three-way intersection of politics, economics, ideas and, 327; United States and, 325, 328n10, 330; universities and, 329–30

Office of Management and Budget (OMB): convergence and, 251–52; influence and, 282, 310; partisanship and, 53–55, 57, 65–66

Office of Technology Assessment (OTA), 273

oil prices, 21

OPEC (Organization of the Petroleum Exporting Countries), 21

organizational theory, 3n4

Organization for Economic Cooperation and Development (OECD): aggregate quantitative data and, 33; convergence and, 241, 260, 274n113; Denmark and, 188, 190; Germany and, 137, 138n42, 157; influence and, 304; policy research organizations and, 32n72

Palmer, Tom, 72–73

parliament: convergence and, 268–69; Denmark and, 173, 175, 177, 196, 200, 203, 269; France and, 86n11, 96, 98–99, 103, 127, 291, 293; future research and, 337; Germany and, 131–32, 142n69, 145, 155, 168, 170, 284, 286; influence and, 284, 286, 291, 293

partisanship: absence of party research organizations and, 51–52; advocacy vs. scholarly organizations and, 46–51; American Enterprise Institute (AEI) and, 43–48, 51, 54, 61–62, 68, 71, 76–78, 82; Center for American Progress (CAP) and, 49, 51–52, 58, 61–62, 74–75, 78n152, 79; Center on Budget and Policy Priorities (CBPP) and, 45, 47n34, 51, 64, 68, 73–74, 77, 78n152; coercion and, 14, 249–53; competition and, 39–43, 57, 59–67, 74, 78, 80–82, 216, 217, 249–53; Congressional Budget Office (CBO) and, 53–57, 62, 65–66, 71, 81, 83; Congressional Research Service (CRS) and, 53–57, 65–66, 71, 83; cooperation and, 26, 31, 39–40, 57, 65–66, 74, 76–82; Council of Economic Advisors (CEA) and, 53–57, 66; credibility and, 74–80; crisis of, 22–23, 26, 69–75, 80–81, 178, 216, 299; current U.S. knowledge regime and, 43–59; Democratic Leadership Council (DLC) and, 52; Democrats and, 39, 42, 45, 52, 55, 62, 68–76, 83, 224, 253, 265, 282–83; Denmark and, 178; Economic Policy Institute (EPI) and, 45–46, 47n34, 51, 58, 61–62, 64, 68, 78n152, 80; excessive, 253; Germany and, 132, 138, 140, 143; Government Accountability Office (GAO) and, 53–57, 65–66, 71–72, 77, 81, 83; inconsistency and, 299–303; influence and, 299–303; institutional complementarity and, 40, 59, 68–69, 82; Internet and, 74; labor and, 41, 46; market of ideas and, 59–67; Massachusetts Institute of Technology (MIT) and, 54; media and, 49, 59,

62–64, 67, 73–74, 76–77, 79, 81; National Center for Policy Analysis (NCPA) and, 48–49, 51, 68, 70–71, 77; National Research Council (NRC) and, 56–57, 65, 81; Office of Management and Budget (OMB) and, 53–55, 57, 65–66; policy analysis and, 43, 45, 48, 52, 53n59, 56, 58, 65; political-economic environment and, 41–43; private organizations and, 60–64; Progressive Policy Institute (PPI) and, 48, 52, 60, 63, 68, 76; prominence of state research organizations and, 52–57; Republicans and, 39, 42, 45, 48, 52, 55, 62, 68–69, 71, 73, 75–76, 83, 224, 282; Resources for the Future (RFF) and, 43, 44n24, 57, 61; think tanks and, 43–44, 46–48, 54, 60–62, 67, 69–78; Third Way and, 48; universities and, 57–59

party research organizations, 30, 51–52

Pedersen, Lars Haagen, 181, 198n93

Pedersen, Ove K., 5n15, 280n11, 335n5, 338n11, 349, 354

Penner, Rudolph, 76, 77, 248, 282, 291

perception: comparative political economy and, 221–22; convergence and, 270; Denmark and, 173, 205; France and, 116n140, 125–26; future research and, 334, 338; Germany and, 130, 134, 149, 169; knowledge regimes and, 8, 11, 15; national crises and, 216; normative implications and, 326; research design and, 351; United States and, 68, 82

permanent scholarly organizations, 180–83

personal networks, 78–79, 103, 152–53, 164, 190–92, 235n5, 285

philanthropy, 42, 44, 104–5, 124–25, 223

Planning Commissariat, 86, 88, 90, 92, 94, 108, 121, 122n165, 272, 346

Podesta, John, 49

policy analysis: comparative political economy and, 220, 223; convergence and, 240–44, 253–56, 259, 263, 266, 275; coordination/compromise policy and, 130, 134, 135n22, 138, 140n57, 143, 148–64, 168; Denmark and, 173, 180, 187, 192–97, 199, 201–6, 211–13; dirigisme and, 89, 91, 93n48, 107, 120, 122n165, 123, 128; France and, 89, 91, 93n48, 107, 122n165, 123, 128, 129; future research and, 335, 339; Germany and, 130, 134, 135n22, 138, 140n57, 143, 148–64, 168; globalization and, 215 (see also globalization); implications of independent, 223–29; influence and, 290, 303, 316–17; knowledge regimes and, 1–2, 7n19, 16, 24–28, 34; negotiation and, 173, 180, 187, 192–97, 199, 201–6, 211–13; normative implications

and, 325; partisanship and, 43, 45, 48, 52, 53n59, 56, 58, 65; taxes and, 13n48, 48, 76, 302, 308, 346; United States and, 43, 45, 48, 52, 53n59, 56, 58, 65, 89, 91, 93n48, 107, 122n165, 123, 128–29

policymakers: comparative political economy and, 219–20; convergence and, 240, 245–46, 253–54, 256, 259–61, 266, 270; Denmark and, 178, 190, 197, 199, 206; France and, 84, 90, 92, 94, 100–113, 123–26; future research and, 334–37, 342; Germany and, 129, 133–37, 142, 144–45, 156, 160, 162, 168–70; Golden Age and, 217 (see also Golden Age); influence and, 276–98, 303–4, 307–8, 316–17, 318n145, 320–21; knowledge regimes and, 2–10, 15–17, 22n64, 23–29; normative implications and, 325–30; public debate and, 2–3, 30, 102, 108, 111–13, 143, 158, 187, 209, 255, 287–89, 294–95, 348; statist regimes and, 14, 23, 27, 31, 33, 86, 89, 125, 129, 168–69, 174, 216–18, 227, 242, 253, 259, 266, 271, 333, 343; United States and, 39–43, 49, 52–54, 58–59, 62, 64, 66, 67–68, 76–77, 82

policymaking regimes: convergence and, 266–69; Denmark and, 175–78, 191, 196, 203, 208–9, 211–12; Evans and, 6–7; France and, 86–87, 93n47, 98, 104–5, 112–13, 123–24; future research and, 332, 336; Germany and, 131, 134, 148, 154, 160, 165–68, 171; influence and, 281; knowledge regimes and, 6–7, 15n55, 17–18, 23–24, 31, 35; methodology on analysis of, 31–35; normative implications and, 325–31; political institutions and, 266–69; reform and, 5n15; Rueschemeyer and, 6–7; Skocpol and, 6–7; Third Way and, 48, 293, 301, 318; United States and, 40, 42, 58–62, 65–69, 73, 75, 81–82

policy recommendations: convergence and, 234, 255; Denmark and, 183, 190, 192, 194–95; France and, 92–93, 96; Germany and, 149–51, 154, 164, 169; influence and, 291, 301, 304, 307, 310–13; knowledge regimes and, 3, 28; normative implications and, 329; research design and, 352–53; United States and, 46, 83

policy research organizations: aggressive, 1; choosing the best, 328–30; comparative political economy and, 220, 223; competition and, 60–64; convergence and, 232–36, 240–73; Denmark and, 172–72, 178–86, 189–202, 205–7, 210–14, 218; France and, 84, 89–98, 101, 103–28; future research and, 333–42; Germany and, 129–30, 134–35, 139–49, 153–56, 160–71; independent

World Bank, 119, 138n42, 174n7, 241, 274n113

YouTube, 63, 73, 247

Zimmerman, Klaus, 150
Zimmern, Bernard, 96–97, 105, 112, 114–15, 117–18, 224, 246, 255, 267–68, 271, 275
Zweiner, Rudolf, 150